PRINCIPLES AND GERRYMANDERS

Principles and Gerrymanders

Parliamentary Redistribution of Ridings in Ontario, 1840–1954

GEORGE EMERY

McGill-Queen's University Press
Montreal & Kingston • London • Chicago

ISBN 978-0-7735-4583-0 (cloth)
ISBN 978-0-7735-9750-1 (ePDF)
ISBN 978-0-7735-9751-8 (ePUB)

Legal deposit first quarter 2016
Bibliothèque nationale du Québec

Printed in Canada on acid-free paper that is 100% ancient forest free (100% post-consumer recycled), processed chlorine free

This book has been published with the help of a grant from the J.B. Smallman Publication Fund, Faculty of Social Science, Western University.

McGill-Queen's University Press acknowledges the support of the Canada Council for the Arts for our publishing program. We also acknowledge the financial support of the Government of Canada through the Canada Book Fund for our publishing activities.

Library and Archives Canada Cataloguing in Publication

Emery, George Neil, 1941–, author
Principles and gerrymanders: parliamentary redistribution of ridings in Ontario, 1840–1954/George Emery.

Includes bibliographical references and index.
Issued in print and electronic formats.
ISBN 978-0-7735-4583-0 (bound). – ISBN 978-0-7735-9750-1 (pdf). – ISBN 978-0-7735-9751-8 (ePUB)

1. Election districts – Ontario – History. 2. Canada. Parliament – Election districts – History. 3. Gerrymandering – Ontario – History. 4. Gerrymandering – Canada – History. I. Title.

JL193.E552 2015 328.71'07345 C2015-906586-0
C2015-906587-9

This book was typeset by Interscript in 10.5/13 Sabon.

Contents

Figures, Maps, and Tables

FIGURES

MAPS

TABLES

Acknowledgments

This book is a team effort. I thank Philip Cercone, director of McGill-Queen's University Press, for his expert management of my file through the vetting process. For their professionalism, timely efficiency, and creativity, I am grateful to the press's team, including Ryan Van Huijstee, Jessica Howarth, Paloma Friedman, Jacqui Davis, and Filomena Falocco. The Press arranged for two expert readers, who reported on three drafts of the manuscript. Their critiques were essential to my development of the manuscript to a standard required for publication. My appreciation also goes to Grace Seybold for her solid work of copy editing. Joel Natanblut and Anne Marie Holland of McGill University's Canadian County Atlas Digital Project made available high-resolution versions of nineteenth-century Ontario county maps. Tim Ziegler, a graphic artist from Toronto, co-ordinated the map work and produced the high-quality images that grace the book. Ian Steele, professor emeritus of Western University, provided some "inconvenient truths" about an early draft of the manuscript. Any faults of the end product, of course, are my responsibility.

Few things seem to excite a member of Parliament so much as a proposal to alter the boundaries of the constituency which elected him ... Of all aspects of parliamentary representation ... the debates on redistribution reveal the Commons at its worst.

Norman Ward, 1950[1]

With respect to the redistribution of seats ... every ten years or so this house is made the theatre of a somewhat unseemly, undignified, and utterly confusing scramble for personal or political advantage.

C.G. "Chubby" Power, Liberal MP, 1939[2]

[A] scheme from end to end for the political aggrandizement of the hon. gentleman [Sir John A. Macdonald] and his friends. There is no excuse whatever for the measure that he has brought in ... Sir, he ought to be ashamed ... to introduce such a measure as this ... he is a traitor to his own Province in its feelings and interests.

Alexander Mackenzie, Liberal MP, 1882[3]

So far from copying British precedents, [the Conservatives] have gone to another source. They are following in the footsteps of predecessors, not in the mother land, but in a neighbouring nation, and directly in the line of operations that can only be criticized as the *summum bonum* of political rascality. I refer to the American system of gerrymander.

John Charlton, Liberal MP, 1892[4]

Introduction

A redistribution of electoral districts (ridings) alters their number, revises their boundaries, or does both at the same time.[5] Its formal purpose is to adjust parliamentary representation to the movement of population: the growth or decline of population, and shifts in its territorial distribution and social composition. Canada's Constitution Act, 1867 – formerly the British North America Act, 1867 – requires a redistribution of federal ridings among the provinces after each decennial census. The Act says nothing about the redistribution of federal ridings within a province, nor about any aspect of redistribution for provincial parliaments.

WHY REDISTRIBUTION MATTERS

Ridings are integral to Canada's system of parliamentary representation. As John C. Courtney reasons, an election requires an institutional framework to elect members and establish the legitimacy of their election.[6] Building blocks of the framework include statutes to determine the franchise and procedures for holding an election; political parties to select the candidates and mobilize the electors on their behalf; and electoral districts, within which "votes can be aggregated, counted, and distributed to elect members."

The redistribution of ridings is part of the larger framework for holding elections. Hence the importance of who does it (the authority for redistribution) and how it is done (its rules, understood principles, guidelines, mechanisms, stratagems, and practices). The particulars of a redistribution set limits on democracy – for example, a vote in one riding has the same weight as a vote in other ridings only if the ridings have approximately equal populations. Another issue is whether or not distinctive "communities" (ethnic, economic, social-class, historical) should have separate representation.

When Parliament is the authority, as it was for Ontario before the 1960s, the government party administers redistribution. Its handiwork, in turn, affects the electoral prospects of candidates and political parties, hence access to power and patronage. Consequently, partisanship and principles may clash in designing adjustments to the ridings. In the circumstances, the government party might be tempted to gerrymander: that is, alter the number and boundaries of ridings to boost its future prospects.

A redistribution can affect outcomes in the next general election. If it under-represents large cities on the basis of population, for example, then it penalizes a party that polls strongly in large cities. Similarly, a gerrymander within a redistribution, if it works, benefits the government party. Thus, the identification of gerrymanders, their frequency, and their efficacy are important empirical issues that play on the legitimacy of elections, the behaviour of the political parties, and the confidence of the electorate in the institutions that govern them. Like "attack ads" in the 2010s, gerrymanders are unsavoury, but a government party may use them if its leaders believe that cheating works.

FROM PARLIAMENTARY REDISTRIBUTION TO COMMISSIONED RIDINGS

The authority for redistribution in Ontario underwent a revolutionary change during the 1960s. Hitherto, Parliament – effectively, the majority party – had administered redistribution for Canada's House of Commons and the Ontario Legislative Assembly. "For decades," opine the distinguished University of Saskatchewan political scientists Norman Ward and John C. Courtney, "redistributions had been carefully managed ... self-interested exercises controlled by the party in office. They often amounted to little more than thinly disguised gerrymanders." Since the 1960s, in contrast, arm's-length provincial boundary commissions, each chaired by a judge, have redrawn the ridings. "Independent electoral boundary commissions," judges Courtney, "stand as one of the success stories of the last half-century of Canadian political institutions ... With the replacement of government-dominated redistributions by independent commissions, partisan gerrymandering as it was once practised in Canada was relegated to history."[7]

WHAT THE BOOK DOES

This book examines the 120 years of parliamentary redistribution in Ontario that preceded the province's commissioned ridings of the 1960s. It unravels how parliamentary redistribution worked: its principles, mechanisms, operational strategies, exposure to partisanship, and influence on the outcomes of general elections. In the process, it gives an historical perspective on the current system of commissioned ridings – what has changed in redistribution, and what continues from the parliamentary era.

The book develops five themes. First, it explores the pre-Confederation roots of redistributions for Ontario. Second, it documents the underlying principles for historical redistributions and appraises their application. Third, it discusses the mechanisms and protocols for redistribution, in particular the bipartisan special committee, introduced in 1903, and its contrasting usage between the Dominion and provincial parliaments. Fourth, it investigates *gerrymandering* – political tampering to benefit the government party – its various forms, frequency over time, extent in given redistributions, and impact on outcomes of elections. Fifth, it contrasts Ontario's parliamentary redistribution with commissioned ridings, which replaced it during the 1960s.

THE LITERATURE FOR REDISTRIBUTIONS OF ONTARIO RIDINGS

The literature for redistributions during the period of study is scanty and patchy. Norman Ward's classic, *The Canadian House of Commons: Representation* (1950), gives an overview of Dominion redistributions for the years 1867 to 1950.[8] John C. Courtney, *Commissioned Ridings, Designing Canada's Electoral Districts* (2001), discusses the commission system, which Canada adopted in 1964.[9] The literature is negligible for pre-Confederation redistributions (1840–67) and provincial redistributions (1867–1954). Donald Kerr discusses briefly the Dominion redistribution of 1872 in *The 1867 Elections in Ontario: The Rules of the Game* (1970).[10]

R. MacGregor Dawson's *The Gerrymander of 1882* (1935) gives a detailed, lively, and useful analysis of John A. Macdonald's infamous Dominion redistribution for Ontario in 1882. Indeed, years later Dawson's article entered parliamentary debate. The Hon. C.G. "Chubby"

Power (Liberal, Quebec South) in 1952 and Pauline Jewett (Liberal, Northumberland) in 1964 cited it as proof that the 1882 redistribution was "the worst redistribution we have ever suffered."[11] Dawson's conclusion is sound, but factual errors, sensational language, and uncritical acceptance of Liberal-Party opinion colour his presentation.[12]

"The Great Gerrymander of 1882," writes J. Murray Beck in *Pendulum of Power*, was "ineffective [in Ontario in the 1882 general election] because of the resentment it aroused, [but] worked decidedly in Sir John's favour" in the 1887 general election.[13] Beck's statement raises an interesting issue: that a given redistribution applies to *all general elections through to the next redistribution* (in this instance, the general elections of 1882, 1887, and 1891). That said, Beck offers no evidence to support his contrasting claims for Macdonald's gerrymander in the 1882 and 1887 general elections. Quite the contrary. His tabular statistics show that Conservative fortunes in the two elections were identical (number of seats won, 55 and 55; popular vote, 50.4 percent and 50.7 percent). In the event, the unexplored empirical issue is how specific gerrymandered ridings, not the whole redistribution, functioned in the general elections of 1882, 1887, and 1891.

Biographies of Dominion prime ministers, Ontario premiers, and other prominent politicians give passing notice to redistribution. Donald Creighton concedes that John A. Macdonald "hived the Grits" in his notorious Representation Act of 1882.[14] P.B. Waite judges that Sir John Thompson's 1892 Dominion redistribution was acceptable to "reasonable men."[15] Joseph Schull gives no mention of Wilfrid Laurier's 1899 and 1900 Redistribution Bills, nor of Laurier's ground-breaking redistribution of 1903.[16] Robert Craig Brown notes Robert Borden's decision to assign the 1914 redistribution to a bipartisan special committee, but does not comment on the redistribution itself.[17] H. Blair Neatby notes, without comment, Mackenzie King's 1924 Representation Act.[18] Roger Graham's biography of Arthur Meighen ignores that redistribution entirely.[19] In their respective biographies of R.B. Bennett, John Boyko, P.B. Waite, and Larry Glassford omit mention of Bennett's Dominion redistribution of 1933.[20] In his biography, *Louis St. Laurent*, Dale C. Thomson treats debates about the 1952 Dominion Redistribution Bill, but not the redistribution itself, other than to say "that the government did not escape the charge of gerrymandering."[21] In *My Life with Louis St. Laurent*, J.W. Pickersgill, who had been in charge of the Prime Minister's Office, gives his insider's perspective on the 1952 Dominion redistribution. He credits Walter Harris, chairman of the parliament's special committee on redistribution, for achieving "the fairest redistribution ever made by parliament. But, however fair, redistribution by Parliament never helps the government in office."[22]

In her biography of Ontario's long-time Liberal premier Oliver Mowat, Margaret Evans avers that redistribution was a political weapon for the government party, second only to patronage in importance, and she discusses Mowat's 1874 and 1885 redistributions in some detail.[23] In his biography of the Tory premier James Whitney, Charles Humphries mentions Whitney's 1908 redistribution, but not his 1914 redistribution, which also escapes notice in Margaret Prang's biography of N.W. Rowell, who led the Liberal opposition.[24] Peter Oliver's biography of the Tory premier Howard Ferguson notes Ferguson's increase of representation for Ontario cities in his redistribution of 1925.[25] Charles Johnston's biography of the UFO leader, E.C. Drury, is silent about that redistribution, but Drury's memoir notes that it was overdue, was done fairly, and satisfied all parties.[26] Donald Ross Spanner's biography of the Tory premier George Henry discusses the 1933 provincial redistribution and its disruptive effect on Conservative distribution of patronage.[27] Roger Graham's biography of the Tory premier Leslie Frost does not mention Frost's 1954 provincial redistribution.[28] Two biographers of the Tory premier John Robarts do not mention Robarts's singular contribution to provincial redistribution, namely the province's adoption of commissioned ridings in 1962.[29] Without exception, redistribution is unmentioned in sketches of key politicians in the *Dictionary of Canadian Biography*.

Conventional wisdom is that Dominion redistributions invariably involved gerrymandering – the redrawing of electoral boundaries to rig the next election in favour of the government party. The Dominion government, writes MacGregor Dawson, used the device of the gerrymander "to a varying degree on three occasions – in 1872, in 1882, and in 1892. The most thorough and ambitious of the Canadian gerrymander Acts was that of 1882 ... it surpassed the others in scope, in apparent skill and shrewdness, in lack of scruple, and in the volume of denunciation and disapproval which it aroused."[30] "After the first decennial census [1871] and each succeeding census," writes Norman Ward, "the Government in power had the opportunity to tamper with the constituencies to its own advantage on a comprehensive scale, a procedure known to American politics as gerrymandering. The tampering was done with some hesitation and pretence of principle in 1872, with a gay abandon in 1882, and with dignity and persistence in 1892."[31] Writing about "federal decennial redistributions carried out between 1872 and 1952," John Courtney finds that "*without exception* each was carefully managed by the government of the day, whether Conservative or Liberal, in its own interest. The great majority, especially the gerrymander of 1882, were partisan and blatantly self-serving affairs."[32]

The House of Commons was the authority for Dominion redistribution. Thus, in each case, explains Ward, government introduced a Representation Bill and then used its parliamentary majority to bulldoze the Bill's passage, with few concessions to the opposition party. In 1903 the Dominion government delegated the preliminary work to a bipartisan special committee on which the government party had a majority. Subsequent redistributions, Dominion and provincial, continued with this mechanism, but, according to Ward, little changed. As opposition-party critics complained, government-party members came to meetings of the committee with fixed schedules, without the constraints of fixed guidelines, and with themselves in the majority on the committee.[33] Ward writes of passive gerrymandering: a failure to act on riding-population inequalities where it was in the governing party's interest to leave the status quo. "The 'do-nothing' rule," he judges, "has perhaps contributed as much to the misrepresentation of the Canadian people as to their representation."[34]

MacGregor Dawson avers that Oliver Mowat's 1874 Representation Act for the provincial parliament "was not a gerrymander, though it probably did not go out of its way to favour the Conservatives. It made a number of changes which appear to have been quite legitimate, such as placing a town, which had been in two counties, in one, and adding new constituencies within the county boundaries. In no instance did Mowat go beyond county limits in creating any new districts."[35] Simply put, the provincial Liberals had clean hands; Dominion Conservatives were "shameless" cheaters.[36]

Gordon Stewart questions the value judgment, such as Dawson's, that partisan manipulation of the ridings was "shameful."[37] Macdonald himself regarded his highly partisan Franchise Act of 1885 as serving the national interest. By helping to keep the Conservative Party in power, the Act protected his two major policy initiatives, the construction of the Pacific Railway and the National Policy, which the Liberal opposition party would dismantle. Effectively, a noble end justified unsavoury means, a logic that applied equally to his 1882 redistribution.

CONTRIBUTION TO THE LITERATURE

This book builds on the enduring work of Ward and Dawson for Dominion redistributions (1872–1952) and breaks new ground for pre-Confederation redistributions (1840–67) and Ontario-provincial redistributions (1874–1954). The book revises conventional wisdom about the principles and mechanisms for parliamentary redistribution. It refines the literature for definitions of gerrymander, the identification of gerrymanders, and the extent of the government party's gerrymandering in parliamentary redistributions. It pioneers the empirical demonstration of whether or not specific gerrymanders worked or failed, and how their fortunes affected results across Ontario in the next general election.

The book's study of redistribution contributes to a larger field of interest: electoral practice. Patronage, for example, was at the heart of Canadian political life before the First World War. "The distribution of patronage," notes O.D. Skelton in his biography of Sir Wilfrid Laurier, "was the most important single function of the government. No other subject bulked so large in correspondence; no other purpose brought so many visitors to Ottawa."[38] "For Laurier, preoccupied with national affairs," writes John English, "patronage was an endless nuisance; for the ordinary member of Parliament it was the lifeblood of political existence ... and an erratic rate of flow could rapidly assure one's political doom." In the circumstances, most Dominion Members of Parliament regarded themselves as delegates for the patronage interests of their ridings, not as trustees for a larger public interest.[39]

But a party's access to patronage required holding office. Thus, patronage-driven parties evolved into "machines for winning elections."[40] Partisan rivalry, in turn, generated lively issues in electoral practice, such as revising the franchise; policing voters' lists; shifting from the voice-vote method of election to the secret ballot method in 1874; amending the process for trials of controverted elections; and committing electoral dirty tricks. Prominent on the list of dirty tricks was the gerrymandered redistribution.

This book's treatment of redistribution draws on the literature for electoral practice. John English's *The Decline of Politics* (1977) is essential reading for Dominion redistributions of the period 1900 to 1925, in particular the relationship between Dominion and provincial branches of parties, and tension between ideals and patronage interests in election campaigns.[41] In their 1986 article in the *Canadian Historical Review*, Ben Forster and his co-authors lay bare John A. Macdonald's notorious

Franchise Act of 1885.[42] In *Patrons, Clients, Brokers: Ontario Society and Politics, 1791–1896*, S.J.R. Noel writes brilliantly about Oliver Mowat's Liberal-Party machine in Ontario provincial politics.[43] André Siegfried's *The Race Question in Canada* is a classic on electoral practice in Canada's 1904 general election.[44] My own *Elections in Oxford County, 1837–1875: A Case Study of Democracy in Canada West and Early Ontario* (2012) discusses election protocols, campaigns, and electoral dirty tricks in the era of voice-voting, which preceded Canada's adoption of the secret ballot.[45]

UNDERLYING PRINCIPLES FOR REDISTRIBUTION

From Confederation into the 1950s, Canadian politicians regarded representation by population – the equalization of population across ridings – merely as one of several principles for redistribution. Their ranking order of importance for principles changed over time due to population growth, urbanization, advances in transportation and communications, and the expansion of suffrage.

Two general principles were a no-gerrymandering rule and minimalism: that is, that government should not revise the boundaries of ridings unfairly to gain partisan advantage (gerrymandering) and that ridings were best left undisturbed (minimalism) where no principle warranted intervention.

Representation by population was a major principle, though seldom a controlling one. The 1867 British North America Act (BNA Act) made population the basis for redistributing seats to the provinces. Thus some contemporaries inferred that it should apply to representation *within* provinces. If the democratic principle of "one man, one vote" was valued, then the weight of a man's vote should not vary from one riding to another. To this end, redistribution should equalize population across the ridings "as far as possible."

A second major principle was that electoral districts should observe municipal lines. "As much as possible," electoral boundaries should coincide with municipal ones. Ridings in cities should follow ward boundaries. Electoral districts for large cities, such as Toronto, Hamilton, and Ottawa, should be revised from time to time to match their civic boundaries, which tended to spread into adjacent county ridings through municipal annexations. Conversely, riding boundaries should not cross county lines or split townships.

A third major principle, which emerged in the 1890s, was that ridings in cities should have larger populations – less representation – than county ridings. Effectively the equalization of riding populations should be applied in two stages, first within cities, and then within counties.

A fourth principle was that each riding should have a compact, symmetrical shape, with its municipalities contiguous to one another.

A fifth principle was that riding boundaries should respect "communities of interest." Some held that city populations should be represented separately from rural populations. Glengarry County warranted separate representation due to the Highland-Scotch character of its population. County boundaries should be respected because the shared experience of municipal elections and functions in local government made each county a community of interest.

Two minor principles were that "historical" ridings with small populations should be left alone, and that, where possible, the territories of Dominion ridings should be made to coincide with those of provincial ridings.

The majority-held principles sometimes clashed in application. The observance of county lines, for example, could work against the equalizing of riding populations. Yet such principles could be reconciled through combination, such as first allotting ridings to counties on the basis of population, and then equalizing riding populations within counties.

Majority principles sometimes collided with minority counter-principles. In 1892, for example, certain Conservatives argued that municipal lines mattered for the provincial parliament, which dealt with local issues, but not for the House of Commons, which grappled with national issues. Some MPs for Toronto ridings argued for representation by population across the board, without distinction between city and county ridings.

GENUINE PRINCIPLES AND THEORIES MASQUERADING AS PRINCIPLES

Eminent University of Saskatchewan scholars Norman Ward (1950) and John C. Courtney (2001) distinguish between "genuine principles" for redistribution and "theories frequently masquerading as principles." "As long as constituencies were regularly adjusted by one party," writes Ward, the growth of *genuine* principles governing the determination of boundaries *was not encouraged*. True, since seats were allotted to the provinces on the basis of population, a fundamental aim in drawing the boundary lines *might seem to be* the equalization of constituency populations. But from the beginning the application of this principle was undermined by the strength of local feeling for the preservation of existing county and town lines. This *sentiment*, however laudable, all too often clashed with representation by population. *The mutual exclusiveness of these two ideas played into the hands of anyone interested in manipulating the boundaries and populations of constituencies for party advantage …*

A total of four separate theories, frequently masquerading as principles, have thus appeared in the history of redistribution in Canada [representation by population, county lines, minimalism, and city-rural differences in representation] … they developed early in Canadian politics, and since the beginning have been used indiscriminately as genuine guiding principles and as excuses to justify perversions of representation.[46]

Courtney endorses Ward's view:

Although Canada's first nine federal redistributions amounted to little more than acts of political expediency, with the passage of time a certain number of "theories masquerading as principles" (Norman Ward's words) were concocted by governments, Commons committees, and individual MPs to justify their self-serving moves. By the mid-twentieth century some five 'principles' had evolved which, in varying degrees, had been brought into play over the course of ninety years. County and town lines were to be preserved as electoral boundaries; party leaders' seats were to be left untouched; ridings might be added to areas of growing populations; urban constituencies were expected to contain larger populations than rural ones; and, however unfeasible this might be given the other constraints, representation was to be determined by population.[47]

The Ward-Courtney position is instructive but ahistorical. Clearly any principle used merely as pretext for political gain ceases to be genuine, as was the case with John A. Macdonald's misuse of representation by population in his infamous gerrymander of 1882. Second, representation by population was not the only genuine principle. The observance of county lines, for example, was a compelling principle, supported with logic, and not merely a "laudable sentiment," as Ward would have it. Third, principles that clashed, such as municipal lines and representation by population, were not "mutually exclusive," but rather were open to combination. Some redistribution Bills decided each county's number of ridings on the basis of population, after which they tried to equalize riding populations within counties. Similarly, the principle that city ridings should have larger populations than country ridings was not mutually exclusive with the population principle; rather, the population principle was applied separately to city ridings and county ridings.

That said, Dawson and Ward give a balanced overview of the principles for Canadian redistributions in *The Government of Canada* (1963).[48] As evidenced in the following excerpt, drawn from evidence in *Debates* for 1882, 1924, and 1962, the authors have moved beyond their initial position of "theories masquerading as principles."

> Two important principles have been accepted in Canada as justifying a departure from the general rule of the approximate equality of the constituencies. First, municipal and county boundaries should be followed when at all possible. It is considered wiser to over- or under-represent an area than to dismember districts which have established traditions, long history, and strong local pride and character.
>
> Secondly, rural areas should be more generously represented than urban, that is, the population of rural constituencies should be definitely less than that of the city constituencies. This is justified on several grounds. The cities have many more spokesmen than the country in the form of boards of trade and various commercial, social, and industrial organizations; and the daily press is entirely an urban institution. It is therefore much more difficult for opinion in the country to become organized and to make itself felt in Parliament and elsewhere. Many representatives of country districts live in the cities most of the year, whereas few city representatives have the same contact with the country. Moreover, the member who represents a rural district has an exceptionally difficult task in canvassing his constituents and in keeping in touch with them. But while this inequality in representation is deliberately sought, it is expected there should be an approximate equality among all the urban districts, and also among all the rural districts. This has not been, and is still not, carried out in practice.

MECHANISMS FOR REDISTRIBUTION

Throughout the nineteenth century, the government party simply introduced a redistribution Bill and used its majority to ram it through Parliament. In 1903 Prime Minister Wilfrid Laurier established a new mechanism, whereby he delegated the details of revision to a bipartisan special committee on which government members were a majority. His intent was to give the minority party a voice and provide a neutral ground for discussion. Laurier's Conservative and Liberal successors continued with the special-committee mechanism through to 1952. Beginning in 1914 the special committee delegated the work to regional subcommittees, one of them for Ontario; thereafter the Ontario subcommittee was the key decider for the province's Dominion ridings. Tory ministries in Ontario's provincial parliament used the special-committee mechanism in 1908, 1914, 1925, 1933, and 1954. In the 1908 and 1914 provincial redistributions, however, a committee of cabinet redrew the ridings and limited the special committee to a ratifying role.

John Courtney posits a three-stage model to explain the change in the mechanisms for Dominion redistributions after 1867.[49] In stage 1, dating from Confederation to the First World War, patronage, constituency politics, and localism characterized Canada's national parties. In the circumstances, the prime minister and his lieutenants micro-managed the details of redistribution. In stage 2, dating from 1900 to the 1950s, parties became preoccupied with regional and provincial interests. Accordingly, the prime minister delegated redistribution to all-party special committees and their regional subcommittees, such as the one for Ontario. In stage 3, dating from 1964, national issues came to the fore. Redistribution shifted to arm's-length boundary commissions to remove party-driven influences from redistribution, thereby making it more democratic and accountable.

THE PERIOD OF STUDY (1840–1954)

The period of study begins with Britain's creation of the United Province of Canada in 1840, and ends with Ontario's last parliamentary redistribution in 1954. The United Province (1840–67) comprised two sections: Canada West and Canada East, formerly the provinces of Upper Canada and Lower Canada (1791–1840), and destined to become the Canadian provinces of Ontario and Quebec upon Confederation in 1867. The twenty-three redistributions in this study include five for Canada West

(1840, 1845, 1851, 1853, and 1867); nine for Dominion ridings (1872, 1882, 1892, 1903, 1914, 1924, 1933, 1947, and 1952); and nine for provincial ridings (1874, 1885, 1894, 1902, 1908, 1914, 1925–26, 1933–34, and 1954).[50]

THE ORGANIZATION OF CHAPTERS

Chapter 1 provides five sections of background information. It opens with a history of Ontario counties, which were the base units for electoral districts. Second, it surveys the evolution of Canada's political parties, which administered redistribution and were potential agents for gerrymander. Third, it describes the movement of population during the period of study – population growth, urbanization, rural depopulation, and the spread of population into Northern Ontario. Fourth, it explains the book's *standard-population* methodology for measuring population inequality across ridings. Fifth, it discusses *gerrymander* as an historical construct, its definitions, methodology for its identification, and methodology for determining if gerrymanders worked in the general election following.

Chapter 2 examines five redistributions for the years of Canada West, 1840–67. This chapter establishes the pre-Confederation roots of Ontario redistribution and the pivotal role of John A. Macdonald in creating the start-up ridings for Ontario (Schedule I in the BNA Act, 1867). Chapters 3 and 4 examine Dominion and provincial redistributions by decades for the 1870s and 1880s. Chapter 5 treats the Dominion redistribution of 1892. Chapter 6 discusses Wilfrid Laurier's redistribution Bills of 1899 and 1900 and his Representation Act of 1903. Chapter 7 investigates the Dominion Redistribution of 1914. Chapter 8 explores the provincial redistributions of 1894, 1902, 1908, and 1914. Chapters 9 and 10 examine Dominion and provincial redistributions by decades for the 1920s and 1930s. Chapter 11 examines the Dominion and provincial redistributions of the 1940s and 1950s. The closing chapter summarizes and interprets the findings for parliamentary redistribution and describes and appraises the transition to commissioned ridings during the 1960s. Appendix B addresses a modern issue of riding boundaries beyond the scope of the main text.

1

The Ontario Setting

This chapter comprises five sections of background information. It opens with a history of Ontario counties, which were the base units for parliamentary representation. Second, it surveys the evolution of Canada's political parties, which administered redistribution and were potential agents for gerrymander. Third, it describes the movement of population in Ontario – its sustained growth over 120 years of time, urbanization, rural depopulation, and spread into Northern Ontario. Population matters because the ridings represented populations, not electors or property owners. Fourth, this chapter explains the standard population for measuring population inequality across ridings. Fifth, it discusses gerrymander as an historical construct; forms of gerrymander; and the book's methodology for identifying gerrymanders, predicting their effect on electoral prospects, and demonstrating empirically whether or not particular gerrymanders worked.

COUNTIES: THE BASE UNITS FOR REPRESENTATION

During the 1840s, counties in Canada West became municipal as well as electoral entities.[1] Initially counties were units for parliamentary representation and organization of the militia, but not for local government, which was given to magistrates meeting in quarter sessions. In 1841 the Legislative Assembly assigned local government to districts, not counties. Then, in 1849, the government's Act for Abolishing the Territorial Division of Upper Canada into Districts gave local government to counties, townships, and incorporated urban places. Therein originated a distinction between an electoral county (with one or more ridings) and a municipal county (with local government).

The province's counties and ridings evolved over time. The 1840 imperial Act to Unite Upper Canada and Lower Canada carried forward the twenty-nine electoral counties of Upper Canada; divided each of three counties (Halton, Northumberland, and Lincoln) into two ridings; made the city of Toronto a two-member riding; and formed seven town ridings (Hamilton, Bytown, London, Kingston, Brockville, Cornwall, and Niagara). An 1845 statute created three new counties: the West riding of Halton became the county of Waterloo; the North riding of Northumberland became the county of Peterborough; and the South riding of Lincoln became the county of Welland.[2] Statutes in 1849 and 1851 increased the number of counties from thirty-two to forty-two.

Provincial statutes united certain counties for representation. The 1845 Act created two *united-electoral counties*: Lennox-Addington and Lanark-Renfrew. The 1851 Act created eight of them through unions involving eighteen counties.[3] The 1853 Act pared the number down to two: Lennox-Addington and Huron-Bruce. One of these vanished with an 1860 statute that merged Lennox and Addington into one county, Lennox & Addington.[4] The other disappeared with the BNA Act, 1867, which separated Huron and Bruce and gave each county two ridings.

Ontario statutes in 1874 created two provisional-municipal counties, Dufferin and Haliburton, which raised the number of counties to forty-three. The province gave full county status to Dufferin in 1881 and Haliburton in 1890. Ontario Premier Oliver Mowat made Dufferin a provincial riding in 1874, and Prime Minister Wilfrid Laurier made Dufferin a Dominion riding in 1903. Haliburton never became a riding due to its persistently small population.

After Confederation, one-member ridings continued to be the norm, except for Ontario's three largest cities. For Dominion elections, Toronto West and Hamilton City were two-member ridings for the years 1872–1903, and Ottawa was a two-member riding for the years 1872–1914. For provincial elections, Toronto City was a three-member riding for the years 1885–1904; Hamilton City and Ottawa City were two-member ridings for the years 1904–08; and four Toronto ridings returned two members for the years 1908–25. In each case, an elector could vote for up to two candidates; hence the number of votes cast generally exceeded the number of electors (persons on the voters' lists).

Redistribution dealt inconsistently with villages that straddled municipal boundaries. The 1867 redistribution gave Mount Forest to a Wellington-County riding, although part of the village was in Grey County. It split Hastings Village between ridings in two counties,

Peterborough and Northumberland. In another three cases – Richmond Hill, Carleton Place, and Lucknow – it split villages between ridings within a county.[5]

Northland Districts and Redistribution

Ontario's territorial boundaries expanded north and west after Confederation: first, north to the 51st parallel in 1874, when the province agreed to pay for construction at Prince Arthur's Landing and the maintenance of a police force at Thunder Bay; second, in 1884, when the province acquired the Lake of the Woods region from a judicial settlement of the Ontario-Manitoba boundary dispute; and third, in 1912, when it acquired part of the Hudson's Bay Territory.[6] The province did not extend the county system of local government into the northlands, with their small, scattered populations. Rather, it created twelve territorial *districts*: Algoma and Nipissing, 1858; Muskoka, 1868; Parry Sound, 1869; Thunder Bay, 1871 (from the western half of Algoma); Rainy River, 1885 (from part of Thunder Bay); Manitoulin, 1888 (from part of Algoma); Sudbury, 1907 (from eastern Algoma and western Nipissing); Kenora, 1909 (from part of Rainy River); Temiskaming, 1912 (from parts of Algoma, Nipissing, and Sudbury); and Cochrane, 1921 (from parts of Temiskaming and Thunder Bay). The province created Patricia District in 1912, but folded it into Kenora in 1927.[7]

The principle of observing county lines in redistribution did not apply to the northland districts, which, unlike counties, had no municipal function, and hence no administrative bodies that were comparable to county councils. Thus, in Ontario's 1925 Representation Act, for example, the "Electoral District of Algoma [was] to consist of parts of the Territorial Districts of Sudbury and Algoma," and the "Electoral District of Cochrane [was] to consist of … portions of the Territorial Districts of Temiskaming, Algoma, Thunder Bay, and Patricia."

United-Municipal Counties

Provincial statutes united certain counties for municipal purposes. In such cases, the united county was the municipal county, the counties within it having no municipal function. The distinction was to become important after Confederation, when the observance of county lines became an important principle of redistribution. The united county had county lines; the counties within the union did not, and could be carved up without trespassing on the principle.

The united-municipal county originated in 1849, when the Baldwin Act transferred local government to counties. A companion statute "providing for temporary unions of counties for judicial and other purposes" folded twenty-one counties into nine united-municipal counties.[8] An 1851 Act grouped thirty-four counties into fourteen united-municipal ones.[9] An 1859 statute grouped twenty counties into nine united-municipal counties.[10] Statutes dissolved some united-municipal counties during the 1860s.[11] The BNA Act, 1867, placed "municipal institutions" under the jurisdiction of provinces.[12] Thereafter, the province of Ontario held four united-municipal counties with nine counties in them (Stormont-Dundas-Glengarry; Leeds-Grenville; Northumberland-Durham; and Prescott-Russell).[13]

Ontario Cities: "Counties of Themselves" for Municipal Purposes

Toronto became an incorporated city in 1834, followed by Hamilton and Kingston in 1846 and Ottawa and London in 1855. Under the Municipal Act, Upper Canada, 1849, an incorporated city was a "county of itself" for municipal purposes.[14] Similarly, under the Act respecting the Territorial Division of Upper Canada, 1859, and subsequent provincial Acts after Confederation, cities "did not form part of the several counties in which they are respectively situate."[15] York County, for example, comprised two municipal counties: the city of Toronto and the rest of York County. By extension, Toronto's city limits were a county line, to be observed in redistribution.

In 1883 Ontario cities began to annex suburban populations on the outskirts of their civic territories (see Appendix A). Toronto annexed forty-six territories during the years 1883–1950; Hamilton, twenty-three during the years 1891–1949; Ottawa, eleven during the years 1887–1950; and London, nine during the years 1885–1950. Each annexation made the city's municipal territory larger than its electoral district. The issue in redistribution was whether or not to enlarge the city's electoral territory to match its municipal territory, thereby observing county lines for cities, those "counties of themselves."

Purely-Electoral Counties

Through the medium of the imperial 1867 BNA Act, and counter to the principle of observing municipal-county lines, John A. Macdonald created the purely-electoral counties of Bothwell, Cardwell, and Monck from parts of seven municipal counties. Redistributions periodically revised these ridings and eventually abolished them: all of them for Dominion elections in 1903; and for provincial elections, Bothwell, 1874; Cardwell, 1908; and Monck, 1914.

POLITICAL PARTIES

Disciplined, centrally financed and directed political parties did not exist in Canada West (1840–67). The base units for provincial politics were local networks of patron-client relationships, in which the patron bestowed material benefits on clients, and the clients responded with loyalty, service, and support for the patron's business and political interests. Brokers organized clusters of patrons for projects such as railways, which were beyond the resources of patrons to complete individually. "Members of parliament," writes S.J.R. Noel, "were typically local magnates, or the nominees of local magnates, with their own independent bases of support and their own patron-client relationships to consider; they were not merely grist to some party mill."[16]

Development of the Province's Infrastructure and Government Patronage

Ontario changed after Confederation, with the development of roads and railway branch lines; urbanization; the emergence of non-local markets; and an increasing level of central-government control over "rural or geographically remote areas that were previously beyond its reach, or to which its reach extended only weakly or intermittently."[17] As J.E. Crawford writes, the Canada West years saw the public service evolve from "a disheartening scene of administrative incompetence" into "an administrative machine which, with few fundamental changes, remained intact after Confederation."[18] In 1841 Governor Sydenham made cabinet ministers responsible for particular departments. Unity of command was vested in the governor until 1849 and then in the cabinet of the province's Legislative Assembly. Permanent deputy ministers gave stability to departments, given the turnover of their political heads. The number of civil servants for the Province of Canada rose from 437 in 1842 to 2,660 in 1867. Headquarters staff (the "inside service") were 21 percent of the 1842 total and 13 percent of the 1867 total, with the balance being field staff (the "outside service"). These numbers excluded "the large judicial staff and the employees of the legislative branch," as well as the personnel of post offices.[19] Civil-service positions were primarily patronage appointments. Although a change of ministry did not bring about wholesale dismissals, as in the United States, ministries did fill positions as they became vacant with partisan interests in mind.

The public service was a key mechanism for governance at the local level. The state regulated, taxed, and delivered services through an army of local agents on commission. For every public servant at headquarters, three were in the field. The postal service exemplified the outreach of the public service into rural communities. In 1842 Canada had some 450 post offices, each staffed by a postmaster who was paid by fees; the province had 840 post offices by 1852 and 2,300 by 1867.[20] In 1862 the Toronto *Globe* likened the (rural) postmaster to a "country storekeeper [who], for the accommodation of his neighbours, takes charge of their letters and papers, receiving therefore the 'paltry' amounts of £5 or £10 per year [$20 to $40]."[21] The commissions for village and town post offices were more substantial. For a nine-month period ending in June 1864, they were $877 for Woodstock and $826 for Ingersoll. Mail-delivery contracts were a second arm of the postal service. In 1865 the postmaster-general let 1,100 delivery contracts at a cost of $130,000 to reach communities that were not on a railway line. In 1864 his office paid $974 to Edwin Doty for operating a mail stage out of Ingersoll, daily to Port Burwell and tri-weekly to the village of Lakeside.[22] Finally, the postmaster-general was a patron of local newspapers. In 1861 he purchased subscriptions to fifty-six local journals in which he advertised local schedules for dispatching and receiving mail, as well as lists of unclaimed letters; his payments to three Oxford County newspapers totalled $51.95.

Political Parties after 1850

Political parties developed by superimposing province-wide, hierarchical structures on local and regional networks of patrons. The lifeblood of the parties was the downward flow of patronage, in return for which they received an upward flow of electoral support. The provincial Liberals, writes Noel, "were compelled to build from the ground up, by promoting the advancement of new local elites whose prospects were closely tied to those of the party. The Conservatives, however, having been long in office and now additionally enriched with federal patronage, naturally preferred to build on their existing foundations. And that meant continuing their old alliance with the quasi-independent patrons who had always been the conservative mainstay."[23]

THE PATRONS AND THE PATRON-AGE.

SIR OLIVER: 'Oh, oh! Gracious, goodness, dear Patron Giant! Take anything, everything you want, but spare, oh, spare this, my pet and favorite che-ild.'

Figure 1.1 Bengough cartoon, 1890s. Control of patronage was the prize for winning elections, hence the government party's temptation to gerrymander.

Social change accelerated during the early twentieth century. As John English writes, "Rapid economic growth, a flood of immigrants, urbanization and consequent rural depopulation of rural Canada, broke down traditional allegiances, disrupted local communities, and promoted social disturbance." These tendencies made growing numbers of individuals dependent on ties with distant outsiders, thereby weakening the traditional social bonds of patron-client networks. Thus, "no longer did constituency boundaries and interests define the party contest."[24]

In *The Decline of Politics*, English shows how the Conservative Party responded to altered circumstances after 1896, when the Liberals, led by Wilfrid Laurier, displaced the Conservatives as the government party in Ottawa, and after 1905, when the Ontario Conservatives, led by James P. Whitney, replaced the Liberals as the government party in the provincial parliament.[25] As leader of the opposition in Ottawa, Robert Borden lacked patronage – the lifeblood of election campaigns – whereas James Whitney, as premier in Toronto, had provincial patronage in abundance. In the circumstances, Borden bypassed the traditional strategy of electioneering through Members of Parliament, with their ties to local notables in the constituencies. Instead, he fought the campaigns of 1904, 1908, and 1911 through Tory premiers in Ontario, Manitoba, and British Columbia. This paid off handsomely with Borden's victory over Laurier in the general election of 1911, but became a liability when the provincial-Tory administrations were toppled, in Ontario by the United Farmers of Ontario in 1919.

There is more to English's argument than patronage. The relevant point here is that parties, and relations between their Dominion and provincial branches, were dynamic and evolving. The close Dominion-provincial Conservative ties under Borden influenced Dominion and provincial redistributions in 1914. Third parties appeared after the First World War.

THE MOVEMENT OF POPULATION, 1852–1954

Ridings represented populations, which changed over time. Ontario's census population increased nearly fourfold during the century after 1852, from 952,293 to 4,597,542. The rate of increase was massive during the 1840s and 1850s, low for the 1880s, 1890s, and 1930s, and substantial for all other decades.

As shown in Tables 1.1 and 1.2, population was differentiated by regions. The GTA (the *Greater Toronto Area*, as represented by the counties of York, Peel, and Ontario) increased from 14 to 29 percent of the provincial total between 1852 and 1956. The northland districts rose from 0 to 12 percent. The statistics for county regions declined accordingly. The Eastern-Ontario region dropped from 39 to 20 percent, and its rate of increase was below average for Ontario. The Western-Ontario region dropped from 47 to 38 percent; its rate of increase was above average through to the 1870s, and then below average.

Table 1.1 Regional distribution of Ontario census populations, 1861–1921

% of Ontario population	*1852 census*	*1861 census*	*1871 census*	*1881 census*	*1891 census*	*1901 census*	*1911 census*	*1921 census*	*1931 census*	*1941 census*	*1951 census*	*1956 census*
Eastern	39%	36%	33%	31%	30%	29%	26%	23%	20%	20%	19%	20%
Western	47%	52%	55%	55%	51%	49%	44%	42%	40%	39%	40%	38%
Northern	–	–	1%	3%	4%	7%	11%	11%	12%	13%	13%	12%
GTA*	14%	12%	12%	12%	15%	15%	20%	24%	28%	28%	29%	29%
Population in 1,000s	952	1,398	1,621	1,846	2,093	2,523	2,516	2,933	2,933	3,788	4,598	5,558
					% population in cities (10,000+ population)							
Eastern	3%	6%	7%	8%	10%	14%	19%	26%	29%	35%	42%	37%
Western	3%	4%	5%	6%	12%	14%	25%	34%	42%	43%	46%	46%
Northern	–	–	–	–	–	–	16%	21%	29%	31%	32%	31%
GTA	23%	25%	31%	42%	57%	63%	75%	74%	69%	67%	59%	49%
Ontario	6%	7%	9%	11%	17%	21%	33%	41%	45%	47%	47%	43%
# of cities	3	5	5	5	9	10	19	26	33	33	41	46

* The counties of York, Peel, and Ontario.

Table 1.2 Between-census population growth by regions, 1861–1951

	1852–61	*1861–71*	*1871–81*	*1881–91*	*1891–1901*	*1901–11*	*1911–21*	*1921–31*	*1931–41*	*1941–51*
Eastern	36%	5%	12%	6%	2%	0%	3%	4%	9%	15%
Western	62%	23%	19%	2%	-2%	5%	12%	12%	7%	23%
Northern	–	–	237%	73%	59%	83%	18%	30%	25%	16%
GTA	26%	10%	21%	38%	6%	52%	42%	32%	11%	26%
Ontario	47%	16%	19%	10%	3%	16%	16%	17%	10%	21%
Cities 10,000+	79%	39%	47%	79%	23%	81%	43%	30%	13%	31%

A growing proportion of the provincial population resided in *cities*. The percentage rose from 6 to 46 between 1852 and 1951. During the 1940s and 1950s, suburban sprawl around the edges of cities was more striking than population growth in the cities. Indeed, Toronto in 1956 had just 249 more individuals than its enumerated population for 1941.

Table 1.3 Ridings per 100,000 population, after redistribution

	Dominion ridings									
	1867	*1872*	*1882*	*1892*	*1903*	*1914*	*1924*	*1933*	*1947*	*1952*
Eastern ridings	6.0	5.9	5.2	5.1	4.3	3.8	3.3	3.4	3.0	2.3
Western ridings	5.7	4.8	4.4	4.4	4.0	3.5	3.1	2.6	2.4	1.9
Northern ridings	23.8	28.5	5.5	2.9	4.1	3.0	3.0	2.4	2.2	2.1
Small cities	6.8	5.5	6.2	4.6	3.6	2.7	2.3	1.8	1.7	1.5
GTA	5.0	5.3	4.4	2.9	3.1	2.4	2.1	1.8	1.6	1.5
Ontario	5.9	5.4	5.8	4.4	3.9	3.2	2.8	2.4	2.2	1.9
	Ontario ridings									
	1867	1874	1885	1894	1908	1914	1926	1933	1940s	1954
Eastern ridings	6.0	5.9	5.1	5.0	5.0	4.7	4.7	3.3	NA	2.7
Western ridings	5.7	5.1	4.5	4.5	4.7	4.5	3.8	2.8	NA	2.1
North	23.8	16.8	10.7	5.4	9.8	4.3	4.7	3.1	NA	2.4
Small cities	6.8	5.2	3.9	3.2	3.5	4.7	3.4	1.9	NA	2.0
GTA	5.0	3.9	4.0	3.3	4.1	3.3	2.6	2.0	NA	1.7
Ontario	5.9	5.4	4.7	4.4	4.9	4.3	3.7	2.6	NA	2.1

Population outstripped the supply of ridings, which produced a declining trend for number of ridings per 100,000 population. Within the declining trend, representation varied regionally. As shown in Table 1.3 for the years 1867–1954, the GTA consistently had below-average representation, and Eastern Ontario consistently had above-average representation. The statistics became lower for the Dominion Parliament than for the Legislative Assembly, which came to have more seats.

THE STANDARD POPULATION AND MEASUREMENT OF INEQUALITY

The imperial 1867 BNA Act set up a Quebec-based standard population to determine the allocation of seats among the provinces. With Quebec's representation fixed at sixty-five seats, the standard population was Quebec's census population divided by sixty-five. Ontario's quota of seats was the number of standard populations in its census population. Quebec's population grew over time, while its sixty-five seats were constant. Perforce, the standard population rose, from 18,331 at

Confederation (1861 census) to 36,283 in the 1921 census. A 1915 amendment to Section 51 of the BNA Act secured a higher quota for Ontario in the 1924 and 1933 redistributions than would have obtained from a strict application of the Quebec-standard population. A 1946 amendment to the BNA Act jettisoned the Quebec-based standard population, first by fixing the number of seats in the House of Commons at 255, and then by setting each province's quota according to its share of the national population.

This book uses the Quebec-based standard population for Dominion redistributions through to the 1930s and the constitutionally modified standard population for the 1947 and 1952 Dominion redistributions. It uses the mean population for all ridings as the standard population for redistributions in Canada West (1840–67) and Ontario's provincial parliament (1867–1954).

The standard population for the Ontario ridings is always 1.00. The chapters report the percentage of riding populations within ±10 percent of the standard population (0.90–1.10) and in the ranges of <0.80, 0.80–0.89, 1.11–1.19, and 1.20+. The range of 0.90–1.10, the book's optimum zone, measures 10 percent tolerance (±10). The three middle ranges (0.80–1.19) measure a 20 percent tolerance (±20). The statutory tolerance for commissioned ridings (1964) is 25 percent (±25, or 0.75–1.25).

THE GERRYMANDER

Definitions

A gerrymander is a redistribution of two or more ridings that unfairly benefits the government party.

Passive gerrymandering refers to leaving alone, for the benefit of the government party, ridings that deserve intervention on the basis of principle, such as ridings with below-average or above-average populations. On the basis of population, for example, Eastern-Ontario ridings were over-represented in Dominion elections. Yet, knowing that these ridings favoured Conservatives, John A. Macdonald left them alone. His inaction was passive gerrymandering.

An intentional gerrymander involves a redrawing of electoral boundaries and occurs in two forms.[26] An outright (intentional) gerrymander is a redistribution that benefits the government party and has no basis in understood principles. A thinly disguised (intentional) gerrymander, a term in the literature, is one in which the government party cites principles to mask its partisan manipulation of ridings.

A political assassination refers to a government party's gerrymandering of an opposition politician's riding in a bid to secure his defeat in the next election.

Origin and the Ontario Context

The term gerrymander originated in 1812, when the majority party in the Massachusetts legislature passed a Bill to redraw the boundaries of the state's electoral districts with the object of preventing the re-election of an opposition-party politician. Elbridge Gerry, the state's governor, signed the Bill. A Boston newspaper editor, noting that the bizarre shape of one revised electoral district resembled the mythical salamander, styled the redistribution a gerry-mander.[27]

By Confederation, the concept of gerrymander was entrenched in Canadian political lore. John Charlton (Liberal, Norfolk North) gleefully recounted the Massachusetts origin of the term during debates on the Tory redistributions of 1882 and 1892. The Conservative Party claimed to revere British precedents, gloated Charlton, but its redistributions followed "the *summum bonum* of political rascality … the system of American gerrymander."[28] The Liberals were no better when they became the majority party, according to Thomas Thomson (Conservative, Grey North). Laurier's 1903 redistribution bore "all the marks of the worst gerrymander ever perpetrated. It bears all the vilest and most vicious features of gerrymanders perpetrated by the local government of Ontario."[29]

"Hiving the Grits"

Hiving is a stratagem to waste opposition-party votes in the next election.[30] A *hive* is a riding in which the opposition party was overwhelmingly dominant in the previous election. With this stratagem, the government party transfers an opposition-leaning township from an adjacent *fighting* riding (a closely contested riding) into the hive riding. The out-transfer boosts the government party's prospects in the fighting riding, while the in-transfer merely adds to the opposition party's certain majority in the hive.

Figure 1.2 Cartoon of the original gerrymander, *Boston Gazette*, 26 March 1812. It depicts the bizarre shape of a district in Essex County, Massachusetts, as a dragon-like monster. Others likened the shape to a salamander. The district had the antithesis of a compact, symmetrical shape, which was the ideal for Canadian ridings.

Edward Blake, leader of the Dominion Liberal Party, coined the term *hiving* on 28 April 1882, when debating John A. Macdonald's redistribution Bill: "He [Macdonald] is detaching townships from their counties and adding them to other counties, and making his divisions under the pretence – and I repeat the word pretence – of equalizing the population, but with the real result of doing what he threatened he would do to an hon. friend of mine not now in this House, hiving the Grits."[31] The term, in Blake's usage, meant "cutting up and carving up the constituencies, by arranging them so as to concentrate, so far as they can, the Liberal strength in a comparatively limited number of constituencies, to weaken as far as he can the Liberal strength in a great many of the constituencies."[32]

On 8 May Blake again used the term: "In fact the Grits are hived into one [Middlesex] riding in order to strengthen the hon. gentleman [Macdonald] in the three other [Middlesex] ridings ... the Reformers are given for the purpose of hiving West Bruce, South Middlesex, West Ontario, [and] East Simcoe, and their strength is closely concentrated in North Brant, South Oxford, North Oxford, West Ontario, East Simcoe, South Middlesex, West Bruce, Central Huron, and West Elgin."[33] Shortly thereafter, the Liberal front-bencher David Mills confirmed Blake as the originator of the term: "As the hon. member for West Durham [Blake] has shown, the right hon. gentleman has taken a number of constituencies in groups and hived, to use his expression, the Reform party within those constituencies."[34] "The only contribution we [Liberals] have made to the gerrymander literature or phrases," recalled John Charlton, during debates on the 1892 Dominion redistribution Bill, "is the one originated during the last gerrymander of 1882, when we originated the phrase, 'hiving the Grits.'"[35]

During the debate on Macdonald's 1882 Bill, writes MacGregor Dawson, "Sir John's attitude throughout was one of cynical amusement, and *it is reported* that he sat in his place in the House rubbing his hands and chuckling to his colleagues: 'I've hived the Grits! I've hived the Grits!'"[36] Regrettably, Dawson cites no source for this hand-rubbing prime minister and his cynical chuckle. Nor does he question its authenticity. Given the novelty of the term "hiving" and its provenance from the Liberal side of the House, Dawson's account most likely is apocryphal.

Nonetheless, two weeks after Parliament's passage of the 1882 Bill, at a "mass meeting of the electors of Toronto held in the Amphitheatre," Sir John did use the term in his colourful way: "Well, the Grits ... complain that they are hived altogether. It seems they do not like the association (laughter) ... So it is with the Grits. They do not like each other's company (renewed laughter). They like to associate with Conservative gentlemen such as you. Your being with them rather gives tone to their society."[37] Such was Sir John's first documented use of the term.

THE GRIT NURSERY.

TROUBLED WITH "HIVES."

Figure 1.3 Bengough cartoon. The cartoon lampoons Macdonald's 1882 redistribution. Bengough's Macdonald offers "partisan returning officer lotion" for relief, a reference to Macdonald's "political assassination" of David Mills in the Bothwell riding.

The Book's "Liberal-Majority" Statistic

A government party's intent to gerrymander is measurable empirically with the Liberal-majority statistic and a modified version of Dawson's descriptive categories. The Liberal-majority statistic is the Liberal candidate's majority over his Conservative opponent, as calculated from returns for the previous election. If the Tory has the majority, then the Liberal-majority statistic has a negative value. One can calculate the statistic for ridings and also for municipal subdivisions within ridings. In a nutshell, these statistics reveal whether or not the government party benefits from transfers of municipalities between ridings, mergers of ridings, and the creation of new ridings. Unless its prospective gain is mitigated by understood principles, the redistribution is an outright gerrymander.

Dawson's categories for Liberal-majority statistics add a useful descriptive tool for nineteenth-century redistributions. As Dawson writes, "a majority of 200 would be considered at that time in Ontario as very safe indeed; one of 100 would be 'reasonably safe'; one of 50 to 100 meant much more than a fighting chance, it would be 'possibly safe'; and only when a majority went below 50 did a seat become really 'precarious.'"[38] Thus, in 1882, writes Dawson, "Sir John Macdonald's natural desire would be to have all seats as safe as could be managed; but he was severely limited by the small number of votes with which he had to work and the restricted amount of territory which could be transferred. He would have to content himself, therefore, with placing as many Conservative seats as possible in the 'reasonably safe' and 'possibly safe' classes, and perhaps even be compelled to leave a few, where unavoidable, in the 'precarious' class." This book uses Dawson's categories with two enhancements: it labels majorities of 500 or more (±500) as hives, and it places acclamations and contests between candidates of the same party in a separate category.

Table 1.4 demonstrates the Liberal-majority statistics and the modified Dawson categories for the Dominion riding of Ontario South, Ontario County, in the 1878 election, which preceded the 1882 redistribution. The data for Pickering Township show a majority of 140 for the Liberal candidate (a Liberal-majority statistic of +140). The data for Oshawa show a majority of 15 for the Conservative candidate (a statistic of -15). For the riding as a whole, the statistic is +206 (very safe, Liberal).

Table 1.4 Population and Liberal-majority statistics for the riding of Ontario South in the 1878 general election and after the Conservative Party's 1882 redistribution

1878 Dominion election *Ontario South riding*	*Glen (Liberal)*	*Gibbs (Conservative)*	*Liberal majority*	*Riding population*
Pickering Township	669	529	+140	6,883
Whitby West	289	249	+40	2,946
Whitby East Township	308	259	+49	3,417
Whitby Town Township	221	229	-8	3,140
Oshawa Town	380	395	-15	3,992
Total before redistribution	1,867	1,661	+206	20,378
<= Pickering, out-transfer			+140	6,883
Subtotal =>			+66	13,495
Reach Township, in-transfer =>			-86	4,949
Port Perry Village, in-transfer =>			+28	1,800
Net =>			+8	20,244

The 1882 Tory redistribution removed Pickering Township (+140) from Ontario South to the riding of Ontario West, but transferred Reach Township (-86) and Port Perry (+28) from Ontario North to Ontario South. These transfers changed Ontario South from very safe, Liberal (+206) to precarious (+8). The drop in the Liberal incumbent's chances for re-election flags the possibility of gerrymander – a judgment, however, which requires evidence about principles.

The Dawson categories are problematic for twentieth-century elections. As population increased over time, so too did the numbers of electors (persons eligible to vote) and voters (electors who voted) in the ridings. Between the 1882 and 1935 general elections, for example, the mean number of voters per Dominion riding rose from 3,290 to 19,613. In this context, the percentage of ridings in hives (±500) rose sharply, from 10 in 1882 to 26 in 1903 and 82 in 1933. The percentages for the provincial parliament were 7 for 1885, 34 for 1908, and 77 in 1933. Effectively, hive majority became the norm, and precarious and possibly safe ridings increasingly were endangered species.

Did Gerrymanders Work? Macgregor Dawson's Empirical Dead End

The concept of gerrymander assumes that the party preferences of voters in a given township are stable and transferable to another riding. "Every Canadian politician knows," opined Sir Richard Cartwright in 1912, "that, in the case of ordinary rural ridings more particularly, it is perfectly certain that certain townships in any given constituency will give a large majority for one party or the other. They also know that once a township has become decidedly Liberal or decidedly Conservative it will, as a rule, continue to vote in that way for many successive elections unless some burning question should arise to over-ride ordinary party associations."[39] Voters did indeed evidence continuity of party preference. In the 1878 and 1882 general elections, for example, voters favoured the same party in 442 of 573 municipalities (78 percent).

Nevertheless, the assumption of transferable, stable party preferences in a given township is problematic. The candidates and election issues differ between the sending riding in the previous election and the receiving riding in the next election. The electoral population in a transferred township undergoes turnover between elections. Some electors exit the township through death or out-migration; other individuals enter the township's electorate through attainment of the age of twenty-one, or through in-migration. Further, the participation of electors is unstable; as Gail Campbell finds in her poll-book-based study of Oxford County electors before 1875, only a minority of electors were repeat voters through two consecutive elections.[40]

So, did gerrymanders work, as government politicians believed, and opposition politicians feared? Dawson's 1935 article nicely shows the ambiguity of evidence for John A. Macdonald's infamous gerrymandered redistribution of 1882:

> The supreme test of any gerrymander is the election. No hiving of votes, no altering of boundaries, no increasing of majorities, is of much use if the votes do not go the way anticipated. The gerrymander of 1882, if judged by this test, was a failure; for the Conservatives, instead of winning 32 seats, as estimated, carried only 18, while the Liberals, who were to have had 14, secured 28. The objection may be urged, however, that these bare results are misleading: for it is possible that had the gerrymander not been

> enacted, the Liberal gains might have been very much greater; the Act may have averted disaster for the Conservatives, and what might have been a rout may have been turned, with its aid, into a mere defeat.[41]

Did Macdonald's gerrymanders fail to deliver expected gains, or successfully staunch losses? Dawson's alternative interpretations seem to be mutually exclusive, yet each is compatible with his evidence. Dawson's conundrum arises from his focus on the whole 1882 redistribution. Many influences act on the outcome of a general election, and one cannot isolate the influence of the redistribution.

Methodology for Escaping from Dawson's Dead End

Escape from Dawson's empirical dead end requires shifting our focus from the whole redistribution to its corrupted parts, the gerrymandered ridings within. First, one identifies the gerrymanders, each of which comprises a cluster of two or more ridings. Second, one pinpoints the target ridings within the clusters, which are the intended fruits of the gerrymander. Examples are opposition-held ridings that the government party expects to capture, or precariously held government-party ridings that have been strengthened to forestall loss to the opposition. Third, one compares the predicted outcomes for the target ridings in the next election with the actual outcomes. A gerrymander works if the government party captures the target riding, or prevents its capture by the opposition, and does so because votes in the municipalities of the target riding go the expected way. In one case, Sir John aimed to shore up the slim Tory majority in Norfolk South to prevent its loss to the Liberals. To this end, he transferred Simcoe Town (-94) from Norfolk North to Norfolk South, which boosted Tory prospects in the South riding from precarious, Tory (-17) to reasonably safe (-111). But this gerrymander failed: Norfolk South returned a Liberal (+26). One culprit was Simcoe Town, which favoured the Tory candidate, as expected, but by a reduced margin (-32, down from -94).

Fourth, one tallies the findings for all target ridings to judge how gerrymanders influenced party fortunes in the next election. Investigation of the 1882 redistribution reveals fifteen target ridings, of which ten returned Liberals in the 1882 general election.[42] Sir John's gerrymanders failed. They did not deliver the expected gains to his party. Nor did they staunch its losses.

Redistribution: Its Impact Beyond the Next General Election

The gerrymandered redistribution of 1882 was in place for all general elections until the next redistribution (1892), and beyond, given that the 1892 redistribution left the gerrymanders undisturbed. Thus, opined the veteran Grit politician Sir Richard Cartwright in 1912, Sir John's gerrymander lasted

> for nearly a quarter of a century. It began in 1882 and was not done away with till the election of 1904 ... for five successive elections, in 1882, 1887, 1891, 1896, and 1900, the Liberal party in Ontario were deprived of their fair share in representation ... while the Liberal party in Ontario almost exactly divided the popular vote in 1882 and 1887, and had a decisive majority in 1891, they were placed in a large minority in 1882 and 1887 and even in 1891 were kept still in a minority, though, of course, not so large a one ... Take for instance the election of 1887. Sir John had a nominal majority of some thirty votes, more or less. Of these thirty votes he owed at least fourteen or fifteen to the gerrymander. Had Sir John come out of that election with a majority of ten or twelve, he could not have kept office for six weeks. It was his gerrymander alone which saved him then and on half-a-dozen occasions between 1887 and 1891.[43]

"The Great Gerrymander of 1882," writes J. Murray Beck in *Pendulum of Power* (1968), was "ineffective [in Ontario in the 1882 general election] because of the resentment it aroused, [but] worked decidedly in Sir John's favour" in the 1887 general election. What is missing is evidence. Indeed, Beck's tabular statistics show that Conservative fortunes in the 1882 and 1887 elections were identical (number of seats won, 55 and 55; popular vote, 50.4 percent and 50.7 percent).[44] Perhaps the fate of our fifteen target ridings in three general elections offers partial comfort to Beck's guesswork. Macdonald's party won five of these gerrymandered ridings in 1882 ("ineffective"), ten in 1887 ("worked decidedly"), and four in 1891.

SUMMARY AND INTERPRETATION

Counties were both electoral and municipal entities after 1849. Ontario's municipal counties numbered nineteen in 1840 and forty-three after 1874. An 1851 Act united certain counties for municipal and judicial purposes (united-municipal counties), and some for representation (united-electoral counties). The schedule of ridings in the 1867 BNA Act abolished the united-electoral counties, but created three purely-electoral counties from parts of seven municipal counties. To the north of the counties were territorial districts, whose numbers increased from three to eleven during the years 1858–1921. With their sparse, scattered populations, territorial districts had no municipal functions and no equivalent to county lines to be observed in redistribution.

The delineation of municipal county had three complications for redistribution. First, the province had several united-municipal counties. In these cases, the united county was the municipal entity, the counties within having no municipal function and no county boundaries to be observed in redistribution. Second, incorporated cities were "counties of themselves ... for municipal purposes." Conversely, for municipal purposes, Toronto, Hamilton, Kingston, London, and Ottawa were not "parts of the counties of York, Wentworth, Frontenac, Middlesex, and Carleton."[45] Effectively, their city limits were county lines for purposes of redistribution. Third, over time, these cities annexed suburban populations in their adjacent townships. Thus, to observe county lines, a redistribution needed to enlarge the electoral territories of the cities to include their annexed territories.

Disciplined, centrally financed and directed political parties developed and evolved after Confederation. Government parties were potential agents for gerrymanders: a redrawing of electoral boundaries for party advantage.

Electoral districts in Canada represented populations. Thus, it mattered how redistribution adjusted ridings to the movement of population. Population rose nearly fourfold during the years of study, with above-average increases for the GTA and northlands and lagging growth in the counties. In this context, representation by population was consistently below average for the GTA and above average for Eastern Ontario. The standard population is this book's tool for measuring inequality of the riding populations.

A gerrymander unfairly boosts the government party's prospects in the next election. Passive gerrymandering leaves alone ridings that favour the government party, yet warrant adjustment on the basis of principle. An intentional gerrymander redraws riding territories. An outright intentional gerrymander benefits the government party but is problematic in terms of understood principles. A thinly disguised intentional gerrymander uses principles to mask a partisan manipulation of ridings. Stratagems for gerrymandering include hiving, the merging of two opposition-held ridings, the division into two of a riding held by the government party, over-representing populations that favour the government party, and under-representing populations that favour the opposition. By focusing on gerrymanders within a given redistribution, one can determine empirically whether or not particular gerrymanders worked, and how their collective performance contributed to the government party's gains or losses across the province.

This survey of counties, political parties, the movement of population, the standard population, and the gerrymander sets the stage for chapter 2, a study of redistribution in Canada West, the Ontario section of the United Province of Canada (1840–67).

2

Redistributions in Canada West, 1840–67

Canada West began and ended with imperial statutes. The 1840 imperial Act to Re-Unite the Provinces of Upper and Lower Canada (Union Act) created a Province of Canada with two sections, Canada West and Canada East, and a constitutional requirement for their equal representation in the province's Legislative Assembly. The imperial BNA Act, 1867, turned the sections into the provinces of Ontario and Quebec; created the Dominion of Canada, a federation of four provinces (Ontario, Quebec, New Brunswick, and Nova Scotia); and made population the basis of provincial representation in the national parliament, the House of Commons.

The 1840 and 1867 imperial statutes each redistributed the ridings. In the interim, Canada West received three redistributions by statutes of the Legislative Assembly (1845, 1851, and 1853). Although the 1867 redistribution came from the imperial BNA Act, its substance came from John A. Macdonald and his Great-Coalition Party in the Legislative Assembly of the Province of Canada.

Meanwhile, two government initiatives reconfigured redistribution. First, the 1849 Municipal Act transferred local government from districts to counties, which turned counties into municipal entities as well as electoral ones. Therein originated the principle of observing municipal-county lines in the drawing of electoral boundaries. Second, the province undertook its first modern census enumerations in 1852 and 1861. These censuses documented that Canada West had an increasingly larger population than Canada East. This generated dissatisfaction in Canada West with the 1840 constitutional requirement for equal representation between the two sections of the Province, and a cry for representation by population on a sectional basis. The censuses also exposed inequalities of population across the ridings, but without consequence for redistribution.

REDISTRIBUTION BY IMPERIAL STATUTE, 1840

Britain's 1840 Union Act established a start-up schedule of ridings, but empowered the Legislative Assembly to "alter the Divisions and Extent of the several Counties, Ridings, Cities, and Towns which shall be represented."[1] Lord Sydenham, provincial governor in the wake of the failed 1837 rebellions, was the principal author of the imperial list.[2] Sydenham's draft Bill, sent to the Colonial Office, proposed seventy-six single-member constituencies, which implied thirty-eight for Canada West. A revised draft from the Colonial Office to Sydenham proposed forty single-member ridings and one two-member riding, Toronto. The Colonial-Office draft, pronounced Sydenham, "will do."

The 1840 imperial Act required that the two sections of the province have equal representation in the Legislative Assembly. Thus, Canada West and Canada East each had forty-two members in the province's Legislative Assembly in 1841, and sixty-five members each after 1853. Toronto was the sole two-member constituency in Canada West under the Union Act. This contrasted with the parliament of Upper Canada, in which twenty-two of the forty ridings had two representatives.

The forty-two constituencies in Canada West included thirty-three for its twenty-nine counties; two for Toronto, the only city; and seven for towns (Kingston, Hamilton, London, Bytown, Cornwall, Brockville, and Niagara). Three counties had two ridings: Halton, East and West; Lincoln, North and South; and Northumberland, North and South. The Act folded four counties into two "united-electoral counties": Lennox-Addington and Lanark-Renfrew.

THE BIRTH OF MUNICIPAL COUNTIES, 1849

In 1841 the twenty-nine counties in Canada West were units for representation in the Legislative Assembly, but nineteen territorial districts administered local government. As "wealth and population" in Canada West increased, government divided some of the districts, and the territories of districts and counties became increasingly similar. In 1849, government judged that the districts were redundant and abolished them, and gave local government to counties.[3] Henceforth counties were municipal entities as well as electoral.

THE REDISTRIBUTIONS OF 1845 AND 1851

Counties had been units for representation in the Legislative Assembly since the creation of Upper Canada in 1791. Perforce, the province's 1845 and 1851 Acts to reorganize counties were redistribution statutes. The 1845 Act, as its title indicated, was "for Better Defining the Limits of Counties and Districts in Upper Canada, for Detaching Townships from Some Counties and attaching them to others, and for Other Purposes relative to the Division of Upper Canada into Townships, Counties, and Districts." The Act transformed three counties each with two ridings – Northumberland, Halton, and Lincoln – into six counties each with one riding: Northumberland and Peterborough; Halton and Wellington; and Lincoln and Welland.[4] This raised the number of counties from twenty-nine to thirty-two. Statutes added three more counties – Lambton, Bruce, and Perth – in 1849. The 1851 Act to Make Certain Alterations in the Territorial Divisions of Upper Canada created seven counties from parts of existing counties.[5] This raised the tally of counties to forty-two.

The 1851 Act folded eighteen counties into eight united-electoral counties and twenty-one counties into nine united-municipal counties. The territories of united-electoral and united-municipal counties sometimes differed. Lambton County, for example, was united with Essex County for municipal purposes, but with Kent County "as the County of Kent" for representation. As discussed in chapter 1, the united-municipal county had county lines to be observed in redistribution, but the counties within it did not.

THE 1852 AND 1861 CENSUSES OF THE PROVINCE OF CANADA

In January of 1852, the Province of Canada completed its first modern census enumeration – one with a comprehensive nominal schedule,[6] and the first of what became a decennial series. The 1861 census revealed that population in Canada West had surpassed population in Canada East. That created opposition in the western counties of Canada West to the constitutional requirement for equality of representation between the two sections of the province. Representation by population on a sectional basis became a Reform-Party battle cry in Canada West and, with Confederation in 1867, a founding principle for provincial representation in the Dominion Parliament.

The 1852 and 1861 censuses exposed sharp inequalities of population across the ridings. Thus, in May 1861, Skeffington Connor, the member for Oxford South, alluded to "the evil of leaving a County such as Huron and Bruce, with a population of 80,000 or 90,000 inhabitants, represented by only one member, whilst the little borough of Niagara [population 4,470] had the same representation."[7] Even so, his exposé did not cause politicians to embrace approximate equality of riding populations as a foundational principle for redistribution. Throughout the pre-Confederation years, that principle was a minor consideration, modest in application.

THE 1853 REDISTRIBUTION

The 1853 Representation Act increased the number of ridings from forty-two to sixty-five. It created fifteen new constituencies through division of county ridings and dissolution of united-electoral counties. It boosted the populations of three town ridings (Niagara, Cornwall, and Brockville), in each case by merging them with a contiguous township. Lastly, it gave Toronto two single-member ridings to replace the city's two-member constituency under the 1840 Act.[8] The 1853 Act provided for two united-electoral counties, down from eight in 1851.[9]

The 1853 Act interfered with municipal lines. By "special provision" and "for the purpose of Representation only," it transferred two Carleton-County townships (Osgood and Gloucester, combined population 8,854) from the riding of Carleton to the county riding of Russell, which had just 6,824 inhabitants.[10] The Act split townships in three instances: Brantford Township, Brant County; Waterloo Township, Waterloo County; and York Township, York County. These splits were to be precedents of consequence thirty years later.

The revised schedule of ridings expressed scant regard for the principle of representation by population. In Table 2.1 the mean population for the sixty-five Canada West ridings in 1852 (14,651) is the standard population (1.00). After redistribution, the standard populations of ridings ranged from 0.38 to 1.69. Just eighteen of the sixty-five ridings (28 percent) were within the optimum range (0.90–1.10). The ridings of Niagara, Cornwall, and London each had less than 0.50. The ridings of Huron & Bruce, Lennox & Addington, and Peel each had more than 1.50, but just one member.

Interestingly, the movement of population equalized the riding populations during the 1850s, without the assistance of redistribution. As

Table 2.1 Canada West, percentage of ridings within 10% of the standard population after the 1853 redistribution

Census	*1852*	*1861*
under 0.80	23%	23%
0.80–0.89	11%	14%
0.90–1.10	28%	35%
1.11–1.20	17%	11%
over 1.20	22%	17%
# of ridings	65	65
Population	952,293	1,398,138
Standard population	14,651	21,510

Table 2.1 reports, the percentage of ridings in the optimum zone was 35 under the 1861 census, up from 28 in 1852.[11]

POLITICAL DEVELOPMENTS DURING THE 1860S

The political climate for redistribution was changing during the early 1860s. First, a two-party system of Conservatives and Liberals (Tories and Grits) was taking root. Second, representation by population on a sectional basis was emerging as a major political issue. Both developments connected to redistribution.

Political Parties

Two political parties were emerging from regional political formations and "loose fish" in Canada West. John A. Macdonald headed a coalition of Conservatives and pro-coalition Reformers. Against him was an array of anti-coalition Reformers, supporters in principle of one-party ministries.[12] In June 1864, most anti-coalition Reformers followed George Brown into a Great Coalition with Macdonald's Conservatives. In December 1865 Brown left the Great Coalition, and in 1867 he held a Reform Convention in Toronto to revive the anti-coalition Reform Party. Some of his former followers – at least seven – stayed with the Great Coalition, thereby becoming Liberal-Conservatives: effectively Conservatives, or colloquially Tories. The rump of Brown's group became known as Liberals, or colloquially Grits or Reformers. The colloquial name *Grits* was ironic for a party founded by George Brown. During the late 1850s Brown had been a fierce opponent of Clear-Grit democracy and had done more than any other politician to marginalize the Clear-Grit movement among anti-coalition Reformers.[13]

In the event, the Canada West section of Parliament held twenty-seven Conservatives and thirty-eight Liberals after George Brown's exit from the Great Coalition. With a two-party system falling into place, gerrymandered redistribution was a growing possibility. If so, the perpetrators were likely to be Tories, the government-in-waiting party for the new Dominion of Canada. Indeed, on the day of Confederation, 1 July 1867, a newly knighted Sir John A. Macdonald became prime minister, and his newly recruited ally in coalition, John Sandfield Macdonald, an anti-Brown Reformer, became premier of the Province of Ontario.

Sectionalism

Representation by population on a sectional basis was a major political issue by the 1860s. The 1840 imperial Act of Union had prescribed equal representation between Canada West and Canada East in the Legislative Assembly. The 1861 census of Canada, however, reported 285,535 more people in Canada West than in Canada East. To followers of George Brown, a leading anti-coalition Reformer, equal representation was the arithmetic for French-Canadian, Roman-Catholic domination of Anglo-Protestants in Canada West. Brown's remedy for this perceived injustice was representation by population on a sectional basis, a revision of the constitution that required imperial enabling legislation.[14] Thirteen Conservatives and five coalitionist Reformers supported the change in divisions of the Legislative Assembly in 1862 and 1863. In the circumstances, the Conservative co-premier, John A. Macdonald, and his successor, the anti-sectionalist Reformer John Sandfield Macdonald, agreed to treat the issue as an open question. Here lay the roots of a key provision in the 1867 BNA Act – the original provinces in Confederation were to be represented in the House of Commons on the basis of population.

Simply put, representation by population on a sectional basis was the new orthodoxy in Canada West. It remained to be seen how the principle of representation by population would play out in Ontario after Confederation: first, to equalize population across ridings; second, to equalize population between sections of Ontario (the slow-growth eastern counties versus the rapidly growing western counties); third, for application to cities; and fourth, for application to emerging northern districts with vast territories and small, scattered populations.

THE AUTHORITY FOR REDISTRIBUTION UNDER THE BNA ACT, 1867

Confederation resolved a sectional deadlock between Canada West and Canada East that had developed from the 1840 constitutional requirement for sectional equality in the Province of Canada's Legislative Assembly. Given that the requirement was fixed by imperial statute, another imperial Act was necessary to change it. Such was the job of the imperial British North America Act, 1867. First, the Act transformed Canada West and Canada East into the separate provinces of Ontario and Quebec. Second, it placed Ontario in a larger federal union in which the founding provinces were to be represented by population in the national parliament, the House of Commons.

In 1867 Ontario was allocated eighty-two seats in the House of Commons, based on a formula for calculation in Section 51 of the BNA Act. The Act fixed Quebec's representation at sixty-five seats, from which was calculated a standard population: the Quebec population in the most recent census, divided by sixty-five, which was 17,108 in 1867. Ontario's representation in 1867 derived from the eighty-two standard populations in its 1861 census population.

The BNA Act made the House of Commons the authority for Dominion redistribution, which in practice meant the majority party. This provision in the Act originated with John A. Macdonald and his Great-Coalition ministry and took three years to evolve.[15] At the Quebec Conference in October 1864, Macdonald himself had moved "that the Legislature of each Province shall divide such Province into the proper number of constituencies and define the boundaries of each of them." The Quebec Conference delegates passed a second motion, movers unknown, that "the Local Legislature of each Province may, from time to time, alter the electoral districts of the Province for the purposes of representation in the House of Commons, and distribute the representatives to which the Province is entitled in any manner such Legislature may see fit." However, between the closing of the Quebec Conference in October 1864 and the meeting of the Canadian Legislature in January 1865, the Conference delegates revised the text to read that "the Local Legislature of each Province may from time to time alter the Electoral Districts for the purpose of Representation in such Local Legislature and distribute the Representatives to which the Province is entitled in such Local Legislature in any manner such Legislature may see fit."

In April 1865, Sir E.P. Taché – prime minister and nominal head of the Great-Coalition ministry[16] – noted the discrepancy between the original resolution, which had been signed by the delegates, and the revised text, and asked the governor-general to advise which document applied. As he noted, "This alteration is not altogether unimportant. In the one copy, the Resolution refers to the House of Commons of the Federal Legislature, in the other, to the Local Legislature alone." The governor-general turned to the actual chief minister, John A. Macdonald, for an answer. The original resolution, wrote Macdonald in May 1865, was an error:

> the proceedings of the Conference towards the close of its deliberations were very much hurried, and it was subsequently discovered that several errors had occurred in revising and re-arranging its numerous resolutions which were adopted in the first instance without that exactness of expression and logical sequence so necessary in an instrument intended to present a complete scheme. Some of these errors were discovered and corrected at Montreal, by the unanimous consent of the Delegates present at a meeting held in that City for the purpose ... The power to alter or re-adjust the Constituencies after Parliament is constituted belongs naturally, logically, and according to every constitutional precedent, to that Parliament [the House of Commons], and not to an inferior Body [the Legislative Assembly of a province].

In January 1867, a note (provenance unknown) attached to Section 25 of a first draft of the BNA Bill stated enigmatically that "the readjustment [is] to be made by an independent authority, as some of the judges, as specified in the imperial act." Nothing came of this query or of the Quebec Conference resolution in its original and altered versions. As the final draft of the BNA Bill stated, "Representation shall be readjusted by such authority, and in such manner, and in such time, as the Parliament of Canada from time to time provides."[17]

The BNA Act said nothing about redistribution for Canada's provincial parliaments. By default the Legislative Assembly became the authority for redistribution, which meant the government party. The provincial parliament could enact redistribution whenever it wished, or not at all – it had no timing requirement. Indeed, the provincial ridings were to go without a redistribution between 1933 and 1954 (twenty-one years).[18]

Similarly, the provincial parliament had no constitutional quota for the number of seats in the Legislative Assembly. In this constitutional void, Oliver Mowat's Liberal-Party ministry was to match the Dominion quota of eighty-eight in 1874, but thereafter the numbers of Dominion and provincial ridings were to differ.

JOHN A. MACDONALD'S REDISTRIBUTION OF 1867

Schedule I in the 1867 BNA Act listed one set of ridings for Ontario's 1867 Dominion and provincial general elections, which each riding was to hold simultaneously. The schedule increased the number of ridings from sixty-five to eighty-two, a rise of seventeen apiece for the Dominion and provincial elections. It established new constituencies, redrew the boundaries of existing ones, and eliminated the last of the united-electoral counties.

Schedule I came in the form of an imperial statute, but the BNA Act merely adopted the schedule that John A. Macdonald had prepared in 1866. The representation for Ontario at Confederation, recalled Edward Blake, leader of the Dominion Liberals in 1882, was "settled by the hon. gentleman [Macdonald] himself in the first instance ... it was settled by the coalition government which passed confederation."[19] Macdonald's letter to Viscount Monck, governor-general of the Province of Canada, in June 1866, provided direct evidence of Macdonald's role: "I have felt it my duty to have confidential conversations with the leading supporters of the Government (Liberal and Conservative) ... The only point, then, remaining unsettled is the redistribution of constituencies. I am now consulting the leading members on this point, in order to prevent discussion in the House. I have prepared and printed a population return, and hope in a few days to perfect a scheme with the consent of my [coalition] Reform colleagues,[20] which we shall submit to Your Lordship, in the first place, and then to Parliament."[21]

The Legislative Assembly ratified Macdonald's schedule in August 1866. The names of two ridings greased the wheels for the schedule's acceptance by the imperial authority – the constituencies of Monck and Cardwell paid homage to Viscount Monck, governor-general, and Viscount Cardwell, colonial secretary in the imperial government.[22]

Details of the 1867 Redistribution

The 1861 census tallied 1,396, 091 people for Canada West, up 47 percent from 1852. The province's western section now had five cities:

Toronto (incorporated 1834); Hamilton and Kingston (incorporated 1846); and Ottawa and London (incorporated 1855). In addition to its forty-one counties, Canada West had two northern districts, Algoma and Nipissing, dating from 1858 and lightly populated (with 4,916 and 2,094 people respectively).

The 1867 redistribution fashioned eighty-two Ontario ridings from the sixty-five of Canada West. It retained forty-three old ridings and created thirty-nine new ones. Of the latter, thirty-five came from divisions of old ridings; Lambton County, for example, was divided into the ridings of Lambton East and Lambton West. Four were created anew: the ridings of Algoma District and the purely-electoral counties of Bothwell, Cardwell, and Monck. Nipissing District (population 2,094) was not given representation.

Documentary evidence for Macdonald's underlying principles is lacking, primarily because Macdonald successfully avoided debate in the Legislative Assembly about the 1867 redistribution. Nevertheless, features of the redistribution indicate scanty support for municipal lines and the equalization of riding populations.

The schedule trespassed on county lines in several cases. The three purely-electoral counties took townships from seven municipal counties: Bothwell from Lambton and Kent; Monck from Haldimand, Lincoln, and Welland; and Cardwell from Peel and Simcoe. As they had been since 1853, the townships of Gloucester and Osgoode were "in the county of Carleton, but united to the county of Russell for Electoral purposes."[23]

Just 24 percent of the eighty-two ridings were in the optimum range for population (0.90–1.10), down from 33 percent of sixty-five ridings in 1861. Ridings in certain counties had unequal populations (Elgin, 1.25, 0.62; Bruce, 0.52, 1.09; Victoria, 0.44, 0.92; York, 1.49, 1.33, 0.67). Macdonald over-represented counties in Eastern Ontario and the northern district of Algoma (0.29). At the low-population extreme were two town ridings, Niagara and Cornwall, with 0.26 and 0.40 standard populations. At the high-population extreme were Oxford North (1.44), Toronto West (1.45), Essex (1.47), and York East (1.49).

Party Advantage in the 1867 Redistribution

Returns for the 1863 general election were John A. Macdonald's raw material for designing the eighty-two ridings of Confederation. By 1866, however, party strengths in the 1863 parliament had shifted, due to by-elections and fallout from the Great Coalition of 1864. Thus, party standings for the sixty-five ridings in Canada West were now thirty-eight Liberals (anti-coalition Reformers) and twenty-seven Conservatives (Conservatives and coalition Reformers).[24] The Conservative-held ridings had a smaller mean population, hence more representation, than the Liberal-held ridings: 20,423 compared to 22,281.

The evidence is mixed for a judgment that Macdonald's redistribution was a gerrymander. To be sure, Macdonald declined to match representation to population for certain ridings whose incumbents were Liberals. The pre-Confederation riding of Huron-Bruce rated five ridings but got four; Oxford County warranted three ridings, but got two; and Essex County merited two ridings but got one. Yet some of Macdonald's changes aided the opposition party. The Liberal-held county ridings of Renfrew and Victoria each merited one riding, but were given two. The redistribution for Wellington County turned two Liberal-held ridings into three. The two Liberal-held Elgin-County ridings presented an opportunity for Tory gain that Macdonald missed. Those ridings had unequal populations (1.25 and 0.62). Given the east-west alignment of the Elgin townships, the only possible within-county adjustment was to move Yarmouth Township and St. Thomas Town from Elgin East to Elgin West. These transfers would have been positive for population equality (1.08 and 0.79) and would have moved Elgin West from precarious, Liberal (+31) to possibly safe, Conservative (-98), a gain for the government party.[25] But Macdonald did not make the change.

If gerrymandering was involved in the division of Lennox & Addington into two ridings, Lennox and Addington, then it was between factions of the Conservative Party. In the 1863 Lennox & Addington general election, Richard Cartwright, then "a loyal back-bencher in Macdonald's party," had defeated Augustus Hooper, the sitting Conservative, in a "factionalized and intensely local contest."[26] Years later, during a heated debate on the Conservative Party's 1892 Representation bill, Uriah Wilson, the Conservative member for Lennox & Addington, accused Richard Cartwright, who by then had become a front-bench Liberal, of having rigged the boundary changes of 1867. "At Confederation," complained Wilson, "those boundaries were changed very peculiarly, because the township of Camden, which would have made Lennox a compact and square constituency, with about the unit of population, was left out, and, I think, for a very good reason, because at the previous general election [1863] it had gone pretty strongly against the hon. member, [who was] then sitting for Lennox and Addington. Is it to be supposed that this change [was] made at confederation without the member for that riding being consulted? He was a strong supporter at the time of Sir John Macdonald."[27] Keeping in mind Wilson's partisan incentive to skewer a Tory apostate, his allegation was plausible. As he alleged, Camden Township, including Newburgh Village, had given a massive majority to Hooper, and was the only municipality to do so; thus, Cartwright stood to benefit in the 1867 election when he stood for Lennox, with Camden in the neighbouring Addington riding. Second, the Lennox riding would indeed have been square and compact had it retained Camden. That said, one could argue principles against placing Camden in Lennox,[28] and direct evidence is lacking about whether or not Cartwright cared about the placement of Camden, or if he did, whether his view carried weight with Macdonald.

Macdonald's formation of three purely-electoral counties – Monck, Cardwell, and Bothwell – offered little advantage for his party. Those ridings stood to add two Liberal seats (Monck and Bothwell) and one Conservative seat (Cardwell) to party tallies. Ridings in the contributing counties were likely to remain unchanged in their partisan preferences, four of them Liberal and three Conservative.[29]

The creation of Monck disrupted Liberals in Welland, which lost the Liberal-leaning townships of Pelham and Wainfleet (+182) to Monck, to the benefit of Welland's Conservatives.[30] When the "Welland Reform Association" met to nominate candidates for the 1867 Dominion and provincial general elections, it voted to seat delegates from Pelham and Wainfleet, but lost its president, Dr John Fraser, whose residence in Pelham placed him outside the Welland riding. Fraser "did not know what the change in the geography of the county would mean politically." For his predicament, he blamed the Conservative member for Welland, Thomas Clark Street, for having "manufactured the change for some reason best known to himself." Fraser himself had defeated Street in the 1854 election for Welland "in an unusually violent contest";[31] he ran unsuccessfully for Monck in the 1867 Dominion election.

SUMMARY AND INTERPRETATION

The 1840 imperial Union Act gave Canada West mostly single-member ridings, a contrast to the many two-member ridings on the Upper Canada list. The governor, Lord Sydenham, in consultation with the Colonial Office, made this determination.

Two government initiatives reconfigured redistributions. The first, the 1849 Municipal Act, made counties municipal units in addition to their previous function as electoral units. This laid the basis for the principle that electoral divisions should follow county lines, although support for the principle was feeble in Canada West. The second initiative, the introduction of modern decennial census enumerations in 1852 and 1861, issued counts of population for municipalities, ridings, and the two sections of the Province. Population statistics made representation by population on a sectional basis an issue during the 1850s and 1860s. In contrast, representation by population for ridings attracted little interest.

The 1845 and 1851 Acts to reorganize counties and the 1853 Representation Act were redistributions by the Legislative Assembly. The 1853 redistribution set a precedent for interfering with municipal lines – it split townships and divided counties – and did little to equalize riding populations. Just 28 percent of the ridings fell into the optimum range for population (0.90–1.10). The province's lack of stable political parties ruled out the possibility of a comprehensive gerrymander. Nevertheless, "log-rolling" – mutual exchanges of political favours – possibly influenced Macdonald's settlement of specific ridings.

Although the 1867 schedule of ridings came from an imperial Act, the list was Canadian-made, coming from John A. Macdonald and his Great-Coalition majority in the Assembly. The schedule showed a lukewarm commitment to equalizing population across ridings; just 21 percent of the ridings were in the optimum range, which was less than the 28 percent attained in the 1853 redistribution. Like the 1853 Act, the 1867 list trespassed on municipal lines, in particular by its creation of three purely-electoral counties. Liberal-held ridings under the 1867 schedule had larger populations than government-held ones. Nevertheless, gerrymandering played little role in John A. Macdonald's 1867 redistribution. In some cases, the opposition party benefited.

The BNA Act, 1867, set the parameters for future redistributions. Parliament was the authority for redistribution. The Dominion government had quota and timing requirements for redistribution, but the provincial parliament had neither. Canada had no constitutional rules for redrawing the ridings within a province. Unwritten principles were to fill the void. Such was the template for the first redistributions in Confederation, one for Dominion ridings in 1872, and the other for provincial ridings in 1874.

3

Sir John A. Macdonald and Oliver Mowat: Redistributions of the 1870s

The 1870s featured two redistributions, one in 1872 for Dominion ridings, which was mandatory under the 1867 BNA Act, and the other in 1874 for provincial ridings. Canada's Conservative prime minister, Sir John A. Macdonald, administered the Dominion redistribution, his second in five years. Macdonald led a majority of twenty nationally and held a majority of the Ontario ridings (forty-nine Conservatives, thirty-three Liberals). Ontario's Liberal premier, Oliver Mowat, managed Ontario's first provincial redistribution. His ministry held a majority of four in the provincial parliament (forty-three Liberals, thirty-nine Conservatives).

During the decade 1861–71, the provincial population increased by 16 percent, led by Western Ontario (23 percent), with the GTA (10 percent) and Eastern Ontario (5 percent) trailing. Toronto was the largest of Ontario's five cities, with 59,000 people, followed by Hamilton, 26,716; Ottawa, 21,545; London, 15,826; and Kingston, 12,407. The five cities held 9 percent of the Ontario population, up from 7 percent in 1861. In 1871 Ontario had five northern districts: Algoma (1858), Nipissing (1858), Muskoka (1868), Parry Sound (1869), and Thunder Bay (1871). Their combined population was 15,728. Only Algoma had representation in 1867, but the riding of Algoma included the newly created Thunder Bay district. Nipissing was to be without provincial representation until 1889 and without Dominion representation until 1892.[1]

Each redistribution was for eighty-eight seats, up from eighty-two at Confederation. This number was Ontario's constitutional quota for Dominion ridings, which Mowat chose to match. The names and territories of the Dominion and provincial ridings, however, began to differ. Both redistributions were modest in scope. The Dominion Representation

Act touched fourteen of the eighty-two original ridings, and the Provincial Act, twenty-one.

The BNA Act gave no guidelines for redistribution within a province for either jurisdiction. In this constitutional vacuum, debates on the redistribution Bills expressed an interplay of evolving, underlying principles. Macdonald and Mowat each valued municipal lines and representation by population, but acted modestly on those principles. In the creation of new ridings, Macdonald favoured cities, whereas Mowat's additions were in the counties.

Macdonald's 1872 redistribution retained controversial features of his 1867 ridings, such as the purely-electoral counties of Bothwell, Monck, and Cardwell, and the small-population ridings of Niagara and Cornwall. Mowat abolished Bothwell and Niagara, but retained Monck, Cardwell, and Cornwall. In 1882 Dominion Conservatives were to allege that Oliver Mowat's 1874 Bill was a gerrymander. The evidence indicates that it was not, and that the Tory allegation was a canard.

THE DOMINION REDISTRIBUTION OF 1872

To reach the Ontario quota of eighty-eight ridings, Sir John A. Macdonald added six seats and eliminated none. His Representation Act made Ottawa and Hamilton two-member ridings instead of single-member ones; gave Toronto a third riding; gave third ridings to the counties of Huron and Grey; and created the riding of Muskoka for the districts of Muskoka and Parry Sound. The Act did little to equalize the riding populations. The percentage of ridings in the optimum range of standard populations (0.90–1.10) moved from 22 to 24. Two transfers crossed county lines, one moving Dunn Township from Haldimand County to the purely-electoral county of Monck, and the other moving four townships (2,329 people) from Victoria North to the new riding of Muskoka (0.38 standard populations).

Principles Underlying the 1872 Redistribution

Macdonald professed several overlapping principles to guide his delineation of ridings.[2] His paramount goal was to advance the equalization of riding populations. His second principle was adherence to municipal lines in the redrawing of electoral districts. "With respect to rural constituencies," elaborated the prime minister,

Figure 3.1 Bengough cartoon. "The veritable John A."

the desire of the government has been to preserve the representation for counties and sub-divisions of counties as much as possible … that rule was broken in 1867 in three constituencies, viz., Bothwell, Cardwell, and Monck; and I do not think, on the whole, that the experiment has proven a successful one … it is obvious that there is great advantage in having counties elect men whom they know …

> All that great advantage is lost by cutting off a portion of two [or] several counties and adding them together for electoral purposes only. The portions so cut off have no common interest: they do not meet together, and they have no common feeling except that once in five years they go to the polls in their own township to vote for a man who may be known in one section and not in another.

His third principle was that "while the principle of population was considered to a very great extent, other considerations were also held to have weight; so that different interests, classes, and localities should be fairly represented, that the principle of numbers should not be the only one." Thus, Macdonald's Bill gave special consideration to "manufacturing and commercial" interests, as opposed to "agricultural" ones; Eastern Ontario as a sectional interest; and northland districts recently opened for settlement. As an accommodation for "manufacturing and commercial" interests, the cities of Hamilton (1.46) and Ottawa (1.18) were made two-member ridings, although they merited only one member apiece on grounds of population. The additional member for Ottawa also balanced representation between Eastern Ontario, a region of slow-growth population, and areas "north and west of Toronto," which were undergoing rapid population growth and received four additional ridings. Algoma (0.38), "a new country just opened for settlement and almost beyond the ken or protection of law," required representation "to give confidence to the settlers going there." Lastly, Macdonald supported the preservation of certain ridings on historical grounds. He intended that his Bill "should not destroy any constituency now existing." Although he referred explicitly to the province's tiny town ridings, Niagara (0.20) and Cornwall (0.39), he valued all existing ridings, which, of course, were of his own creation in 1867.

Liberals espoused similar principles. Edward Blake, premier in the provincial legislature and member for Durham West in the House of Commons, urged that equality of population should be "regarded as far as possible," but not pushed "too far."[3] Malcolm Colin Cameron, the member for Huron South and an adopted son of the Union-era politician Malcolm Cameron, insisted that ridings "ought ... to be as compact as possible ... Another object should be that the Townships forming a riding should be contiguous."[4]

The Liberal Critique

Macdonald's Bill was wanting in Grit eyes. Alexander Mackenzie, soon to be leader of the Dominion Liberal Party, characterized Macdonald's

Bill "as having been drawn solely to enable the Government to obtain political advantage." Mackenzie rejected Macdonald's premise that cities (Toronto, Hamilton, and Ottawa) were the exclusive domains of "manufacturing and commercial" interests, and that counties exclusively represented "rural" or "agricultural" concerns. His own Lambton-County riding, for example, had "a larger and wealthier manufacturing interest than in almost any other constituency in Canada, and there were 200 or 300 engines pumping oil, and there were extensive refineries."[5] As for equalizing population, noted David Mills, the member for Bothwell and a future minister, the Bill left alone the small-population ridings of Niagara and Cornwall, and also high-population ridings that were ripe for division: Simcoe North (1.84), Bruce South (1.71), Essex (1.80), and Lambton (1.75).[6]

Case Studies

HAMILTON AND OTTAWA: GERRYMANDERING THROUGH OVER-REPRESENTATION

Macdonald's Act made Hamilton City (1.46) and Ottawa City (1.18) two-member ridings, despite each having less than 1.50 standard populations.[7] Conversely, it withheld second ridings for Lambton and Essex Counties (1.75 and 1.80), a third riding for Simcoe County (3.13), and fourth ridings for the counties of Middlesex (3.65) and Huron (3.61). Macdonald's justification was that cities represented "communities of manufacturing and commercial interest," and as such, deserved over-representation on the basis of population. Macdonald's party stood to benefit. Ottawa was a Conservative hive (-943). The incumbent for Hamilton, Charles Magill, was Liberal, but he broke ranks with his party and voted for Macdonald's Bill, with its increased representation for his city. Magill's defection failed to save him. In the 1872 general election, the Conservatives swept all four seats for the two cities. Front-bench Liberals disputed Macdonald's pronouncement that cities alone represented business interests and that the counties were entirely agricultural.

RIDINGS LEFT WITH UNEQUAL POPULATIONS

Based on understood principles, the equalization of population applied first to counties, then ridings. That is, the number of ridings in a county was to match its number of standard populations, and ridings within the county were to have approximately equal populations.

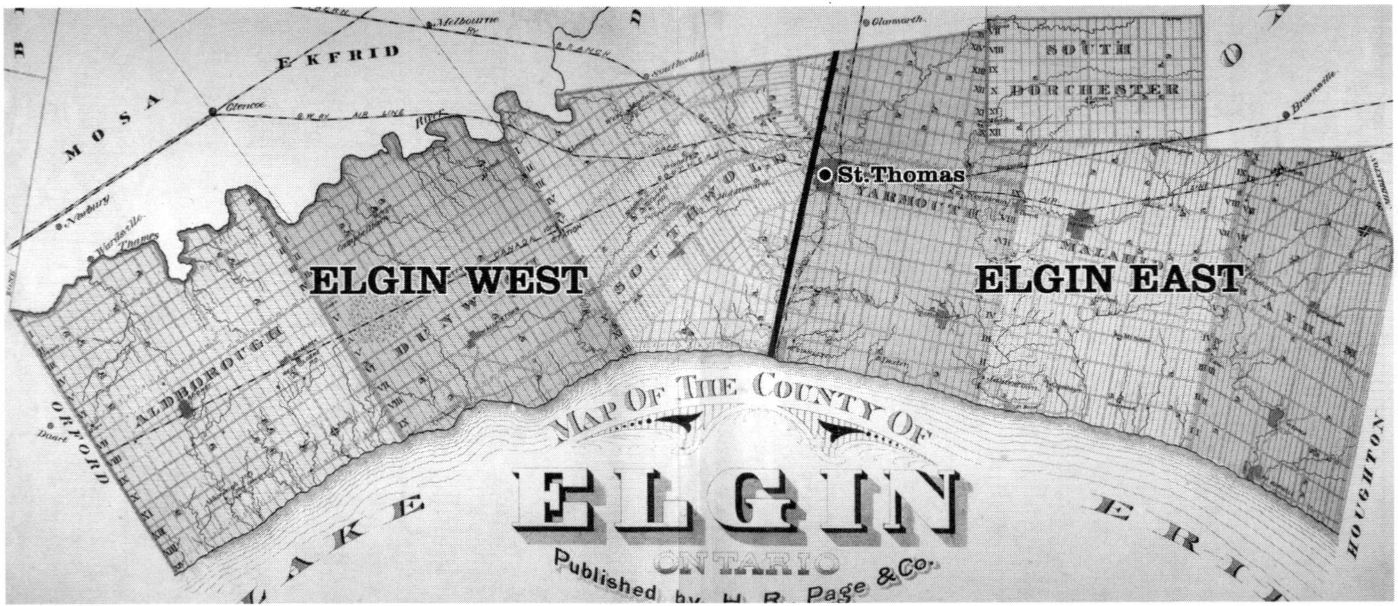

Map 3.1 Elgin County, Dominion ridings, 1872

Elgin County (Map 3.1) had two left-alone ridings with unequal populations: Elgin West, 0.70, and Elgin East, 1.14. Had Macdonald transferred St. Thomas Town – in the dead centre of the county and on the boundary of the ridings – from Elgin East to Elgin West, then the populations would have been more equal (1.02 and 0.82). The consequences for the political parties would have been small.

Peterborough County (Map 3.2) had two left-alone ridings with unequal populations: Peterborough East, 1.02, and Peterborough West, 0.64. Had Macdonald transferred Douro Township from Peterborough East to Peterborough West, the populations would have been more equal (0.87 and 0.79). The Tories held both ridings (very safe, -312, and precarious, -29) and this would have continued, albeit with changed levels of security (reasonably safe, -158 and -183).

Brant County (Map 3.3) had two left-alone ridings with unequal populations: Brant North, 0.63, and Brant South, 1.13. Macdonald might have transferred Tuscarora Township from Brant South to Brant North to equalize the populations (0.76 and 0.99), without giving advantage to either party. The inhabitants of Tuscarora were Six Nations Indians who had no votes, just population.

"CHERRY-PICKING" LIBERAL RIDINGS FOR DISTURBANCE

Seventeen of the eighty-two Ontario ridings had less than 0.80 standard populations. Of these, the government party held fourteen, and the opposition Liberals, three. Macdonald's Bill touched just two of these low-population ridings – Victoria North and Wellington South – two of the three with Liberal incumbents. Conversely, Conservatives held fourteen of the fifteen left-alone ridings, an indication of passive gerrymandering, and doubtless of intra-caucus lobbying by the sitting Tory MPs. In the 1872 general election, however, eight of the fifteen returned Liberals. The passive gerrymander failed.

LEFT-ALONE TINY TOWN RIDINGS, NIAGARA AND CORNWALL

During debate, the government party defeated a Liberal amendment to abolish the "glaring anomalies" of Niagara (0.20) and Cornwall (0.39). Macdonald defended the status quo on the principle of "not sweeping away" original ridings. "If the matter were done *de novo*, he could not say that Niagara or Cornwall would have a member, but they were established in 1791, and on a subsequent occasion, so averse was the government of the day (Baldwin-LaFontaine) to extinguish them that they attached to them the townships immediately adjoining, so as to

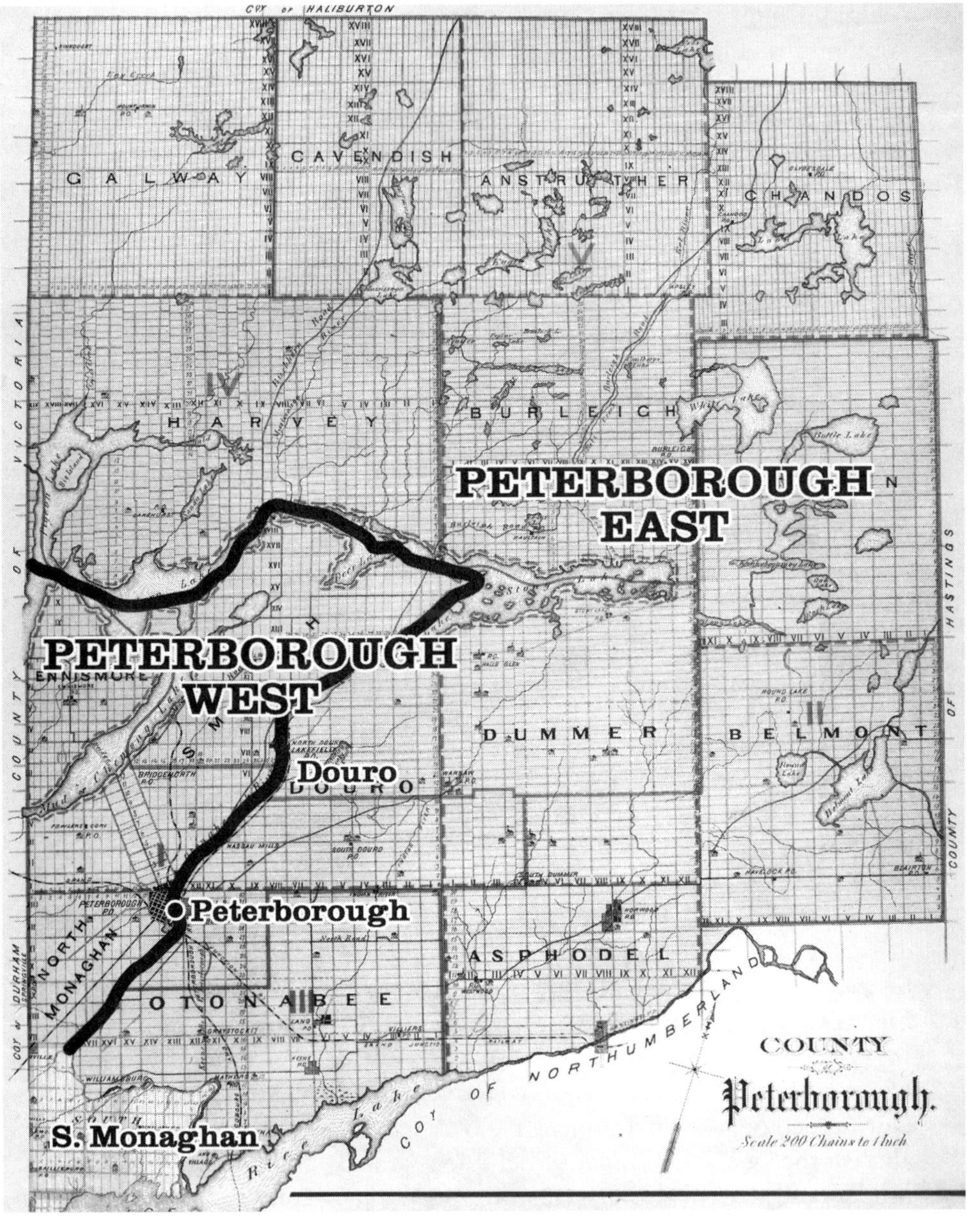

Map 3.2 Peterborough County, Dominion ridings, 1872

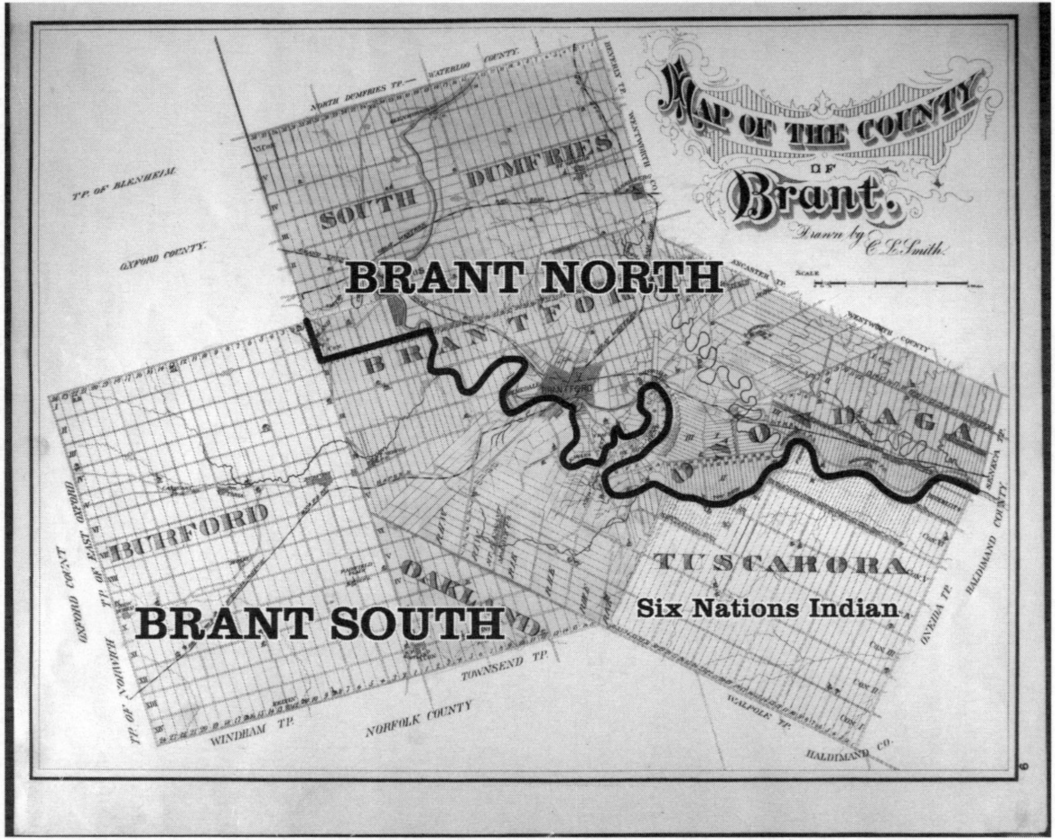

Map 3.3 Brant County, Dominion ridings, 1872

justify their having a representative. The principle ... obtained in England, and a constituency was seldom destroyed that had not by bribery or corruption or some other means forfeited all claims to consideration. If this principle ... were acknowledged, the measure would be found a good one."[8]

Macdonald's history of the ridings was as specious as his argument. Neither riding was original to 1791, as the prime minister claimed. Niagara dated from 1824 and Cornwall from 1834. The town ridings were attached to their "townships immediately adjoining" in 1853, which was two years after the Baldwin-Lafontaine ministry had left office. The 1853 attachments, moreover, set a precedent for interfering with original ridings. What did matter to Macdonald in 1872 was politics. A merger of Cornwall and Stormont would cost his party a seat. Stormont was a Tory hive (-592) and Cornwall was represented by John Sandfield Macdonald, Sir John's ally in the coalition government. A merger of Niagara and Lincoln portended another loss to the Tory side: whereas the tiny Niagara riding (0.20) was possibly safe, Conservative (-50), an 1868 by-election had turned neighbouring Lincoln, a much larger riding (1.13), into a Liberal hive (+600).

WELLINGTON BUT NOT MIDDLESEX: A PARTISAN SELECTION

The counties of Wellington and Middlesex each had three ridings with unequal populations. The population of Wellington was appropriate for three ridings (3.45), but Middlesex (3.65) warranted consideration for a fourth riding. Macdonald equalized riding populations in Wellington, but withheld redistribution for Middlesex – a passive gerrymander.

Partisan calculation invited Macdonald to equalize population in Wellington but not Middlesex. His interference with the Wellington ridings caused no harm to the prospects of the government party and, indeed, helped them in Wellington North, whose incumbent was George Alexander Drew, grandfather to his namesake, George Drew, a future premier of Ontario (1943–48). The redistribution stripped Drew's riding of its sole Liberal-leaning township, Peel, thereby improving Drew's Liberal-majority statistic from -222 to -268. Passive gerrymander suited Macdonald for Middlesex. He could have issued four compact ridings with relatively equal populations (1.02, 0.86, 0.94, and 0.83). The prospective benefit, however, would have gone to the opposition party: Liberal wins in three of the four ridings, versus two of three without redistribution – the actual outcome in the 1872 general election.[9]

GREY COUNTY: A CARELESS REDISTRIBUTION

Macdonald missed an opportunity for party gain when giving a third riding to Grey County (3.24). The populations of the new ridings were unequal (1.21, 1.01, and 1.02). Before redistribution, each party held one seat; Grey North was very safe, Liberal (+256), and Grey South, precarious, Conservative (-13). The new ridings (Map 3.4) were Grey East, precarious, Liberal (+15); Grey North, very safe, Liberal (+362); and Grey South, reasonably safe, Conservative (-134) – a gain of a seat for the opposition party.

A hypothetical alternative redistribution would have placed Proton Township in Grey South rather than Grey East. This would have equalized the riding populations (1.09, 1.01, and 1.14), and would have gained, prospectively, one seat for the government party.[10] Partisan strengths under the alternative redistribution would have been Grey East, precarious, Conservative (-25); Grey North, unchanged at very safe, Liberal (+362); and Grey South, reasonably safe, Conservative (-94).

HURON COUNTY: A THINLY DISGUISED GERRYMANDER

The devil was in the details for Huron County, which received a third riding, but not a fourth, for its 3.61 standard populations (Map 3.5). The Liberal incumbent for Huron South, Malcolm Colin Cameron, was shocked to learn that Goderich Town (+125) and Tuckersmith Township (+194), from opposite sides of his Huron-South riding, were now in Huron Centre.[11] Consequently his reasonably safe riding (+171) had become precarious, Tory (-29).

The Huron redistribution was a thinly disguised gerrymander that forecast a gain of two seats for the government party. The opposition Liberals held both ridings before redistribution (Huron North, +622; Huron South, +171), but, prospectively, the government party would win two of the three redistributed ridings (Huron Centre, +826; Huron North, -29; Huron South, -4). The redistribution hived the Grits in the Centre riding to favour the Tories in the other two.

The riding populations were relatively equal, but on the high side of optimum (1.24, 1.19, and 1.17) for want of a fourth riding for the county's 3.61 standard populations. My hypothetical redistribution for four ridings would have produced relatively equal populations (0.87, 0.86, 0.98, and 0.90) and predicted Liberal wins in three of the four seats (+642, +243, +14, and -106): a gain of one seat for each party, as opposed to a gain of two seats for the government party in the actual redistribution.

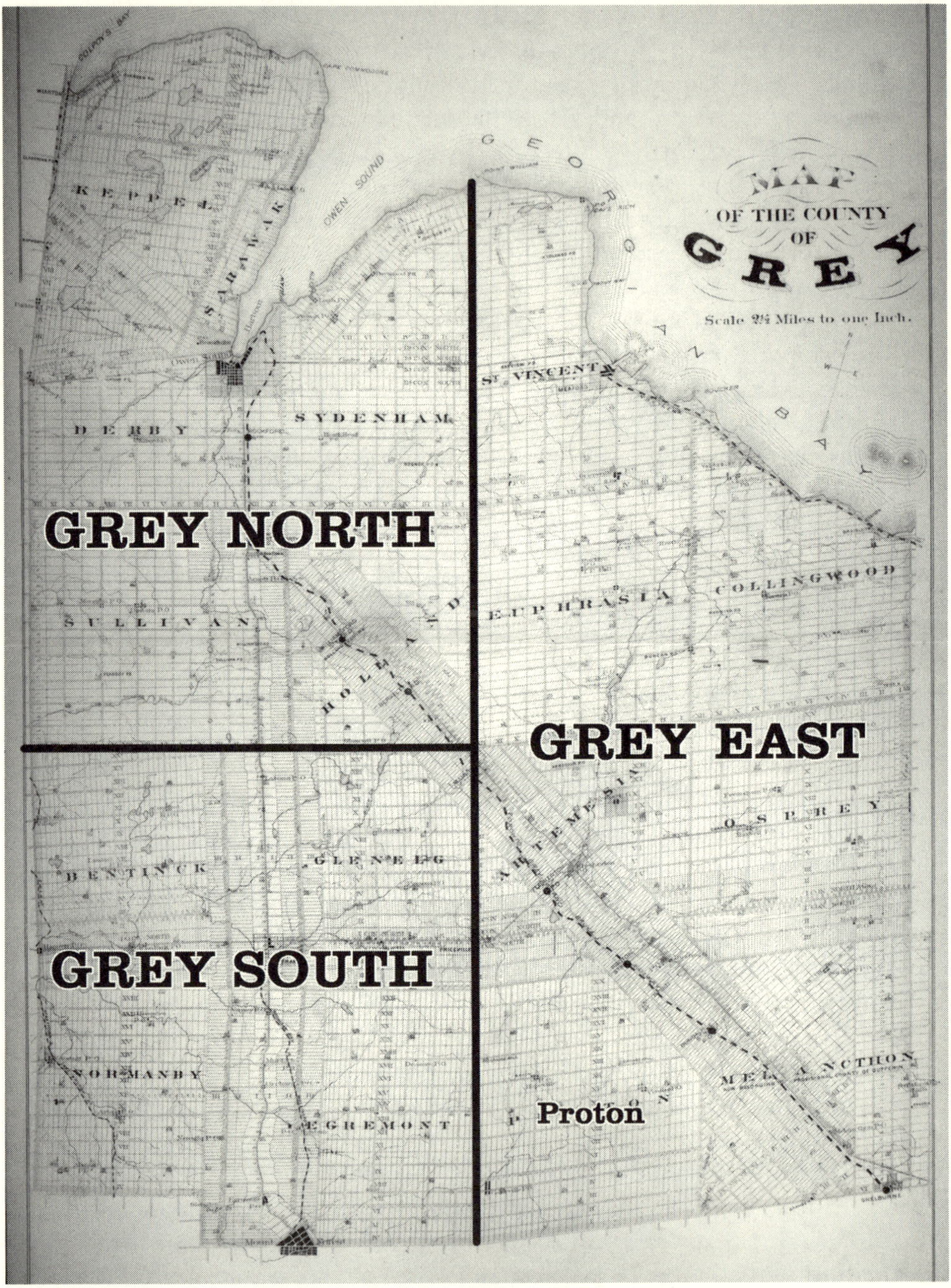

Map 3.4 Redistribution for Grey County, Dominion ridings, 1872.

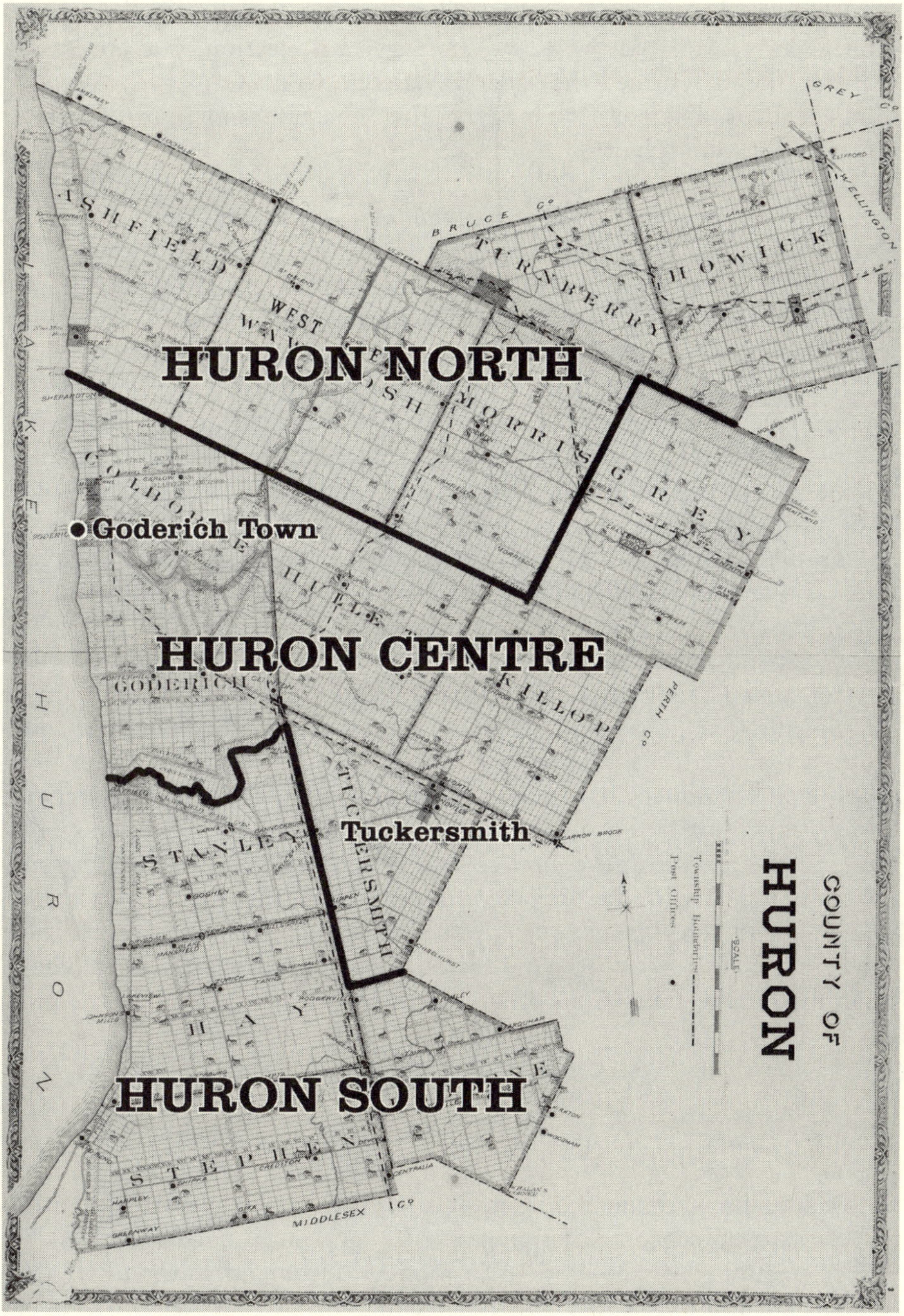

Map 3.5 Redistribution for Huron County, Dominion ridings, 1872

The gerrymander produced mixed results for the Tories. They gained one seat, Huron North, in the 1872 general election, but not two. Huron South returned the Liberal Malcolm Colin Cameron, over an Independent, Thomas Greenway, a Tory apostate and future Liberal premier of Manitoba.[12]

Summary of the 1872 Dominion Redistribution

The 1872 redistribution was flawed in fairness, design, and execution. It retained three purely-electoral counties, which Macdonald acknowledged as failed experiments. It over-represented Hamilton and Ottawa. When disturbing low-population ridings, it "cherry-picked" ridings with Liberal incumbents. It left alone the counties of Elgin, Peterborough, and Brant, whose ridings were unequal in population. It left alone the small-population town ridings of Niagara and Cornwall. It missed a chance for party gain in Grey County.

As summarized in Table 3.1, the redistribution added six ridings to Ontario and a predicted increase of five to the government party's tally of ridings in the next general election. Against prediction, the 1872 general election gave the Conservatives a loss of fifteen seats in Ontario (thirty-nine Conservatives, forty-nine Liberals) and a reduced majority nationally. The gerrymander by over-representation for Hamilton and Ottawa worked in the 1872 general election: Conservatives swept the two-member ridings. In contrast, Macdonald's passive gerrymander for fifteen low-population ridings failed: eight returned a Liberal, up from one in the previous general election. His redistribution for Wellington County failed, with the opposition Liberals sweeping the three ridings. His passive gerrymander for Middlesex County failed also, with the Liberals gaining a seat from the Tories. Clearly, Macdonald's sharp practice did little to staunch his party's losses.

THE PROVINCIAL REDISTRIBUTION OF 1874

The BNA Act, 1867, was silent about redistribution for provincial parliaments. Thus, Ontario had no quota for the size of its parliament and no census-based timing requirement for redistribution. Nevertheless, the Act's start-up schedule of ridings for the provincial parliament was a Tory creation, the handiwork of Sir John A. Macdonald. In 1874 Premier Oliver Mowat unfolded his Liberal vision.

Table 3.1 Distribution of Dominion seats by party and level of safety, before and after the 1872 redistribution

Liberal-majority statistics from 1872 election	*Before 1872 redistribution*			*After 1872 redistribution: Predictions for 1872 election*		
	Conservative	*Liberal*	*All parties*	*Conservative*	*Liberal*	*All parties*
hive (500+)	16%	18%	17%	19%	15%	17%
very safe (200–499)	16%	30%	22%	20%	27%	23%
reasonably safe (100–199)	18%	12%	16%	17%	9%	14%
possibly safe (50–99)	18%	9%	15%	15%	12%	14%
precarious (< 50)	18%	3%	12%	19%	3%	13%
acclamation/same party	12%	27%	18%	11%	33%	20%
# of ridings	49	33	82	54	33	88
Not counted		0			1 new northland riding	

Mowat's Representation Bill raised the number of provincial ridings to eighty-eight, which, as Mowat intended, matched the 1872 constitutional quota for Dominion ridings. But Mowat's provincial ridings differed from Macdonald's Dominion ridings. Macdonald had added six seats and abolished none; Mowat created eight ridings and abolished two.[13] Macdonald added three new seats for cities; Mowat gave none. Macdonald left alone the three purely-electoral counties; Mowat abolished Bothwell. Under the BNA Act (s. 92.8), municipal institutions were exclusively in the domain of the provincial parliament. Thus, Mowat did what Macdonald could not do: he changed county lines. In 1874 he combined townships from three counties to create Dufferin as a provisional-municipal county and a provincial riding. Also in 1874, he combined twenty-three townships from two counties, Peterborough and Victoria, to create Haliburton as a provisional-municipal county; he then attached Haliburton to the riding of Victoria North for electoral purposes, the Haliburton population being too small for separate representation.

Whereas John A. Macdonald's 1872 Dominion Act touched fourteen of the eighty-two ridings of 1867, Oliver Mowat's 1874 provincial Act touched twenty-one. Whereas the Dominion Act increased the percentage of ridings in the optimum range (0.90–1.10) from 22 to 24, the Ontario Act raised the percentage from 20 to 30. These statistics, of course, require a nuanced interpretation because the county, not the riding, was the first stage for equalizing populations.

Principles

Given that a *Hansard* did not exist for Ontario's Legislative Assembly, newspaper reportage is the chief documentary source for information about Mowat's principles for redistribution. The Toronto *Globe* serves the purpose, if one keeps in mind that it was a partisan Liberal organ and spotty in its coverage of the debates.

In the *Globe*'s reportage, Mowat's major principles were the equalization of riding populations and the observance of municipal boundaries for electoral districts. Local opinion mattered to Mowat. His Bill retained the low-population riding of Cornwall, ostensibly because electors in the neighbouring ridings wanted their riding boundaries undisturbed. Mowat created the municipal and electoral county of Dufferin "upon petitions from the localities interested ... The counties from which it was cut are ... of enormous size" and "after a vote of the people had been taken in each locality ... affirming the view that those townships and municipalities which constituted Dufferin should be constituted into one municipal county."[14] Similarly, Mowat created the provisional county of Haliburton "in response to the strongly expressed desire of the settlers in those townships."[15]

On Mowat's Splitting of Townships and Gerrymander

A hotly debated issue in the Dominion parliament in 1882 was whether or not Mowat's 1874 Act interfered with municipal-county lines, thereby abandoning "an historic Liberal principle," as alleged by Sir John A. Macdonald. A related issue was whether or not Mowat's Act was a gerrymander. MacGregor Dawson's answer is negative on both counts: "The Mowat redistribution Act of 1874 was not a gerrymander, though it probably did not go out of its way to favour the Conservatives. It made a number of changes [that] appear to have been quite legitimate, such as placing a town, which had been in two counties, in one, and adding new constituencies within the county boundaries. In no instance did Mowat go beyond county limits in creating any new districts."[16]

Dawson refers to municipal counties, not the purely-electoral counties of Cardwell, Monck, and Bothwell. Municipal counties, with their function of local government, were communities of common interest; the purely-electoral counties, functioning solely in elections at five-year intervals, were not. The distinction put Mowat in the clear. He abolished Bothwell, an electoral county only, and recast it as a riding within Kent, a municipal county. Similarly, he established Dufferin as a provisional-municipal county when making it an electoral riding.

Contrary to Dawson's claim, Mowat did trespass on municipal lines for certain of his adjustments. Cardwell, a purely-electoral county, acquired Tecumseth Township from Simcoe South. Muskoka & Parry Sound, a new riding, took eight townships from Victoria North. Mowat's most extraordinary departure from municipal lines, however, was to split three townships in Huron County, as discussed below.

Yet contrary to Macdonald's claim in 1882, Mowat's interference with municipal lines, including the splitting of townships, set no precedent. The 1853 Representation Act had split townships in the counties of Brant, Waterloo, and York, and transferred two townships from Carleton County to Russell County. As for trespassing on county lines, Macdonald's three purely-electoral counties of 1867 included parts of seven municipal counties.

Case Studies

Eight case studies follow below to unpack the nature of Mowat's 1874 redistribution. The findings, with the exception of the Huron-County ridings, are positive for Mowat's observance of key principles – population equality and county lines. They show balance between the two parties in the prospective benefits of the changes. Thus, as MacGregor Dawson judges, Mowat's 1874 redistribution was not a gerrymander.

HURON COUNTY

Mowat's redistribution divided Huron North and Huron South into three ridings: Huron East, Huron South, and Huron West. It gave the ridings approximately equal populations[17] and predicted a Liberal sweep of those ridings in the next provincial general election – a gain of one seat for the government party.

Mowat trespassed on principles. First, he split townships, rather than observing county lines. He divided Goderich Township along "the line known as the 'cut line,'" and the townships of Hullett and Turnberry along "the road commonly called the Gravel Road" (Map 3.6). Second,

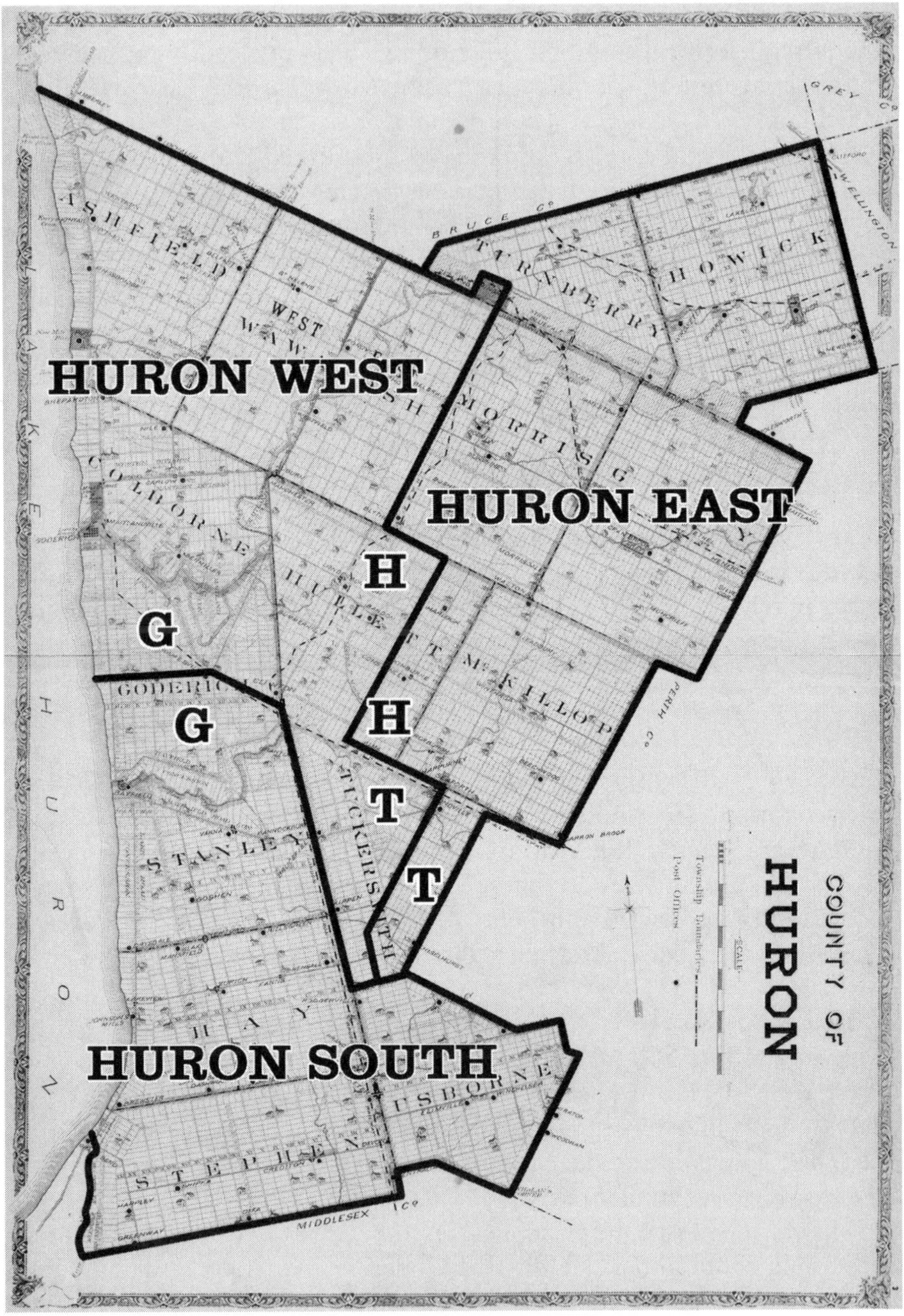

Map 3.6 Huron County, provincial ridings, 1874

his new ridings of Huron West and Huron East lacked symmetrical, compact shape. Third, the riding populations were reasonably equal, but on the high side of optimum; the county's population (3.65) sufficed for a fourth riding.

The distribution was not a gerrymander, in that the government party did not profit from its trespass on principles. The evidence derives from comparison of Mowat's actual redistribution with possible alternatives that did not split townships, one for three ridings and one for four. The three-riding model produces similar results for riding populations and predicted-partisan strengths.[18] Mowat's splitting of townships served no purpose. The four-riding model balances riding populations and predicts a Liberal sweep of the four ridings: a gain of two for the government party.[19] Without a fourth Huron riding, Mowat's redistribution did not maximize advantage for his party, as in a gerrymander.

BOTHWELL

The redistribution abolished the purely-electoral county of Bothwell; repatriated its townships to their municipal counties, Kent and Lambton; and divided Kent and Lambton Counties into four ridings, Kent East, Kent West, Lambton East, and Lambton West. These changes benefited the government party, which held all three original ridings (Bothwell, Kent, and Lambton) and could expect to win all four replacement ridings in the next general election. Nevertheless, the redistribution was grounded in principle. Its provision of a fourth riding was warranted by the counties' collective 4.30 standard populations. It equalized populations,[20] and it restored county lines in Kent and Lambton. The redistribution helped the government party, but it was not a gerrymander.

NIAGARA, LINCOLN, AND ESSEX

Niagara Town was an "historical" small-population riding (0.20) with a Tory incumbent, the Hon. Stephen Richards. A draft version of Mowat's Bill would have transferred three municipalities (Stamford Township, Chippawa Village, and Clifton Town) from the Welland riding into Niagara. These transfers would have given Niagara 0.50 standard populations, modest for separate representation, but a step in the right direction. However, the Tory incumbent, Richards, challenged the province's constitutional authority to alter the number of ridings the province had held at Confederation. He might better have stayed quiet. Mowat responded by abolishing the Niagara riding by folding it into the

Tory-held riding of Lincoln, thereby merging two Tory-held ridings into one. The change was neutral for population equality: it removed an English-style rotten borough, but moved the Lincoln riding further out of the optimum range (from 1.13 to 1.33).

In Mowat's calculus, however, the abolition of Niagara freed up a seat, which he used to divide Essex (1.80) into Essex North (0.98) and Essex South (0.80).[21] In the 1871 general election, Essex had been very safe, Liberal (+468). With division, Essex North became a Liberal hive (+532) and Essex South became possibly safe, Conservative (-64). Effectively, the division of Essex created an expected gain of one for the Conservatives, which offset their loss of one from the merger of Niagara and Lincoln. Both Essex ridings returned Conservatives in the 1875 general election.

BROCKVILLE AND LEEDS (MAP 3.7)

The Act transferred two townships (Front of Yonge and Rear of Yonge & Escott) from Leeds South (1.13) to the riding of Brockville (0.57). The transfers were positive for equalizing populations. Leeds South and Brockville moved from 1.13 and 0.57 standard populations to 0.76 and 0.94. Conservatives held both ridings, Leeds South (acclamation) and Brockville, precarious (-7), and were forecast to retain them in the 1875 general election. Mowat's Liberals, however, won Brockville.

CORNWALL AND STORMONT (MAP 3.8)

Mowat declined to merge two Tory-held ridings with below-average populations: Cornwall Town (0.39) and Stormont (0.65). Such a merger would have created a riding with an optimum population (1.04) and benefited Mowat's party by substituting one Tory-held constituency for two. Mowat ostensibly passed up the merger in deference to local opinion. "Cornwall alone is left untouched," reported the Toronto *Globe*, "in obedience, certainly not to any political exigencies, but to the very strongly expressed desire of the surrounding constituencies, to remain for the present without alteration – a desire it was the more easy to gratify, because there was no reason to suppose a change would be made in the political character of the representation of the district by any reasonable scheme of readjustment that could be devised."[22] The *Globe*'s rationalization is unconvincing, but none better was on offer. Cornwall, of course, had been the riding of John Sandfield Macdonald, a coalition Reformer and Ontario's first premier, who had died in 1872.[23]

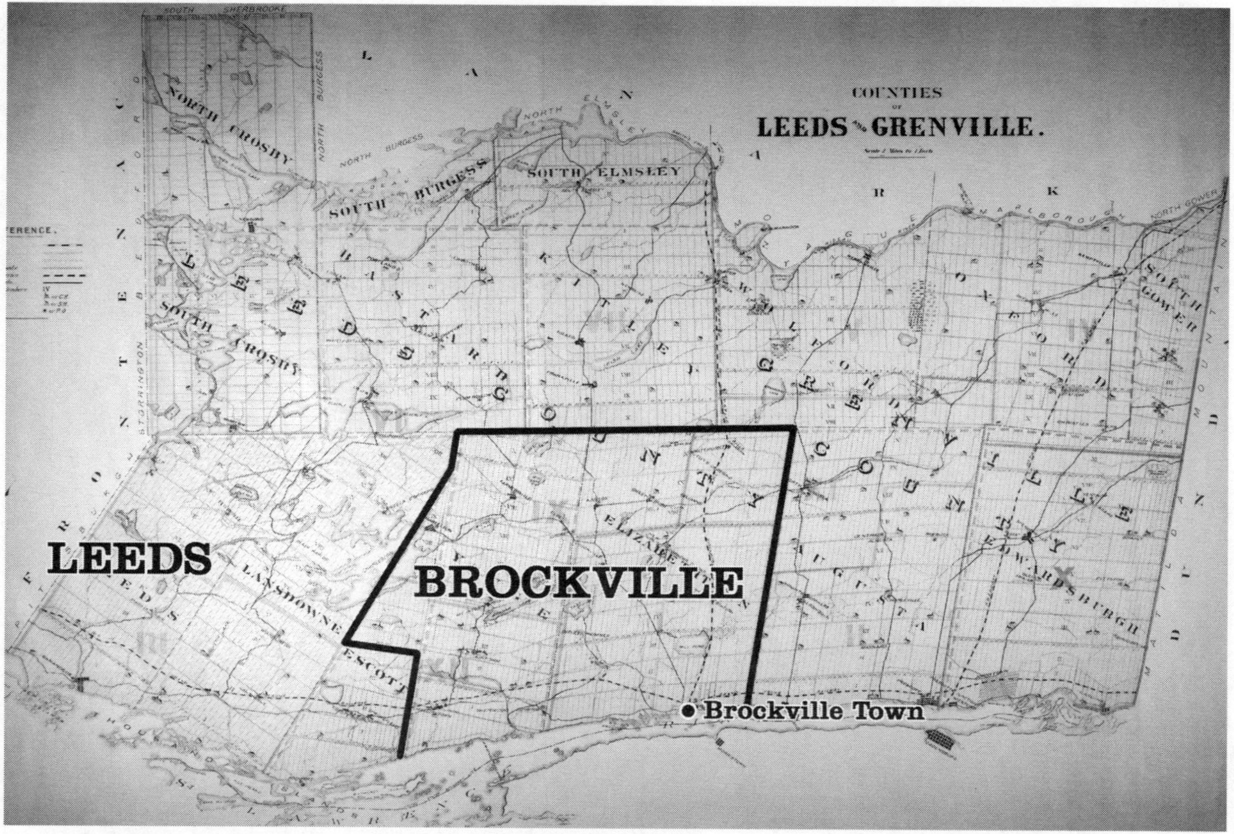

Map 3.7 Leeds and Brockville, provincial ridings, 1874

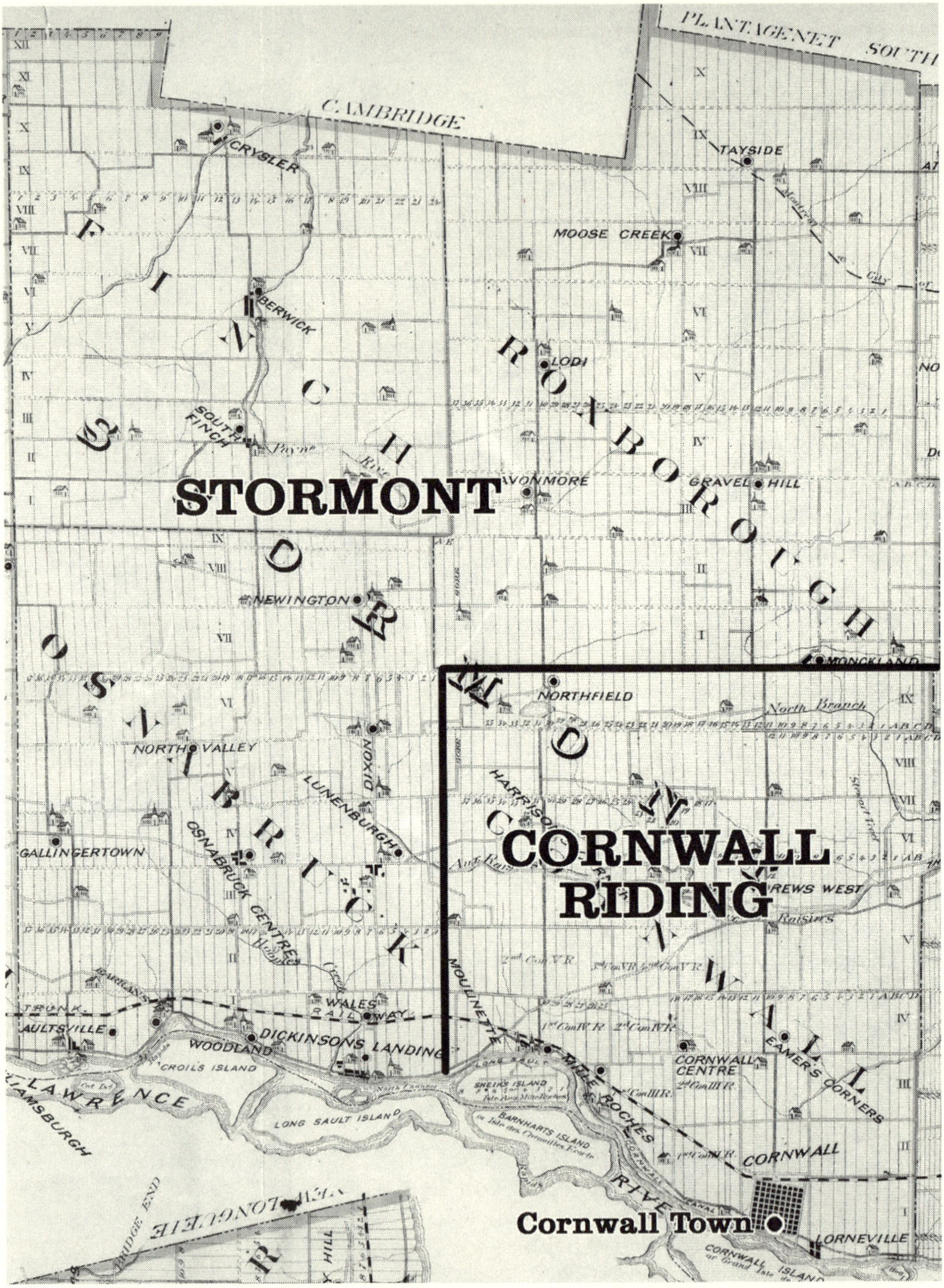

Map 3.8 Cornwall and Stormont, provincial ridings, 1874

DUFFERIN COUNTY

Mowat took townships from five ridings in four counties to create Dufferin as a provisional-municipal county and provincial riding in 1874.[24] "The scheme did not originate with the Government at all," reported the *Globe*, "but with persons of both political parties resident in the district."[25] The *Globe* expected Dufferin to return a Tory in the 1875 general election. In the 1871 election, four of its townships collectively had been very safe, Conservative (-363), and a fifth township had come from Simcoe South (Conservative, acclamation). The creation of Dufferin had minor partisan consequences for the ridings that furnished its townships. Grey South had been a Tory hive (-682); with the loss of one township (-165) to Dufferin and three townships (-463) to Grey East, Grey South was reduced to possibly safe (-90). Wellington North (now Wellington West) and Wellington Centre had been and remained Liberal hives. Cardwell, hitherto very safe for the Tories, was likely to remain so: although it lost Mono Township (-143), it acquired Tecumseth Township and Bolton Village from Simcoe South, whose Tory member had been acclaimed. The redistribution was positive for equalizing population in the five ridings involved. It was no gerrymander. The 1875 general election went as predicted for Dufferin, Cardwell, Simcoe South, Grey South, and Wellington Centre, but not for Wellington West (+599), which returned a Tory.

SIMCOE COUNTY

Mowat's Bill gave Simcoe County a third riding, but transferred two of its townships out of the county, one to the purely-electoral county of Cardwell, and the other to the new county riding of Dufferin. These changes were positive for population equality. Simcoe North and Simcoe South had respectively 1.84 and 1.29 standard populations, compared to 0.82, 1.04, and 1.02 standard populations for the three replacement ridings. Conservatives represented the original ridings (very safe, -313, and acclamation) and were favourites to win the three new ridings (very safe, -234; hive, -734; and acclamation). Thus, the Bill, prospectively, produced an additional seat for the opposition party, not the government party, as in a gerrymander.

PETERBOROUGH COUNTY

Mowat's Act transferred three townships from Peterborough East to Peterborough West and twenty townships from Peterborough East to Victoria North (as part of the provisional county of Haliburton, created in 1874). The changes smoothed differences in population for the Peterborough ridings (from 1.02 and 0.64 to 0.84 and 0.71) without benefit to the government party. The Peterborough Tory-held ridings were very safe (-299) and possibly safe (-53) before redistribution, and reasonably safe (-148 and -105) after.

NORTHLAND DISTRICTS

Like Macdonald, Mowat favoured representation for low-population districts with vast territories that had recently been opened to settlement. Thus, he left alone Algoma, with 0.38 standard populations, and created the riding of Muskoka & Parry Sound, with 0.38.[26] Like Macdonald, he transferred townships from Victoria North to the Muskoka–Parry Sound riding (0.30 without the transfers); unlike Macdonald, he gave Victoria North four townships from Peterborough East, thereby boosting Victoria North from 0.60 to 0.74 standard populations. Mowat's transfers equalized population for the Victoria and Peterborough ridings and, prospectively, helped the opposition Tories in both counties.[27]

The 1874 Redistribution: No Gerrymander

Contrary to Dominion-Tory allegations in 1882 and 1892, Mowat's 1874 redistribution was no gerrymander. As shown in Table 3.2, the 1874 redistribution forecast a Liberal majority of five, an increase of one. The redistribution touched five of thirty-one ridings that were precarious, possibly safe, or reasonably safe for the incumbent (either party, ±199). The Liberals prospectively lost ground in four and gained in one. Mowat's Liberals did better than predicted in the 1875 general election, taking fifty-one seats, against thirty-seven for the Conservatives, a majority of fourteen, nine more than forecast.

SUMMARY AND INTERPRETATION

The 1872 Dominion redistribution and the 1874 Ontario-provincial redistribution were modest in scope. The two Representation Acts each added six ridings to the original eighty-two ridings of Confederation, but the Dominion and provincial ridings began to differ. Even where the names of the ridings matched, their municipal territories often did not. Macdonald's riding of Peterborough East, for example, was the same riding that he had created in 1867. In contrast, Mowat's redistributed provincial riding of Peterborough East had a smaller population

Table 3.2 Distribution of provincial seats by party and level of safety, before and after the 1874 redistribution

Liberal-majority statistics from 1871 election	*Before 1874 redistribution*			*After 1874 redistribution: Predictions for 1875 election*		
	Conservative	*Liberal*	*All parties*	*Conservative*	*Liberal*	*All parties*
hive (500+)	5%	7%	6%	7%	7%	7%
very safe (200–499)	21%	49%	35%	15%	46%	31%
reasonably safe (100–199)	26%	16%	21%	27%	20%	23%
possibly safe (50–99)	5%	5%	5%	7%	2%	5%
precarious (< 50)	23%	7%	15%	17%	9%	13%
acclamation / same party	21%	16%	18%	27%	17%	22%
# of ridings	39	43	82	41	46	88
Not counted		0		1 new northland riding		

(0.84 standard populations versus 1.02 for the Dominion riding) and about half the number of the original townships. The divergence between the Dominion and provincial ridings was a predictable outcome of party differences. Macdonald, the Conservative, had produced the 1867 schedule of ridings and their redistribution in 1872, and Mowat's Liberals held power provincially.

Both redistributions departed from municipal-county lines in certain cases. Macdonald retained his three purely-electoral counties (Cardwell, Monck, and Bothwell), despite characterizing them as a failed experiment. Mowat's Act split three townships in Huron County, and dispatched two Simcoe townships to ridings outside the county. Yet Mowat's interference with municipal lines, including his splitting of townships, was no precedent, as Macdonald was later to allege. Rather, the precedents were in the 1853 Representation Act and Macdonald's 1867 and 1872 redistributions.

Mowat's redistribution for Huron County created two ridings with asymmetrical, non-compact shape. Curiously, this passed without comment from the Tory benches, even though the splitting of Huron townships did not. Sir John was to create three asymmetrical, non-compact ridings in his 1882 redistribution, but again, without citing Mowat as a precedent to justify his handiwork.

Representation by population animated both Acts, provided that the principle was not "pushed too far." Just 22 percent of the 1867 ridings were within 10 percent of the standard population; with redistribution, the statistic moved to 24 percent for Dominion elections and 30 for provincial elections. Compared with Macdonald's Dominion Act, Mowat's Ontario Act was the more aggressive in acting on low-population ridings. Both redistributions over-represented ridings that were territories of recent and ongoing settlement, such as Algoma and Muskoka and Victoria North. Neither reduced the over-representation of ridings in the Eastern-Ontario region.

The Dominion redistribution favoured cities (a third riding for Toronto and premature second members for the Hamilton and Ottawa ridings), whereas the provincial adjustments did not, in particular refusing Toronto (3.06) a third riding. Macdonald treated cities as the exclusive representatives of industrial and manufacturing interests, and therefore over-represented them in relation to population. Dominion Liberals countered that county ridings as well as cities had manufacturing and commercial interests.

The Dominion and Ontario Bills differed in their treatment of "historical" and small-population ridings. Macdonald urged the preservation of the ridings of 1867, including "historical" small-population ridings such as Niagara, and advanced the principle of "some diversity" in the sizes of riding populations. Mowat abolished "historical" Niagara, although he left alone "historical" Cornwall.

In certain cases, Mowat's redistribution ostensibly deferred to local opinion. Mowat left alone the small-population riding of Cornwall, because the electors of neighbouring ridings opposed changes in their boundaries. Similarly, he created Dufferin as a provisional-municipal and electoral county, allegedly because electors in the area wanted the change for municipal purposes.

The 1872 Dominion redistribution was flawed in design, fairness, and execution. It retained the purely-electoral counties, which Macdonald acknowledged as failed experiments. It gerrymandered Hamilton and Ottawa by over-representing them with two-member ridings. Among seventeen low-population ridings (0.20 to 0.79), it disturbed two of the three with Liberal incumbents, while leaving alone fourteen with Tory incumbents. In counties with more than one riding, it left alone ridings with unequal populations. It left alone the small-population town ridings of Niagara (0.20) and Cornwall (0.39). It missed a chance for party gain in Grey County. Macdonald's sharp practice failed to staunch his party's losses in the 1872 general election. Against predictions of a gain of five seats, the Conservatives lost fifteen.

Mowat's 1874 Representation Act was notably free of gerrymandering. Indeed, its transfers appeared to benefit the opposition Tories more than the government party. Over the next three decades, however, Dominion Conservatives were to seize on Mowat's splitting of three townships in Huron County. With the distorting spin that Mowat had disregarded county lines, the Conservatives were to style Mowat's handiwork as archetypal foul practice and a brush for the tarring of Mowat's federal cousins. Chapter 4 notes this development in Macdonald's "great gerrymander" of 1882.

4

Sir John A. Macdonald and Oliver Mowat: Redistributions of the 1880s

Sir John A. Macdonald administered his second Dominion redistribution in 1882, and Oliver Mowat his second provincial one in 1885. Their Representation Acts set high-water marks for intervention. Macdonald disturbed fifty of the eighty-eight Ontario ridings (57 percent), and Mowat, forty-five (51 percent). Also unmatched were their advances in the equalization of population across ridings. The percentage in the optimum range for population (0.90–1.10) moved from 24 to 43 for Dominion ridings, and from 30 to 39 for provincial ridings.

What stood out for Dominion Liberals, however, was Macdonald's spectacular trespass on county lines – in contradiction to his stated principles of 1872. In twenty-two transfers, his Act uprooted fifty-three townships, towns, and villages from their municipal counties. In reaction, Dominion Liberals championed county lines as paramount in redistribution, with representation by population important, but secondary.

Macdonald was unapologetic for his transgressions. Municipal lines were a constraint on equalizing population, hence cast aside. Dominion Liberals were hypocrites in denouncing his Bill, whose organizing principle, representation by population, had come from the Reform Party program of pre-Confederation years (a disingenuous claim given that the Reform platform had been representation by population on a sectional basis, not by counties and ridings). Moreover, Ontario's Liberal premier Oliver Mowat had split townships in Huron County in his redistribution of 1874, so why should Macdonald observe municipal lines? The Tory prime minister's charge was a *tu quoque* ("you too"), a canard or red herring, a charge without substance whose purpose was to put his accusers on the defensive. Dominion Liberals took the bait, but insisted that Macdonald's redistribution was a shameless gerrymander, of which his disregard of county lines was a telling clue.

THE DOMINION REPRESENTATION ACT OF 1882

Population in Ontario increased by 19 percent during the decade 1871–81. The regional statistics were Eastern Ontario, 12 percent; Western Ontario, 19; the GTA, 21; and the five northland districts (population 52,992), 237. Toronto was the largest of Ontario's five cities, with 86,415 people. The populations of the other cities were Hamilton, 35,961; Ottawa, 27,412; London, 19,746; and Kingston, 14,091.[1]

The 1881 census entitled Ontario to ninety-two seats, an increase of four. To arrive at the quota, Macdonald's Bill abolished the town ridings of Niagara and Cornwall and added six ridings for counties. Essex and Lambton received second ridings; Bruce, Ontario, and Simcoe, third ridings; and Middlesex a fourth.

The Bill left alone the purely-electoral counties of Bothwell, Monck, and Cardwell, as well as the electoral districts of cities. Ottawa (1.31) still lacked the population to warrant its two members; Hamilton (1.72) now had sufficient population for its two; and Toronto, with three ridings, was under-represented (4.13). The principle that city populations should have less representation than country populations had yet to take root – Ontario cities were too small to provoke the issue.

Macdonald's Underlying Principle

"The principle upon which the readjustment of the constituencies is arranged in this Act," stated the prime minister at the Bill's first reading, was "to equalize as much as possible the population of Ontario [ridings] ... Of course there is not and cannot be a perfect adherence to the principle ... It is a Bill which equalizes the population, which acknowledges the principle which was pressed to a successful completion by the Liberal party – the old Reform party of Canada – since that time adopted by all parties as being the true principle, the real basis of representative institutions."[2]

The prime minister's homage to Grit tradition was bogus, and front-bench Liberals were outraged at the Bill. "Over fifty constituencies are to have their boundaries changed by this measure," exclaimed Edward Blake (Durham West), leader of the Liberal opposition.

Figure 4.1 Bengough cartoon. Macdonald's method of redistribution.

> The political map of Ontario is to be entirely reconstructed. What is the excuse? The excuse is that four seats had to be added to the Province of Ontario … that he is obliged, by the strong sense of justice which animates him, to see that [inequalities of population] are removed in consequence of the addition of four members. What is he doing in order to accomplish this? Disregarding … wholly the principle which he himself stated … ten years ago … the principle … of having regard for the municipal boundaries and divisions … He is wholly disregarding that principle now. He is detaching townships from their counties and adding them to other counties, and making his divisions under the *pretence* – and I repeat the word *pretence* – of equalizing the population, but with the real result of doing what he threatened he would do to an hon. friend of mine not now in this House, hiving the Grits.[3]

"The hon. gentleman professes that he is anxious to equalize the representation of the people in the Province of Ontario," noted the Hon. David Mills (Bothwell), minister of the Interior and superintendent of Indian Affairs in the ministry of Alexander Mackenzie (1876–78) and one of Blake's chief lieutenants. "I deny that the hon. gentleman has any such object in view. His object is to legislate himself and his friends into Parliament."[4] For the Hon. Alexander Mackenzie (York East), the former Liberal prime minister (1873–78), the Bill was "a scheme from end to end for the political aggrandizement of the hon. gentleman and his friends. There is no excuse whatever for the measure that he has brought in. I was surprised to hear him say that his reason for doing so was that the principle of representation by population had never been asked for in the other Provinces, but as Ontario had demanded it as a recognized principle, he used it to aggrandize his own followers. Sir, he ought to be ashamed ... to introduce such a measure as this ... he is a traitor to his own Province in its feelings and interests."[5]

Violations of Principle in the 1882 Act

The Act achieved gains in the equalization of population at the cost of Macdonald's previously held principles. The ridings of 1882 trespassed on county lines in 58 percent of Ontario's forty-three municipal counties.[6] Three redistributions, affecting Bruce, Huron, and Oxford Counties, violated the principle that each riding should be compact and symmetrical, with its townships contiguous to one another. The prime minister's elimination of the Cornwall and Niagara ridings clashed with his principle that "historical" small-population ridings should be left alone.

Both political parties, although in different ways, subscribed to the ideal of combining the equalization of population with municipal lines. Macdonald had supported the latter ideal in 1872 and professed to support it still. His 1882 Bill had thrown aside the ideal, he claimed, because Mowat's 1874 provincial Bill had violated it.[7] As he had contended in 1872, "it was of great importance that the municipal counties should be the electoral districts, and I gave my reasons: that young men would first become councillors, then reeves and then wardens, and there would be municipal as well as political uniformity. But we see that the Ontario government [has] disregarded that ... Mr. Mowat split townships and villages in two; and when I find that Ontario had, by a Liberal government, acting on Liberal principles, born, cradled, and raised in accordance with the principles of responsible government, disregarded that principle, drawing a distinction between electoral and municipal representation, the whole object of my argument is gone and the impropriety of the change, if there be an impropriety, rests upon the Liberal government of Ontario."

Edward Blake shredded the logic of Macdonald's *tu quoque*. "I think so still," Blake had Macdonald saying, "I would not withdraw a word of it; those words express my opinion of today but the whole state of things is altered because Mr. Mowat passed a Bill in the Ontario Legislature to readjust representation, and that was quite wrong; the Bill was a very bad one, it violated my principles and views; it was contrary to my opinions, which I still hold ... but I am going to follow him; as he did wrong, I shall do wrong too." Blake indignantly denied that Mowat's Act had disturbed municipal boundaries.[8] Macdonald's *tu quoque* was posturing.

Mackenzie Bowell (Hastings North), a future prime minister (1894–96), was the sole Conservative to reject the principle of municipal lines. "There may be some argument in favour of retaining municipal divisions for the Local House," he allowed, "but it does not apply in any sense to the Dominion Parliament. The Provincial Legislatures have exclusively to deal with municipal corporations, and with all local matters pertaining to the Provinces. They have nothing whatever to do in their legislative capacity with the general politics of trade and commerce of the Dominion."[9]

Interestingly, the sole Conservative to style Mowat's 1874 redistribution a gerrymander was Albert Boultbee (York East). Like his Liberal opponents, Boultbee equated the disregard of municipal boundaries with certain gerrymandering. Thus an 1882 Liberal-Party pamphlet, entitled "The Alleged 'Gerrymander' by Mr. Mowat, in 1874," defended the Ontario premier on both issues, county lines *and* gerrymandering.[10]

Macdonald's Trespass on County Lines: The Evidence

After Macdonald's redistribution, 97 of 671 Ontario municipalities (14 percent) were in ridings that were outside their municipal counties.[11] Transfers in his 1882 Act provided 50 percent of the total, and the balance derived from two other sources. First, the 1882 Act left alone anomalies in Macdonald's 1867 redistribution. These included the county riding of Russell, which held three Carleton-County municipalities, and the purely-electoral counties of Bothwell, Monck, and Cardwell, which comprised twenty-one municipalities from seven municipal counties.

Second, the 1882 Act ignored the provincial government's recent changes to municipal territories: its creation of two provisional-municipal counties, Dufferin and Haliburton, in 1874, and its dissolution of a united-municipal county, Lennox & Addington–Frontenac. The Dominion redistribution had no Dufferin riding; perforce, it left the eight Dufferin municipalities outside their municipal county. Haliburton, with 0.26 standard populations, lacked the population normally required for a county riding; thus, the Act divided the twenty-three Haliburton townships between the ridings of Victoria North and Peterborough East.[12] In the defunct united-municipal county of Lennox & Addington–Frontenac, Macdonald stranded thirteen Frontenac townships in the Addington riding, hence outside Frontenac, which had replaced the united-municipal county as their municipal county.

The Principle of Compact, Symmetrical Shape

OXFORD AND NORFOLK

Macdonald's redistribution violated the principle that ridings should be compact and symmetrical in shape, with their municipal parts contiguous. One instance concerned the transfer of Dereham Township and Tillsonburg Town from Oxford South to Norfolk North. Dereham was like Cyrano's nose on the adjusted territory of Norfolk North. If the government party insisted on transferring municipalities from South Oxford into North Norfolk, then the two Norwich townships were the natural geographical choice.

As shown in Map 4.1, the south and east boundaries of South Norwich Township, and part of the east boundary of North Norwich Township, were contiguous with Norfolk. Yet the Bill transferred Dereham Township and Tillsonburg, a small part of whose south boundaries touched Norfolk territory. John Charlton, the Liberal incumbent for Norfolk North, accurately stated the reason for Macdonald's preference: "the township of Norwich gives a Reform majority, while the township of Dereham gives a Conservative majority."[13] Interestingly, Dereham and Tillsonburg polled a Liberal majority for Charlton (+57) in the 1882 general election.

BRUCE COUNTY

A second transgression of the compact-riding principle occurred in Bruce County, whose population (3.12) warranted a third riding. Macdonald's Bill, on its first reading, created three ridings: Bruce North, Bruce East, and Bruce West. At this stage, the West riding included Port Elgin Village on Lake Huron and its home township, Saugeen, which surrounded the village on its land border (Map 4.2).

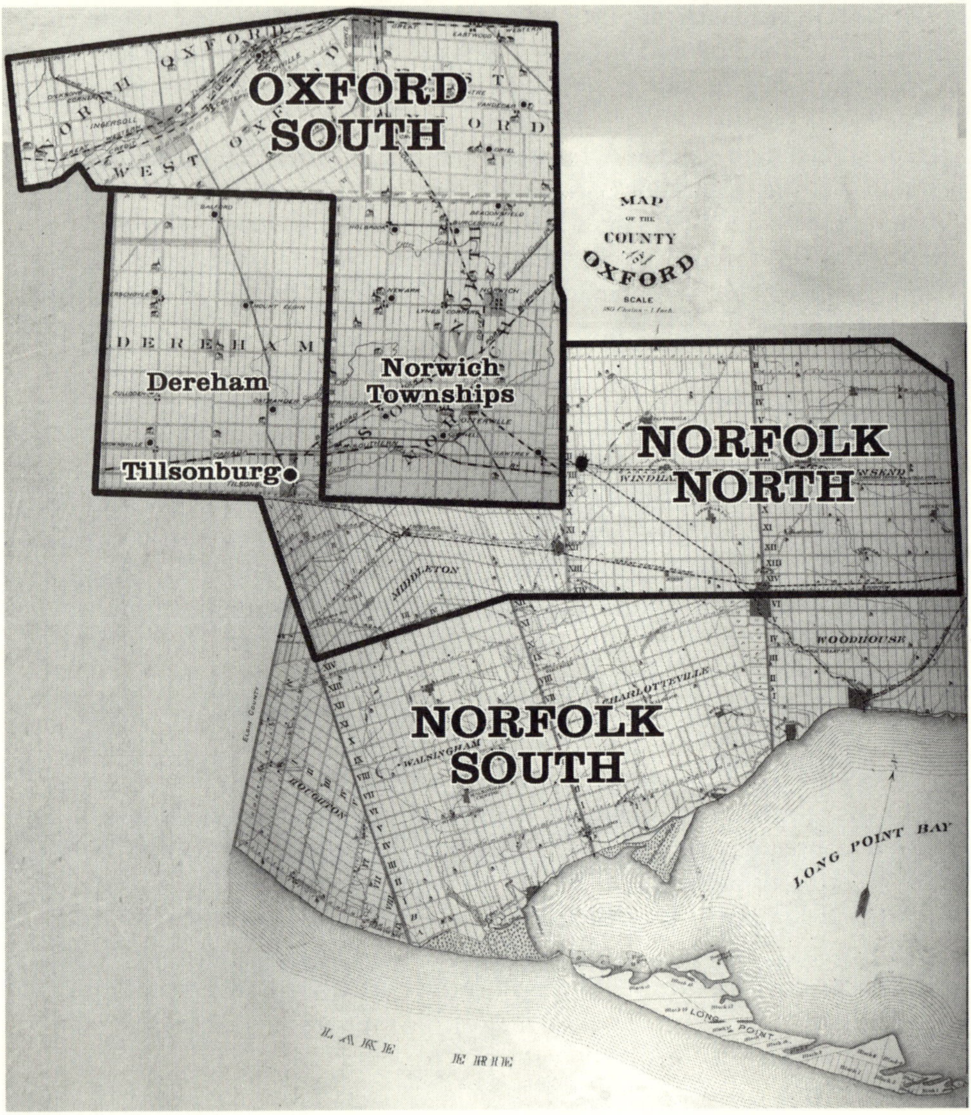

Map 4.1 Asymmetrical shape of Norfolk North, Dominion ridings, 1882

On the third reading of the Bill, however, William Paterson (Liberal, Brant South) sought to place Port Elgin and Saugeen in the North riding to further equalize the riding populations. But in an ill-chosen strategy, Paterson attempted his transfers in two stages.[14] First, he moved to transfer Port Elgin to the North riding, which Macdonald accepted.

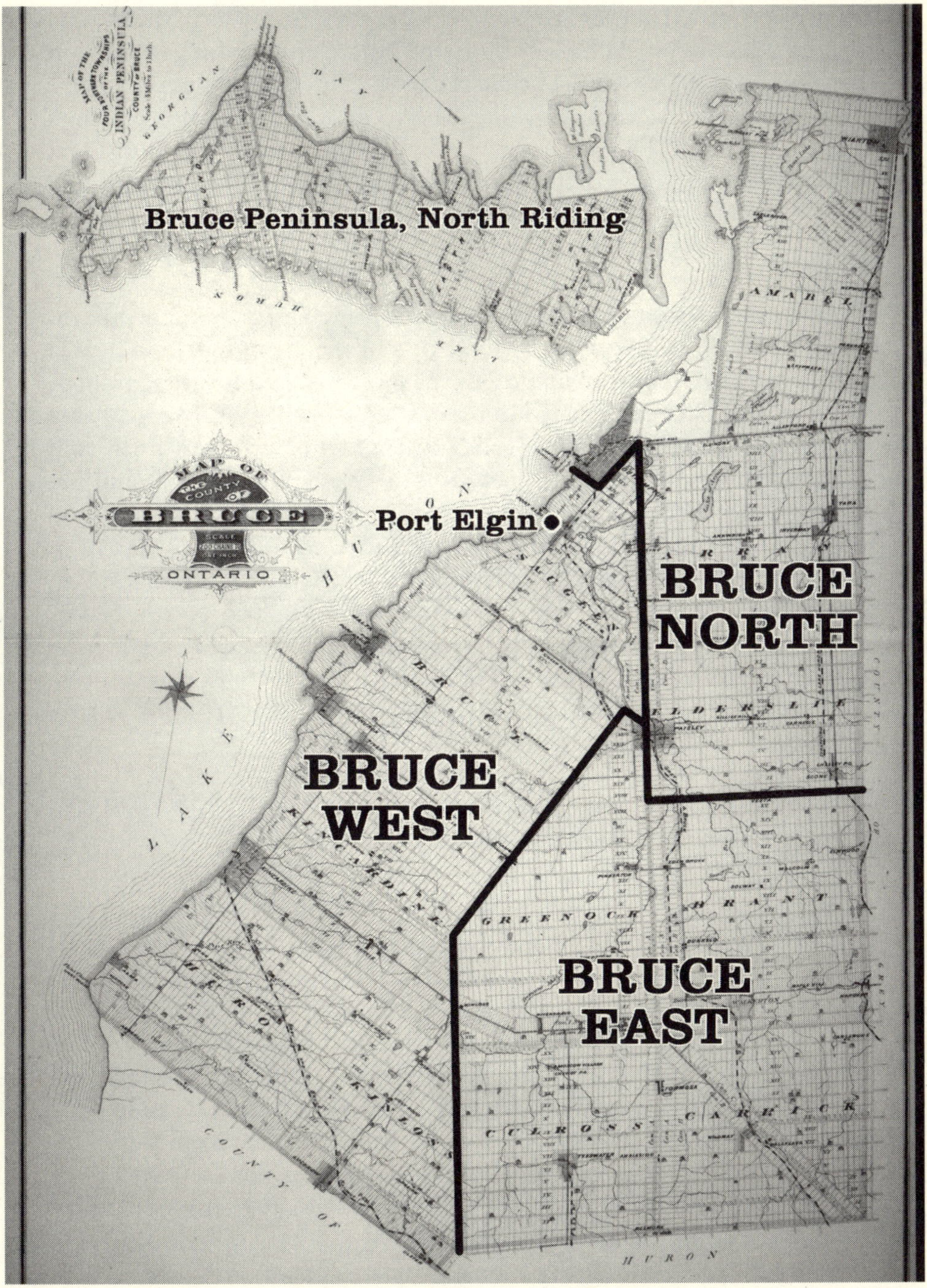

Map 4.2 Saugeen Township and Port Elgin Village, Dominion ridings, 1882

Then he moved to transfer Saugeen to the North riding, which Macdonald refused. "We offered half a loaf by giving Port Elgin to North Bruce, and they voted for it," stated the prime minister. "Now they want me to give them the whole loaf and allow Saugeen to go into North Bruce. I shall vote against that." The result was a geographical fiasco, with Port Elgin separated from the rest of its North riding by Saugeen Township, still in the West riding.

ONTARIO COUNTY

A third transgression of the compact-riding principle occurred in Ontario County, which received a third riding, despite having only 1.72 standard populations. To boost population to the level required for three ridings, Macdonald's Bill relocated six municipalities from Muskoka & Parry Sound to the new riding of Ontario North, and three municipalities from York North to the new riding of Ontario West. Within the county, it relocated Reach Township and Port Perry Village, but not the island township of Scugog, from Ontario North to Ontario South (Map 4.3). As Edward Blake remarked, this left Scugog, which was adjacent to Reach Township and Port Perry, marooned in Ontario North, eleven miles from the rest of its riding.[15] The placement of Scugog made little difference to the equalization of populations, nor to Conservative prospects in the three ridings, but Macdonald refused to reunite Scugog with Reach Township and Port Perry.

Tory Remorse about the 1882 Gerrymander Act

As John Ross Robertson (Independent Conservative, Toronto East), proprietor of the *Toronto Evening Telegram*, recalled in 1899, he had "not hesitated to speak, as a humble adherent of the Conservative party, against the Redistribution Act of 1882. I denounced that measure to the full limit of my power as a newspaper man. The gerrymander of 1882 was wrong – that was my opinion in 1882 and that is my opinion this minute. From a party standpoint, the gerrymander of 1882 was unnecessary. The Conservatives were then strong enough to win without such unfair tactics. The gerrymander of 1882 was a mistake from the country's standpoint, because it looked like an attempt on the part of the Government to load the dice. I do not believe that any party should play the game of politics with loaded dice."[16]

In 1892 D'Alton McCarthy (Conservative, Simcoe North) had regrets: "Perhaps it will be said that I was as deep a sinner as any of them in

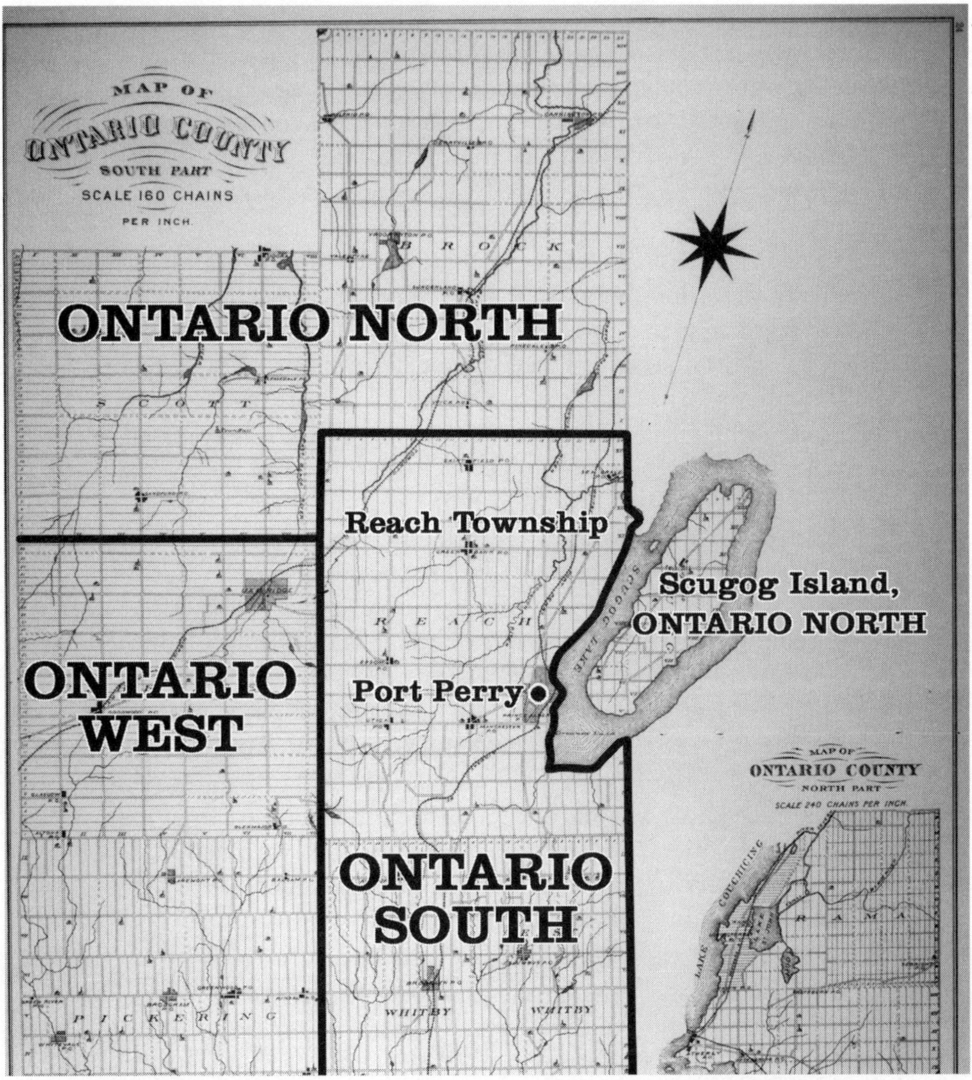

Map 4.3 Ontario County: Scugog Island, Port Perry, and Reach Township, Dominion ridings, 1882

1882 ... I can only say that, if so ... I have the merit of not persisting in my iniquity ... I fully realize by this time that in every sense, party and political, the Act was a gross mistake ... the party, to which I have the honour to belong, gained nothing by it. I venture to say that [the bad Bill of 1882] has had the effect of attaching to the party the stigma of having done what was wrong, and enabling Sir Oliver Mowat in the Local House to do what was wrong with the sanction of public opinion."[17]

"The Bill of 1882," agreed William E. O'Brien (Conservative, Muskoka), comrade-in-arms of D'Alton McCarthy, was "based on no principle, and it violates every principle ... The carefully laid plans of 1882, like many other plans of men and mice, went vastly agee, and many a constituency which had been carefully arranged to return a Conservative, though it had a majority of Conservative votes, turned around and returned an opponent of the Administration. I have very little faith as to the results expected from any system of gerrymander. It matters little, though, whether these results are attained or not. It is the principle which is at issue. It is the injustice which is done to the minority. The minority has surely some rights. It has its fair rights, according to the expressed opinions of the people, to be represented in this House, and for the majority to attempt by legislation to prevent that expression of opinion is an act of tyranny just as much when perpetrated by a majority in this House as if it were perpetrated by any individual despot who ever lived."[18]

In 1892 Richard C. Weldon (Conservative, New Brunswick) spoke "after having reconstructed the old political map of 1867, and having gone over the counties of Ontario one by one as they were then defined by the British North America Act, and having compared the old map with the map of 1882." He found "townships scattered like flocks of birds upon which the dogs had pounced, one being here, and another being there, so that it was hard to find them and place them in their old positions – after this study, I am free and frank in saying that I think the Redistribution Act of 1882 was one that reflected very little credit on the Parliament of Canada that passed it."[19]

Anecdotal Evidence of Gerrymander in 1882

An army of agents did Macdonald's dirty work, claimed front-bench Liberals.[20] "All the sitting members and political aspirants," alleged Alexander Mackenzie, "were called together from Dan to Beersheba, in order to make known to the head of the clan the precise measures necessary to secure success in each of their districts." "Why, Sir, we know how this has been going on," exclaimed Edward Blake. "We know there have been caucuses, gatherings, meetings of local politicians, interviews with the Tory candidate members, and discussions from one point of view only ... 'How shall we be the strongest.'"[21] "Not one of the Tory Party in Ontario, from the lowest to the greatest, [had] not been consulted in

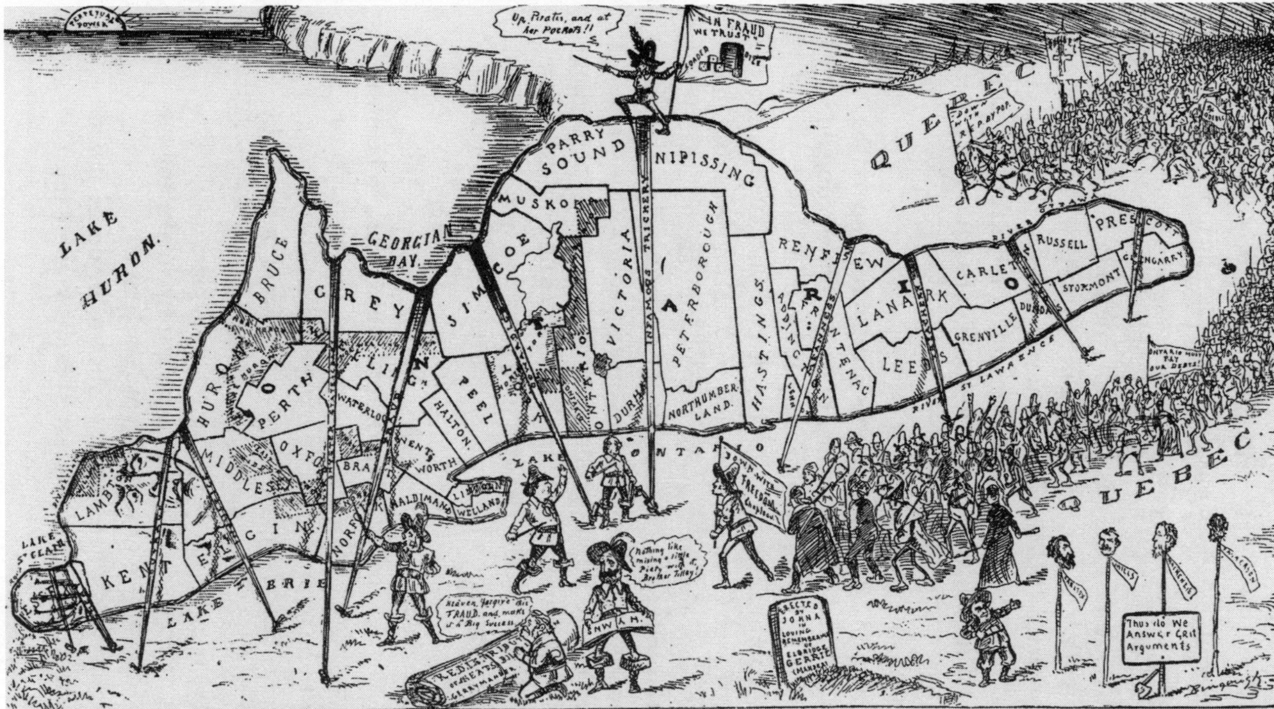

GULLIVER GERRYMANDERED;

OR, ONTARIO IN THE POWER OF MITEY SMALL STATESMEN.

Figure 4.2 Bengough cartoon. Under the pretence of "equalizing the population," in 1882 the Macdonald government introduced the Redistribution Bill for the redistribution of seats throughout the Dominion. In Ontario the changes made were almost invariably in the interests of the Conservative Party, and the measure has been known ever since as the "gerrymander bill." *Grip*, 6 May 1882.

this matter," opined Joseph Rymal (Liberal, Wentworth South). "I could see [Tory partisans] two weeks after the beginning of the Session, coming in day after day, and they were received by certain members who had the matter in charge."

Dramatic evidence of Tory tampering – "the Hague letter" – surfaced in 1899, seventeen years after the enactment of the 1882 Bill. In a signed letter to the Montreal *Herald*, a Liberal organ,[22] John Hague, editor of the *Journal of Commerce* (Montreal),[23] claimed to have done the clerical work for the comprehensive Tory gerrymander of 1882. His detailed account, reproduced in full from the Toronto *Globe*, another Liberal organ, follows below.

> On September 15, 1881, I received notice from a member of the Senate, who represented the government of Sir John Macdonald in Toronto, asking me to call upon him at a certain hour. I was informed that in compliance with the constitution the government proposed to re-arrange the constituencies of Ontario. I was told that the work of preparing a chart showing the boundaries proposed had been entrusted to officers of the Department of the Interior, of which Sir John held the portfolio, but they had failed to draft a workable plan. I was asked if I would undertake to construct a chart according to the ideas and suggestions of the speaker. On hearing my assurance that I felt equal to such a task, the Senator proceeded to say that he wished a chart made showing the boundaries of the electoral districts, the voting strength of each of them, and the majority at the last election. He wished me to make this chart quite large and to exhibit the statistics desired on small tickets, which were to be pasted over each district, the one fixed on a place which had returned a Liberal member to be pink, and the one over a district which had chosen a Conservative to be blue. These tickets were prepared by Williams, Sleeth & McMillan, printers, Toronto; they were the same size as a street car ticket. I strongly opposed this plan, as likely to prove cumbrous and very difficult to operate from in altering the boundaries, but was induced to put the plan to a test.
>
> The next question was where was the work to be done? It was represented as one demanding the greatest secrecy; there must be no risk of the chart being seen by any outsider. After various suggestions had been made and rejected, I offered to do the work at my own house, where I would give up my study to the service of the Government, and use the help of some members of my family in

filling in the tickets and other mechanical work. This was agreed to. I secured an electoral map about eighteen inches by twelve, and raised all the lines up, so as to be a reproduction on a large scale, the chart I made being five feet and a half by four feet. After the most tedious work, extending over several weeks, for I only devoted my evenings to it, the chart, with its mass of pink and blue tickets, was finished, and a pretty foolish affair it was, as I had predicted. Ontario, so treated, looked like some fabulous animal, covered with loose scales, blue and pink, which fluttered like so many tiny wings. The thing was condemned, and the author of it was puzzled. He saw that it was impossible to re-arrange the electoral districts from such a chart, and invited me to advise as to the best way of proceeding.

I was informed that what the government wished to effect was a re-arrangement of the electoral districts so far as possible recognizing a common unit of representation. This, however, was to be made sufficiently elastic to allow the grouping of different sections of the district, so as to detach Conservative voters from places where they were in excess for the needs of a majority, and the attachment of such voters to districts where the new accession would turn the scale of an election in favour of a Conservative candidate where a Liberal one had hitherto been returned. Electoral districts which were hopelessly Liberal were, if possible, to be abolished, or the constituencies so arranged so as to put Liberal voters altogether in one district, especially where they could be drawn away from a district where they menaced the Conservative candidate. The process was afterwards called 'hiving,' which is quite appropriate, though while the work was being done for the act of 1882 this word was never used. After making a colossal chart, I took each electoral district and its surroundings in hand, and wrote upon each the number polled for each party at the two previous elections, the total number of electors, with the majority in each case. I coloured each district to show at a glance its political complexion. I then made a thorough study of the official returns of the last two elections, and took out hundreds of statistics for comparison and readjustment. Some of the districts were most difficult to alter so as to secure the results desired. It was said that the configuration of some of these represented nothing on earth, in the heavens or in the waters under the heavens. Quite true, they simply represented an effort to fix the boundaries of electoral districts according to two rules: first, on the principle of equal representation to equal numbers of voters; second, on the principle that electoral districts should be arranged to serve the interests of the party in power ... These rules do not work well together, hence the highly eccentric shape of some of the districts on the chart ... When nearly complete it was taken down to Ottawa.

I was assigned to a room close to that of the Minister of the Interior. Into that room I was instructed to prohibit the entrance of anyone, even of a cabinet minister unless brought in by the Senator. I remember the petty rage of one minister to whom I refused admission. One day the hon. Mr. Aikins, Minister of Inland Revenue, came in and saw the chart, upon which he made no comment. His silence elicited the remark: 'Why Aikins, I am surprised at such a straight-laced fellow as you being in such company,' to which Mr. Aikins gave his usual placid smile. One by one several members were consulted as to the changes made in their districts, among others being the late J.C. Rykert, Col. O'Brien, and Mr. Mackenzie Bowell. The latter made a little fuss over some feature, but it passed off. When the final touch was put to my chart, it was shown to Sir John Macdonald. After closely examining the work done on the boundaries, the statistics written on the face of the map and the schedule I wrote on the side, showing the result of the changes, Sir John exclaimed: 'That takes a great load off my shoulders.'

The gerrymander act, as it was called, was simply the chart I had constructed, expressed in legal language. The changes were estimated to have given an absolute gain to the Conservative party of four seats, and a better fighting chance in a number of others. I remember remarking at the time that all such arrangements proceeded on the very doubtful assumption that future elections would proceed on the same lines as past ones, and that each party in the future would command the same support, no more and no less, than it had previously done. On my saying this to Sir John, he said, 'Quite true, but constituencies are governed a good deal by tradition, and Grits are very conservative in sticking to their party!'

My experience in this matter should be a warning to young men when asked to do work for a Government apart from a stated salary. My advice is: insist upon a written agreement for a fixed sum to be paid on the completion of the work. The work done by me in preparing the charts for the redistribution of seats cost me over $500. When payment was asked, Sir John put me off with vague promises of a handsome reward. Yet I never received one cent remuneration for labor which took all my pleasure for months, and drained me of

> a very large sum which I paid for assistance, besides giving up one room in my house for the Government service. Some member should move for the production of that chart. If it is not now in the possession of the Government, it has been stolen from the buildings, where I handed it over to the Premier, the late Sir John Macdonald, by whose instructions it was constructed.[24]

The *Herald* adds:

> Inquiry at the Department of the Interior to-day showed that there was an impression that the map from which the gerrymander of Ontario in 1882 was drawn, as described by Mr. John Hague, was at one time kept in the department, but that it is no longer there. The description of the map as given to the *Herald* correspondent corresponded to that given by the man who claims to have been its author. The *Herald* correspondent made another discovery, however, that the Hague map is not the only representation of the voting geography of Ontario that was made under the direction of the Conservative gerrymanderers. In the department is a large map, measuring six feet by ten feet, and representing the Province of Ontario and the Quebec counties of Ottawa and Pontiac. The map itself is a well-finished one, prepared by the draughtsman of the Post Office department in 1891, and representing the counties as they exist municipally. Over this are carefully-drawn the lines of the constituencies as gerrymandered by the act of 1882. The work is finished with a nicety of detail. Each township, town, and village is there, with the voting strength of the two parties marked in blue characters. The available vote and the actual vote are each marked. Then follow the Conservative vote, marked (c), and the Reform vote, marked (r). Altogether the chart is a most ingeniously contrived and neatly executed piece of political machinery, evidently used in the gerrymander of 1892, when an attempt was made to make the work of the sweeping gerrymander of 1882 more complete by calling into requisition the surgical knife to supplement the axe used in hacking to pieces the county organizations, in order to stifle the electorate and 'hive the grits.'[25]

Norman Ward appropriately cautions that the authenticity of such a letter is always in doubt, but finds that its content matched "the spirit and practice" described in Dawson's "careful examination" of the evidence in his 1935 article.[26] Information in biographical dictionaries lends weight to Ward's guesswork.[27] Hague (1829–1906) was a native of Yorkshire, a former banker in England, a resident of Canada since 1871, and in Canada an author who wrote on "financial and social topics." He had "rendered able service to the Con. party as the writer and compiler of campaign literature." His credits included "Ten Years of Lib. Govt. in Ontario" and "Analysis of Public Accounts during the Mackenzie *Régime*." A cousin, George Hague (1825–1915), was a prominent Montreal banker.

John Hague's Tory credentials may explain why an unnamed Conservative senator approached him about the gerrymander project. Although his labours, he claimed, left him out of pocket for a considerable sum ($500), the party was an ongoing source of patronage for an author of campaign literature. Thus, his seventeen-year silence makes sense. In 1899, of course, he placed his signed tell-all letter in a Grit newspaper (the Montreal *Herald*). Perhaps the Liberal Party's ascension to office in 1896 changed Hague's party allegiance and source of patronage.

If the Hague letter was authentic, then doubts about its claims remain. In September 1903, during debates on Laurier's Representation Bill, Thomas Sproule (Conservative, Grey East) debunked an important section of the Hague letter, which read: "I was assigned to a room close to that of the Minister of the Interior. Into that room I was instructed to prohibit the entrance of anyone, even of a cabinet minister unless brought in by the Senator." "I was there," exclaimed Sproule. The chart was "simply a map with the ridings as they existed shown in one colour, and the ridings as they were proposed shown in another colour." "The chart remained in the room for anyone to see ... a similar chart was put in room 16, and I have no doubt that it was seen by dozens of Liberal members of the House, because some of them looked at it with myself. There was no endeavour to keep it secret." Sproule had never heard of Hague "until tonight." The Hague letter was "simply trash."[28]

Hiving the Grits: Liberal-Majority Statistics from the 1878 Election

The object of hiving was to waste opposition-party votes. In the 1882 redistribution, hiving entailed the transfer of a Liberal-leaning municipality from a fighting riding (±200) to a Liberal hive (+500 or more) that the Liberals were likely to win anyway. Conversely, a Tory hive (-500) wasted Tory votes and hence was a candidate for dismantling, either by removing some of the Tory surplus votes to another riding, or absorbing the intake of a Liberal-leaning municipality.

Macdonald's Bill created six Liberal hives for the 1882 general election: Brant North, Bruce West, Huron South, Ontario West, Oxford North, and Oxford South. Conversely, the Bill dismantled two Tory hives: Kent and Grey East. The Liberal-majority statistic is unavailable for three more de facto Tory hives – Leeds & Grenville, Carleton, and Middlesex East – ridings in which both candidates in the 1878 general election had been Conservatives.

HURON COUNTY: A GERRYMANDER AND "POLITICAL ASSASSINATION"

The redistribution turned the ridings of Huron Centre, Huron North, and Huron South into the ridings of Huron East, Huron South, and Huron West. The new ridings bore the Huron name, but had lost some of their Huron-County substance. To shed 10,465 surplus inhabitants from three Huron ridings (3.68), the redistribution exported two townships (Stephen and Usborne) and two villages (Exeter and part of Lucknow) to ridings in Perth, Middlesex, and Bruce; this left the new ridings with 2.81 standard populations. Second, the redistribution rearranged the municipalities in what remained of the original ridings. These changes equalized the riding populations.[29]

The redistribution prospectively gained a seat for the government party in the general election to follow. Before adjustment, the Liberal-majority statistics were: Huron North, possibly safe, Conservative (-84); Huron Centre, very safe, Liberal (+371); and Huron South, reasonably safe, Liberal (+165). After readjustment, the statistics were Huron South, a Liberal hive (+689); Huron West, reasonably safe, Conservative (-122) and Huron East, reasonably safe, Conservative (-170). Effectively, the redistribution "hived the Grits" into Huron South to give prospective Tory majorities in the other two ridings.

A bonus for Macdonald was the redistribution's "political assassination" of the Right Hon. Sir Richard John Cartwright, the Liberal incumbent for Huron Centre. Conservatives reviled Sir Richard for having bolted their party in 1873 (over the Pacific Scandal), and serving as Finance minister in Alexander Mackenzie's Liberal administration (1873–78). They had exulted over Cartwright's defeat in Lennox in the 1878 general election. To keep Cartwright in Parliament, Horace Horton had made way for him in Huron Centre, a very safe Liberal seat (+371), which returned Cartwright in an 1878 by-election. In March 1882, Cartwright received the Liberal re-nomination for Huron Centre, only to find himself in the Tory crosshairs once again with the enactment of

Macdonald's redistribution Bill in May. Cartwright acknowledged his "political assassination" in an open letter to his constituents: "the very name of this riding Centre Huron is to be henceforth blotted out on the list of Canadian constituencies," in consequence of it having "selecting a representative who is personally exceedingly noxious to the faction now in power."[30] Suddenly without a constituency, he accepted an offer of nomination for Wellington Centre, which he lost in the 1882 general election.[31]

In the 1882 general election, Macdonald's gerrymander succeeded in Huron East (-60), but failed in Huron West (+29), where four of seven Tory-leaning municipalities favoured the Liberal candidate. Against prediction, the Liberals, not the government party, captured two of the three Huron ridings. When Cartwright lost in Wellington Centre, John McMillan obligingly "made way" for Sir Richard in Huron South, which Cartwright carried in an 1883 by-election.[32] Cartwright was back in a Huron riding to torment his Tory enemies in Parliament.

OXFORD, BRANT, AND NORFOLK COUNTIES

As shown in Map 4.4, a set of between-county transfers turned Oxford South and Brant North into Liberal hives and continued Oxford North as a Liberal hive. Oxford South received Oakland and Burford Townships (+225) from Brant South and gave up Dereham Township and Tillsonburg (-102) to Norfolk North; these changes moved Oxford South from very safe, Liberal (+361) to hive (+688). Brant North acquired Ancaster Township (+271) from Wentworth South and Blenheim Township (+220) from Oxford North; and gave up Onondaga Township and Paris Town (-16) to Brant South. These transfers moved Brant North from reasonably safe, Liberal (+197) to hive (+579). Oxford North lost Blenheim (+220) to Brant North, but gained North Easthope and South Easthope Townships from Perth-County ridings (+482); thus, it started as a Liberal hive (+903) and remained more so (+1,165).

The expected fruits of Macdonald's manipulation were in ridings that fed the hives. Brant South, reasonably safe, Liberal (+198) was now precarious, Conservative (-43). Wentworth South, possibly safe, Liberal (+74) became reasonably safe, Conservative (-103).[33] Perth North, possibly safe, Conservative (-83) became very safe (-288). Perth South, possibly safe, Liberal (+77) was now reasonably safe, Conservative (-118).[34] Norfolk North remained reasonably safe for its Liberal incumbent, John Charlton (from +144 to +136); his riding's intake of Tory-leaning Dereham and Tillsonburg (-102) was offset by its loss of Simcoe Town

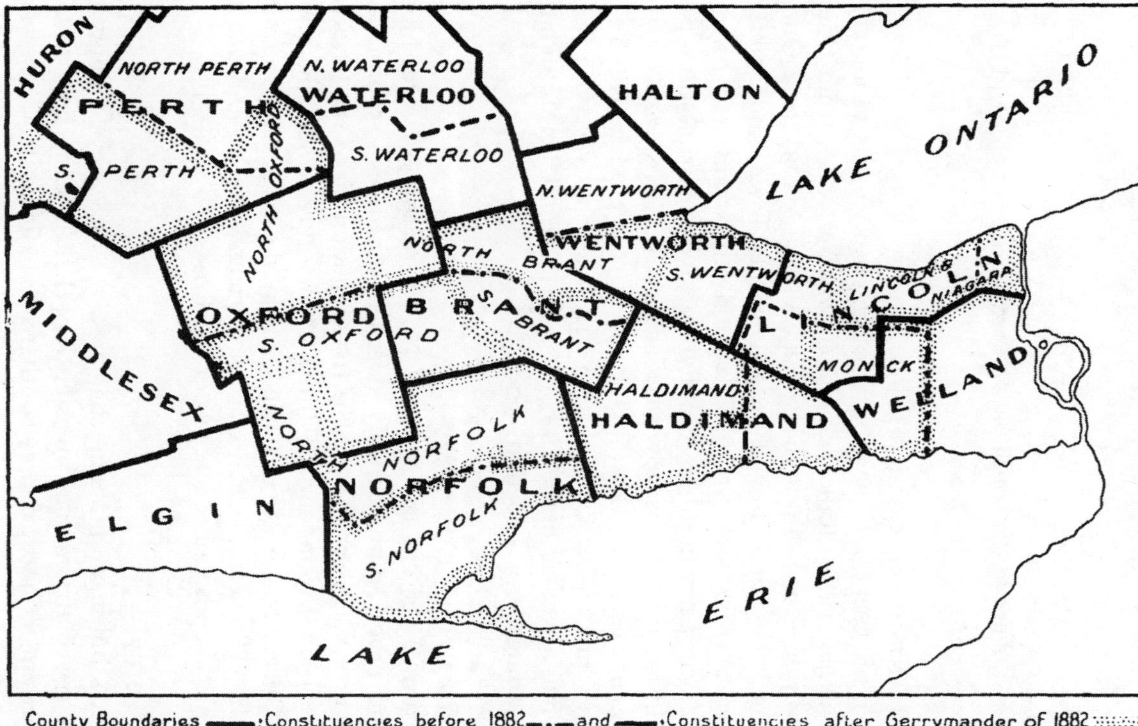

Map 4.4 Dawson's map of Macdonald's gerrymandering of eight counties

(-94) to Norfolk South, the real target of the hiving. Once precarious, Conservative (-17), Norfolk South was now reasonably safe (-111). Macdonald's gerrymander failed in the 1882 general election. Liberals won all four redistributed ridings intended for Tory capture: Brant South (+176), Wentworth South (+48), Perth South (+179), and Norfolk South (+26).

ONTARIO AND YORK COUNTIES

Macdonald's Act set up the new riding of Ontario West as a Liberal hive (+609). The new riding took Pickering Township (+140) from Ontario South; Uxbridge Township and Uxbridge Village (+309) from Ontario North; and Whitchurch Township, Newmarket Town, and Stouffville Village (+162) from York North. These and other transfers[35] benefited the government party in ridings that fed the hive. Ontario North, possibly safe, Liberal (+54) was now reasonably safe, Conservative (-198); Ontario South, very safe, Liberal (+206) was now precarious (+8); and York North, precarious, Conservative (-14) was now very safe (-202). The gerrymander failed in the 1882 general election: Liberal candidates swept the ridings (+59, +50, and +109).

BRUCE COUNTY

The Act turned the ridings of Bruce North, reasonably safe, Liberal (+156) and Bruce South, possibly safe, Conservative (-75) into three ridings (North, East, and West). The redistribution hived the Grits into Bruce West (+971) to favour the Tories in the other two ridings (Bruce East, -520; Bruce North, -331), whence a gain of one for the government party. In the 1882 general election, the gerrymander failed in Bruce East (+176). The Liberals gained a seat, not the Tories.

GREY COUNTY

Macdonald's Bill made just one change to the three Grey-County ridings: it removed Artemesia Township (-153) from Grey East to Grey South. The transfer boosted Grey South from possibly safe, Conservative (-81) to very safe (-234). It dropped Grey East from hive, Conservative (-531) to very safe (-378). Effectively, by de-hiving Grey East, the redistribution shifted wasted Tory votes to Grey South, a fighting riding. The transfer helped to equalize riding populations within Grey County.[36] The Tories held all three original Grey ridings and were predicted to hold all three redistributed ones. That did not happen. The 1882 general election returned the Tory incumbent in Grey East, the Tory-hive riding, but not in Grey North (left alone) or Grey South, the target riding for this thinly disguised Tory gerrymander.[37]

BOTHWELL

Macdonald's Bill manufactured a Tory capture of Bothwell through a complex set of transfers that involved six ridings in three municipal counties: Elgin, Kent, and Middlesex.[38] The transfers moved Bothwell from very safe, Liberal (+285) to reasonably safe, Conservative (-189). Macdonald's goal, apart from gaining a seat for his party, was the "political assassination" of the Hon. David Mills, his front-bench Liberal opponent from the riding.

Sir John A. Macdonald, the Tory cheater, briefly prospered. Mills lost Bothwell by sixteen votes (1,520 to 1,504) in the 1882 general election due to sharp practice by the returning officer, James Stephens of Dresden, a Tory. The returns submitted by Stephens excluded the votes from two polls (Camden, No. 1 and Dawn, No. 3) that favoured Mills (seventy-two to forty-four). A certified judicial recount included the polls and found a twelve-vote majority for Mills (1,576 to 1,564). However, Stephens did not act on the judge's findings, ostensibly because the judge had not recounted the votes at the two polls, but had merely accepted the unsigned statements of the deputy returning officers. However, Mills was to regain his seat in February 1884, when a judicial review ruled that the votes refused by Stephens should be counted.[39] Thus, Macdonald's "political assassination" of Mills succeeded for two years but ultimately failed.

Redistribution Without Hives

BROCKVILLE: A GERRYMANDER

Conservatives held the ridings of Leeds & Grenville (Conservative versus Conservative), Lanark South (very safe, -324), and Brockville (reasonably safe, -127). Macdonald's redistribution transferred Kitley Township from Leeds & Grenville to Brockville, and Smiths Falls Village (+87) from Lanark South to Leeds & Grenville. These transfers boosted the Conservatives in Lanark South (from -324 to -411) and Brockville (amount unknown), without unduly weakening the party in Leeds & Grenville. The transfers were negative for the equalization of population.[40] The redistribution was a gerrymander that strengthened Tory prospects in three Tory-held seats. The government party swept the three ridings in the 1882 general election, but barely held Brockville (precarious, -5, a drop from reasonably safe, -127). No seats changed hands; the evidence is ambiguous about whether or not the gerrymander mattered to the outcomes.

LAMBTON: NOT A GERRYMANDER

Macdonald's division of Lambton County into two ridings, Lambton East (1.04) and Lambton West (1.00), gained a seat for his party, but was not a gerrymander. The Liberals held the original riding (reasonably safe, +146). The new Lambton East riding was possibly safe, Conservative (-85), and Lambton West, very safe, Liberal (+231). A hypothetical division of Lambton into North and South ridings would have produced similar results (North, +235; South, -189). Simply put, a division was warranted on the basis of population, and the Tories, prospectively, would have gained a seat regardless of its details.

ESSEX: A RARE TORY MISSTEP

Macdonald's division of the Essex-County riding (2.25) into the ridings of Essex North (1.23) and Essex South (1.02) copied Oliver Mowat's 1874 provincial ridings. This, prospectively, gained a seat for the opposition. Whereas the county riding was very safe, Conservative (-278), the new ridings, Essex North and Essex South, were very safe, Conservative (-430) and reasonably safe, Liberal (+152). An alternative division of Essex into East and West ridings would have predicted Tory wins in both ridings (possibly safe, -53, and very safe, -225): a gain of a seat for the government party. It also would have given the ridings more equal populations (1.11 and 1.14, versus 1.23 and 1.02).

STORMONT AND CORNWALL MERGE: THE TORIES LOSE A SEAT

The 1882 Act merged two low-population ridings, Cornwall (0.47) and Stormont (0.64), to form the riding of Cornwall & Stormont (1.11). Before redistribution, Cornwall had been precarious, Conservative (-38) and Stormont very safe (-200). The merger cost the Tories a seat.

NIAGARA REGION: A GERRYMANDER

The government party prospectively gained from the 1882 Act's provisions for the ridings of Niagara, Lincoln, Monck, Brant North, and Wentworth South. The Act turned five ridings (3.51 standard populations) into four. It transferred the Lincoln-County municipalities of Grimsby Township and Grimsby Village (+60) from the riding of Lincoln to Wentworth South; the Lincoln-County municipality of Caistor

Table 4.1 Distribution of Dominion seats by party and level of safety, before and after the 1882 redistribution

	Liberal-majority statistics, 1878 election			*After the 1882 redistribution: Predictions for 1882 election*		
	Conservative	*Liberal*	*All parties*	*Conservative*	*Liberal*	*All parties*
hive (500+)	11%	8%	11%	8%	15%	11%
very safe (200–499)	26%	19%	24%	45%	13%	32%
reasonably safe (100–199)	15%	38%	22%	11%	28%	18%
possibly safe (50–99)	21%	19%	20%	17%	21%	18%
precarious (< 50)	20%	12%	17%	13%	18%	15%
acclamation / same party	7%	4%	6%	6%	5%	5%
# of ridings	61	26	88	53	39	92

Township (+34) from Monck to Wentworth South; and the Wentworth-County municipality of Ancaster Township (+271) from Wentworth South to Brant North. Then it merged the rump of Lincoln with the low-population riding of Niagara (0.16) to form the riding of Lincoln & Niagara (1.11). The redistribution was positive for the equalization of population, but, of course, flouted county lines.

It was a gerrymander. Prospectively, the government party gained one seat and the opposition lost two. Before redistribution, the Liberals held three of the five seats; the redistribution cut them down to one of four.[41] In the 1882 general election, however, each party won two ridings. Against prediction, the government party failed to gain one seat, and the Liberals lost one seat, not two.

The 1882 Redistribution: A Tory Gerrymander

The redistribution as a whole was gerrymandered. As shown in Table 4.1, the 1882 redistribution boosted a Tory majority of thirty-five into a prospective Tory majority of forty-five, a gain of ten seats for the government party. Hiving was Macdonald's weapon of choice. A notable feature of the 1882 redistribution was the rise in the percentage of hives among the prospective Liberal-held seats, and the drop in the percentage of hives among the prospective Tory-held seats. Of county ridings that continued in name, the redistribution touched twenty-five that were fighting ridings (either party, ±199); twenty-one of these cases benefited the Conservatives and four the Liberals.

The 1882 election demolished the predictions arising from Macdonald's scandalous redistribution. The electors returned fifty-two Tories, fourteen fewer than predicted, and forty Liberals, fourteen more. Macdonald's hive-based gerrymander failed in ten of twelve ridings that had been predicted for Tory gain.[42] To revisit Macgregor Dawson's conundrum of mutually exclusive interpretations, electoral outcomes in the gerrymandered ridings did not staunch losses for the government party, but rather contributed to them.

MOWAT'S PROVINCIAL REDISTRIBUTIONS, 1885 AND 1889

Mowat's 1885 Act increased the number of ridings from eighty-eight to ninety. For the first and only time, the provincial parliament had fewer Ontario ridings than the House of Commons (ninety-two). To reach the new number, Mowat's Act added four seats and eliminated two. It made Toronto a three-member riding instead of two one-member ridings; divided Muskoka & Parry Sound into two ridings, Muskoka and Parry Sound; divided Algoma into two ridings, Algoma East and Algoma West; and gave Bruce County a third riding. Turning to reductions, the Bill merged Cornwall and Stormont into the single riding of Cornwall-Stormont, and turned three ridings – Grenville, Leeds & Grenville, and Leeds – into two county ridings, Leeds and Grenville. Thus, Mowat increased representation in the northlands and Toronto and reduced it in the eastern counties.

A fifth northland constituency followed four years later, with Mowat's Act to Give Representation to the District of Nipissing, 1889. The district population had been 1,774 in 1881 but was to be 10,654 in 1891. Hitherto, Nipissing District had been without representation.

Underlying Principles

The Hon. Arthur S. Hardy, Mowat's provincial secretary and point man for rough politicking, introduced the Bill "to divide Algoma and otherwise adjust the representation" and outlined its underlying principles.[43] The Bill's provisional title underscored its focus on the northlands. As Hardy explained, Algoma "stretches west from the French River on the east to Lake of the Woods across to Fort Francis and Rat Portage, making in all some 1,000 miles in length. That is an extensive territory which no candidate can be expected adequately to canvass and which scarcely any candidate can be expected to visit during the short time available. Its interests are varied as its numerous resources are of a different character." The "unsettled nature of the Manitoba Boundary question," noted Hardy, had delayed the division of Algoma by "some years." With redistribution, the northlands had four ridings for 2.53 standard populations: Algoma East, 0.57; Algoma West, 0.57; Muskoka, 0.62; and Parry Sound, 0.68. Like the 1882 Dominion Representation Act, the 1885 provincial Act made no provision for Nipissing District, but as noted above, an 1889 statute did.

Three principles animated the Bill's provisions for Southern Ontario. Hardy's first principle was "not to increase the membership of the House except for new territory ... in the event of requests for new members due to growing population, it is thought better to even up those places than to increase the number provided for them." Thus, Hamilton City, with 1.72 standard populations, was refused a second member, and Perth County, with 2.56 standard populations, did not get a third riding. Hardy's second principle was to preserve municipal boundaries in the drawing of electoral districts. His third principle was the equalization of riding populations. As the provincial secretary elaborated, "We are moving in [the] direction of equalization ... with reasonable fairness and reasonable discretion ... but to make each district equal [would] require a more extensive scheme than we contemplate now."

The provision for Toronto, a single riding with three members, was an experiment in "minority representation," in which each elector could vote for up to two candidates. England's provision for "Manchester ... and other large cities" was the model for this arrangement. Although England's 1885 Redistribution of Seats Act abandoned the model, "it [was] thought advisable to try it here." On the basis of population, the Bill under-represented the province's two largest cities – Hamilton (one seat, 1.72) and Toronto (three members, 4.14) – but not Ottawa (1.31), London (0.94), or Kingston (0.67).

The 1885 Act touched forty-five ridings: 51 percent of the province's eighty-eight. The percentage of the provincial ridings in the optimum range for standard populations (0.90–1.10) moved from 30 to 39. The provincial Act interfered with municipal boundaries in two cases. Three transfers repatriated townships to their municipal counties.[44] The Act produced an expected gain of one seat for each party.

"Hiving the Tories" was not on Mowat's agenda. The Act created no Tory hives and left alone four of five Liberal hives: Waterloo North (+783); Wellington Centre (+518); Brant South (+559); and York North (+854). Wellington Centre was the only hive riding from which the Act relocated wasted Liberal votes to fighting ridings nearby.

Details of the Redistribution

Five case studies unpack features of Mowat's redistribution: equalizing riding populations in Brant, Arthur Hardy's home county; an expansion of the Toronto electoral district to match the city's expanding civic boundaries; an unavoidable creation of non-compact ridings in Wellington County; a violation of the principle of minimalism in Grey County; and a successful equalization of populations in the five ridings of Simcoe and Peel Counties and the purely-electoral county of Cardwell.

BRANT: ARTHUR HARDY'S HOME COUNTY

Liberals held both county ridings, Brant North (acclamation) and Arthur Hardy's riding, Brant South (+559). Hardy's redistribution transferred Tuscarora Township (population 2,891) from the South riding to the North riding. It equalized population between the two ridings, from 1.06 and 0.57 to 0.92 and 0.71, but made no change to prospective party strengths. Tuscarora Township had population but no voters – its 2,891 inhabitants were disenfranchised Aboriginals on the Six Nations reserve.

YORK RIDINGS AND TORONTO'S EXPANDING CIVIC BOUNDARIES

Toronto annexed three suburban populations in York County during the years 1883–84 (Yorkville Village, Brockton Town, and Riverside Village). These annexations were the city's very first additions to its original civic territory of 1834.

Mowat's redistribution enlarged Toronto's electoral district to include these fragments of the municipal city, and also, immediately to the south of Brockton, Parkdale Village, which Toronto was not to annex until 1889. These transfers added 7,501 people to the city's electoral district, a rise of 7 percent. Then Mowat increased the city's representation from two ridings (for 4.14 standard populations) to a single three-member one (for 4.49). The redistribution left the York ridings with unequal populations, caused by its failure to transfers parts of the left-alone York

North riding into the depleted city-border ridings of York East and York West.[45] Its transfer of Parkdale Village trespassed on municipal lines.

With the redistribution, the opposition Tories prospectively gained a seat in Toronto, but lost a seat to the government party in the Yorks, with all three ridings prospectively going to the Liberals.[46] The opposition Tories did better than predicted in the 1886 general election, returning three members in Toronto, as predicted, but also holding York West.

WELLINGTON COUNTY: NON-COMPACT RIDINGS BUT NO GERRYMANDER

Before and after redistribution, the Wellington County ridings were neither compact nor symmetrical in shape (Map 4.5). In Wellington West, Minto Township was a square balanced precariously on its southeast corner to connect with the rest of the riding. The South riding had the shape of a tuning fork, whose prongs (Pilkington and Eramosa Townships) nearly surrounded the West riding's Nichol Township. As James McMullen (Dominion Liberal MP, Wellington North) explained, Wellington County was "the most peculiarly shaped county in the Province of Ontario, and I defy any man to form three constituencies out of that county without making them very awkward in shape. It is impossible."[47] Mowat's 1874 redistribution was responsible for the awkwardly shaped county, having given three of its townships and the town of Orangeville to his newly created county of Dufferin.[48]

Mowat's Bill improved the prospects for his party in Wellington County. Liberals held all three county ridings: Wellington Centre, a hive (+518); Wellington West, very safe (+469); and Wellington South, precarious (+33). The Bill transferred Pilkington Township (+98) from Wellington East to Wellington South, and Arthur Township and Mount Forest Town (-29) from the West riding to the East riding. These transfers de-hived the Centre riding to boost Mowat's party's prospective margin of safety in the other two ridings.[49] But the redistribution was not a gerrymander. Odd-shaped ridings were unavoidable in this odd-shaped county, and the redistribution was positive for the equalization of the riding populations.[50] The government party retained the three ridings in the 1883 general election.

GREY COUNTY: A TRESPASS ON MINIMALISM

Mowat's Act turned the ridings of Grey North, South, and East into the ridings of Grey North, South, and Centre. It reorganized the ridings

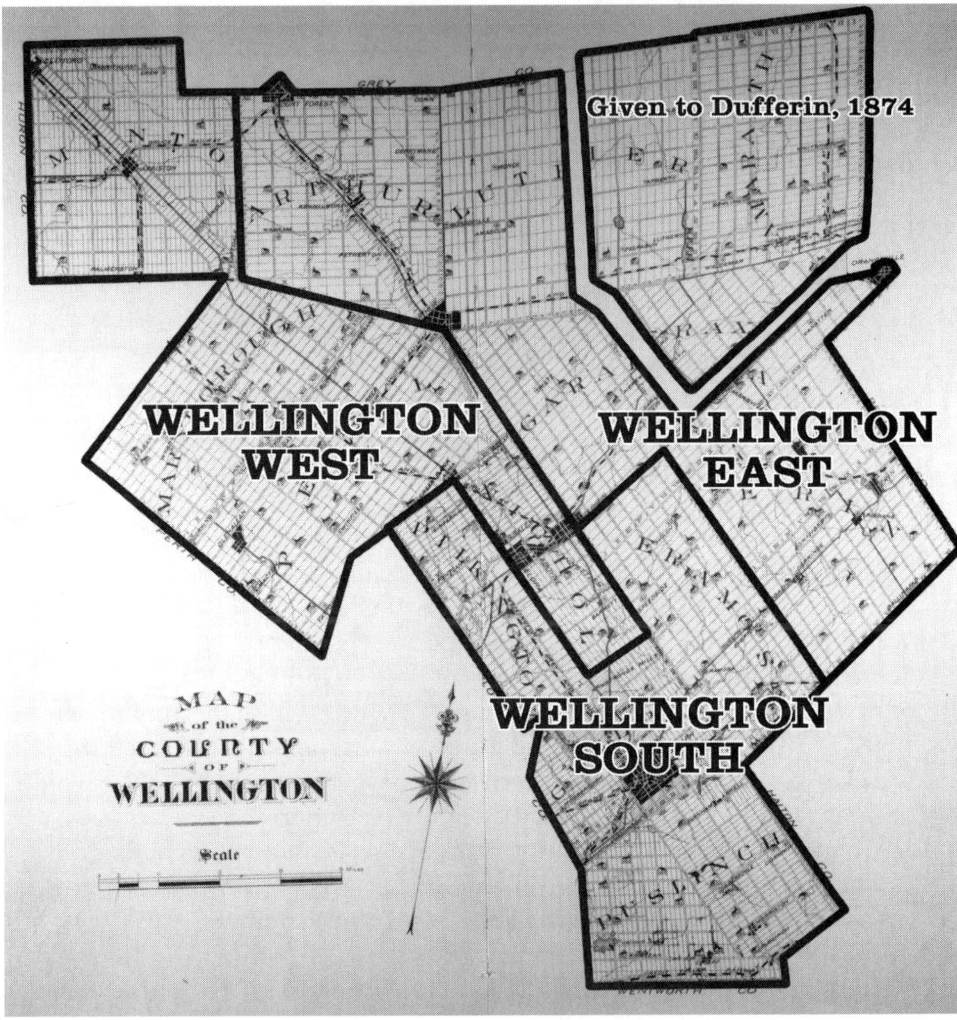

Map 4.5 Odd-shaped ridings in Wellington County, after redistribution

without equalizing populations,[51] a violation of the principle of minimalism. Yet its changes did not clearly benefit the government party. Before adjustment, all three ridings were reasonably safe for the Tories (-155, -179, -167). After rearrangement, they were precarious (-20); reasonably safe (-181); and very safe (-300). Perhaps Mowat plotted to capture the now-precarious North riding, at the cost of giving ground in the two other ridings. In the event, the opposition Tories retained the three ridings in the 1886 general election.

Table 4.2 Distribution of provincial seats by party and level of safety, before and after the 1885 redistribution

	Before 1885 redistribution			*After redistribution: Predictions for 1886 election*		
	Conservative	*Liberal*	*All parties*	*Conservative*	*Liberal*	*All parties*
hive (500+)	5%	8%	7%	5%	6%	6%
very safe (200–499)	30%	18%	23%	42%	20%	29%
reasonably safe (100–199)	32%	28%	30%	16%	39%	29%
possibly safe (50–99)	16%	14%	15%	18%	12%	14%
precarious (< 50)	11%	24%	19%	16%	12%	16%
acclamation	5%	8%	7%	3%	10%	7%
# of ridings	37	50	88	38	51	90

SIMCOE, PEEL, AND CARDWELL: A SUCCESSFUL EQUALIZATION OF POPULATION

The redistribution for the municipal counties of Simcoe and Peel and the purely-electoral county of Cardwell successfully equalized population in their five ridings. None of the original ridings had population in the optimum zone (0.90–1.10). After redistribution, four of them did.[52] The redistribution reinforced the partisan preferences of the five ridings. Cardwell, possibly safe, Conservative (-80) became very safe (-403); Peel, reasonably safe, Liberal (+166) became very safe (+230); two other Simcoe ridings moved from precarious, Liberal (+35 and +22) to reasonably safe (+192 and +184); the other Simcoe riding moved from reasonably safe, Conservative (-168) to very safe (-271).

The 1885 Redistribution: Not a Gerrymander

Mowat's redistribution of 1885 was free of intentional gerrymanders. As shown in Table 4.2, it forecast a Liberal majority of thirteen, the same as the pre-redistribution majority. The redistribution touched seventeen ridings that were precarious, possibly safe, or reasonably safe for the incumbent (either party, ±199); ten cases benefited the Liberals and seven the Tories. The 1886 general election returned fifty-seven Liberals, six more than predicted, and increased Mowat's majority to twenty-four.

SUMMARY AND INTERPRETATION

The Dominion and provincial ridings became sharply different from each other during the 1880s. Macdonald's 1882 Act abandoned the principle of observing municipal boundaries, whereas Mowat's 1885 Act reinforced the principle. Macdonald's Act violated the principle of compact, symmetrical ridings in three cases; Mowat's Act appeared to do so in Wellington County, but this was unavoidable, for reasons of geography. Mowat's Act featured new ridings for the sparsely settled northlands, Algoma in particular, whereas Macdonald's Dominion Act did not. Both Acts achieved never-to-be-equalled progress towards the equalization of populations for ridings.

Toronto's first-ever annexations in 1883–84 expanded its municipal territory beyond the confines of its ridings. Mowat's aggressive response made the electoral district the larger by adding Parkdale Village, as well as the recently annexed municipalities, to the city's electoral district. Macdonald's Dominion redistribution had preceded the annexations and therefore had not faced the issue.

Sir John A. Macdonald's 1882 Representation Act was a comprehensive gerrymander that was to deepen partisan rancour for years to come. Mowat's 1885 Representation Act, like his 1874 Act, was above-board, although Tory political lore claimed otherwise.

Macdonald's Dominion gerrymander failed in the 1882 general election. Electoral outcomes in his gerrymandered ridings helped the opposition Liberals, not his government party. To revisit Macgregor Dawson's conundrum of mutually exclusive interpretations ("failed" versus "staunched losses"), Macdonald's mischief did not staunch losses for his party, but rather contributed to them.

Macdonald's gerrymandered redistribution lasted through three general elections: 1882, 1887, and 1891. It remained to be seen how it would fare with the next redistribution, by another Tory ministry in 1892 (chapter 5). Mowat's 1885 Act was the last large-scale redistribution until 1908, when a Tory ministry under James P. Whitney, elected in 1905, responded to thirty-three years of Liberal management of the ridings (chapter 8).

5

John Thompson's 1892 Dominion Redistribution

Sir John Abbott was prime minister in 1892, Sir John A. Macdonald having died in office in 1891. But it was Sir John Thompson, minister of Justice, the de facto head of government, and prime-minister-in-waiting, who administered the redistribution. The Liberal opposition demanded nothing less than the overturning of Sir John A. Macdonald's "Gerrymander Act" of 1882, in particular a restoration of municipal lines in electoral districts. That is not what Thompson gave them.

The Ontario population increased by 10 percent during the 1880s. The regional percentages were the northland districts, a 73 percent increase; the GTA, 38; Eastern Ontario, 6; and Western Ontario, 2. Toronto, with 174,414 people (a rise of 101 percent), was the largest of the province's cities, now nine in number. Cities held 17 percent of Ontario's 1891 census population, up from 10 percent in 1881. The nine northland districts held 89,236 people (a rise of 68 percent).

Ontario's 1891 census population entitled the province to ninety-two seats in the House of Commons, the same as in 1881. With the quota unchanged, the 1892 Representation Act added two seats, for a prospective gain of two for the Conservative benches, and eliminated two, for a prospective subtraction of two from the Liberal tally. For addition, the Act made Toronto West a two-member riding and created the riding of Nipissing, the Nipissing District's first-ever representation.[1] For subtraction, it eliminated two ridings in the counties through transfers and mergers. Brant North and Wentworth North became the merged riding of Wentworth North & Brant; Haldimand and Monck became the merged riding of Haldimand & Monck. The Act touched twelve ridings, down from fifty under the 1882 Act. The percentage of ridings with population in the optimum range (0.90–1.10) moved from 33 to 36, down from 43 percent under the 1882 redistribution.

In the judgment of the distinguished biographer, P.B. Waite, "The opposition press made a great deal of noise about not very much ... Reasonable men by and large accepted as sensible the redistribution of 1892."[2] Clearly Thompson's redistribution, touching only twelve ridings, did not do "very much." It restored two of Macdonald's misshapen ridings to compact, symmetrical shape, but its two mergers of ridings were gerrymanders.

From the viewpoint of the opposition Liberals, however, Thompson's Representation Act was outrageous for what it did not do: restore county lines that Macdonald's "Gerrymander Act" had obliterated in 1882. James David Edgar (Ontario West), a key Liberal organizer and fundraiser and future speaker of the House,[3] made the Liberal case: the governing Tories had "taken upon their shoulders the whole burden of justifying the gerrymander of 1882; because, Sir, if they do not justify it, they are bound, before this Bill becomes law, to rectify it ... I cannot disassociate the Act of 1882 from the present Bill, and therefore I say that although Quebec and Prince Edward Island and other parts of the country suffer more additional wrong than Ontario does under this Bill, the effect is cumulative in the Province of Ontario, and we have all the wrongs of 1872 and 1882 to redress before we are finished with this legislation."[4]

Principles of the 1892 Representation Act

On introducing the 1892 Bill, Thompson misstated his mandate. In his understanding, the 1867 BNA Act required that "after the completion of each decennial census, the representation of the various constituencies in this House shall be readjusted on certain well-known and well-defined principles."[5] In fact, the BNA Act said nothing about the readjustment of constituencies, and the principles for readjustment, although well-known, were evolving and contested. Indeed, the BNA Act did not require any redistribution for Ontario in 1892, given that the province's quota of seats was unchanged.

Nevertheless, Thompson stated the principles that animated his Bill.[6] In addition to the standard no-gerrymander pledge, these were, first and paramount, the equalization of riding populations; second, to interfere only "in those districts where additional representation for increased population has to be provided" (minimalism); third, additional representation for large cities, hence an additional member for Toronto; fourth, an increase of representation for developing northern districts; and fifth, the principle of compact ridings: "geographical proximity" in Thompson's language. Thompson's list was missing what mattered most to the Liberals – the restoration of municipal lines that Macdonald had shattered in 1882.

John Haggart (Lanark South), minister of Railways and Canals and the government's chief planner for the 1892 schedule of ridings, added a sixth principle: to balance representation between Eastern and Western Ontario. As he elaborated, "I divided Ontario so that one-half of the 92 constituencies would lie on one side and the other half on the other side, and I placed the dividing line between York and Peel and ran it up to Georgian Bay, and I added Algoma to the east. That made 46 constituencies on each side."[7] Haggart's division placed Toronto in the Eastern Ontario region, as well as Algoma, whose territory extended west to Thunder Bay. Haggart rejected the principle of municipal boundaries for his schedule, noting that enactment of that principle would change "70 odd constituencies" and create uproar on the opposition benches.

Tory Dissent: The McCarthy-O'Brien Motion

Two Conservatives, D'Alton McCarthy (Simcoe North) and William E. O'Brien (Muskoka), moved an amendment to send the Bill back to the drawing board. These men had a history as Tory rebels and adversaries of the Justice minister, McCarthy having seconded O'Brien's motion for disallowance of Quebec's Jesuits Estates Act in 1889.[8] After lengthy debate, their amendment was lost by a vote of 109 to 62. Sixty Liberals supported their amendment; McCarthy and O'Brien were the only Tories to do so.

Nevertheless, their motion sparked debate on issues of principle that crossed party lines. First, they condemned the 1892 Bill and its 1882 predecessor for not delivering on their professed organizing principle, the equalization of riding populations, and hence for having no principles. Second, they called for a restoration of municipal lines in electoral divisions – effectively, an overturning of the redistribution of 1882. Other principles in the motion included full representation by population for Toronto; representation for "communities of interest"; and compact shape for ridings. More generally, their motion acknowledged that the 1882 Act was a gerrymander: a "gross mistake" for the Conservative Party and the parliamentary system. In O'Brien's description, "it was based on no principle and it violated every principle." As such, it required correction, which Thompson's 1892 Bill did not deliver.

The text of the McCarthy-O'Brien motion was:

> that the said Bill be not now read a second time, but that it be resolved, that the distribution of seats of the members of this House should, so far as is practicable, be based on equality of population, due regard being had to the community of interest existing in localities, a full and fair expression of public opinion and the permanence and stability of constituencies.
>
> That the most effectual way of accomplishing these ends is to assume county and city boundaries as the natural limits of electoral districts, with equitable divisions thereof constituted with compactness as regards geographical position, and based on well-known existing areas where the population entitles the city or county to two or more representatives.
>
> That the system now prevailing, and proposed to be continued by the said Bill, fails to secure equality of population, ignores community of interests, disregards geographical compactness, renders stability impossible, and is liable to gross abuse in affording opportunities in the arrangement of electoral districts for promoting party aims and obtaining party advantages regardless of the considerations which ought to determine the settlement of the representation of the people in this House.[9]

R.C. Weldon (Conservative, New Brunswick) in 1892 conceded that his party's 1882 Act was a gerrymander, but argued for "building on what we have" for stability, rather than a massive overturning of the electoral map that the motion required. As he argued, Ontario had undergone three elections with the corrupt 1882 redistribution, but the gerrymander had failed – the Liberals had done well in Ontario, and the Tories, the party that was intended to benefit, had suffered.[10] Thomas Sproule (Conservative, Grey East) objected to one feature of the motion: full representation by population for Toronto. In the event, party discipline, not points of principle, sealed the Tory vote and the motion's fate.

The Liberal Critique of the 1892 Bill

Liberals championed the restoration of municipal lines in the ridings. The Hon. David Mills (Bothwell), minister of the Interior and superintendent of Indian Affairs in the government of Alexander Mackenzie and resurrected from "political assassination" in 1882, made the case: "the only way we can obtain anything approaching permanency in the electoral districts is by recognizing the permanency of municipal boundaries." Municipal boundaries unite people "with those with whom they have social affinities, and with whom they are co-operating for other purposes ... These organizations in large measure grow up. In the first instance, they are a matter of convenience. You associated certain people together in a certain district as one township. They are associated in their schools, in their county councils, in their agricultural societies, and so they are in a political sense one organization, and the business of this House ought to recognize these facts." The 1892 Bill made three transfers across county lines. What mattered more to the Liberals was the Bill's failure to restore municipal lines that Sir John had violated in 1882.

Mackenzie Bowell (Conservative, Hastings North), soon to be prime minister (1894–96), conceded the relevance of "municipal or county lines" for the provincial parliament, which dealt with local issues, but not for the House of Commons, which dealt with "great principles," such as "the broad question of the National Policy." Richard Weldon, a New Brunswick Conservative, cared "very little for the counties of Ontario, but [did] care for the maintenance, as far as they can be maintained, of the boundaries of the old electoral districts."[11] Possibly he referred to the ridings of Confederation, such as the purely-electoral counties of Bothwell, Monck, and Cardwell.

Liberal critics noted sectional bias – sectional balance in John Haggart's parlance – in the Bill's application of the principle of representation by population. "It is only necessary to look at the census," exclaimed David Mills, "to see that the portion of the Province of Ontario which lies west of Toronto is under-represented at the present time, and the portion which lies to the east ... is over-represented, but the hon. gentleman and his colleagues have taken away two members from the district which is already under-represented [the merged ridings of Wentworth North with Brant North, and Haldimand with Monck] and have left that section of the province which at the present time and all along has been over-represented."[12] "The blot on this measure, as everyone knows perfectly well," fumed the Hon. Sir Richard Cartwright (Oxford South), "is this: that the constituencies ... which lie west of the city of Toronto are scarcely represented in accordance with their population. The 35 constituencies which lie east of Toronto are at this moment represented utterly disproportionately to their numerical strength." Accordingly, noting government's need to make room in the 1892 quota for two additional members (for Nipissing and Toronto West), Cartwright proposed to eliminate two seats in "the district which lies east of Toronto … Let us take the four smallest constituencies in Ontario, which as it happens lie contiguous to one another, and let us unite those four 2 and 2."[13] He had in mind Leeds & Grenville (0.59) and Grenville South (0.56) for a merged riding with 1.15 standard populations; and Frontenac (0.59) and Lennox (0.65) for a merged riding with 1.24 standard populations. Admittedly, Cartwright had an axe to grind; although now representing Oxford South, he had originally represented Lennox as a Conservative, changed parties in 1873, been defeated in Lennox as a Liberal in 1878, and been the victim of "political assassination" in Huron Centre in 1882.

Mowat's 1885 Gerrymander: A Tory Canard

Sam Hughes (Conservative, Victoria North) mocked the pretended innocence of his Liberal foes: "We are treated on every occasion when [the Liberals] address the House to the same old story of purity in elections. They are the only party, they are the only persons, in whom purity is to be found." The "infamous gerrymander" of their provincial cousin, Oliver Mowat, belied their pretension, pronounced Hughes.[14] His first proof of Mowat's roguery was the popular vote in the 1890 provincial general election, which, he claimed, had given the Tories a majority of 1,458. Thus, Mowat's "majority on the floor of the House of 28 to 30 members [was] not due to the votes of the people, but to the gerrymander by the Government." Hughes's second proof was the "extraordinary shape of some of the ridings for the Ontario Legislature," as evidenced by the constituencies in Wellington and Waterloo counties. In Wellington,

> the [riding] in the centre with the indescribable outline represents East Wellington. It is hung in the middle and is almost cut in two, and yet hon. gentlemen in the opposition do not go into a rage over the shape of that riding. Alongside of it is West Wellington, and as a gentleman pointed out the other day, you have to step across a corner about an inch wide to get from the northern part of the riding to the southern part. Hon. Gentlemen can also see the fantastic shape of South Waterloo. That the House may properly appreciate South Waterloo is doctored up and to what extreme these purists of the Liberal party will go to gerrymander a county, I shall read you a

description of the County of Waterloo from the Revised Statutes of Ontario ... This is the description of the county from the Act itself: '*The said northerly portion of the township of Waterloo shall include and consist of that part of the said township lying within the following limits, that is to say: Commencing at the south-west angle of lot number forty-six ... thence easterly along the southerly limits of the said lot, and of the lots numbered forty-seven, forty-eight, fifty, fifty-one, and fifty-three, and the prolongation thereof, to the middle of the Grand River; thence along the middle of said river, against the stream to the prolongation of the limit between lots one hundred and thirteen and one hundred and fourteen, and along the prolongation of the limit between the said lots ... northerly and easterly, to the westerly limits of the said lot number one hundred and seven, northerly to the northern limits thereof; thence along the northerly limits of the said lot one hundred and seven, and of lots numbers one hundred and six, eight-four, and ninety-six, easterly to the easterly boundary of the said capital township.*'

You will notice that lots 49 and 52, as well as other lots which happen to be occupied by Tories, are omitted so as to make the gerrymander complete.

Hughes, noted one of his biographers, "usually spoke with absolute confidence, sometimes without much forethought." According to another of his biographers, Hughes "was a skilful practitioner of inflammatory rhetoric, back-room deals, and parish-pump patronage."[15] So it was with Hughes's allegation against Mowat. His statistics for the popular vote in the 1890 provincial election, which showed a Tory majority of 1,458, were a modified version of the official statistics.[16] A simple tally from the 1890 election returns shows a Liberal majority of 8,680.[17] The electoral division of Waterloo Township in Waterloo County was unusual, but it dated from the redistribution of 1853, two decades before Mowat became premier.[18] "There never was an alteration in the County of Waterloo by Mr. Mowat," exclaimed James McMullen (Liberal, Wellington North). "That constituency remains as it was when Mr. Mowat came to power. Yet the hon. gentleman tries to show people in this House who do not know what was done that Mr. Mowat gerrymandered and he is trying to make an impression on the House that is not true; and if he did not know it, then he ought to have known it." As Hughes noted, none of the three Wellington-County ridings was compact and symmetrical. However, as McMullen explained, Wellington was "the most peculiarly shaped county in the Province of Ontario, and I defy any man to form three constituencies out of that county without making them very awkward in shape. It is impossible."[19] In this regard, Wellington was an awkwardly shaped rump of the original county (Map 4.5); Mowat's 1874 redistribution had taken three of its townships and the Town of Orangeville for the new county of Dufferin.

Mowat's alleged trespass on county lines was a trailing issue. Sam Hughes, claimed McMullen, "stated that the Hon. Oliver Mowat, the Premier of Ontario, has made many invasions of county boundaries in that province." McMullen challenged Hughes "to show one single instance in which a county boundary has been invaded by any Act which the Hon. Oliver Mowat has passed for readjustment of constituencies." Clarke Wallace (Conservative, York West) interjected that Mowat had "destroyed township boundaries, let alone county boundaries." McMullen would have none of that: "I say that there is not a single case in which the Hon. Oliver Mowat has invaded county boundaries; if there are any such cases, they existed before Mr. Mowat became Premier, and they have been left as they were." Although Hughes and Wallace had no response, McMullen's denial was too sweeping. Mowat had split townships in 1874. His 1885 redistribution had transferred Parkdale Village from York County to Toronto, four years before Toronto annexed the village.

Toronto: An Emerging "Elephant in the Room" for Redistribution

The population of Toronto, the provincial metropolis, was 174,414 in 1891, a rise of 101 percent from a decade earlier.[20] With the city's twelve annexations of suburban territories during the years 1883–90, a growing population of city residents were situated outside the limits of the three Toronto ridings. With three seats, Toronto had been fully represented on the basis of population in 1872 (3.06 standard populations), under-represented in 1882 (4.13), and markedly under-represented in 1892 (7.62 for the municipal city, 6.29 for the city ridings). Other Ontario cities – Hamilton (2.06) and Ottawa (1.70) with two seats each, and London and Kingston with one – were fully represented.

Toronto alone was an "elephant in the room" for redistribution. On the basis of its civic population (7.62), the Toronto municipality merited eight ridings, compared to its current three. Yet the Ontario quota for ridings was unchanged at ninety-two. Accordingly, if redistribution gave five additional ridings for Toronto and one for the northlands, then six county ridings were headed for extinction. Montreal posed the same problem for representation in Quebec.

Thus, for the first time, members from both sides of the House advanced the principle that city ridings should have larger populations – less representation – than county ridings. In practice, "cities" was code for Toronto and Montreal. In the 1892 parliament, noted Wilfrid Laurier, leader of the opposition since 1887, residents of cities represented several county ridings, as well as ridings in their cities of residence, thereby giving additional representation for city interests. Richard Weldon (Conservative, New Brunswick) agreed: "The cities of the country should be underrepresented, partly for the reason given by the leader of the Opposition, and still more largely for these reasons, that cities by reason of daily newspapers published there, influence the political thinking of the people, by reason of the influence of their wholesale merchants and banking institutions and universities the feelings and opinions of the cities are projected upon the country outside, so that the cities, independent of their representatives, have an enormous influence upon political opinion in the country."[21]

James David Edgar (Liberal, Ontario West), a Toronto lawyer who represented a county riding, and George Cockburn (Conservative, Toronto Centre) were on the other side of the debate. Edgar, a Liberal, agreed with apologists for the Tory Bill that "the city of Toronto … needs more representation." He differed from some of his Liberal colleagues who judged "that because a member from an outside constituency happens to live in Toronto, he represents Toronto." Cockburn, a Conservative, disputed

> the objection to the increased representation of cities [on the grounds] that in each city there is a number of residents who have seats for other constituencies, and who indirectly represent the interests of the city in which they reside … while we have in Toronto perhaps four or five gentlemen who represent constituencies in other parts of the Dominion, I have never gone to one of them to ask him any help with regard to the representation of Toronto or its special interests … cities are not being fairly treated in this Bill [i.e., one additional seat is not enough] … they represent more particularly commercial and manufacturing capital. They are the seats of science, literature, and arts; they are the seats of our universities and centres of intelligence … we must bear in mind that while the counties are constantly diminishing in population the cities are increasing, and there is no use in trying to stem the torrent in that direction.[22]

Interestingly, all three Toronto City ridings and York West were Tory hives (-502, -1,464, -1,757, and -806), while York East was precarious for the Liberals (+26). Thus, any additional seats for the GTA would benefit the government party. Nevertheless, the county lobby prevailed. The 1892 Bill retained three ridings for Toronto, but made Toronto West a two-member riding, for a net increase of one member (not four or five).

The Electoral and Municipal Territories of Cities

During the years 1883–91, Ontario cities began to annex suburban populations in adjacent townships. Toronto annexed twelve territories from York County; Hamilton, two from Wentworth County; Ottawa, two from Carleton County; and London, two from Middlesex County. Thus, by the 1892 redistribution, the municipal territories of these cities had extended beyond the limits of their electoral districts. Inasmuch as a city was a "county of itself" for municipal purposes, its municipal limits were a county line to be observed in redistribution.

But county lines were not a priority for the Tories of 1882 and 1892. Hence Thompson's Bill enlarged the electoral district of Hamilton to match its civic boundaries, but did not do so for the other cities. "The electoral district of the city of Hamilton," stated Thompson's Bill, "shall consist of the city of Hamilton as at present constituted." This captured two parcels that the city had annexed in 1891 (see Map 9.1). In contrast, the Bill left alone Toronto's electoral territory, which remained "as constituted on 14 June, 1872." This left 17 percent of the city's population (30,391 people) in two city-border York ridings; conversely, Toronto residents were 50 percent of the population in York East and 30 percent in York West. "The electoral district of the city of Ottawa," read Thompson's 1892 Bill, "shall consist of the city of Ottawa, except that part thereof known as New Edinburgh" – the city's Rideau Ward since 1887 (Map 5.1). The left-alone London-City riding excluded the villages of London East and London South, which the city had annexed in 1885 and 1890 respectively.

Compact Ridings

Macdonald's 1882 Act had flouted the principle of compact-shaped ridings in three instances: one in transferring Dereham Township and Tillsonburg Town, rather than two Norwich townships, to the riding of Norfolk North; one in separating Port Elgin from its home township, Saugeen, in Bruce County; and one separating Scugog Township from its

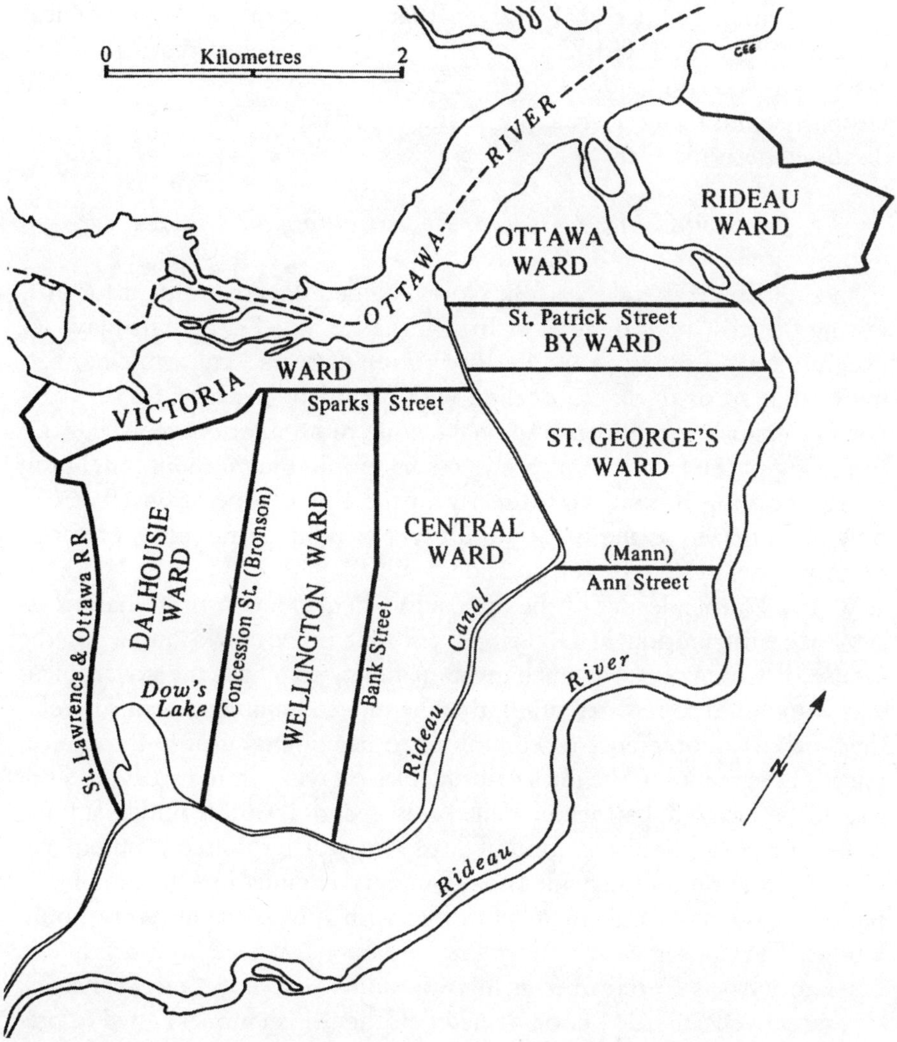

Map 5.1 Wards of Ottawa, 1889

contiguous municipalities, Port Perry and Reach Township, in Ontario County (see Maps 4.1, 4.2, and 4.3).

John Thompson acknowledged the principle of "geographical proximity," and he reversed two of Macdonald's departures from that principle. His Bill reunited Scugog Township with Port Perry Village and Reach Township, and rejoined Port Elgin Village to Saugeen Township. Ironically, the latter change assisted the government party by boosting Bruce North from precarious, Conservative (-39) to reasonably safe

(-137). Rather hypocritically, given that restoration of "geographical proximity" squared with Grit principle, Liberals alleged that this restoration was a gerrymander. Perhaps Thompson did the right thing for the wrong reason: using a principle to mask partisan advantage – a thinly disguised gerrymander.

A Neutral Mechanism for Redistributing the Ridings

John Charlton (Liberal, Norfolk North) chided the government for professing "British precedents and British justice and British fair-play," as exemplified in Britain's 1885 Redistribution of Seats Act, "while not acting in that spirit to-day in dealing with a similar measure. So far from copying British precedents, they have gone to another source. They are following in the footsteps of predecessors, not in the mother land, but in a neighbouring nation, and directly in the line of operations that can only be criticized as the *summum bonum* of political rascality. I refer to the American system of gerrymander."[23]

Wilfrid Laurier, leader of the opposition, denied a constitutional necessity for redistribution in Ontario, given that the Ontario quota for the House of Commons was unchanged at ninety-two.[24] If the government was committed to redistribution, then he moved an amendment to "refer the work to a conference or committee to be composed of both political parties to agree upon the lines or principles on which a redistribution Bill should be drawn." Laurier modelled this proposal on his understanding of Britain's 1885 Redistribution of Seats Act, which resulted from bipartisan consultation and provided for boundary commissions to establish a national system of single-member ridings with approximately equal populations. The Conservative majority in Parliament rejected his amendment, but Laurier was to return to it in 1899 and 1903. The New Brunswick Conservative Richard Weldon denied that the British model aimed to preserve the balance between parties; British statutes did not mention party.[25]

A Gerrymander for the Niagara Region

The Niagara region held four counties: Wentworth, Haldimand, Lincoln, and Welland (Maps 5.2, 5.3, and 5.4). During the 1880s, the standard populations for these four counties had declined from 5.17 to 4.69 – still sufficient for five ridings. Nevertheless, Macdonald's 1882 Representation Act had transferred Ancaster Township from Wentworth to Brant North, which was outside of the region. Without Ancaster, the four counties had 4.39 standard populations, which sufficed for four ridings.

As it happened, the status quo, inherited from 1882, was six ridings: Haldimand, Lincoln & Niagara, Welland, Wentworth North, Wentworth South, and Monck. Five of the six ridings had below-average populations (0.72, 1.10, 0.71, 0.67, 0.64, and 0.73). None of the six ridings observed county lines. Monck was a purely-electoral county that included six municipalities from Haldimand, two from Welland, and one from Lincoln. The Wentworth ridings, as noted above, were missing Ancaster, and Wentworth South included the Lincoln-County townships of Caistor and Grimsby.

Thompson's 1892 Representation Act reorganized eight ridings, the six of the four counties plus the ridings of Brant North and Norfolk South. Like Macdonald's 1882 Act, Thompson's Act disregarded county lines. It transferred the Haldimand township of Walpole from the Haldimand riding to Norfolk South; merged Wentworth North with Brant North to form the riding of Wentworth North & Brant; merged the rump of Haldimand with Monck to form the riding of Haldimand & Monck; and used transfers within the region to balance the ridings' populations. The result was six ridings for 6.32 standard populations, with four ridings in the optimum zone for population.[26]

As shown in Table 5.1, the Act's reduction of eight ridings to six prospectively removed two from the Liberal count of seats. The Tory count held at three, with higher levels of safety (Haldimand, -78, to Haldimand & Monck, -444; Wentworth South, from -1 to -200; Norfolk South from -412 to -459). For the purpose, the redistribution hived Liberal votes into Wentworth North & Brant (+1,121) and Lincoln & Niagara (+596) to boost Tory prospects in Wentworth South, Haldimand & Monck, and Norfolk South. Monck (+260), for example, was stripped of two Liberal-leaning townships (Pelham and Gainsborough, +548), which were given to Lincoln & Niagara (moving it from +48 to +596). The Tory-leaning rump of Monck (-319) was then merged with Haldimand (-78) to form a very safe Tory riding (-444). Effectively, the Niagara-region redistribution was a gerrymander: it damaged Liberal prospects with hiving and trespass on county lines.

The net outcome in the 1896 general election (three Liberal and three Tory seats) matched the predicted net outcome. That said, the gerrymander flopped. Contrary to prediction, the very safe, Tory riding of Wentworth South (-200) elected a Liberal (+187), and the very safe, Liberal seat of Welland (+447) elected a Tory (-169). The municipal-level statistics elaborated the failure of the gerrymander for Wentworth South. The riding's three newly added municipalities, with a Tory majority (-144) in their previous riding of Wentworth North, delivered no majority – zero – in the 1896 general election.

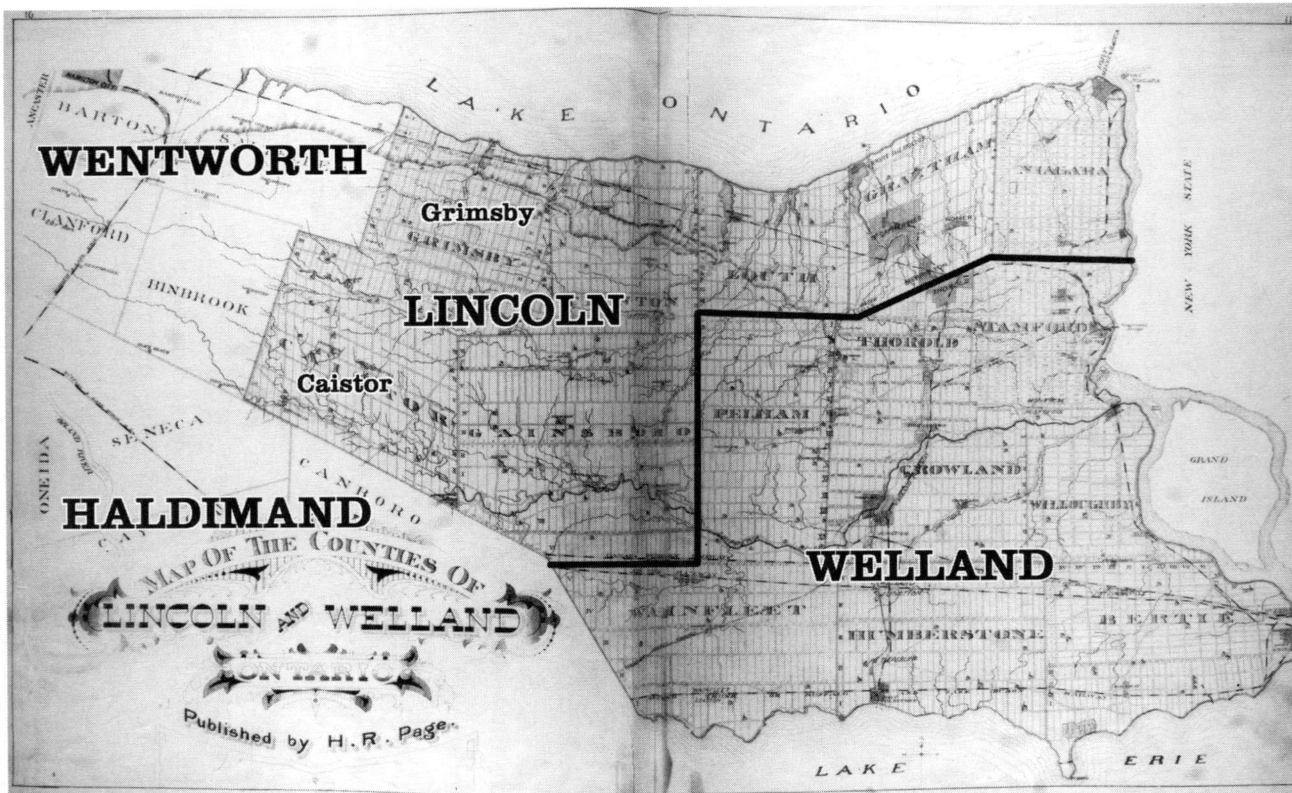

Map 5.2 The four counties of the Niagara region, Dominion ridings, 1892

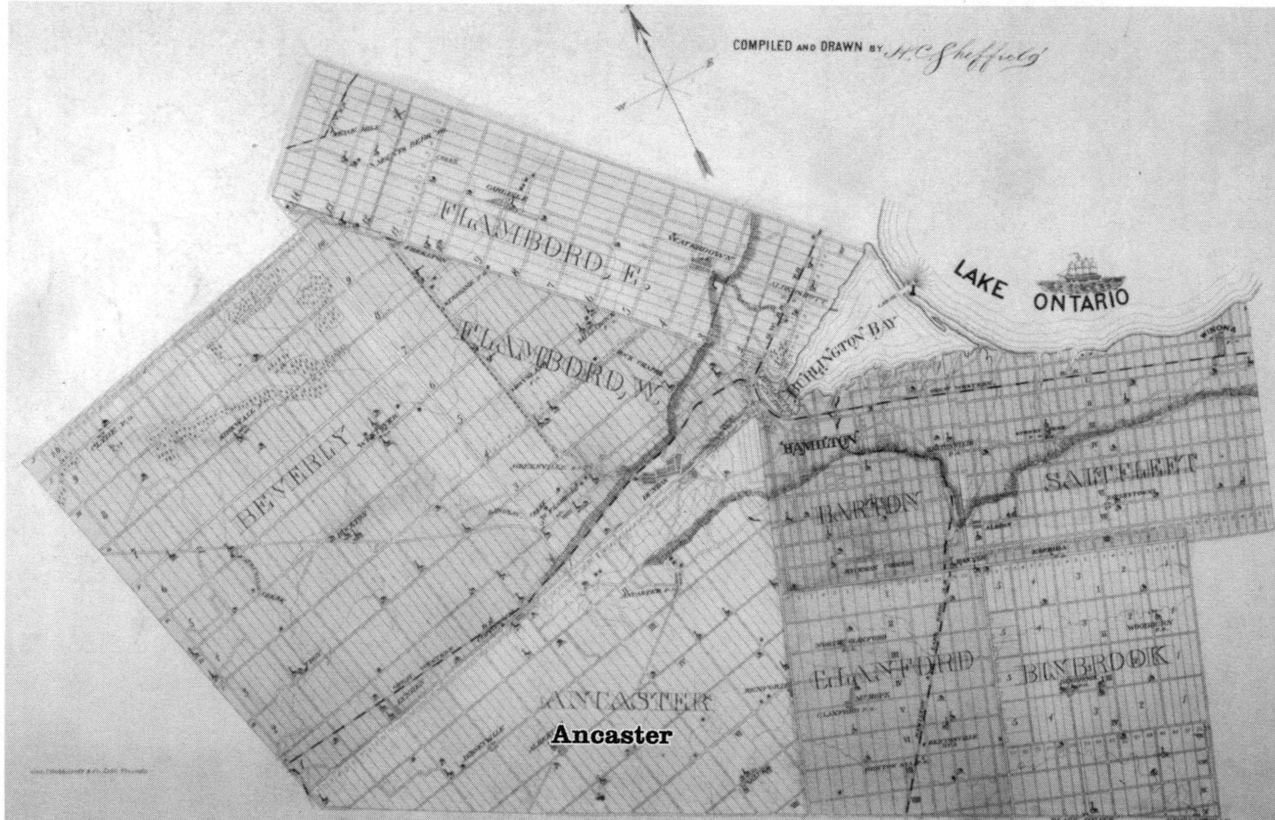

Map 5.3 Wentworth County, Dominion ridings, 1892

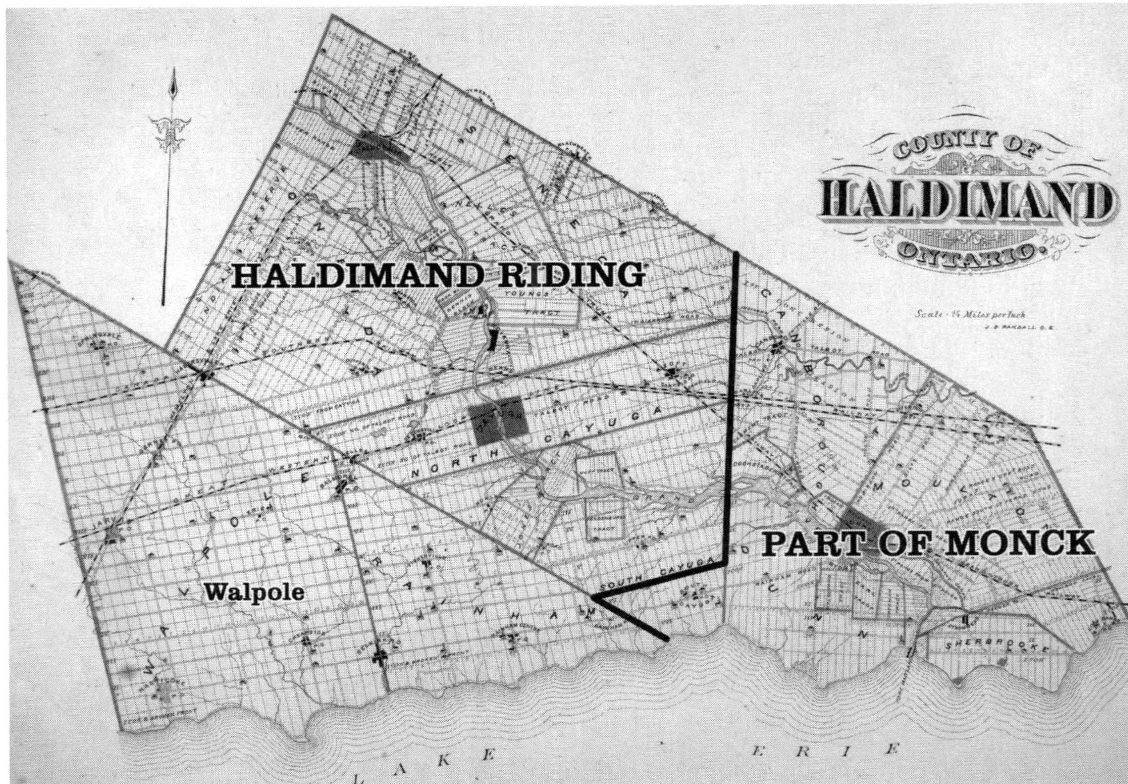

Map 5.4 Haldimand County showing the Haldimand riding and Haldimand townships in Monck, Dominion ridings, 1892

Table 5.1 Dominion redistribution in the Niagara region, 1892: Predicted and actual outcomes for the 1896 general election

Original ridings	*1891 election*	*Redistributed ridings*	*Predicted 1896 election*	*Actual 1896 outcome*
Brant North	+1,116			
Wentworth North	+206	Wentworth North & Brant	+2,582	+1,121
Monck	+260			
Haldimand	-78	Haldimand & Monck	-444	-713
Wentworth South	-1	Wentworth South	-200	+187
Welland	+447	Welland (left alone)	+447	-169
Lincoln & Niagara	+48	Lincoln & Niagara	+596	+422

SUMMARY AND INTERPRETATION

The 1892 Representation Act touched just twelve ridings, down from fifty under the 1882 Act. It boosted the percentage of ridings in the optimum zone from 34 to 38. Its interventions were selective in leaving alone the small-population, Tory-leaning ridings of Eastern Ontario – a large-scale passive gerrymander. Alternatively, as the Conservatives advertised, the Act's minimalism preserved balance in representation between the province's eastern and western sections. The Act restored compact shape to two ridings, with transfers of the municipalities of Port Elgin and Scugog. Correction of the third anomaly, Macdonald's placement of Dereham Township and Tillsonburg Town in Norfolk North, awaited Laurier's redistribution of 1903.

The redistribution did little to equalize the riding populations, which purportedly was its animating principle. For the Liberals, however, the chief fault of the Act was its failure to reverse the Tory gerrymander of 1882 by restoring the principle of county lines. The Act left alone most of Macdonald's mischief of 1882, and it disregarded municipal lines in the Niagara region, which it gerrymandered, albeit unsuccessfully.

The provincial metropolis posed an emergent problem in representation. In 1892 Toronto held 7.62 standard populations, yet had just three seats. At the same time, Ontario's constitutional quota for representation was unchanged from 1882. Perforce, each additional seat for Toronto required the elimination of a country riding. Grits and Tories alike responded with a new principle for federal ridings: that cities

Table 5.2 Distribution of Dominion seats by party and level of safety, before and after the 1892 redistribution

	Liberal-majority statistics, 1891 election		*After the 1892 redistribution: Predictions for 1896 election*		*Actual result of the 1896 general election*	
	Tory	*Grit*	*Tory*	*Grit*	*Tory*	*Grit*
hive (500+)	25%	27%	24%	31%	22%	32%
very safe (200–499)	33%	30%	38%	29%	35%	32%
reasonably safe (100–199)	13%	14%	16%	14%	15%	14%
possibly safe (50–99)	8%	16%	6%	17%	13%	16%
precarious (< 50)	19%	14%	14%	10%	11%	17%
acclamation/ same party	2%	0%	2%	0%	4%	0%
# of ridings	48	44	50	42	46	44
% Ontario seats won	52%	48%	54%	46%	50%	48%
not counted					2 (Patrons)	

– specifically Toronto – should have less representation than country regions on the basis of population. Accordingly, the Act gave Toronto one additional seat, not the four or five that the city's standard populations warranted.

The 1892 redistribution enlarged Hamilton's electoral district to match its expanded municipal boundaries, but did not do so for Toronto, Ottawa, or London. This was unsurprising given Thompson's indifference to the principle of county lines.

As Table 5.2 shows, statistics for the redistribution predicted a gain of two seats for the government party and a loss of two seats for the Liberals. The 1896 general election, however, delivered a loss of two seats for the government party and a gain of two seats for a new third party, the Patrons.

"The opposition press made a great deal of noise about not very much," writes the eminent biographer, P.B. Waite, adding that "reasonable men by and large accepted as sensible the redistribution of 1892."[27] "Not very much," however, was precisely the issue. Effectively,

John Thompson's handiwork was a large-scale passive gerrymander that left intact Macdonald's notorious gerrymander of 1882. Its elimination of two ridings added two gerrymanders more. Furious Liberals under Laurier were to take their revenge with the next redistribution, in 1903.

6

Hitting Back: Wilfrid Laurier's Redistribution Bills of 1899, 1900, and 1903

The Liberal Party replaced the Conservatives in office for the years 1896–1911. Its ascendancy gave Prime Minister Wilfrid Laurier a chance to overturn the Tory "Gerrymander Acts" of 1882 and 1892. But the Conservative majority in the Senate defeated Laurier's Representation Bill of 1899 and a nearly identical Bill in 1900. Each Bill would have "de-gerrymandered" ridings in the western counties by restoring them to county lines. In the event, the Senate accepted Laurier's 1903 Bill, thereby enacting the first-ever Dominion redistribution by a Liberal administration. In general, Laurier's Act restored municipal lines to ridings in Western Ontario, and gerrymandered ridings in Eastern Ontario.

Senate obstruction fanned the flames of Liberal outrage, but also caused both sides of the House to explore ways to dampen partisan warfare in redistribution. The ascension of Robert Borden, a courteous and respectful politician,[1] to the Tory leadership in 1901 helped Laurier to arrive at a promising middle ground. Also helpful was that policy differences between the parties had diminished, in particular by Laurier's acceptance of the National Policy in 1896. The upshot, in 1903, was Laurier's agreement with Borden to delegate the details of redistribution to a bipartisan special committee.

THE LAURIER BILLS OF 1899 AND 1900

Following Wilfrid Laurier's ascension to office in 1896, the House of Commons passed Representation Bills in 1899 and 1900.[2] After the Senate rejected the 1899 Bill, the House passed a nearly identical 1900 Bill, which the Senate also rejected. In each case, the Liberal government's purpose was to "right" the Conservative "wrongs" of the 1882 and 1892 "Gerrymander Acts." To this end, Laurier made the restoration of municipal boundaries in electoral districts his controlling principle, with the equalization of population secondary. The Bills provided for the redistribution of seats in a two-step process. First, Parliament (the government party) would set the number of ridings that each county was to receive, based on its population. Second, a government-appointed Board of Commissioners, consisting of three Ontario Superior Court judges, would draw the boundaries of ridings within counties that were to receive more than one riding.

The Bills were unusual for their "out-of-season" timing. The 1867 BNA Act made a redistribution mandatory on the completion of a new census. The Laurier Bills were introduced several years after the census of 1891, on the eve of a new census in 1901, which would require another redistribution. A second feature of the Bills was their limited scope. They proposed to restore county lines to districts in the Western Ontario region, but left alone ridings in Eastern Ontario. A third feature was their provision for a judicial commission to do part of the work, and a fourth was their deliberate under-representation of Toronto in relation to population.

The Tories vigorously opposed the Bills. Sir Charles Tupper, predecessor to Laurier as prime minister and leader of the Conservative Party, regarded the 1899 Bill as "a violation of the constitution ... according to which no Redistribution Bill can be passed except after a decennial census." A redistribution "can only be done after a decennial census, an inference [from the BNA Act] that has been respected by every Government of Canada and every party in Canada from confederation down to the present hour." Robert Borden (Halifax), who was to succeed Tupper as leader of the Conservative Party in 1901, conceded that the House of Commons had the legal power to pass a redistribution Bill, but to do so was inexpedient. Such an action, he worried, might lay down the principle "that whenever a party comes into power and is not satisfied with the distribution which has been made under the last decennial census, it should immediately seek to gain an advantage by an act of this kind." Alexander McNeill (Bruce North) insisted that previous Tory "out-of-season" Representation Acts were no precedent for the 1899 Bill: "the changes they made were insignificant; whereas this is a great measure of change, an absolutely new departure."[3] Similarly, the Conservative majority in the Senate rejected the 1899 Bill as "inexpedient" and "a violation of the spirit of the BNA Act," and gave the 1900 Bill "six months' hoist."[4]

Conservatives objected to the content of the Bill as well as its timing. Representation by population was, in their view, the proper controlling principle, which the Liberal Bills sacrificed on the altar of municipal lines. The provision of a two-stage process in the Bills was a recipe for gerrymander. Clarke Wallace (York West), for one, had no hope that the Liberals would submit to a fair and equitable representation, preferring, as they did, "to follow the Mowat gerrymander of Ontario, as iniquitous a scheme as was ever planned, to rob the Conservatives of their franchise in every portion of the province."[5]

The Liberals insisted that their Bills were constitutional. The BNA Act required a redistribution of seats among the provinces after a decennial census, but said nothing about a redistribution within a province at another time. Previous Conservative administrations had passed redistribution Bills between censuses to correct clerical errors and provide clarifications. By extension, the 1899 and 1900 Liberal "out-of-season" Bills responded to an "urgent need" to repeal the 1892 Representation Act, which had failed to undo the gerrymander of 1882. The Bills also redeemed a pledge, made at the party's 1893 convention and on which the party had been elected in 1896, to introduce a remedial Bill at the earliest opportunity. Effectively, the between-census Liberal Bills were constitutional and expressed the will of the electorate.

The Role of the Judges

In his provision for a judicial determination of boundaries, Laurier took inspiration from a bipartisan process that had produced Britain's 1885 Redistribution of Seats Act. Britain's Liberal prime minister, William Gladstone, after taking into account the Conservative majority in the House of Lords, had negotiated with the leader of the opposition, Lord Salisbury, about setting up single-member seats for each borough and county, based on their populations. A Boundary Commission, headed by two senior civil servants, one a Liberal and the other a Conservative, worked out the details of the riding boundaries. Its mandate was to produce ridings with approximately equal populations and compact shape, taking into account areas of local government and different communities of interest (urban versus rural). The commissioners consulted with the public and representatives of the political parties in each locality. And they worked quickly. The bipartisan process in Britain, opine D.J. Rossiter and his co-authors, was a resounding political success, producing approximately equal populations across regions and between boroughs and counties.[6]

Like Britain's Prime Minister Gladstone, Laurier faced an Upper House with an opposition-party majority, and hence pressure to reach accommodation with the Tory minority in the House of Commons. In 1892, as opposition leader, he had proposed to "refer the work to a conference or committee to be composed of both political parties to agree upon the lines or principles on which a redistribution Bill should be drawn."[7] Then his 1899 redistribution Bill had provided for a judicial commission to do part of the work. Redistribution was to unfold in a two-stage process. The House (effectively, the majority party) was to determine the number of ridings for each county and urban municipality, after which the judicial commission was to draw the boundaries of ridings within a county or city. The commissioners, appointed by the Laurier ministry, were to work without guidelines, without holding court for pubic consultation, and without recourse to Parliament.[8]

John Ross Robertson (Independent Conservative, Toronto East) opposed the 1899 Bill's provision for a judicial role. Though he did not doubt that judges were honest men, he was sceptical of the "impartiality of judges in political cases," and noted that the Liberal government "retained the power to nominate the judges who will suit them best ... The government rebukes the Opposition for its unwillingness to trust the judges who have been Liberals, but it reserves power in such a way as to show its unwillingness to trust judges who have been Conservatives."[9]

The Conservative leader, Sir Charles Tupper, moved an amendment to place the entire redistribution process in the hands of an arm's-length judicial commission "consisting of the chief justices in each of the provinces of Canada." The commission was to "consider the distribution of population according to the latest census of Canada and the public interest and convenience, and shall particularly have regard to the principle of representation by population, and also have regard as far as practicable to the boundaries of counties, municipalities, and cities."[10] The amendment closed by providing "that such commission shall be appointed as soon as possible after the completion of the next census." Laurier rejected the amendment, on the grounds that it was irrelevant to the subject at hand – his Bill now before the House – although he was gratified that both parties now supported the principle of using judicial authority at some future time.

The Scope of the 1899 and 1900 Bills

The Bills applied exclusively to ridings in Western Ontario. "We are not undertaking at this moment to deal with all the objectionable features of the Acts of 1882 and 1892," explained Laurier, "but only with their most salient features."[11] As Peter Macdonald (Liberal, Huron East), elaborated, "We have commenced at the present time to go as far as we deem necessary. We have commenced the work that we will complete, probably in 1902. We will be in power in 1902, and after the census is taken, we will complete the work we have commenced, and try to undo the evil done by the Gerrymander Bill of 1882."[12]

The Bills proposed changes to fifty-four of the ninety-two ridings.[13] Features of the Bills presaged those of the 1903 redistribution. First, the proposed changes applied exclusively to Western Ontario and Toronto. Essex, Halton, and Waterloo were the only western counties whose ridings were left alone. Second, county lines were to be restored in the ridings of seventeen counties. Third, the judges would redistribute the ridings for fifteen counties that had more than one riding. Fourth, the Bills would abolish the purely-electoral counties of Bothwell, Cardwell, and Monck ("ridings that have no counterpart in our municipal institutions"). Fifth, Dufferin, formed as a county in 1874 but not given a member, was to be a riding. Sixth, the electoral districts of Toronto, Hamilton, and London were to assume the territories of their municipal districts, including annexed territories that were currently in county ridings. Seventh, Toronto was to be under-represented by population. Eighth, the riding of Muskoka–Parry Sound was to be divided into two district ridings, Muskoka and Parry Sound, and the counties of Ontario and Middlesex were each to lose one riding.

The Representation for Toronto

The 1900 Bill proposed five members for Toronto, an increase of one from the current city ridings and also from what had been proposed in the 1899 Bill. The increase was for Toronto as municipally constituted in 1899.[14] For Toronto's electoral district, this added fourteen territories that the city had annexed during the years 1883–93. With a 17 percent increase of population (1881–91), Toronto's enlarged electoral district would hold 7.62 standard populations for five members. As Laurier maintained, "We cannot, under present circumstances, give the same representation, according to population, to urban as to rural constituencies. Were we to do that, we would have in this country of sparse population, counties which would be equal in extent to kingdoms or empires. If we were to give eight or nine members to Toronto, we would have to add together three or four or five counties, already too large for the convenience of any man who has to represent them."[15] Nor did Toronto need additional representation. "If the large commercial centres like Toronto and Montreal have not been given the representation that their population would entitle them to," noted William Mulock (York North), Laurier's postmaster-general and a resident of Toronto,

> it is because they have a power and influence that carry weight independent of any representation ... if a question comes up here which affects the interests of Toronto, the able reporters for the Toronto papers who sit in the Gallery, and who are so thoroughly posted on every question, flash the news to their press. That announcement appears in the morning papers, and if there is anything by which the interests of the city are jeopardized and representations are to be made to the government, they do not need to depend on their representatives in this House alone. The Board of trade can be summoned within an hour, if need be; the city council can be convened, and deputations of prominent citizens can be sent to present their case. In rural constituencies the case is far different. They cannot be reached in that way, nor can they act in that way.[16]

Residents of Toronto, noted William McGregor (Liberal, North Essex), represented several county ridings as well as Toronto ridings: "In looking over this House to-day we find Mr. Ross Robertson, Mr. Osler, Mr. Bertram, Mr. Clarke, Mr. Maclean, Mr. Campbell, Mr. Edgar, Mr. Wallace, and Mr. McCarthy from the city of Toronto." One of the city men, James David Edgar (Liberal, Ontario West), noted fourteen Toronto men in the Senate.[17]

John Ross Robertson (Independent Conservative, Toronto East) wanted "to see this [1899] Bill annihilated, and [was] prepared to justify any constitutional means which will protect the people [of Toronto] I represent from a contemptible attack on the sacred right of representation by population in this House ... the first minister hives over 40,000 people from East and West York in the city of Toronto and gives them only one additional member."[18] Effectively, Robertson rejected the principle that city populations should have less representation than rural populations, although his party did not.

Conservative Reverence for "Original" Electoral Districts

Conservatives professed to revere historical electoral districts, regardless of their congruence with municipal-county lines. Hence their distaste for the Bill's proposed abolition of Bothwell, Cardwell, and Monck, the purely-electoral counties of 1867. Conservatives disputed the proposed return of Pelham Township to the riding of Welland, its municipal county, from its current riding, Lincoln & Niagara. The Hon. John Haggart (Lanark South) opposed the transfer on principle. "The [1867] Imperial Act, making the electoral districts of the country," insisted Haggart, had set apart Welland "in precisely the same state as it is found at the present day. There has been no change from that time down to the present, and all of the reasons which apply to municipal or county boundaries apply more strongly to Welland, because the people have been accustomed within that district, to return members for that particular portion of it. It is sanctioned by a higher authority than even municipal or county boundaries. The district was set apart by imperial Act at the time of confederation. Surely that is a stronger reason for no interference with it than the application of the principle of county boundaries, which may be altered from time to time by provincial authority."[19]

David Henderson (Halton) elaborated the Tory spin with pure fabrication: "The township of Pelham, away back at the union, was in the county of Lincoln. It was put into the county of [Lincoln] for good reasons ... by such men as the Hon. George Brown, Sir Oliver Mowat, and other good Liberals who at that time helped frame the British North America Act. Now it is proposed, for the first time in thirty-two years to change the boundaries of this old historic riding ... As I said before, men like the Hon. George Brown and Sir Oliver Mowat agreed that there was fairness in the arrangement made in 1867. Her majesty the Queen assented to the Bill and, as Mr. Speaker says, signed it by her own hand, declaring that it was considered fair and proper, and that no injustice was done as between one side and the other."[20]

The Haggart-Henderson facts were fantasy. Pelham had always been in Welland County for municipal purposes and had been in the riding of Welland before Confederation. Macdonald's 1867 redistribution had placed the township in Monck. There it remained until 1892, when Thompson's redistribution had placed it in the riding of Lincoln & Niagara. The schedule of ridings in the 1867 BNA Act came from John A. Macdonald and his coalition-Liberal allies. George Brown and Oliver Mowat had no part in its determination.

A Liberal Gerrymander

To Conservatives, the Laurier Bill was a gerrymander. "Every Liberal constituency is to have a small population," charged Clarke Wallace (York West), "so that the Liberal population will send far more representatives to Parliament than the Conservatives ... They fixed the whole thing up and they attempt to shield themselves behind the judges, who can do nothing." Whereas the standard population was 22,901, Simcoe County, which usually sent Conservatives to Parliament, had an average of 27,569 people for each of its three members; yet Brant County, which usually returned Liberals, had just 16,608 people for each of its proposed two ridings.[21] "As I understand it," ventured the Hon. David Tisdale (Norfolk South), "Parliament lays out the field and says whether a county shall have one member, two members, or three members, and then to make it look fair, the government ask the judges to come in and divide what cannot be divided in any other way than to give the government a political advantage. That is a farce ... I hold that under our constitution county boundaries as the basis of representation should not override the question of representation by population."[22] The Bill, exclaimed William Bennett (Simcoe East), was "an engine for the destruction of the Conservative party."[23]

THE DOMINION REDISTRIBUTION OF 1903

During the decade 1891–1901, the Ontario population increased by 3 percent, its smallest decadal growth ever. The rise was 59 percent for the northland districts, the sole region with robust population growth. The other regional statistics were Western Ontario, -2; Eastern Ontario, 2; and the GTA, 6. Toronto, with 208,040 individuals, was the largest of the province's cities, now ten in number, an increase of one. Cities held 20 percent of the provincial population, up from 17 percent in 1891.

The municipal territories of Toronto, Hamilton, Ottawa, and London were larger than their electoral territories. Toronto's electoral district excluded seventeen parcels annexed during the years 1893–1903; Hamilton's electoral district excluded three parcels annexed during the years 1902–03; Ottawa's electoral district excluded the city's Rideau Ward, annexed in 1887; and London's electoral district excluded three parcels annexed during the years 1885–98.

The 1901 census returns entitled Ontario to eighty-six seats in the House of Commons, a reduction of six. At the same time, shifts of population since 1891 pressed government to create new ridings for Toronto and the northlands. Yet each new seat added required a subtraction from existing ridings, in addition to the mandatory reduction of six. Perforce, county ridings bore the brunt of reductions in 1903.

Sir Wilfrid Laurier's 1903 redistribution touched seventy-six ridings: 83 percent of the ninety-two Ontario constituencies – the highest ever. It added four ridings: three for northland districts and one for Toronto. It divided Algoma into East and West ridings, partitioned Muskoka & Parry Sound into separate district ridings, and created the new riding of Thunder Bay & Rainy River. This increase of four seats required the government to eliminate ten county seats to reach the quota of eighty-six. The loss for counties divided evenly between Eastern and Western Ontario.

Like the doomed Bills of 1899 and 1900, the 1903 redistribution restored county lines in ridings of the western counties; abolished the purely-electoral counties of Bothwell, Cardwell, and Monck; made Dufferin County a riding; and enlarged the electoral districts of Toronto and London to include their annexed territories currently in county ridings. In contrast to the earlier Bills, the 1903 redistribution was province-wide in scope; but like them, it treated Eastern Ontario differently from the rest of the province.

The 1903 Act took place in a politically charged atmosphere. For the first time, a Liberal ministry administered a Dominion redistribution Bill. The Liberals were still smarting, moreover, from the Tory-led Senate rejections of its 1899 and 1900 redistribution Bills, which had aimed at dismantling the alleged Tory gerrymanders of 1882 and 1892. Thus, the Laurier ministry came to the task with pent-up frustration, and also a new set of underlying principles.

Laurier's controlling principle for redistribution was the restoration of municipal lines in electoral districts. His second principle was that "rural constituencies are entitled to more representation than urban." The Hon. James Sutherland, minister of Public Works, expressed another Liberal principle – that Dominion electoral districts should adhere to Ontario-provincial electoral districts "as far as possible … because the people have political connections and interests within these bounds, which it is well to preserve, everything else being equal."[24] With these Liberal priorities, the principle of equalizing riding populations faded into the background. Thus, the redistribution Act increased the percentage of ridings in the optimum range from 28 to 33 – a drop from 38 under the 1892 Representation Act.

Conservatives averred that the controlling principle should be the equalization of riding populations, not municipal lines. The Hon. David Tisdale (Norfolk South), minister of Militia and Defence in the previous ministry, opined that party differences of principle had evolved since Confederation.[25] During debate on the 1872 Redistribution Bill, both parties respected the principles of representation by population and the preservation of municipal lines. In 1882 the Conservatives focussed on representation by population and abandoned county lines. In 1899, 1900, and 1903 the Liberals gave priority to county lines, at the expense of representation by population. Nevertheless, both parties accepted that cities should have a higher unit of population than county ridings.

The Liberal course, asserted Tisdale, was mistaken for a party that had introduced universal manhood suffrage, the formation of small polling divisions, and the abolition of the property qualification and plural voting.[26] "The principle of county boundaries [was] inconsistent with the principle of manhood suffrage ... The old counties of Ontario were not surveyed with the slightest reference to representation, but largely to combine settlements or expected settlements ... But the idea has grown up that there is almost something sacred in these county boundaries ... Another strong objection to our recognition of these county boundaries is that county boundaries in Ontario can at any time be changed by the legislature of the province of Ontario."

Edging Towards a Non-Partisan Tribunal

By 1900 both parties were considering the adoption of a non-partisan mechanism to administer redistribution. Their quest was animated by a British process – a series of "conferences" between the two parties – that led to Britain's 1885 Redistribution of Seats Act. Laurier's 1900 Representation Bill, which the Senate had rejected, proposed a judicial commission for part of the redistribution process. The House (effectively, the majority party) was to determine the number of ridings for each county and urban municipality, after which the judicial commission was to draw the boundaries of ridings within a county or city, without recourse to Parliament. The Conservative leader, Sir Charles Tupper, agreed in principle with the judicial mechanism, provided that it managed all of the redistribution, not just a mopping-up of details.[27]

In 1903, however, Laurier discarded the judicial mechanism in favour of a bipartisan special committee on which the government party had a majority. Following second reading of the Bill, and with the consent of the opposition party, Sir Wilfrid referred details of the redistribution – the schedule of ridings in the Bill was deliberately left blank – to a special committee of four Liberals and three Conservatives. The members of the committee were heavyweights. The Liberals were the Hon. James Sutherland (Oxford North), minister of Public Works; the Hon. Charles Fitzpatrick (Quebec), minister of Justice; Charles S. Hyman (London), soon to be minister-without-portfolio; and Thomas Osborne Davis, successor to Wilfrid Laurier in his riding of Saskatchewan and a future senator (1904). The three Conservatives were Robert Laird Borden (Halifax), the party leader since 1901; Frederick D. Monk (Jacques Cartier), Borden's lieutenant for the Quebec wing of the party; and the Hon. John G. Haggart (Lanark South), minister of Railways and Canals in the previous ministry and chief architect of Sir John Thompson's 1892 redistribution.

The motion to create the committee had passed unanimously, but Borden had concerns about the committee's role. A special committee with government members in the majority would be simply an ordinary committee, whose nature was to "represent the views of the majority of the House." A conference, in contrast, was "designed for the purpose of agreement." If the special committee was to function as a conference, then it should "be composed of an equal number of members on each side of the House."[28]

When equal representation on the special committee did not happen, Borden launched a second initiative to enable the committee to function as a conference. At the organizational meeting of the special committee, Borden proposed rules to guide its work and dampen partisan ardour. Laurier had given the special committee two general rules – to give priority to municipal-county lines and to give rural constituencies more representation than city constituencies. Borden, seconded by Haggart, moved that the special committee adopt Laurier's rules and additional Borden-Haggart ones:

1 In accordance with the principle laid down by the Prime Minister in the House of Commons introduction of the Bill, municipal county boundaries shall be observed.
2 Where separate representation is given to cities the municipal boundaries of such cities shall be observed.
3 The municipal county boundaries shall be those set forth in Chapter 3, Revised Statutes of Ontario, 1897, and the word 'county' herein

shall include any provisional county or territorial district established by the said Act.[29]

4 The separate representation to be allotted to cities of Ontario shall be first fixed and determined before proceeding with the representation of the rural constituencies.

5 The unit of representation for such rural constituencies shall be determined by deducting from the total population of Ontario the combined population of the said cities and by dividing the remainder by the total number of seats to be allotted to rural constituencies.

6 The population of any city receiving separate representation shall be excluded in computing the population of the county within which it is situate.

7 The allocation of the representation to counties:

(a) Each county having a population of not less than two-thirds of the unit shall be entitled to one member. Any county not entitled to one member shall be added to that adjoining county to which it is related as a judicial district, or with which it is connected for judicial or municipal purposes and the representation of such combined counties shall be dealt with upon the principles already and hereafter stated.

(b) Counties having a population larger than the unit. Each county or combined county having a population of not less than 50 per cent above the unit shall be entitled to two members, and each county or combined county having a population of not less than 150 per cent and not more than 250 per cent above the unit shall be entitled to three members.

(c) If after applying these principles it is found that any seats remain to be allotted, such seats shall be allotted to the counties or combined counties approaching most closely to the conditions which, under the above rule, would entitle them to additional representation.

8 Division of cities or counties into ridings. In the division of cities or counties into ridings, the geographical limits of such riding shall be as symmetrical and compact as may be possible, always having regard to equalities of population.[30]

The Liberal majority on the special committee refused to adopt the Borden-Haggart rules. As they rationalized, it was premature to consider the rules until they could learn how they "played out." It was unwise to "tie the hands" of the committee in dealing with unforeseen situations.[31] Subsequently, as discussed below, the Liberal majority followed all but three of the Borden-Haggart rules, but found ways to subvert Borden's purpose for them.

The Bill's passage into Act unfolded over a six-month period. Laurier introduced the Bill on 31 March, without a schedule of ridings – the schedule was for the special committee to prepare. The special committee completed its work over a three-month period, with many informal meetings and regular formal meetings with minutes that produced "nearly 400 pages of foolscap minutes of closely typewritten matter."[32] At times the committee's proceedings were open to the House. The House went into committee of the whole to consider the report on 9 September, and on 25 September the Bill passed its third reading.

The three Conservatives on the special committee subsequently differed about whether or not its meetings had functioned as conferences. Frederick Monk, Borden's leader for the Quebec wing of the party, gave his experience mixed reviews:

> I have used indiscriminately the words 'conference' and 'committee.' No doubt, to make the proceedings more regular, we proceeded pretty much as a regularly constituted committee. But ... the object in view in creating that committee was to follow the example set in England, and in reality to constitute a conference of both parties in order, if possible, to arrive at some unanimous conclusion on this important matter of redistribution ... Although during proceedings of the committee it was found in many cases ... agreement between members of the conference was impossible, and although ... we found it necessary to protest against the conclusions which the majority of the committee have arrived at ... the House itself is not absolutely bound by the decisions to which the conference may have arrived. Furthermore ... there [was] no misunderstanding in the committee itself as to the character of the committee. It was a conference. It is sufficient to glance at the pages of the report of the proceedings of the committee to see that these proceedings were considered to be the proceedings of a conference purely and simply.

Even so, Monk recalled "counties where difficulties [had occurred] and where the majority was not guided by the lofty principles laid down [by the Prime Minister] that there should be absolute justice, absolute equity in the proceedings. These defects in [the committee's] work – and serious defects they are – will be pointed out by Hon. members of the House ... and it is the duty of this House, if it finds that the minority of the committee were in the right, to modify the conclusion at which the majority of the committee arrived." Disagreements between parties, he opined, resulted from the committee's want of rules of equity. Accordingly, he challenged Laurier to spell out such rules in the House and apply them to the cases at hand. Otherwise there was "no reason for saying that [the bipartisan special committee] method of proceeding, [although] different from the method adopted in 1882 and 1892, [was] a method calculated to give satisfaction to everybody. It will remain a ground of complaint that [the redistribution is] what is commonly called a gerrymander, although that gerrymander has not been carried out in the same way as it is alleged was carried out previously, we can say in this instance it has been carried out in a veiled and concealed manner."

The two other Tory members (Borden and Haggart) answered firmly in the negative. Prime Minister Laurier, recalled Borden, had "suggested that this committee – *conference* he called it in the first instance; *committee* he calls it now – was designed to effect and did effect a very fair distribution. Well, I do not know of one important proposition ... emanating from the minority, which was accepted by the majority ... It was not a conference but simply a partisan committee, upon which there were four Liberal members and three Conservatives." Although the Liberal members on the committee were "friendly and courteous and frank," they also "were very firm." Borden considered resigning from the committee, but remained "as a matter of form only."[34] John Haggart agreed that the committee had accepted "not a single compromise ... between the two parties on the committee and ... not a single proposition" from the Conservative minority.[35] Although the prime minister reported the special committee's unanimous agreement in thirty-nine cases, Laurier's list included Ottawa, Carleton, Russell, and Peterborough; in these cases, alleged Borden, the Liberal majority had obtained the committee's unanimous consent through blackmail (discussed below).[36]

On Laurier's motion to pass the third reading of the Bill, John Haggart moved to refer the Bill back to the committee of the whole House with instructions to amend the schedule in accordance with the Borden-Haggart rules. As he elaborated, "It would have been ... in the interests of both parties that the delimitations should not take a political tinge, and be decided by the majority on the committee. That is what I object to. I believe firmly that [Laurier], when he left the matter to a committee, was of the opinion that some principles would have been adopted by that committee which would have guided them from beginning to end, and that such a delimitation would be made of the constituencies as would not be the result of majority vote, but of a conference between the parties." As it happened, "the committee was not guided by any principles at all." Thus, concluded Haggart, "the stern cold facts show that the result of the action of the committee will be, taking the vote of Ontario as given at the last election, to give political advantage to the government."[37]

"A conference," agreed James Clancy (Conservative, Bothwell), "is a meeting of certain gentlemen on common neutral ground, where men are bound to stand by what is right ... but a conference in this case was not of that description. It was simply a committee called to ratify foregone conclusions and adjust the constituencies in the interests of government."[38] Of course, Clancy had an axe to grind: his riding of Bothwell was slated for extinction. Bothwell, as a purely-electoral county, was abolished on principle. Nevertheless, Clancy was a convenient target for "political assassination": he had defeated the Liberal front-bencher, the Hon. David Mills, in the 1896 general election.[39]

The Work of the Special Committee

The special committee developed its report in stages. First, it fixed the number of ridings for Toronto at five – an increase of one. Second, it constructed a standard "unit of population" to determine the number of ridings to which each county was entitled. For calculation, the special committee subtracted the population of Toronto from the provincial population and divided the remainder by eighty-one, the number of seats remaining for allocation. This calculation produced 24,381 as the unit of population. Thus, as a rough guide, a population of 16,662 (0.667 of the unit) was the minimum for one riding; 26,572 (1.50), two ridings; and 60,953 (2.50), three ridings.[40]

Third, the special committee sorted out the ridings to fit municipal-county boundaries. To reconstruct Oxford County for electoral purposes, for example, it recovered Blenheim Township from Brant County, and Dereham Township and Tillsonburg Town from Norfolk County; conversely, it gave up South Easthope and North Easthope Townships to Perth County and returned Oakland and Burford Townships to Brant County.

Fourth, proceeding by counties in alphabetical order, the special committee allocated ridings to counties on the basis of their 1901 census populations. Thus, it reduced Norfolk County, with 1.15 units, from two ridings to one, whereas it allowed Oxford County, with 1.91 units, to retain two ridings. Fifth, on the basis of rank order of population, it awarded an extra seat to certain counties whose populations were under the threshold for the allocation. Sixth, to circumvent the intent of the rank-order-of-population rule, it made transfers of townships after the allocation of ridings had been set (discussed below).

Representation for Cities

TORONTO AND YORK COUNTY: A GERRYMANDER

Before redistribution, Toronto had three ridings and four seats (Toronto West being a two-member riding) for 6.15 standard populations. York County (4.45) had three seats, two of them, York East (1.59) and York West (2.12), bordering the city ridings. The Toronto city ridings excluded seventeen parcels, with 51,942 people, which the city had annexed during the years 1893–1903. These outlying city wards constituted 25 percent of Toronto's municipal population, 56 percent of the population in the York East riding, and 55 percent of the population in York West.

Laurier's Bill enlarged Toronto's electoral district to include city fragments in the York ridings and gave the city five single-member ridings, an increase of one for its enlarged population (8.20). York County retained three ridings for its shrunken population (2.55), but with a severe rearrangement of the riding territories (discussed below). The redistribution for Toronto and York County restored county lines, the municipal city being "a county unto itself." It followed the principle that city ridings should have larger populations than the county ridings and equalized populations in the York ridings.[41]

Among the province's cities, Toronto alone was severely under-represented in relation to its population. Apart from Toronto, the Laurier ministry needed to eliminate nine seats in the counties (six from the reduction in Ontario's constitutional quota to eighty-six and three to allow additional seats for Northern Ontario). If Toronto were to receive eight seats, as its 8.20 standard populations warranted, then the ministry would need to find twelve county seats for elimination. "You could not do that," exclaimed Laurier; "there would be a rebellion, almost."[42] In any case, Toronto's interests were amply represented. Charles S. Hyman, a Liberal on the special committee, named eight Toronto residents who represented county ridings in the House of Commons.[43]

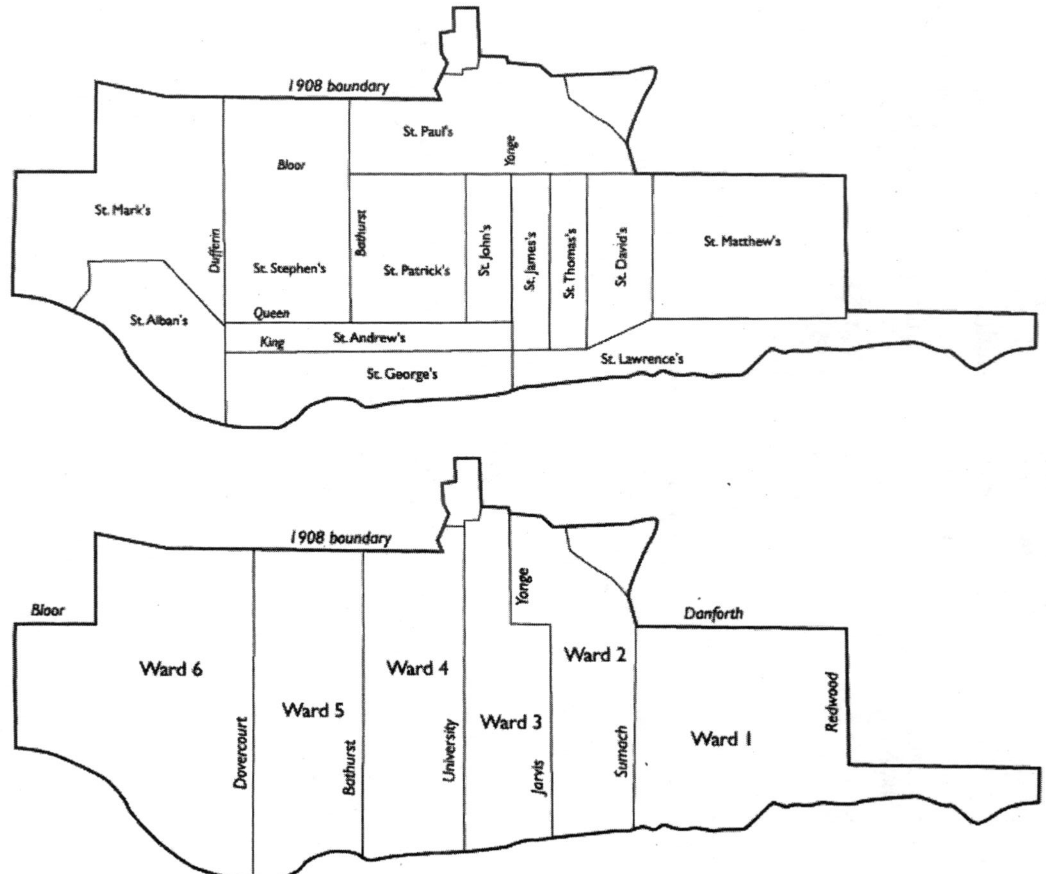

Map 6.1 Toronto, 1891: From parish wards to numbered wards

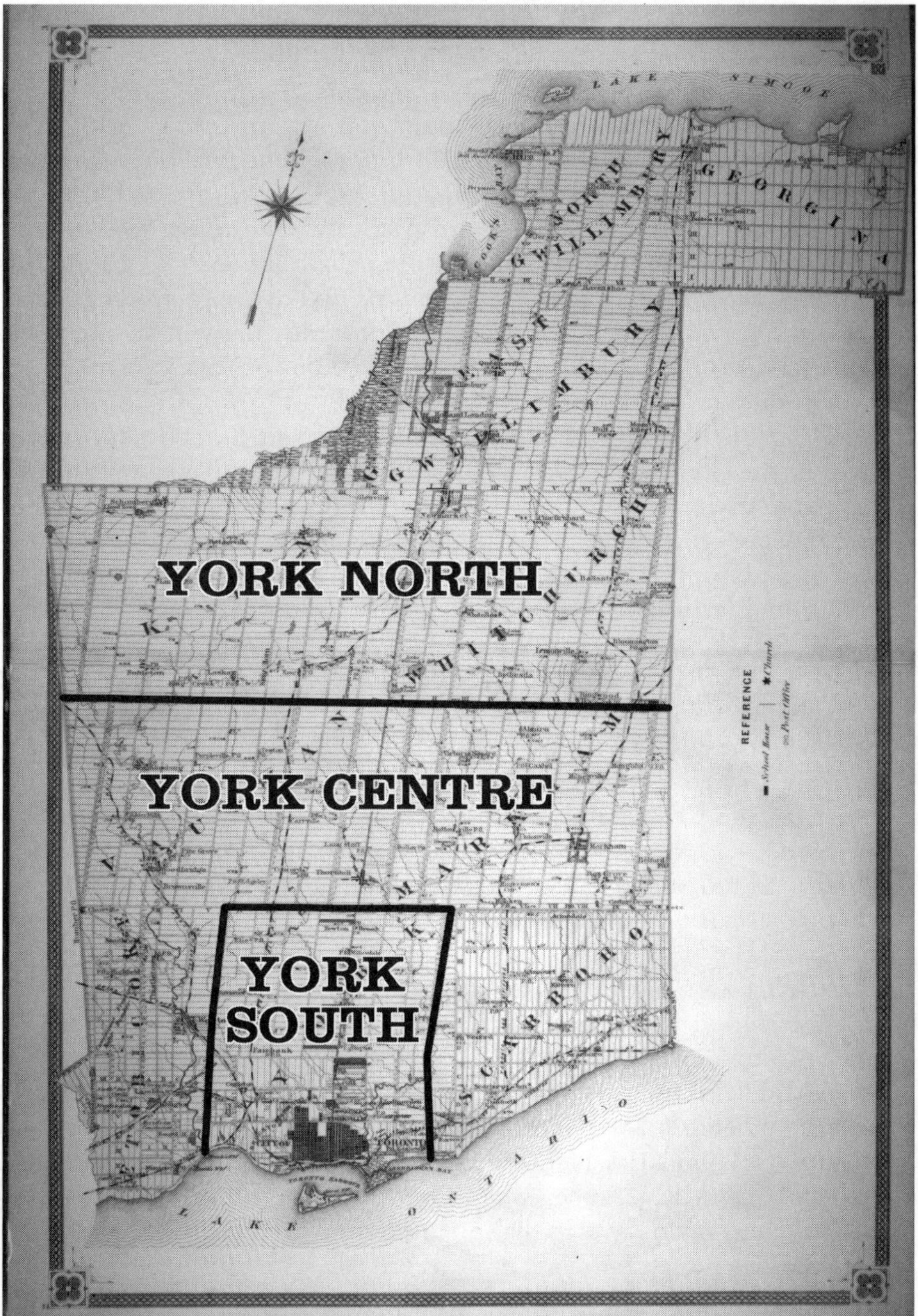

Map 6.2 York County riding after the 1903 redistribution

The redistribution for Toronto and York County, prospectively, gained a seat for the government party. Before redistribution, the Toronto ridings were Tory hives and the city fragments in the York ridings were Tory-leaning. The transfers of city fragments into Toronto's electoral district and the Bill's provision for a fifth city riding gave the opposition party the prospect of five Toronto seats in the next general election, a gain of one. However, the Tories prospectively lost a seat in the York ridings, and the Liberals gained one. Before redistribution, the Liberals held York North (+297) and the Tories held the two city-border ridings, York East (-642) and York West (-820). The redistribution favoured the Liberals in York North (+545) and the new riding of York Centre (+303); York South belonged to the Tories (-754).

The redistribution for the county ridings was a gerrymander. The loss of the city fragments to city ridings contributed to the turnaround in party strengths in the county ridings, but only partly so: the rumps of the pre-redistribution city-border ridings were still Tory-leaning (-103 and -348). The deciding influence was a drastic readjustment of the riding territories. The redistribution replaced two city-border ridings, York East and York West, with one, the redistributed riding of York South. The South riding consisted exclusively of York Township, which had a Tory-leaning suburban population and served as a buffer between the city and the two rural ridings to the north. Effectively, the transfers hived the Tories into York South to boost the Liberals' prospects in the Centre and North ridings. The gerrymander issued two asymmetrical, non-compact ridings (Map 6.2). York South formed a U-shaped territory around the city ridings, and York Centre formed a U-shaped territory around the South riding.

LONDON AND MIDDLESEX COUNTY

Redistribution reduced five ridings – London and four county ridings (4.07) – to four (3.65). First, it restored county lines by repatriating five non-Middlesex municipalities to ridings in their home counties (Lambton, Elgin, and Huron). Second, it enlarged the city riding to match London's 1903 civic boundaries. Before redistribution, the city ridings had excluded London East Village, annexed in 1885, London South Village, annexed in 1890, and London West Village, annexed in 1898. Third, it folded the four county ridings into three.[44] In accordance with principle, the consolidation left the city riding with a larger population (1.50) than the county ridings (0.80, 0.65, and 0.71). The government party held three of the five ridings before redistribution, and, prospectively and accurately, three of the four after – a loss of one seat for the opposition Tories.

HAMILTON AND WENTWORTH COUNTY

The redistribution was mixed for the observance of principles. Before redistribution, Hamilton was a two-member riding. The county of Wentworth held the ridings of Wentworth South and Wentworth North–Brant; each included townships from other counties. Wentworth South held parts of Hamilton that the city had annexed during the years 1902–03.

The redistribution restored county lines by uniting all Wentworth municipalities into a single county riding, Wentworth. It repatriated Ancaster Township from the former riding of Wentworth North–Brant, and it transferred the Welland-County townships of Grimsby and Caistor from Wentworth South into the county riding of Welland. Second, it turned Hamilton from a two-member riding into two single-member ridings. However, it left Hamilton's recently annexed suburbs in the county riding of Wentworth.[45] This trespassed on the principle of county lines – the municipal city being "a county unto itself." It also ignored the principle that city ridings should have larger populations than county ridings; the standard populations were Hamilton East, 0.95; Hamilton West, 1.13; and Wentworth, 1.06.

OTTAWA, CARLETON, AND RUSSELL: A PASSIVE GERRYMANDER

Before redistribution, the observance of Carleton-County lines was in disarray (Map 6.3). The two-member Ottawa riding excluded the city's Rideau Ward (annexed 1887), which was situated in the riding of Russell. The riding of Carleton excluded two Carleton townships in the riding of Lanark North (Huntley and Fitzroy) and two Carleton townships in Russell (Gloucester and Osgoode). The redistribution transferred Huntley and Fitzroy Townships to the riding of Carleton, but not Gloucester or Osgoode. It left the Rideau Ward in Russell.

A complete observance of county lines would have given the Carleton riding 1.46 standard populations, enough to spark Tory hopes for a second Carleton seat; city ridings would have had larger populations per member (1.18) than the county ridings (Russell, 0.80, and two Carleton ridings, 0.73 each); the populations of the county ridings would have been equalized; and the city's electoral and municipal territories would have matched. However, the Conservatives, prospectively, would have gained two seats: one from the division of the Carleton riding (-727), and one of the Ottawa seats. The incumbents for the two-member city riding were very safe, Tory (-478) and precarious, Liberal (+17); with an in-transfer of Rideau Ward (-43), the Liberal incumbent would have been vulnerable.

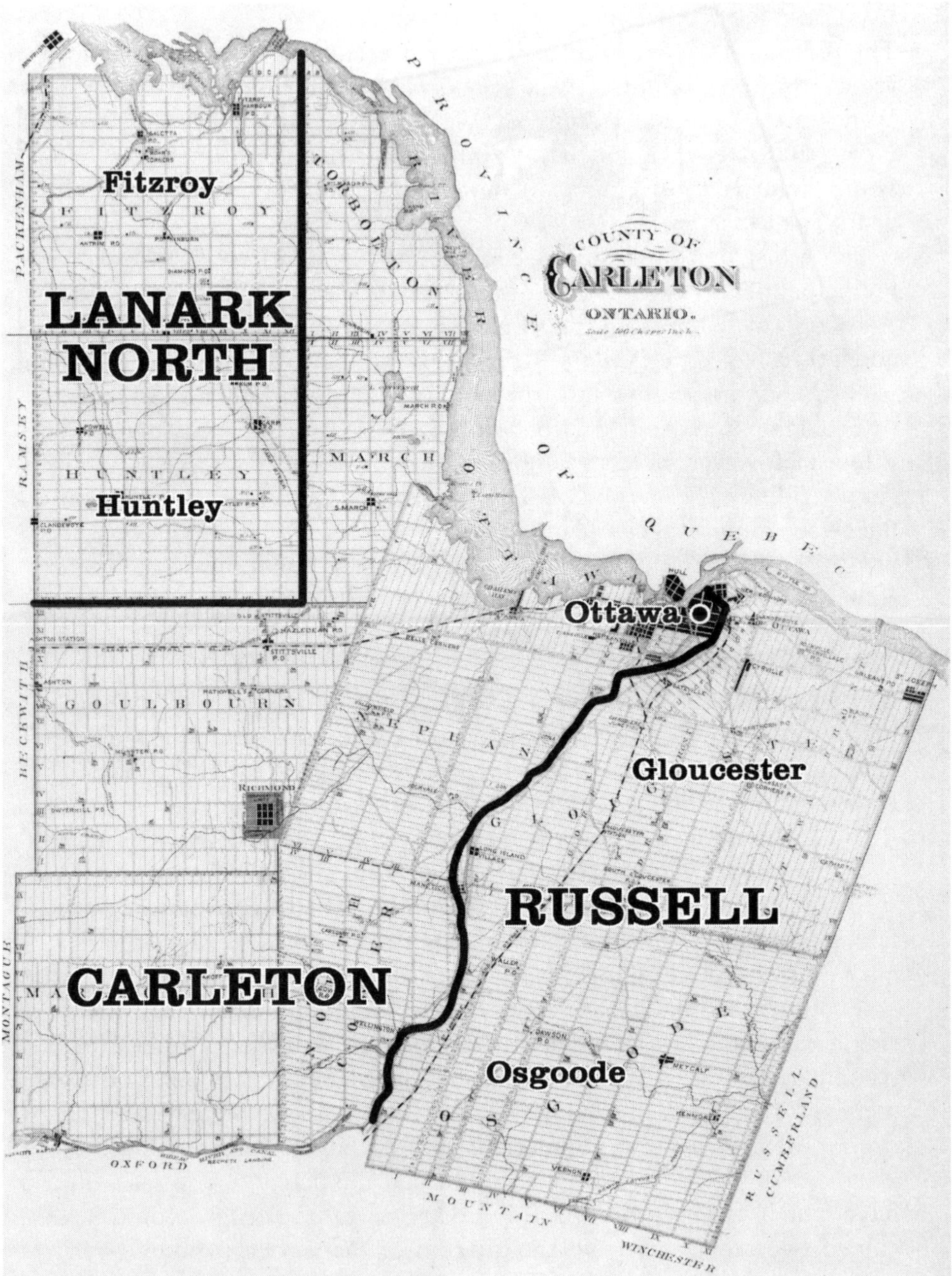

Map 6.3 Carleton County townships and their ridings, 1903

KINGSTON AND FRONTENAC COUNTY

The riding of Kingston matched the city's 1903 civic boundaries, but with a small population for a city riding (0.71). The riding of Frontenac included just half of Frontenac County and had an undersized population for a county riding (0.47). The redistribution boosted the populations of the Kingston and Frontenac ridings to 0.78 and 0.98 standard populations respectively. First, it transferred Portsmouth Village from the Frontenac riding to Kingston. Second, it transferred the Frontenac townships in the Addington riding to the riding of Frontenac. Thus, the redistribution was positive for equalizing populations and county lines, but, contrary to principle, left the city riding, Kingston, with a smaller population than Frontenac, its home county. The redistribution made little difference to prospective party strengths in the ridings.

CITY RIDINGS AND COUNTY RIDINGS

One of Laurier's principles was "that members for city constituencies should represent a larger population than the members for rural populations." As noted by Andrew Ingram (Conservative, Elgin East), the Liberal majority applied that rule to Toronto and London, but not Ottawa, Hamilton, or Kingston. Thus, "out of the five cities affected, three of them are outside the rule laid down by the government."[46]

The redistribution did follow a companion Liberal guideline, that a county riding containing a city should have a larger population than a wholly rural riding in the same county. Thus, Essex North, which included Windsor City (incorporated 1892), was given a larger population than Essex South. Similarly, in allotting two new ridings to Brant County, Brant and Brantford, the special committee declined to make Brantford a stand-alone city riding on the grounds that it would have a smaller population (0.66) than rural Brant (0.85). Accordingly, it placed Oakland Township and part of Brant Township in the Brantford riding. This gave the riding of Brantford 0.78 standard populations, compared with 0.72 for the riding of Brant.

Representation for Counties

The Liberal majority on the committee applied the letter, though not the spirit, of the proposed Borden-Haggart rules (1, 2, 7, and 8) for the allocations to counties.[47] Under those rules, county lines, including the municipal boundaries of cities, were to be observed. Population then applied. Each county with two-thirds (0.67) of the unit of population was entitled to one seat; a county with less than 0.67 was to be attached to an adjoining county for representation; each county with from 1.50 to 2.50 units was entitled to two ridings; and each county with from 2.50 to 3.50 units was entitled to three ridings. Then, "if after applying these principles it is found that any seats remain to be allowed, such seats shall be allotted to the counties approaching most closely [to the minimum number of units] which would entitle them to additional representation." Lastly, "the geographical limits of ridings" were to be "as symmetrical and compact as possible, always having regard to equalities of population."

CARLETON AND THE UNITED COUNTIES: COMPROMISE OR BLACKMAIL?

As noted above, a full application of county lines to the Carleton riding would have given it 1.46 standard populations, enough to stoke Tory hopes for a division of the riding and the prospect of two Conservative members-elect in the 1904 general election. This did not happen and Carleton remained one riding. Conservatives on the special committee differed about whether the outcome for Carleton came from bipartisan compromise or Liberal blackmail. John Haggart defended the outcome as a compromise: "As a compromise the Minister of Justice [Fitzpatrick] waived the opinion he had in reference to the division of united counties ... and he gave us a member for the county of Leeds, to which it is doubtful if we were entitled, and got in return two members for Peterborough. We consented to Peterborough ... because the probabilities are that we will carry the two Peterboroughs ... It was a compromise of principle which we intended to carry out in the delimitation of the different constituencies. We got only one member for Carleton ... [but] with Osgoode and Gloucester in the county of Russell, we have hopes of carrying that county ... It is a matter of compromise, we sacrificing one member in the county of Carleton, in getting one in Leeds, while the Hon. gentleman thinks he has one in Peterborough, though I think he is mistaken."[48]

What was compromise to Haggart was blackmail to Robert Borden. As he stated to the Liberal chair of the special committee, James Sutherland, "I will tell my Hon. friend why there was a compromise in the case of Carleton. It was because after we had accepted [to serve on a bipartisan special committee] for the purpose of endeavouring to arrive at some agreement, we were told that certain united counties were going to be carved up without regard to their actual county boundaries for the purpose of inflicting a gerrymander on the Conservative party if we did not compromise; and having to choose one of two evils, we saw fit to give away our rights in the county of Carleton, because otherwise we were threatened with that gerrymander. We understood that section one of Chapter three of the revised statutes was to be adopted.[49] Instead of that, afterwards, when it was seen it would suit the purposes of my right Hon. friend somewhat better, we were referred to section three and told: Stormont, Dundas, and Glengarry form a united county; we will carve it up as we see fit, and will give you a dose of something you do not like very well. Leeds and Grenville, Northumberland and Durham, Prescott and Russell, will be treated in the same way."[50]

The Liberal position was that Ontario's four united-municipal counties were each a municipal county, but that the nine counties within them had no municipal function and were merely geographical entities. As such, the nine non-municipal counties could be "carved up" without trespass on municipal-county lines. Therein lay the potential gerrymander to which Borden referred.

Having had its way over Carleton, the Liberal majority treated Stormont, Dundas, Glengarry, Leeds, Durham, Grenville, and Prescott as if these were municipal counties, namely by reconstituting them as electoral counties. In contrast, the redistribution trespassed on the county limits of two united-municipal counties. It left Russell with two Carleton-County townships (Gloucester and Osgoode), which were outside the territory of the Prescott-Russell united county, and it gave the Northumberland-County township of South Monaghan to Peterborough West, which was outside the territory of the Northumberland-Durham united county.

LIBERAL ARITHMETIC FOR VICTORIA, HALIBURTON, PETERBOROUGH, AND NORTHUMBERLAND

Under Borden-Haggart rule 6, "Each county having a population of not less than two-thirds of the unit shall be entitled to one member. Any county not entitled to one member shall be added to that adjoining county to which it … is connected for judicial or municipal purposes." If, after allocating seats to the counties on the basis of population, "it is found that any seats remain to be allotted, such seats shall be allotted to the counties … approaching most closely to the conditions which, under the above rule, would entitle them to … representation." In the situation at hand, the special committee had two unallocated seats for three counties, each with two ridings and less than 1.50 standard populations. Only two of the three counties could retain two ridings. The committee's criterion for selecting the two was rank order of population.

The special committee's first task was to restore county lines to ridings in the three counties. To this end, it reconstituted Haliburton County by taking seven Haliburton townships from the riding of Victoria North and six Haliburton townships from the riding of Peterborough East. Then it repatriated the Northumberland township of South Monaghan from the riding of Peterborough West to Northumberland West.[51] At this stage, Haliburton County, with 0.27 standard populations, was not a riding and was temporarily without representation.

With Haliburton in electoral limbo, the transfers left Peterborough County with 1.48 standard populations; Northumberland County, 1.38; and Victoria County, 1.31. On the basis of rank order of population, the committee left Peterborough and Northumberland Counties with two ridings apiece, but merged Victoria County's two ridings into one.

The Liberal majority promptly turned its redistribution into a farce by making post-redistribution transfers of townships (Map 6.4). After its redistribution, it attached Haliburton County to the newly merged riding of Victoria, which gave Victoria 1.58 units of population, sufficient for two ridings. Then, having transferred South Monaghan Township to Northumberland County for allocation, it returned South Monaghan to Peterborough East! This left Northumberland County with 1.32 units for its two ridings, and Peterborough County with 1.52 units for its two ridings. Victoria, with the largest of the three populations, had the least representation.

Partisan considerations made Victoria an attractive target for the special committee's Liberal majority. Conservatives held both Victoria ridings. Ergo, their merger into one riding guaranteed the loss of a seat for the opposition party. The counties of Peterborough and Northumberland each had one Tory incumbent and one Liberal incumbent, which made the elimination of a Tory member through merger less certain.

An added attraction for the Liberal majority was the prospect of "politically assassinating" Sam Hughes, the controversial, outspoken Tory incumbent in Victoria North. By 1903, explains Ronald Haycock, Hughes's biographer,

> Sam had 'seniors' status in both the Commons and the Conservative-party apparatus – so devastated by the Laurier defeat and the leadership crises of the 1890s. Orange (but not too Orange *in extremus* [sic]), a chief organizer in the Tory Midland consortia of riding associations, a Lieutenant-Colonel of the Non-Permanent Active Militia, an experienced Boer war veteran (well self-advertised), an

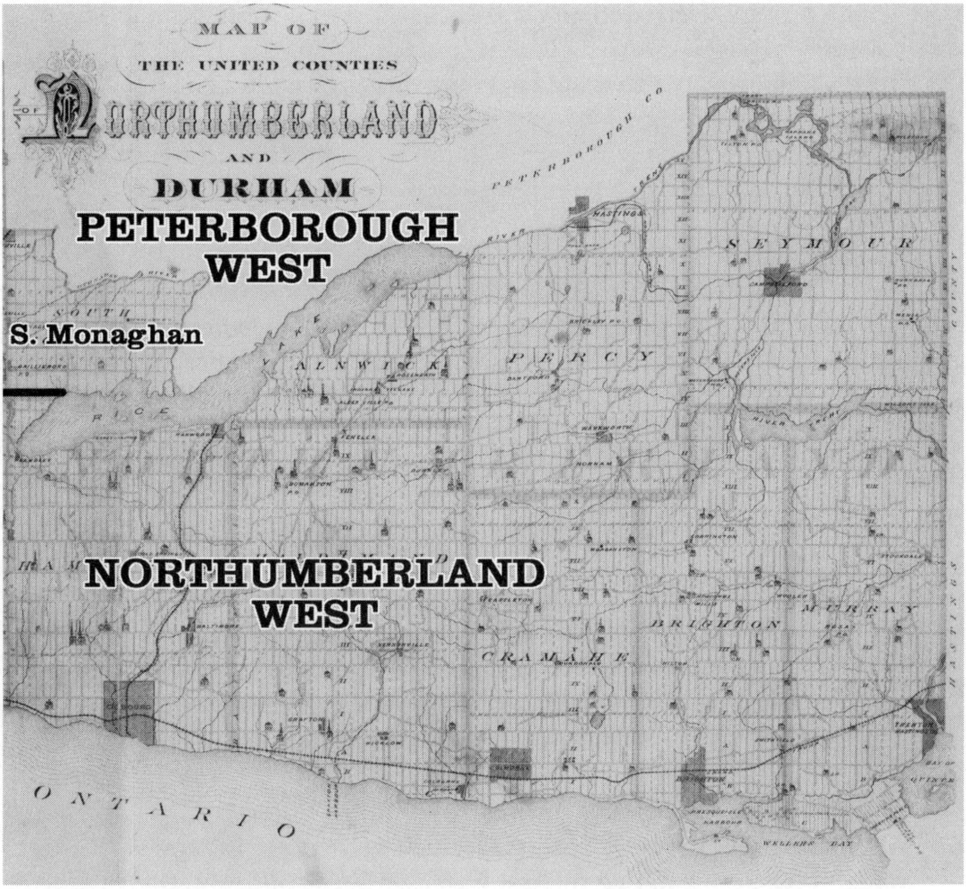

Map 6.4 Northumberland County, with South Monaghan Township, Dominion ridings, 1903

early Robert Borden loyalist, the official opposition Militia critic in the Commons, a leading militia reformer, well connected internationally, a known imperialist (even if a disguise for his nationalism) – Sam was a political power to be reckoned with. Removing him in a gerrymander was a tempting and attempted Grit tactic (that 'boodle gang' of a party in power as Sam labelled it!). In fact, the Grit 'wire-pullers' – another favourite Hughes description for the Liberals – had tried it earlier by facilitating his military service in South Africa. In the autumn of 1899, the arrogant British GOC of the Canadian Militia, E.T.H. Hutton, had removed Sam's name from the list of

> those officers selected to go overseas in the initial contingent. It was the Liberals who allowed Hughes to go to South Africa, and they even paid his way there and back. On the surface it looked like the Laurier cabinet was taking compassion on Sam, wronged by Hutton – but a Sam out of the country and not available to defend his riding in an election surely to be called soon – was also a very attractive political thing – and a nearly perfect device in its application and justification. One supposes that the thought might even have gone through some of the Grit hopefuls' minds that Sam would succumb to the silky whine of a Boer Mauser ball somewhere far away from the Commons. Sam surprised them all and came home (after being fired for his uncontrollable pen critical of bad British generalship!) to defend and win once again his riding in 1900.[52]

Given that the Liberal cause was weak in the merged Victoria riding, a key to Hughes's "political assassination" in the 1904 general election was that the incumbent for Victoria South, Dr Adam Vrooman, would best Hughes for the Tory nomination. Whereas Hughes's North riding was just reasonably safe (-129), Vrooman's South riding was very safe (-216). Moreover, Hughes "was neither as well-liked nor as well-known" in the South riding as he was in his North riding.[53] Against the odds, Hughes bested Vrooman for the Tory nomination and was elected in 1904.

WATERLOO COUNTY: THE LIBERAL MAJORITY YIELDS

Waterloo County had two ridings, Waterloo North and Waterloo South, whose boundaries split Waterloo Township but were otherwise congruent with county lines. The populations of the ridings were approximately equal and in the optimum range (1.07 and 1.00). The ridings were "historical," dating from 1853. Their "community-of-interest" populations differed, Germans predominating in the North riding and Scots in the South riding. The shape of the ridings was compact and symmetrical. But Conservatives held both ridings, the North by acclamation and the South in the range of very safe (-218), and the Liberals could not leave well enough alone. Their Bill would unite the split township of Waterloo, make the unified Waterloo Township a riding in its own right (Waterloo North), and assign the remaining municipalities to the riding of Waterloo South. The proposed revision predicted a Liberal win in the South riding, a gain of one for the government party.[54] Its ostensible purpose was to gather the urban populations of Berlin, Waterloo Town, Hespeler, and

Preston into one riding, Waterloo North. Effectively, a rural-urban divide would trump the German-Scotch ethnic one. However, the urban North riding would have a smaller population than the rural South riding, a Liberal principle overturned. The proposed change was slightly negative for population equality. In the event, following a reasoned, polite defence of the status quo by George Clare, the Conservative incumbent for Waterloo South, the Liberals backed down and left the Waterloo ridings undisturbed.

HURON COUNTY: THE STRANGE CASE OF MORRIS TOWNSHIP

The 1903 redistribution for Huron County was unexceptional. To restore county lines, it retrieved three Huron municipalities from the out-of-county ridings in which Sir John A. Macdonald had placed them in 1882. Their Liberal-majority statistic was negative (-185), so the special committee buried them in the South riding, whose 1878 election had been between two Liberals. The government party held all three Huron ridings before redistribution and, prospectively, all three after. They were to lose all three in the 1904 general election. But the returns for Morris Township in the 1900 general election, the basis for calculation of the Liberal-majority statistic, were odd. Through eight consecutive general elections (1882–1911), Morris Township was in the riding of Huron East. In the 1900 general election alone, however, the township's polls were divided between the ridings of Huron East and Huron South! Both candidates in Huron South were Liberal: John McMillan, a long-serving incumbent, and George McEwen, an Independent Liberal, past reeve of Hay Township and past county warden. McEwen rode a massive majority in his home township (326) to defeat McMillan. The rogue–Morris Township vote gave its majority to McMillan (98), but failed to save him. The unsolved mystery is, how did it get there?[55]

On the Restoration of County Lines

Laurier's 1903 redistribution largely reversed Sir John A. Macdonald's trespass on county lines. After Macdonald's 1882 redistribution, the Dominion ridings crossed county lines in twenty-five of Ontario's forty-three municipal counties (58 percent). Laurier's redistribution reduced the number of trespasses to five (12 percent).[56] Similarly, Macdonald's redistribution placed 97 of 671 Ontario municipalities (14 percent) in ridings that were outside their municipal-home counties. Laurier's 1903 redistribution reduced their number to 16 of 711 (2 percent).

In 1902 the comparable number for provincial-election ridings was ten of forty-three municipal counties (23 percent) – the same five counties as for Dominion ridings in 1903 and five others. Similarly, 34 of 711 Ontario municipalities were in ridings that were outside their municipal-home counties (5 percent). In 1914 the Ontario government was to abolish the purely-electoral riding of Monck; that would reduce its number of counties with trespass to seven (16 percent) and its number of municipalities with trespass to twenty-six (4 percent). Simply put, the observance of municipal-county lines had become the dominant feature of the Dominion and provincial electoral maps.[57]

SUMMARY AND INTERPRETATION

The newly elected Liberals were keen to overturn the Tory gerrymanders of 1882 and 1892, but the Senate, with its Conservative majority, rejected Laurier's Representation Bills of 1899 and 1900. Both Bills, claimed the Tories, were "out of season": they were introduced on the eve of a new decennial census, rather than following one. Even if either Bill had passed into law, the BNA Act would have required another redistribution following the issuance of the 1901 census. Nevertheless, a notable outcome of debates on the two Bills was an agreement in principle of both parties that an arm's-length mechanism – a commission of judges – should manage future redistributions. The Bills applied exclusively to Western Ontario and Toronto. They proposed to abolish Macdonald's three purely-electoral counties (Bothwell, Cardwell, and Monck); to make Dufferin County a riding; to transfer city fragments in county ridings to the electoral districts of cities that had annexed them; and to under-represent Toronto.

Laurier's 1903 redistribution, the first ever by a Liberal administration and the most extensive in Ontario's history of redistribution, was also the first to require a reduction in the number of Ontario ridings, in this case from ninety-two to eighty-six. To reach the reduced quota, the ministry created four additional ridings, three for Northern Ontario and one for Toronto, and eliminated ten ridings in the counties. The loss for counties divided evenly between Eastern Ontario and Western Ontario.

The restoration of municipal boundaries was the controlling principle of the redistribution and the spearhead of the Liberal ministry's determination to reverse the Tory gerrymanders of 1882 and 1892. The under-representation of cities on the basis of population was another key Liberal principle. The opposition Tories chided the Liberals for giving municipal lines priority over the equalization of riding populations, their key principle of preference. Nevertheless, like the Liberals, they accepted that rural regions should have a smaller unit of population than cities.

The Liberals were innovative in their approach to redistribution. Laurier dropped the idea of a commission of judges, but introduced, with Borden's assent, the bipartisan special committee on which government members were a majority. His ideal for the committee, imperfectly realized, was to have it function as a conference of parties, in which the minority Tories had a voice. In this way, it was to be a departure from previous redistributions, in which the government alone drafted the revised schedule of ridings and used its majority to ram it through Parliament.

Reality on the special committee was mixed in terms of opposition-party expectations. The committee evidenced bipartisan agreement on principles, but also Liberal-Party bullying, blackmail, and gerrymanders for redistribution in Eastern Ontario.

The 1903 special committee made three notable applications of principle. First, it restored county lines in the ridings of Western Ontario. Gone were the purely-electoral counties of Bothwell, Cardwell, and Monck, which dated from Confederation. Gone were the gerrymandered redistributions of 1882 and 1892. Dufferin, a county since 1874, became a Dominion riding. Second, the committee introduced a protocol to give Toronto ridings higher populations – less representation – than other ridings. The committee first set the number of Toronto ridings, giving them a high unit of population, and then calculated a lower unit of population for the rest of the province. This enabled it to minimize the elimination of county ridings to meet the province's quota of seats. The principle of under-representing Toronto dated from 1892, but the protocol was new. Third, the 1903 committee was the first to match the electoral districts of cities to their municipal territories, which, dating from the 1880s, had been spreading through annexations. Although the committee matched the electoral and municipal territories for Toronto and London, it did not do so for Hamilton (a departure from the 1899 and 1900 Bills) or Ottawa. The co-operation of the opposition party facilitated the changes discussed above. Under the leadership of Robert Borden and as evidenced by the Borden-Haggart rules, the Conservatives had left behind their "gerrymander Acts" of 1882 and 1892.

The special committee's solid bipartisan achievements, however, were offset, even overshadowed, by the Liberal majority's gerrymandering of ridings in Eastern Ontario. As shown in Table 6.1, the 1903

Table 6.1 Distribution of Dominion seats by party and level of safety, before and after the 1903 redistribution

	Before the 1903 redistribution			*After the 1903 redistribution: Predictions for 1904 election*		
	Conservative	*Liberal*	*All parties*	*Conservative*	*Liberal*	*All parties*
hive (500+)	25%	29%	26%	47%	13%	28%
very safe (200–499)	32%	20%	27%	29%	48%	40%
reasonably safe (100–199)	23%	26%	24%	11%	25%	19%
possibly safe (50–99)	4%	9%	5%	5%	6%	6%
precarious (< 50)	12%	9%	11%	5%	6%	6%
acclamation/ same party	5%	9%	7%	3%	2%	2%
total	100%	100%	100%	100%	100%	100%
# of ridings	57	35	92	39	47	86

redistribution prospectively transformed a Tory majority of twenty-one seats into a prospective Liberal majority of eight, a gain for the Liberals of twenty-nine seats – the greatest shift in favour of the government party in Ontario's history of redistribution. This dramatic shift resulted partly from the Liberal reversal of the Tory-gerrymandered redistributions of 1882 and 1892: that is, by way of restoring county lines that the Tories had destroyed. But it also resulted from sharp practice by the Liberal majority for York County and the ridings of Eastern Ontario. The allocation of seats for the counties of York, Peterborough, Northumberland, and Victoria were gerrymanders and an outrageous perversion of the Liberal Party's professed principles. The Liberal majority ignored county lines for the ridings of Carleton, Russell, and Ottawa to help the Liberal cause and used blackmail (the threat of a partisan redistribution for the united counties) to bludgeon the Tory members into submission. As shown in Table 6.1, a notable effect of the 1903 redistribution was the rise in the percentage of hives among the prospective Tory-held seats, and the drop in the percentage of hives among the prospective Liberal-held seats.

The Liberal gerrymanders worked. The 1904 election returned one Tory for Victoria, not two; one Tory for Carleton, not two; two Liberals in the Peterborough ridings (a gain of one); and one Liberal and one Tory in the Northumberland ridings (versus the predicted loss of a Liberal seat, had the Northumberland ridings been merged).

Yet the Liberals did poorly across the province. The 1904 election returned thirty-seven Liberals, ten short of prediction, and forty-eight Tories, nine more than predicted. The Liberals lost fourteen ridings that they had been predicted to win and won four ridings that they had been predicted to lose. Ten of their fourteen unexpected losses were in Western Ontario, where they had restored county lines, and three of their four unexpected gains were in Eastern Ontario, which they had gerrymandered. Effectively, the gerrymanders staunched Liberal losses across the province.

A Liberal prime minister, Sir Wilfrid Laurier, oversaw the 1903 redistribution, and Robert Laird Borden led the opposition Conservatives. Their roles were exactly reversed for the next redistribution, in 1914. In each case in this remarkable reversal of fortune, the opposition party held a majority in the Senate.

7

Reversal of Fortune: Robert Borden's Dominion Redistribution of 1914

Robert Borden's Conservatives defeated Sir Wilfrid Laurier's Liberals in the 1911 general election, helped by a massive Tory majority in Ontario (seventy-three of eighty-six seats).[1] Consequently, the two party leaders underwent a reversal of fortunes between the 1903 and 1914 redistributions. In 1903, Laurier was prime minister, Borden led the opposition, and Borden's opposition party had a majority in the Senate. In 1914, Borden was prime minister, Laurier led the opposition, and Laurier's opposition party had a majority in the Senate. In the 1903 redistribution, Laurier had been out to avenge previous Tory gerrymanders and had gerrymandered eastern Ontario. In 1914, Borden chose a conciliatory approach, not retaliation.

Lateness of the Bill

Borden's 1914 redistribution Bill was late, given the constitutional requirement for one "on the completion of the census." The 1911 census was completed in mid-February 1912. In December of that year and into 1913, the Liberal opposition pressed the government for a Bill, unsuccessfully.[2] Political deadlock over naval policy explained the prime minister's two-year delay. Borden wanted his Naval Bill enacted before redistribution and the next general election. The Liberals pressed for redistribution and a general election before settling the fate of Borden's naval policy. [3] To this end, they stalled Borden's Naval Bill with endless debate in the House of Commons and then blocked it with their majority in the Senate. What raised the stakes in this party warfare was an assumption that redistribution would boost Liberal prospects in the next general election; as both parties knew, the 1911 census warranted twenty-two additional ridings for the western provinces, where the Liberals had been competitive, and four fewer ridings for Ontario, where they had not.

The Liberal strategy prevailed during the first six months of 1914. In February, Borden finally introduced a redistribution Bill, with its increase of representation for western Canada. In May, the Senate, with its large Liberal majority, rejected Borden's Naval Aid Bill, leaving Borden's naval policy in limbo for the current parliamentary session. Borden countered with a Constitution Bill, which would enable him to appoint eleven Tory senators for western Canada and thereby overcome Liberal opposition in the Upper House.[4] Still in May, the Senate amended the Constitution Bill to provide for its implementation simultaneously with the redistribution Bill. Borden briefly refused the Senate amendment and threatened to kill the redistribution Bill, before backing down on 12 June, the day that prorogation ended the parliamentary session.

The Liberals appeared to have won. A redistribution Act, with its increase of representation for western Canada, was in place before the next general election and with Borden's naval policy in limbo. The stage was set for a general election on Borden's naval policy. In Ottawa, reported the Toronto *Globe*, rumours were rife about a general election in October.[5] Then, abruptly, the Liberal bubble burst. The outbreak of the Great War in September postponed the next general election until 1917, amidst the greatly altered circumstances of Union Government, the conscription issue, and a shattered Liberal Party.

Borden's Collaboration with the Ontario Premier

Borden had close ties with Premier James P. Whitney's provincial Tories. The Conservative Party had one organization for Dominion and provincial elections in Ontario, and both party leaders held redistributions in 1914. Before Whitney launched his provincial redistribution Bill, W.J. Hanna, Whitney's provincial secretary, and his party organizer, J.S. Carstairs, visited Ottawa to confer with Borden's ministers from Ontario and with Conservative members of the Dominion redistribution committee. As reported in the Toronto *Globe*, "the coming Provincial redistribution has a bearing also on the Federal redistribution of Ontario, and hence Mr. Hanna has been called into consultation before the operation is performed."[6]

Figure 7.1 Cartoon mocking the materialism of Canada's patronage-based parties, 1905. George Alcorn represented Prince Edward as a Conservative. The central figure is Laurier. On the left, a poorly drawn Borden?
Source: National Archives of Canada, C-141175.

Despite Borden's collaboration with the Whitney government, the Dominion and provincial parliaments differed sharply in their numbers of seats and therefore in their respective redistributions. The 1911 census returns entitled Ontario to eighty-two seats in the Dominion parliament, a drop of four and a return to its quota at Confederation. Ontario's provincial parliament had no quota and could add new constituencies without eliminating old ones. Thus, the provincial redistribution increased the size of the House from 105 to 111 – twenty-nine more seats for Ontario than in the House of Commons.

The Movement of Population

The Ontario population increased by 16 percent during the decade 1901–11. The regional statistics were the northland districts, 83 percent; the GTA, 52; Eastern Ontario, 0; and Western Ontario, 5. Ontario cities now numbered nineteen, up from ten; they held 32 percent of the provincial population, up from 21 in the previous census. Toronto, with 376,538 people (an increase of 81 percent), was the largest of the province's cities, followed by Ottawa, 87,062; Hamilton, 81,969; and London, 46,300.

THE BORDEN BILL

The quota for Ontario seats was eighty-two, down from eighty-six in 1903. To arrive at Ontario's reduced quota, the Dominion Act added four ridings: two for Northern Ontario, one for Toronto, and one for York County; and eliminated eight seats through consolidation of county ridings.[7] The redistribution touched thirty-three of the eighty-six ridings and boosted the percentage of ridings in the optimum range (0.90–1.10) from 12 to 20.

Principles

Robert Borden posited five principles, which, he ventured, had support from both sides of the House.[8] His two controlling principles were the observance of municipal boundaries and the equalization of riding populations, recognizing that these principles were "constantly brought into opposition with each other." A third principle was that urban constituencies should have larger populations than rural constituencies. Compared to rural constituencies, cities had "greater solidity and compactness," "more uniform interests," and a capacity to communicate their interests "more cogently and effectively." Cities received support from city men who represented country ridings. Those on the land had more stable interests than "a certain floating element of city populations." Two more principles for consideration were geographical "compactness" for ridings and representation for a "community of interests."

Sir Wilfrid Laurier, former prime minister and since 1911 the leader of the opposition, was in broad agreement with Borden. Representation by population should be the guiding principle – a departure from his emphasis on municipal boundaries as the paramount principle in 1903. Other principles "of almost equal importance" were "regard for the compactness of the constituency, and, as far as possible, for the county unit. Under our system, the county is the unit of population, so far as public life is concerned. The county is the base of ... our municipal and judicial system." Yet another principle was "that the unit of population cannot be the same in urban as in rural constituencies ... Without going into all the reasons, there is one supreme reason, namely, that in a country like Canada, where there is a very large territory with a sparse population, if you were to give the same unit of population to cities and counties, in rural constituencies you would have such a large area of territory as to be almost impossible to control or cover."

Borden's Bipartisan Special Committee

Borden proposed, and Laurier accepted, to refer the work of redistribution to a bipartisan special committee, which represented parties according to their strength in the House. This was the mechanism that Laurier had introduced in 1903. Borden's special committee, in turn, appointed "sub-committees ... made up of groups of two representing the Maritime Provinces, Quebec, Ontario, the western provinces and British Columbia. Each of these two-man groups met, and by discussion, friendly overtures, and negotiation settled the boundaries of the various constituencies, discussed and determined the various units of population both urban and rural, and by this method agreed upon a measure which was presented to the House and adopted practically unanimously."[9]

As a courtesy to Laurier, Borden agreed to increase the size of the committee from seven to nine, to allow four Liberals rather than three for staffing the five regional subcommittees. The Hon. Robert "Bob" Rogers (Conservative, Winnipeg), Borden's minister of Public Works, chaired the national committee. Prominent members of the national committee included the Hon. John Dowsley Reid (Conservative, Grenville), Borden's minister of Customs; the Hon. Henri Béland (Liberal, Beauce, Quebec), a former postmaster-general in the Laurier ministry; and Frederick Forsythe Pardee (Liberal, Lambton West), Laurier's chief party whip. The two Ontario members of the national committee, Reid for the Tories and Pardee for the Liberals, acted as its subcommittee for Ontario.[10]

Rogers was a "skilled practitioner of patronage."[11] During his tenure as minister in Manitoba's Conservative provincial government, he had organized Borden's 1904, 1908, and 1911 election campaigns in western Canada. The Toronto *Globe* described him as a master of "the smooth touch," as opposed to the "strong-handed" methods of Frank Cochrane, another organizer in Borden's cabinet. "The selection of Mr. Rogers as Chairman," warned the *Globe*, "is taken to indicate that a gerrymander is in sight."[12] Rogers was to confound the *Globe*'s prediction.

In 1903, Borden had judged that Laurier's special committee had failed to function as a neutral-ground conference of the two parties. He had not known "of one important proposition ... emanating from the minority, which was accepted by the majority ... It was not a conference but simply a partisan committee, upon which there were four Liberal members and three Conservatives."[13]

Borden had moderated his view by 1914. His party had been "inclined in the first instance to speak of [the special committee] as a committee and to say that it should have been a conference, and afterwards we were inclined to take the ground that, properly understood, it was a conference. It was not a *conference* precisely in the sense implied by the British precedent which was invoked by my Right Hon. friend [Laurier]. Yet, on the whole I think it did its work fairly well. There were undoubtedly differences of opinion on [that] occasion. But I venture to state that a small committee of that kind [is] better able to reconcile, as far as possible, those differences of opinion, and to reduce the basis of representation to some fixed principle than it would possibly be done in this House."

Laurier put the special-committee mechanism in perspective.[14] "It has been suggested on the floor of this House more than once," noted the opposition leader, "that Parliament should create an independent body, say a commission of judges, to make after every census the apportionment of the representation between the different provinces ... Up to the present time," however, neither party had "been willing to transfer to any other hands than its own the duty and responsibility ... to determine what shall be the representation in this House." In the circumstances, the special-committee mechanism improved on what had preceded it. The first three redistributions (1872, 1882, and 1892) had given no satisfaction to the Liberal minority or even to the whole of the Conservative Party. "The method which was followed was to bring in a Bill which was cut and dried, and in the preparation of which the minority, the Opposition in this House, had no voice. They had nothing to do but offer criticism or approval; they were not allowed any voice whatever in the preparation of the measure." Hence in 1903 his Liberal administration had brought in "a Bill with the schedule in blank, leaving to a Committee of the House the full work of preparing the map which it is the duty of Parliament to prepare. The committee was composed of seven members, and on that occasion, as on the present and similar occasions, of course, the majority must have the deciding voice ... it is a part of our parliamentary system. The system will work well if the majority on the committee will be guided, not by a desire to have an advantage over a minority, but simply by the principles of equity, justice, and fair play. I am aware that on the committee which was appointed in 1903, there were sometimes very severe cleavages of opinion and some very hot discussion; but I think I can claim, to the credit of the committee, that when its report was presented to the House, it was, after all, in the main, accepted as fair."

The task of the 1914 special committee would not be easy, opined Laurier. It had "two principles to work upon: first, equalization of population between constituency and constituency, and, secondly, maintenance of county boundaries ... occasions may arise when these two things may clash, and then the committee will have to come from some decision as to what to do under such circumstances. In the majority of cases, however, there ought to be no more difficulty in maintaining the principle in 1914 than there was in 1903."

The special committee of 1914 realized the hopes of the party leaders to have it function as a conference. As Edward M. Macdonald (Pictou, Nova Scotia), a Liberal member of Borden's committee, later recalled, the special-committee method allowed Parliament to settle the schedule of ridings "through discussion, negotiation, and agreement among members of the committee." In 1914, as in 1903, "the Bill was thus more a matter of production by parliament as a whole than by the government of the day."[15] As reported in the Toronto *Globe*, a Liberal organ, the Tory chair of the committee, the Hon. Robert Rogers, "was cheered from both sides of the Chamber when he formally presented 'the second and final report of the Redistribution Committee.' The report was the result of months of discussion and compromise, and its results are embodied in the Bill." Similarly, the *Globe* expected that "[t]he Bill will ... be passed through the House before prorogation ... with comparatively little discussion. There are only three or four cases where there is any marked diversion of opinion by the two parties concerning the compromise reached by the committee in addition to the two Ontario cases mentioned." This proved to be the case. The Kent ridings and the proposed merger of Glengarry-Stormont received discussion, but all other proposed changes went through "practically without comment."[16]

The Work of the Special Committee and Its Ontario Subcommittee

The parliamentary debates were silent about the special committee's approach to redistribution for Ontario. How independently, if at all, did the two-man subcommittee of one Tory and one Liberal function without the government party having a majority on it? Did the special committee start by setting the ridings for Toronto alone, as in Laurier's 1903 redistribution? Or for all cities, as prescribed by the 1903 Borden-Haggart rule 4 on the 1903 special committee? We do not know.

Electoral versus Municipal Territory for Large Cities

By 1914, all four cities had civic territories outside of their electoral boundaries. These were, for Toronto, fifteen territories annexed during the years 1905–12; London, four territories annexed in 1912; Hamilton, nine territories annexed since 1902; and Ottawa, the Rideau Ward (1887), and six territories annexed during the years 1907–11.

The 1914 redistribution completely disregarded the 1903 Borden-Haggart rule 2: "Where separate representation is given to cities the municipal boundaries of such cities shall be observed." Borden's redistribution kept the status quo, with ridings given for "the city of Toronto, exclusive of those portions thereof allotted to the electoral districts of East York, West York, and South York"; "the city of Ottawa, exclusive of ... that part of the city of Ottawa formerly known as Hintonburg, Bayswater, and Mechanicsville, and also exclusive of the Rideau Ward"; "the city of Hamilton, exclusive of those parts thereof allotted to the electoral district of Wentworth"; and "the city of London, exclusive of the portions thereof ... formerly in the township of London, now in said city ... [and] formerly in the township of Westminster, now in said city."[17] Indeed, the redistribution moved 6,562 residents of Toronto from the city's electoral district into the York ridings, thereby turning the principle on its head. The redistribution for the ridings of Carleton, Russell, and Ottawa (two members) elaborates the workings of the Rogers special committee. If county lines mattered, then the riding of Russell would give the Rideau Ward to the two-member Ottawa riding and three municipalities to the Carleton riding (the townships of Gloucester and Osgoode, and Eastview Village). These transfers would equalize populations,[18] give the city riding higher per-member populations than the county ridings, recognize the municipal-city riding as a "county unto itself, " and observe municipal lines for the two county ridings. Simply put, the transfers would be on-side with principles and inconsequential for predicted party strengths in the three ridings.

The special committee decided otherwise. As the Hon. John Reid, the Tory on the two-man Ontario subcommittee, explained: "I would like to have seen Rideau ward remain in the city of Ottawa, and it was proposed that it should remain part of the city, but we finally agreed that the electoral divisions should remain as they were, and that we should submit our report to the House and let the House decide." To this end, Reid supported an amendment, moved by two Conservative MPs, Alfred Fripp (Ottawa) and William Garland (Carleton), to transfer the Rideau Ward to the Ottawa riding. John Chabot, the other Ottawa MP and also a Tory, spoke for the amendment. So too did W.F. Maclean (Independent Conservative, York South), who urged that "the principle involved is that of community of interest, and this principle has been violated in Ottawa and Toronto. It may be that convenience suggests the adoption of a plan of combining urban and suburban communities in one electoral district, but, certainly, it is a wider departure from the principle of community of interest than that which has prevailed in the past." Against the motion were two Liberal MPs, the Hon. Charles Murphy (Russell), past secretary of state for External Affairs, and Edmund Proulx (Prescott), who argued that the Rideau River was a natural geographical boundary between the Rideau Ward and the rest of the city, and hence the Rideau Ward should be left in Russell. What doomed the amendment was Prime Minister Borden's indifference to the principles at stake: "The city of Ottawa has grown out into Russell and into Carleton, and if for municipal purposes portions of those counties have been taken within the city limits, nevertheless, for electoral purposes, they have been regarded for a number of years as properly appertaining to the adjoining counties that I have mentioned. The same condition prevails in the city of Toronto [and] in regard to the county of Middlesex and the city of London." Even John Reid, although personally favouring the transfer to Ottawa, did "not think it [made] much difference either way." As noted, the Liberal MPs for Russell and Prescott opposed the transfer, regardless of its grounding in Liberal-held principles. By contrast, the provincial riding of Ottawa had included the Rideau Ward (annexed 1887) since Oliver Mowat's redistribution of 1894.

The Northland Ridings

Borden's redistribution increased the number of northland-district ridings from six to eight. Before redistribution, the ridings were Algoma East, Algoma West, Muskoka, Parry Sound, Nipissing, and Thunder Bay & Rainy River. The redistribution divided Thunder Bay & Rainy River into two ridings, Fort William & Kenora and Port Arthur & Rainy River, and divided Nipissing into two ridings, Temiskaming and Nipissing.

The nature of the ridings in the northland districts had changed considerably since Confederation. The two ridings of the 1872 redistribution had tiny census populations (0.38 each) to allow for their small, scattered settlements and vast territories to be covered by their Members of Parliament. Algoma, "a new country just opened for settlement and almost beyond the ken or protection of law," stated Sir John A. Macdonald, required representation "to give confidence to the settlers going there."[19]

In contrast, the 1911 census reported the first northland cities – Fort William, population 16,499; Sault Ste. Marie, 14,920; and Port Arthur, 11,220. And the ridings of 1914 had above-average populations – Algoma East, 1.22; Algoma West, 0.93; Fort William & Rainy River, 1.04; Temiskaming, 1.41; Port Arthur & Kenora, 1.24; and Nipissing, 1.42. Only the southernmost district ridings, Muskoka and Parry Sound, had below-average populations (0.69 and 0.86).

Case Studies: Glengarry and Kent

"Ontario Liberals are severely militated against in the measure as it stands tonight," reported the Toronto *Globe*.[20] In particular, the Bill's proposed changes for Kent and the united-municipal county of Glengarry-Stormont-Dundas provoked the wrath of that Liberal-Party organ. Before redistribution, Kent County had two ridings, Kent East and Kent West. The redistribution merged the Kent ridings to form a single riding of Kent. Before redistribution, Glengarry, Stormont, and Dundas were stand-alone ridings within the united-municipal county of Glengarry-Stormont-Dundas. The redistribution Bill transferred two Stormont townships (Finch and Osnabruck) to the riding of Dundas. It then merged Glengarry with the rump of Stormont to form the riding of Glengarry-Stormont.

The *Globe*'s complaints differed in the two cases. The Glengarry-Stormont merger violated the principle of communities of interest: "the historic Scotch county of Glengarry loses its individuality and will hereafter be known as Glengarry and Stormont."[21] Otherwise, the opposition Liberals benefited; the redistribution removed one from the Tory count of seats. Glengarry had been very safe, Liberal (+246) and Stormont had been reasonably safe, Conservative (-131). The merged riding of Glengarry-Stormont, with the loss of two Stormont townships to Dundas, would be very safe, Liberal (+272). Dundas had been a Tory hive (-644) and would remain so (-821).[22] The united-municipal county had 2.06 standard populations, which supports the reduction in its number of ridings from three ridings to two. The two redistributed ridings, however, had unequal populations: Dundas, 0.84, and Glengarry-Stormont, 1.24.

By normal criteria, the merger of the Kent ridings was a spectacular gerrymander, which benefited the government party by mocking the principle of equalizing riding populations. The amalgamated riding, observed the *Globe*, would have "some 60,000 population, and some 16,500 voters, while the County of Grenville" – the riding of the Hon. Dr Reid, a Tory member of the special committee – was "left unchanged, [yet] has a population of only 17,500 and 4,000 voters." Indeed, the two Kent ridings had 1.82 standard populations, enough to warrant being left alone. The Kent ridings had Liberal incumbents; thus their merger removed one from the opposition tally of seats.

Curiously, Archie McCoig, the Liberal incumbent in Kent West, meekly asked the special committee to modify the proposed merger, not to nullify it. He had in mind a transfer of Zone and Camden Townships, including the villages of Dresden, Thamesville, and Bothwell, from Kent to the riding of Lambton East to reduce some of Kent's oversized population. Although the proposed transfer would trespass on county lines, it would reduce Kent to 1.61 standard populations (still high), while boosting Lambton East from 0.72 to 0.93 (in the optimum zone). It was politically viable – the townships in question favoured the Tories (-95), and a Conservative held the receiving riding, Lambton East (very safe, -484). The member for Lambton East agreed to the proposed transfer, and the special committee made the change.

A general issue, raised by the case of Kent, was the special committee's criteria for the selection of ridings for elimination. Clearly, population was not its controlling principle. Whereas the amalgamated riding of Kent would have 1.82 standard populations, nine two-riding counties with smaller populations were left alone: Ontario (1.33), Peterborough (1.35), Elgin (1.44), Oxford (1.53), Bruce (1.62), Renfrew (1.67), Perth (1.69), Lambton (1.76), and Wellington (1.76). Even the counties of Middlesex and Huron, each of whose three ridings were to be reduced to two, had fewer standard populations than Kent County (1.66 and 1.72).

Two objectives possibly influenced the special committee. One was to preserve a regional balance in ridings between Eastern and Western Ontario, an approach used explicitly in the Tory redistribution of 1892.[23] Under the provisions of the Bill, the two regions each were to lose four ridings. The second consideration was to balance the prospective party losses from the redistribution. Under the provisions of the 1914 Bill, each party stood to lose two from its count of seats.

In terms of the twin considerations of regional and party-strength balance, Kent was attractive for selection, first, because of its location in the Western Ontario region, and second, because the amalgamation of its ridings guaranteed the elimination of a Liberal-held seat. Kent was the only two-riding county in the western region in which Liberals held both seats. Conservatives held both ridings in the left-alone counties of Elgin, Bruce, and Perth and one of the two ridings in the left-alone counties of Oxford, Lambton, and Wellington. One may speculate, therefore, that the special committee selected Kent as part of a grand bargain between its majority and minority members. This could explain the mildness of Archie McCoig's critique of the Kent merger and the applause for Robert Rogers, from both sides of the House, when he submitted the special committee's final report.

With the exceptions of Kent and Glengarry-Stormont-Dundas, and the observance of municipal boundaries for cities, the 1914 Borden redistribution followed understood principles. To those it added two principles: one of maintaining regional balance in representation between Eastern Ontario and Western Ontario; and the other, ensuring that the two parties shared equally the losses of seats arising from the consolidation of county ridings. On balance the redistribution was a fair one and a tribute to the work of the special committee. Table 7.1 summarizes the effect of the 1914 redistribution on prospective party strengths in the Ontario ridings. With redistribution and the net loss of four seats, each party was projected to lose two seats. The Tories gained four seats from the addition of four Tory-leaning ridings and lost six seats through mergers of county ridings.

Both parties had an unusually large proportion of their ridings in the hive and very safe categories. This resulted in part from a trend toward rising numbers of voters in the ridings. One also must allow for the possibility of "horse trades" between parties on the committee to shore up each other's ridings. This "log-rolling" would have fit well with the unvoiced principles of regional balance and equality of prospective party losses from the distribution.

The alignment of parties changed before the next general election, which the outbreak of the Great War delayed until 1917. By then, the government was Unionist, an alliance of Conservatives and pro-conscription Liberals. Laurier loyalists, who opposed conscription, were the opposition. In wartime circumstances, the 1914 redistribution was largely irrelevant to the outcome of the 1917 general election.

Table 7.1 Distribution of Dominion seats by party and level of safety, before and after the 1914 redistribution

	Before 1914 redistribution			*After redistribution: Predictions for 1914 election*		
	Conservative	*Liberal*	*All parties*	*Conservative*	*Liberal*	*All parties*
hive (500+)	55%	38%	52%	59%	36%	56%
very safe (200–499)	18%	23%	19%	18%	36%	21%
reasonably safe (100–199)	14%	15%	14%	10%	9%	10%
possibly safe (50–99)	5%	15%	7%	4%	9%	5%
precarious (< 50)	7%	0%	6%	6%	0%	5%
acclamation/ unclassed	1%	8%	2%	3%	9%	4%
# of ridings	73	13	86	71	11	82

SUMMARY AND INTERPRETATION

Robert Borden's Tory ministry administered the 1914 Dominion redistribution, working closely behind the scenes with the Ontario premier, James P. Whitney, who administered a provincial redistribution in the same year. Like Laurier in 1903, Prime Minister Borden referred redistribution to a bipartisan special committee, which represented parties according to their strength in the House. Borden professed conventional principles for his 1914 Dominion redistribution – no gerrymander, equalization of riding populations, recognition of municipal boundaries, a rural bias in representation, symmetrical-compact shape for ridings, and recognition of communities of interest.

Borden's 1914 redistribution was fair to the two political parties – it was the least partisan of all redistributions that a Dominion parliament ever enacted. This achievement was a tribute to the respectful relationship between Borden and Laurier,[24] whose roles as prime minister and opposition leader had been reversed since the 1903 redistribution, and the "smooth touch" of the Hon. "Bob" Rogers on the special committee. Indeed, the Hon. Robert Rogers "was cheered from both sides of the Chamber when he formally presented 'the second and final report of the Redistribution Committee.'" Rogers's partisan fairness derived from two unstated principles of his committee: first, to maintain a regional balance in representation between Eastern Ontario and Western Ontario, and second, to require equality between the two parties in net seats lost through redistribution.

Fairness to the political parties cost faithfulness to principles. The redistribution for the ridings of Kent mocked the equalization of population. The special committee was singularly indifferent to observing municipal limits as a county line for the cities of Toronto, Hamilton, Ottawa, and London. Indeed, it transferred 6,562 Toronto residents from city ridings into the York-County ridings. Concerning the proposed transfer of Ottawa's Rideau Ward (annexed 1887) to the Ottawa riding, John Reid, the senior Ontario Tory on the special committee, did "not think it [made] much difference either way." Similarly, Prime Minister Borden was oblivious to the principle that he had advanced as a member of Laurier's special committee in 1903: that "where separate representation is given to cities the municipal boundaries of such cities shall be observed."

The 1914 redistribution had small influence on party fortunes in the next general election, which was expected in 1914, but which the outbreak of war postponed until 1917. By then the alignment of parties had changed. Nor was Borden's redistribution a template for the next redistribution, that of 1924, which was to occur in the altered circumstances of a Liberal prime minister, a hung Parliament, and a three-party system (see chapter 9). In the meantime, Ontario had four provincial redistributions between 1894 and 1914. Chapter 8 considers them.

8

Four Provincial Redistributions, 1894–1914

Ontario had four provincial redistributions between 1890 and the First World War. The first two, by Liberal administrations in 1894 and 1902, were minor in scope and purpose. Sir Oliver Mowat (knighted in 1892) was the premier in 1894, and George Ross held the office in 1902. The last two, by Conservative administrations in 1908 and 1914, were major undertakings. James P. Whitney, whose Conservatives turned the Liberals out of office in 1905, administered the 1908 redistribution. Whitney's provincial secretary, the Hon. William Hanna, managed the 1914 redistribution, Premier Whitney having been invalided by a heart attack, and absent from Parliament. The government's Representation Act, 1914, was enacted on 1 May. Whitney passed away on 25 September.

The provincial parliament had neither a timing requirement nor a quota for redistribution. With no timing requirement, government commonly redistributed the ridings midway between censuses, rather than immediately after the issuance of one. With no quota, it could create additional ridings for cities and northern districts without eliminating seats in the counties. Thus, whereas the number of Dominion ridings for Ontario fell from ninety-two to eighty-two between 1885 and 1914, the size of the provincial parliament rose from ninety to one hundred eleven.

The Movement of Population, 1881–1911

The provincial population grew moderately during the 1880s (10 percent), slumped during the 1890s (3 percent), and boomed during the 1900s (16 percent). Percentage-decadal increases were above average for cities and northlands districts. The statistics were, for Toronto, 102, 19, and 81 percent; Hamilton, 36, 28, and 31; Ottawa, 42, 54, and 45; London, 62, 19, and 22; and the northlands, 73, 59, and 83.

Annexations enlarged the municipal territories of cities. During the years 1894–1914, Toronto annexed twenty-six suburban territories in York County; Ottawa, ten in Carleton County; Hamilton, eleven in Wentworth County; and London, eight in Middlesex County. With each annexation, a city's municipal territory became larger than its electoral territory. Thus the issue again arose whether or not to match a city's electoral territory to its expanded municipal territory. The underlying principle was that city limits were county lines, each city being "a county of itself" for municipal purposes. As discussed below, the redistributions of 1894, 1908, and 1914 ignored the issue, and the 1902 redistribution did not face it, being exclusively for Northern Ontario.

SIR OLIVER MOWAT'S MINIMALIST REDISTRIBUTION, 1894

Mowat's Representation Act boosted the number of seats from ninety-one to ninety-four and gave the increase exclusively to cities.[1] Mowat divided Toronto's three-member riding into four one-member ridings with approximately equal "voting populations."[2] His Act divided the riding of Hamilton City (2.18 standard populations) into the ridings of Hamilton East and Hamilton West, and made Ottawa (1.73), a single-member riding, into a two-member riding. Elsewhere, the Act transferred Kingston Township from Kingston City (1.06) to Frontenac Township (0.63), thereby reducing Kingston to 0.94 standard populations and raising Frontenac to 0.89. With the 1894 Representation Act touching few ridings, the percentage with populations in the optimum range (0.90–1.10) moved from 38 to 39. Among the cities, Toronto alone remained under-represented on the basis of population, with 6.23 standard populations for its four ridings.

William Meredith, the Tory leader, opposed the creation of the new seats, apparently because he could not credit the government with making any changes without calculating partisan advantage.[3] In fact, the redistribution was neutral for prospective partisan strengths in the next election. The governing Grits gained prospectively from the additional representation for Hamilton, a possibly safe, Liberal seat (+86), and Ottawa, a Grit hive (+1,415). The opposition Conservatives gained from the increased representation for Toronto; although the 1890 general election returned two Tories and one Grit for the city's three-member riding, the Tories polled 66 percent of the votes. Tory incumbents represented Kingston (precarious, -29) and Frontenac (possibly safe, -98) and held their ground with redistribution (precarious, -20 and reasonably safe, -107). The 1894 general election went as predicted in the redistributed seats: the Conservatives swept the four Toronto ridings, Kingston, and Frontenac, and the Liberals captured the four ridings in Hamilton and Ottawa.

GEORGE ROSS'S MINIMALIST REDISTRIBUTION OF 1902 (LIBERAL)

In 1896 Mowat quit the premiership to enter Wilfrid Laurier's Dominion cabinet. His successors were Arthur S. Hardy (1896–99) and then George W. Ross (1899–1905).

On becoming premier in 1899, Ross judged that his party was losing popularity after twenty-eight years in office. To staunch the party's wounds, he sought a "sphere of operation" which would "attract the masses" to the Liberal standard. In most areas of legislation ("education, municipal law, the jurisdiction of the courts, public institutions, agriculture") government had "little to do except to advance with the growing demands of each case." Ross could identify "only one field for enterprise, which, though not entirely new, was likely to command public attention and benefit the Province ... that [field] was the development of the district between the Canadian Pacific Railway and Hudson Bay, now known as 'New Ontario.'"[4]

Ross's 1902 Representation Act increased the number of ridings for northland districts from five to nine. The Act divided Algoma West into two ridings: Port Arthur & Rainy River, and Fort William & Lake of the Woods. It divided Algoma East into three ridings: Sault Ste. Marie, Manitoulin, and Algoma. It partitioned Nipissing into two ridings, Nipissing East and Nipissing West.[5] These changes raised the number of seats in the provincial parliament from ninety-four to ninety-eight – fourteen more than the number of Dominion ridings. The three adjusted constituencies (Algoma East, Algoma West, and Nipissing) had 4.62 standard populations – sufficient for five ridings on the basis of population, although not for the seven given in redistribution. With all other provincial ridings left alone, the percentage of ridings in the optimum range for population (0.90–1.10) increased from 25 to 27.

All three pre-redistribution ridings had Liberal incumbents: Algoma East (+224), Algoma West (+400), and Nipissing (+38).[6] Thus, the splitting of these three ridings into seven was promising for the government party. The 1905 general election did not deliver on the promise: James P. Whitney's Conservatives won five of the seven redistributed ridings: Algoma, Manitoulin, Nipissing East, Nipissing West, and Port Arthur & Rainy River, but not Sault Ste. Marie or Fort William & Lake of the Woods.

JAMES P. WHITNEY'S 1908 REDISTRIBUTION

The 1908 provincial redistribution, the first ever by a Conservative administration, increased the size of Parliament from ninety-eight to one hundred six seats. Premier James P. Whitney's Representation Act added four seats for Toronto and four for Northern Ontario (Kenora, Sturgeon Falls, Sudbury, and Temiskaming). It abolished the purely-electoral county of Cardwell (created in 1867) and repatriated its municipalities to their municipal counties, Peel and Simcoe (in the form of a new riding, Simcoe South). Elsewhere, the Bill changed Ottawa from a two-member riding to two single-member ones.

Principles

"The Premier is keeping his redistribution ideas to himself, and we are just as much in the dark as anyone else," reported "a Conservative member" on the eve of the Bill's introduction. Nevertheless, Whitney's piecemeal statements and the throne speech in April 1908 indicated four principles.[7] First was the provision of additional ridings for the northlands, owing to its "rapid increase of population" (59 percent during the 1890s and 83 percent during the 1900s), and for Toronto (increases of 19 percent and 81 percent). Whitney's second priority was respect for county lines. Indeed, as he announced at a banquet given in his honour in March, his Bill would reunite municipalities that an earlier redistribution had divided – a reference to Oliver Mowat's splitting of three Huron-County townships in 1874. His third principle was a partial equalization of population in the county ridings to remove "some of the anomalies and injustices which resulted from previous redistributions." He refused a general application of the equalization principle because the 1901 census statistics were found to be unreliable for use in 1908. "A more complete redistribution of the constituencies, with a view to equalizing the representation in accordance with the population, should take place after the next decennial census."

Whitney's fourth principle was that Toronto ridings should have larger populations than county ridings. As the Toronto *Globe* pronounced, the average population for provincial ridings was 21,000, so "Toronto, with 272,000 people, has an eighth of the population of the Province, and on a strict division, would have twelve members. That, of course, no government would propose. Even the suggestion of eight is looked upon with no great favour by the rural members on either side of politics, and Hon. A.G. Mackay [leader of the Liberal opposition] intimated yesterday that Toronto, with four Cabinet Ministers resident in it, might do very well with six members." Whitney rejected the notion that "the Ministers residing in this city and representing outside constituencies should be considered as representing the city because they lived in Toronto."

Whitney's fifth principle was his willingness to increase the size of Parliament, from ninety-eight to one hundred six seats, to accommodate eight additional ridings for the northlands and Toronto, rather than eliminating county ridings to cap the size of the House at a lesser number – this despite the view of "a prominent Conservative" that a parliament with more than a hundred members was "too large."

Whitney Emasculates His Bipartisan Special Committee

Whitney foreswore changing the ridings for party advantage. Ostensibly to promote fairness, and following in the footsteps of Laurier, Whitney referred the details of redistribution to a bipartisan special committee, composed of five Conservatives and three Liberals.

Compared with the Dominion special committee, Whitney's committee had little to do. Laurier in 1903 had brought in a Bill with no schedule, it being the task of the committee to prepare one. Whitney, in contrast, decided in advance which ridings needed change. As reported in the Toronto *Globe*, a Grit organ, "The constituencies found satisfactory to the Government, and consequently not to be changed, were submitted in groups as the Government had agreed on them, before it was submitted to the committee. Then came the various gerrymanders ... when the committee assembled, composed of five Conservatives, including the Premier and two Cabinet Ministers, and three Liberals, they found no opportunity for usefulness, except in adopting, with or without division, the successive gerrymanders arranged in secret by the Government ... The Liberal members on the committee appealed to the Premier for advance information as to what was intended to be done with the various constituencies, but this was invariably refused." Simply put, the committee was a mere ratifying body.[8]

The three Liberals on the special committee submitted a minority report, which accepted the proposed changes for two counties, but disputed the proposed changes for ten. It supported the increase of representation for Northern Ontario, but opposed the increase of representation for Toronto.[9] It offered an alternative to the committee's proposed reorganization of ridings in Huron County.

The Liberal Critique

The Liberal leader Alexander Grant McKay (Grey North), faulted Whitney for failure to "act upon, what he declared to be his policy, the principle that the population of constituencies should be equalized. [McKay] quoted constituency after constituency which had not been touched where the differences in population ran into thousands. Only where political advantage was to be gained had the cry of equalization been raised for the obvious purpose of gerrymander."[10] McKay's criticism lacked weight: Premier Whitney had committed only to a partial equalization, in part to avoid relying upon dated 1901 census data.

A second Liberal indictment was that the redistribution was "out of season," taking place long after the 1901 census and on the eve of the 1911 census.[11] As maintained in Mackay's "Fourth Letter to the People of Ontario," redistribution should happen shortly after a census, when the statistics are fresh. By the premier's own admission, he had been "working in the dark" with dated 1901 population statistics. His only possible motive for doing so, judged McKay, was to gerrymander the opposition in the next election. This criticism too was a stretch. Ontario did not have a census-based timing requirement for redistribution. Moreover, Ontario's previous provincial redistributions (1874, 1885, and 1894), all by a Liberal premier, Oliver Mowat, had been "out of season."

Third, Liberals opposed the proposed doubling of representation for Toronto. As the *Globe* reasoned, "The city has the ear of the Cabinet at all times. Ministers representing outside constituencies are also in a measure representatives of Toronto, and the same is true of other residents of Toronto who hold seats for outside ridings." Thomas Preston (Liberal, Brant South) moved to allocate six members to Toronto (an increase of two rather than four), but his amendment was defeated.

Fourth, McKay criticized the form of the representation for Toronto. Here the Act added "four new members without altering the present constituencies." Each of the four single-member ridings became a two-member constituency, with two simultaneous elections: "A" and "B," the one for a "senior" member and the other for a "junior." Thus, complained McKay, each elector had two votes, one in each of his riding's two elections, "whereas electors in the rural ridings would still have only one." Here again, McKay's protest was on shaky ground. Oliver Mowat's redistributions had made Toronto a three-member riding in 1885 and Ottawa a two-member riding in 1894; in each case, the elector could vote for up to two candidates. Moreover, Whitney's 1908 Bill proposed changing Ottawa, a two-member constituency, into two one-member ridings, which the Liberal minority on the special committee opposed.[12]

The Minority Report

The three Liberals on Whitney's farcical special committee issued a minority report to the House. Their opposition to the changes proposed for Ottawa, Middlesex, Peterborough, and Northumberland was minor, but this was not so for the changes proposed for Toronto, Huron, Essex, Leeds, Brockville, Cardwell, and Peel. Charges of gerrymander were on the table.

REPRESENTATION FOR TORONTO: A GERRYMANDER

An understood principle was that Toronto ridings should have larger populations – less representation – than county ridings. "In the city," claimed John Auld (Liberal, Essex South), "a man could represent 100,000 people easier than 20,000 in a rural district." At first glance, the increase of representation proposed for Toronto was reasonable. Based on the dated 1901 census and the proposed 106 ridings, Toronto had 10.20 standard populations, sufficient for ten ridings. Given Toronto's robust population growth during the 1900s, the city had a far larger population in 1908 than was indicated by the 1901 census. The Toronto *Globe*, a Liberal organ, placed the city's population at 272,000 (13.3 standard populations). Whitney placed the population at "away over 300,000" (14.7 standard populations). The 1911 census was to enumerate 376,538 people (18.5 standard populations).

The rhetoric was misleading. The increase of four seats was for Toronto's 1894 electoral district, which excluded annexed territories other than Parkdale. Proof was in the returns for the 1911 general election, which reported 11 percent of Toronto electors in the ridings of York East and York West. Toronto's electoral district possibly held

7.66 standard populations (the 1901 census statistic for Dominion ridings); or, as estimated from statistics for electors, 9.1 standard populations. Either way, the increase from four to eight seats was excessive in principle.

The mode of doubling the city's redistribution was unusual and controversial. Rather than giving the city eight ridings for eight members, it allotted a second member to each of the four current ridings. Second, rather than holding one election to elect two candidates (a common arrangement for a two-member riding), each riding was to elect its two members in separate elections.[13] Third, the redistributed ridings had unequal populations per member (0.83, 0.96, 1.05, and 1.71).[14]

Simply put, the redistribution for Toronto was a gerrymander, largely through the stratagem of over-representing populations that favoured the government party. The government party masked this stratagem by presenting population statistics for the municipal city of Toronto, rather than for its smaller electoral district. The pre-redistribution ridings were massive Tory hives (-2,373, -1,485, -1,072, and -3,223). With the doubling of representation for the four ridings, the Conservatives prospectively gained four members. Such, indeed, proved to be the case in the 1908 general election.

LEEDS AND BROCKVILLE: A GERRYMANDER

The redistribution for the ridings of Leeds and Brockville (Map 8.1) was a gerrymander. It moved two Tory-leaning townships, Kitley and South Elmsley (-156), from Leeds to Brockville; and a Liberal-leaning township, Front Yonge & Escott (+99), from Brockville to Leeds. The exchange used wasted Tory votes in Leeds, a Conservative hive (-910), to turn Brockville from reasonably safe, Liberal (+169) to possibly safe, Tory (-86): a prospective gain of a seat for the government party. The exchange was neutral for the equalization of riding populations. This gerrymander worked as predicted in the 1908 general election. The Liberal-majority statistics for the transferred municipalities were, for Kitley and South Elmsley, -189, versus the predicted -156; and for Front Yonge & Escott, +88, versus the predicted +99. Both ridings returned Tories: Brockville, -511, versus the predicted -86; and Leeds, -189, versus the predicted -655.

ESSEX COUNTY: A GERRYMANDER

The redistribution for Essex County (Map 8.2), which transferred Tilbury North Township (+140) from Essex South to Essex North, was a

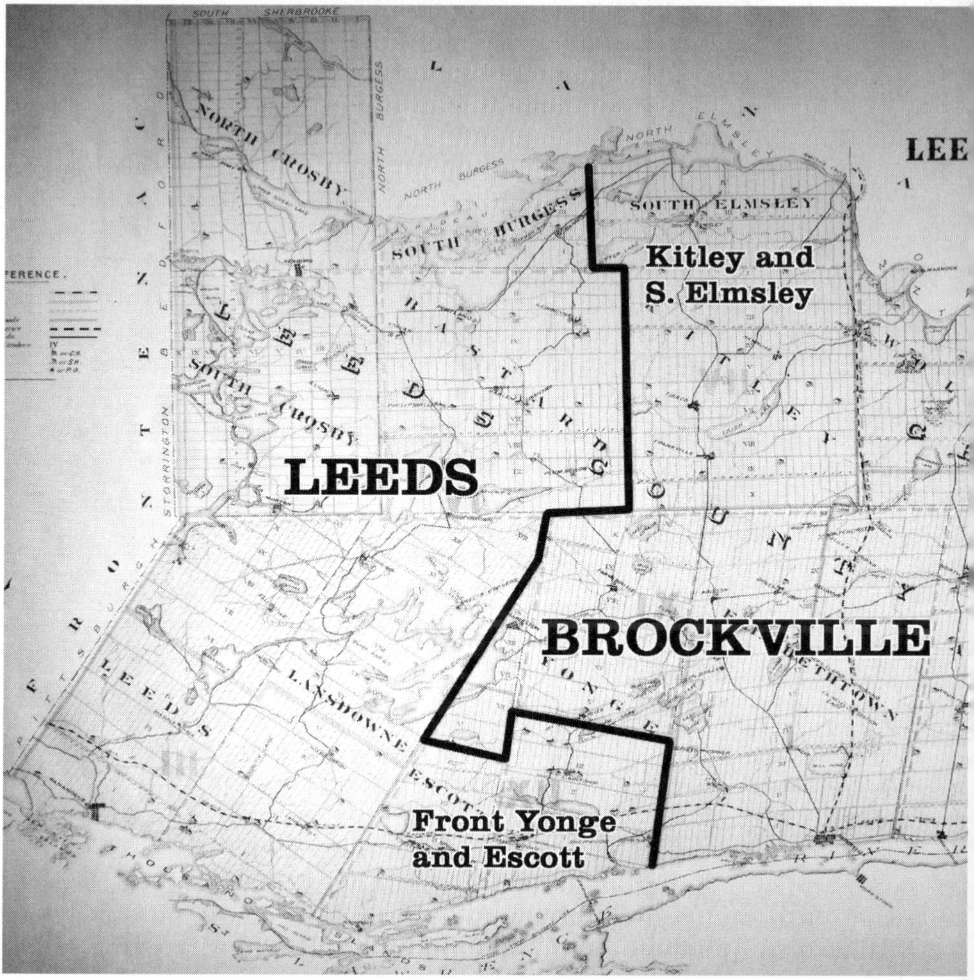

Map 8.1 Leeds and Brockville ridings, provincial ridings, 1908

gerrymander. The transfer did not matter for the North riding, a Tory hive (-836), but turned Essex South from reasonably safe, Liberal (+139) to precarious, Conservative (-1). The transfer increased inequality of population between the two ridings. This gerrymander worked as predicted in the 1908 general election. Both ridings returned Tories: Essex North, -1,280, versus the predicted -696; and Essex South, -78, versus the predicted -1. The out-transfer of Tilbury North Township (+82 in 1908) sunk the Liberals in Essex South.

CARDWELL, PEEL, AND SIMCOE: A THINLY DISGUISED GERRYMANDER

Whitney abolished Cardwell, a purely-electoral county and a Tory hive (-889), and returned its municipalities to their home counties, Peel and Simcoe. This gained a seat for the government party. The repatriation of Albion Township and Bolton Village from Cardwell turned Peel from precarious, Liberal (+32) to reasonably safe, Tory (-128). The balance of Cardwell became the riding of Simcoe South, which, like the defunct Cardwell, was a Tory hive (from -889 to -729).

The redistribution was positive for county lines, Whitney's first principle, but negative for equalizing populations.[15] With mixed support from principles, the dismantling of Cardwell was borderline for a judgment of "thinly disguised" gerrymander. If so, the gerrymander worked. In the 1908 general election, the Liberal-majority statistic for Albion Township and Bolton Village was -182, better than the prediction, -160; even without the in-transfers, the Tory candidate in Peel had a majority. Simcoe South, as predicted, was a Tory hive (-729).

MIDDLESEX COUNTY: A GERRYMANDER

According to municipal censuses, complained Charles Bowman (Liberal, Bruce North), the proposed changes in the ridings of North and West Middlesex made a disparity of 2,800 in population, whereas the old ridings had only a difference of 500. The premier responded that the municipal censuses were "often unreliable and done in a slovenly manner. Therefore government had to reply on the Dominion census."[16]

Even so, this redistribution was a gerrymander. Its transfers helped the government party but were neutral for equalizing populations, hence a trespass on minimalism.[17] It moved Lobo Township (-235) from Middlesex North to Middlesex West, in exchange for Metcalfe Township and Strathroy Town (-55) from Middlesex West. Middlesex West moved from possibly safe, Conservative (-67) to very safe (-247). Middlesex North moved from reasonably safe, Liberal (+124) to possibly safe, Liberal (+69).

HURON COUNTY: NOT A GERRYMANDER

The Bill's reorganization of three Huron-County ridings was not a gerrymander. The Bill transformed Huron East, Huron South, and Huron West into the ridings of Huron Centre, Huron North, and Huron South. A feature of the reorganization, and a fulfilment of Whitney's pledge, was the reunification of Goderich, Hullett, and Turnberry Townships,

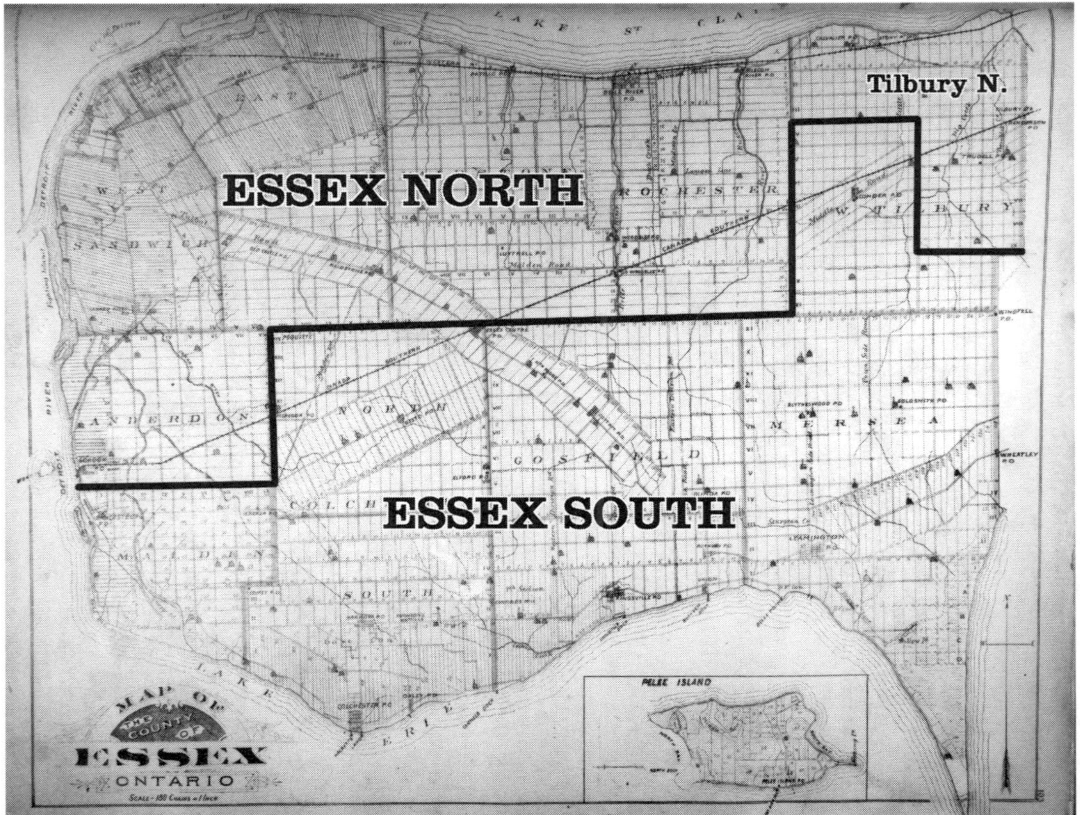

Map 8.2 Essex County ridings, provincial ridings, 1908

which Oliver Mowat's 1874 redistribution had split. Before redistribution, the Huron ridings were reasonably safe, Liberal (+142); very safe, Tory (-411); and precarious, Liberal (+35). After redistribution, they were very safe, Liberal (+442); very safe, Conservative (-205); and very safe, Conservative (-426) – a Tory gain of a seat. In their minority report, the Liberals on the special committee proposed alternative boundaries, which would have retained the prospective Tory gain of a seat, but would have turned all three seats into fighting ridings (+126, -41, and -274). Both the redistribution and the Liberal alternative were positive for the equalization of riding populations.[18] With both adjustments defensible on principle, it would have been asking a lot of the Tories to pick the one from the opposition party.

Summary of the 1908 Provincial Redistribution

Premier Whitney's Act increased the size of Parliament from ninety-eight to one hundred six. It added four seats for Toronto and four for Northern Ontario. It touched twenty-two ridings and increased the percentage of ridings in the optimum zone from 24 to 35.

Ontario's 1908 redistribution, the first ever by a Conservative ministry, was indebted to Canada's Liberal prime minister, Wilfrid Laurier, for two of its features. First, Whitney made county lines his foremost principle, rather than the equalization of populations, which Dominion Tories had favoured during the 1880s and 1890s. Second, Whitney adopted the mechanism of the bipartisan special committee. Unlike the Dominion committee, however, Whitney's committee was a mere ratifying body for details settled in the premier's office.

Whitney's 1908 redistribution was, overall, a "thinly disguised" gerrymander, which paid lip service to principles, emasculated the bipartisan special committee, and predicted an increase in his legislative majority from forty to fifty-two (Table 8.1). This prospective twelve-seat gain came from new seats created from Tory-leaning original ridings, and gerrymanders in Toronto and the counties.[19]

The 1908 general election delivered on the predictions. Whitney's party won eighty-six seats, eight more than predicted. It swept all eight Toronto ridings, all eleven northland ridings, and six county ridings for which redistribution had forecast a gain from the Liberals (Peterborough East, Huron North, Huron South, Brockville, Essex South, and Peel).

Table 8.1 Distribution of provincial seats by party and level of safety, before and after the 1908 redistribution

	Before 1908 redistribution			*After 1908 redistribution: Predictions for 1908 election*		
	Conservative	*Liberal*	*All parties*	*Conservative*	*Liberal*	*All parties*
hive (500+)	43%	10%	34%	46%	11%	37%
very safe (200–499)	32%	31%	32%	24%	37%	28%
reasonably safe (100–199)	12%	28%	16%	15%	15%	15%
possibly safe (50–99)	10%	7%	9%	8%	15%	10%
precarious (< 50)	3%	24%	9%	6%	22%	10%
acclamation/ same party	0%	0%	0%	0%	0%	0%
# of ridings	69	29	98	78	26	106
not counted		0			1	

THE 1914 REDISTRIBUTION

Given the serious illness of Premier Whitney, his provincial secretary, William J. Hanna, introduced the 1914 Bill and piloted it through the Legislative Assembly. Hanna, a corporate lawyer from Sarnia, a gifted orator, and a practitioner of "rough politics," was then favoured to succeed the ailing Whitney as premier.[20]

By 1914 Whitney's provincial Tories had close ties with Robert Borden's Dominion Tories.[21] In 1907 Borden and Whitney had created one organization for their two parties, with J.S. Carstairs, an historian, as organizer and A.E. Kemp as financial manager. Whitney's men ran the organization and planned Borden's 1908 and 1911 campaigns in Ontario. Frank Cochrane, Whitney's minister of Mines, and J.S. Carstairs organized Borden's 1911 campaign in Ontario, to the point of influencing the selection of Tory candidates for the Dominion election. In March 1914 both Conservative Parties prepared to hold redistributions. Thus, before introducing the provincial Bill, Hanna and Carstairs visited Ottawa to confer with Borden's ministers from Ontario and Conservative members of the Dominion redistribution committee. "The coming Provincial redistribution," reported the Toronto *Globe*, "has a bearing also on the Federal redistribution of Ontario, and hence Mr. Hanna has been called into consultation before the operation is performed."[22] Ontario's Representation Act, 1914, came into force on 1 May. The Dominion Act followed on 12 June.

Urbanization, rural depopulation, and settlement of the northlands had developed apace during the decade 1901–11. The percentage increase of population was 16 for the province, but 83 for the northland districts, and 52 for the GTA. Toronto had 381,833 people, an 81 percent increase from 1901. The northland districts held 266,170 people.

The redistribution boosted the size of the provincial parliament from 106 to 111. To arrive at an increase of five ridings, Hanna abolished the purely-electoral county of Monck and set up six new ridings: St. Catharines, Niagara Falls, and Windsor, which were part-city ridings; two Toronto ridings, Parkdale and Riverdale; and Cochrane, which comprised parts of the districts of Temiskaming, Algoma, and Fort William.

The government's ostensible purpose for redistribution was to equalize population.[23] In response to a Liberal query about the "unit of population," however, Hanna stated that "we have been given a pretty wide latitude as between high and low." In the event, Hanna struck the now-customary bipartisan select committee, whose task, as in 1908, was merely to react to schedules prepared by a committee of cabinet. Hanna, chair of the 1908 committee, now chaired the 1914 committee, which met on three occasions in April. The *Globe* did not report the size of the committee or the names of its members, but its reportage identified seven members: four Conservatives and three Liberals. Given that government held 81 percent of the seats, the committee is likely to have included six or seven Conservatives in total – a tidy majority for the government party. The committee included the Hon. Isaac B. Lucas, the provincial treasurer, and Newton W. Rowell, leader of the Liberal Party. Also on the committee was William Proudfoot (Liberal, Huron Centre), who, in 1913, had charged Hanna with corruption. Although the charge did not stick, it left a blemish on the Whitney record.[24]

Perhaps because of Proudfoot's presence on the committee, Hanna managed it roughly. At the first meeting of the committee, Newton Rowell

> asked if the Select Committee on Redistribution would meet before Easter. Opposition members of the committee would like an opportunity to consider changes proposed by the Government and consult their friends in the ridings affected. The Government has had plenty of time to formulate its program, and it would not be giving the

> members of the opposition an opportunity of dealing properly with the proposed changes unless a few weeks' time was provided to let them study the changes.
>
> 'There would be a great deal in the hon. member's argument if there [were] going to be any substantial changes,' said Mr. Hanna. 'It may relieve the hon. member to know that there will be very few changes.' 'If there will be very few changes it should not be necessary to keep us waiting so long.' 'I think I have eliminated the worst of it,' said Mr. Hanna, with a smile.[25]

At the final meeting of the committee, two weeks later, Hanna presented a complete draft schedule of proposed ridings and wanted the committee to report to the House forthwith, "without discussion, without consideration. To this Mr. Rowell would not consent: 'Do we understand that we are not going to have an opportunity to consider these proposals?' he asked with amazement. 'We should have the opportunity of hearing from different parts of the Province before making these changes. The government has had a year to consider its proposals, and they had only been laid before the committee a few moments ago: surely it was only fair that the opposition should have time to consider them.' Replied Mr. Hanna, 'You are just as well equipped to make any comment on these schedules now as you will be a year from now.'"[26]

Case Studies

Four case studies unpack features of the 1914 redistribution. In Bruce County, a gerrymander "hived the Grits" and left Bruce with more ridings than its population warranted. In Essex County, redistribution benefited the opposition Liberals, which was the antithesis of a gerrymander. In the Niagara region, redistribution benefited the government party, with more ridings than population warranted. Redistribution for Toronto retained unusual features of the city's electoral district and added to its complexity.

BRUCE COUNTY: A GERRYMANDER

Liberals held all three Bruce County ridings (+104, +391, and +305). The redistribution hived the Grits into Bruce West (+1,041) to give the government party prospective majorities in the North and South ridings (-234 and -6) – a prospective gain of two seats for the government party. Although the redistribution equalized population in the three ridings,[27] the county's 2.10 standard populations sufficed for two ridings, not the three retained.

The gerrymander worked. Two of the three ridings returned Tories in the 1914 general election (a gain of two for the government party).[28] All but three of the twenty-eight Bruce-County municipalities retained their party preferences from the 1911 general election. However, a recount for Bruce North (-23) gave the victory to the Liberal (+7).

ESSEX COUNTY: THE OPPOSITION DID WELL

Essex County, with 2.82 standard populations, merited a third seat. The redistribution divided Essex North (1.78) and Essex South (1.05) into the ridings of Essex North (1.03), Essex South (0.80), and Windsor, which comprised the city of Windsor and the towns of Walkerville and Sandwich (0.96). It was not a gerrymander. It observed county lines and equalized populations, and, prospectively, it benefited the opposition Liberals. Before redistribution, Conservatives held Essex North, possibly safe (-53) and Essex South, reasonably safe (-130). With redistribution, Essex North became, prospectively, reasonably safe, Liberal (+137); Essex South became reasonably safe, Conservative (-174); and the new riding of Windsor was very safe, Conservative (-290). Thus, the opposition Liberals, prospectively, gained a seat. The Liberals gained two seats in the 1914 general election by sweeping all three Essex ridings. Possibly the Liberals would have done well without an assist from redistribution. As Jack Cécillon judges, Liberal fortunes in the Essex ridings turned on the issue of French-language rights in Roman Catholic schools.[29]

THE NIAGARA REGION: TOO MANY RIDINGS

The redistribution for the Niagara region abolished the electoral county of Monck and repatriated its municipal parts to their home counties of Haldimand, Lincoln, and Welland. Additionally it created the part-city riding of St. Catharines, by separating it from Lincoln, and the part-city riding of Niagara Falls, by separating it from Welland (Map 8.3).

The redistribution benefited the government party. Each party held two seats before redistribution: the Liberals held Monck (+154) and Haldimand (+425), and the Tories held Lincoln (acclamation) and Welland (-805). Redistribution prospectively gave the Tories three seats (St. Catharines, acclamation; Niagara Falls, -428; and Welland, -438), and a chance for a fourth (Lincoln, a mix of +374 and Tory acclamation, hence no prediction). It favoured the Liberals in one riding (Haldimand, +227, down from +425).

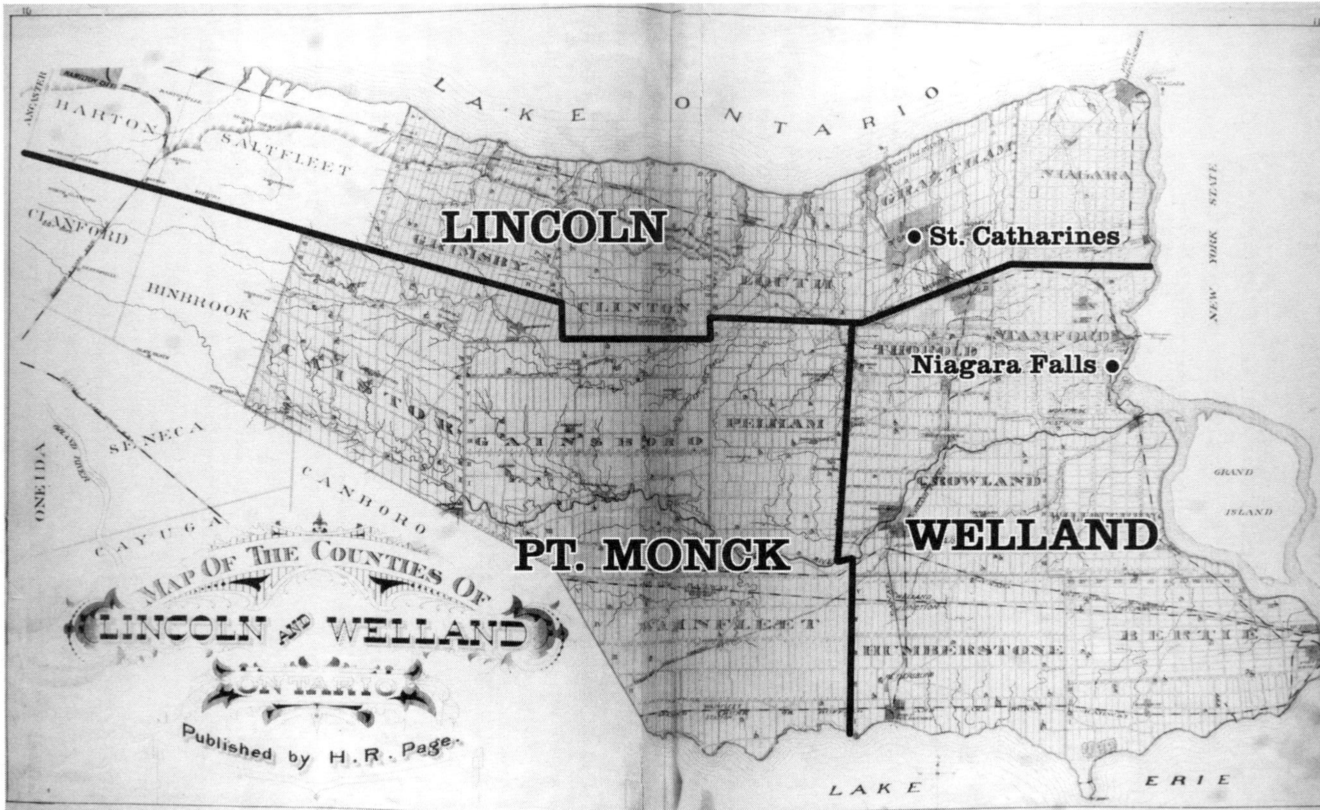

Map 8.3 Ridings of Lincoln, Welland, and (part) Monck, provincial ridings, 1914

The redistribution equalized populations,[30] and its abolition of Monck restored county lines that John A. Macdonald had shredded in 1867. Yet redistribution increased the number of ridings from four to five, one more than the region's 4.36 standard populations warranted. It was a thinly disguised gerrymander, which used principles – county lines and population equalization – to mask partisan gain from its establishment of too many ridings.

The gerrymander worked in the 1914 general election. In the five ridings overall, just five of the forty-three municipalities changed their party preference. The Tories won four of the five ridings, all but Lincoln (no prediction). Against prediction, the government party won Haldimand, where the four in-transfers from the defunct Monck riding (-197) gave the Tory candidate an unexpectedly large majority (-457).

TORONTO CITY AND THE YORK RIDINGS

A principle in Dominion redistribution was that ridings in Toronto should have larger populations than other Ontario ridings. Inasmuch as the province had no quota for the number of seats, it could add ridings for cities without pressure to eliminate ridings in the counties. Effectively, it could offer city ridings fuller representation, for smaller populations, than could a Dominion special committee.

Before redistribution, Toronto had four ridings and eight members for 13.79 standard populations. Any increase in representation stood to strengthen the Tory benches in the next general election. The Liberal-majority statistics for the incumbents ranged from -708 to -3,950. City voters in the York ridings also favoured the Conservatives: their statistics were -459 in York East and -663 in York West.

The 1914 provincial redistribution for Toronto had three features. First, it left the city's electoral territory unchanged. Toronto's recently annexed territories remained in the York ridings. Second, it carved out two new single-member ridings within the existing electoral territory: Parkdale, from part of Toronto West, and Riverdale from part of Toronto East. Third, it retained the four two-member simultaneous-election constituencies of the 1908 redistribution. Thus, the city's representation increased from four ridings and eight members to six ridings and ten members, a prospective gain of two members for the Tory benches. The riding populations were unequal, and, contrary to principle, city ridings had lower population than two county ridings (York East, 1.85, and York West, 2.18). The redistribution predicted a Tory sweep of the Toronto and York-County ridings. The 1914 general election delivered as forecast.

Overview of 1914

The 1914 redistribution was a mild gerrymander, thinly disguised. First, it prospectively boosted the government party's count of seats from eighty-one to eighty-nine, and its majority from fifty-six to sixty-seven. The prospective gains included all six new ridings and two other ridings taken from the Liberals.[31] As in 1908, the special committee of 1914 was an empty shell, a mere ratifying body for decisions issuing from the government party. The case studies revealed elements of gerrymandering, including "hiving the Grits" and leaving too many ridings in Bruce County, and creating more ridings than population warranted in the Niagara region.

Local redistributions, gerrymandered or not, worked for the government party in the 1914 general election. The party was less successful overall. The election returned eighty-four Tories, five short of prediction. The government party won just four of the new seats, not six. It lost thirteen seats that it was predicted to win and won seven seats that it was predicted to lose.

Redistributions and Municipal-City Territories, 1894–1914

Annexations enlarged the municipal territories of cities during the years 1894–1914. As discussed below, the redistributions of 1894, 1908, and 1914 ignored the issue, and the 1902 redistribution did not face it, being exclusively for Northern Ontario.

HAMILTON

The 1894 Representation Act divided "the city of Hamilton ... into two electoral districts," Hamilton East and Hamilton West. The two ridings, in turn, comprised those parts of the city lying east and west "of the centre line of Hughson Street" and proceeding "to the southerly limit of said city." Returns for the 1898 general election do not report any city polls in the Wentworth County ridings. One might infer, mistakenly, that the 1894 Act divided the municipal city into two ridings, which included Hamilton's annexed territories. The 1908 and 1914 Representation Acts repeat verbatim the 1894 delineation of the Hamilton ridings, and returns for the 1908 and 1914 general elections do not report city polls in Wentworth-County ridings. Here again, one might infer that the city ridings for all three redistributions (1894, 1908, and 1914) included Hamilton's recently annexed territories.

Such an inference would be incorrect. Returns for Wentworth South in the 1923 general election report eight polls, 2,137 electors, and 774 voters for "East Hamilton" (Hamilton East). This was possible only if the 1914 redistribution, and possibly the 1894 and 1908 redistributions, had left some city fragments outside the city ridings. The safest assumption is that all provincial redistributions left the Hamilton ridings undisturbed, with the annexed territories in the county ridings.

LONDON

One may assume that none of the 1894, 1902, 1908, and 1914 provincial redistributions enlarged London's electoral district to include annexed territories. Oliver Mowat's 1885 redistribution transferred London East Village (annexed in 1885) to the riding of London City, but the redistributions of 1894 and 1902 left London City alone. Consequently, the city riding of 1902 excluded London South Village (annexed in 1890) and London West Village (annexed in 1898). Returns for the 1890 and 1898 general elections report polls for London West Village in the riding of Middlesex East, but the returns for the 1905 general election do not, even though London West Village, like the never-mentioned London South Village, was still in the riding. Effectively, a non-mention of city polls in returns belies their presence.

In this context, the 1908 and 1914 Representation Acts each list "the city of London" as an electoral district, and returns for the 1908, 1911, and 1914 general elections each make no mention of city polls in the Middlesex East riding. Nevertheless, returns for Middlesex East in the 1923 general election report nine polls, 3,168 electors, and 1,193 polled votes for "London Annex." This was possible only if the 1908 and 1914 redistributions had left the villages of London South and London West in the county riding.

TORONTO

One might assume, mistakenly, that none of the 1894, 1902, 1908, and 1914 provincial redistributions enlarged Toronto's electoral district to include annexed territories. The 1894 and 1908 Representation Acts each divided the "City of Toronto" into four electoral districts (Toronto East, Toronto North, Toronto South, and Toronto West), with the West Toronto riding including "the remainder of the city not included in the other three electoral divisions." Returns for the 1898, 1905, and 1908 general elections do not report city polls in York-County ridings.

Yet returns for the York ridings in the 1911 general election, with no intervening redistribution, do. This means that the 1908 redistribution, and possibly the 1894 redistribution, left annexed territories in York-County ridings. The 1914 Representation Act did so explicitly. York East included "that part of the City of Toronto which was formerly the town of North Toronto, and that part of Ward 1 of said City which lies east of Woodbine Avenue and its production northerly and southerly to the city limits"; and York West included "that part of the City of Toronto known as Ward 7."

OTTAWA

Oliver Mowat's 1894 redistribution placed all of the municipal city of Ottawa in the city's two-member riding. It also gave the city riding "the incorporated villages of Ottawa East and Hintonburg and the unincorporated village of Mechanicsville," ostensibly due to Mowat's belief that the city was about to annex them.[32] His belief was misplaced: their annexations awaited the years 1907–09.

The 1908 Representation Act divided the two-member Ottawa riding into two one-member constituencies, each comprising four wards; by this time, the wards included five newly annexed territories, two being Ottawa East and Hintonburg.

The 1914 Representation Act gave the riding of Ottawa West five wards as constituted on 1 January 1911. This deadline excluded Mechanicsville, which the city annexed in 1911. Thus, bizarrely, Mechanicsville was in the city riding for seventeen years, when it was not part of the municipal city; then, three years after the municipal city annexed it, the 1914 redistribution placed it in the county riding of Carleton.[33]

SUMMARY AND INTERPRETATION

The Ontario population boomed during the 1880s, stagnated during the 1890s, and flourished during the 1900s. In this context, the Liberal redistributions of 1894 and 1902 were minor in scope and the Tory redistributions of 1908 and 1914 were major affairs.

THE MINOR REDISTRIBUTIONS OF 1894 AND 1902

Ontario's Representation Act of 1894 was exclusively for cities. It added three new seats, one for each of Toronto, Hamilton, and Ottawa. The Act left Toronto under-represented by population, but not the province's other cities. It ended the ministry's experiment with Toronto as a three-member riding, but made Ottawa a two-member one.

George Ross's 1902 redistribution increased the representation for Northern Ontario from five members to nine. It made no other changes. It served Ross's belief that a focus on "New Ontario" was the key to the survival of his administration. The division of three northland constituencies, all with Liberal incumbents, into seven ridings was beneficial to Liberal-Party prospects.

WHITNEY'S 1908 REDISTRIBUTION: A GERRYMANDER

The 1908 redistribution was the first major revision of provincial ridings since 1885 and the first-ever by a Conservative administration. Yet Premier Whitney's approach borrowed from the Dominion Liberals. First, he made municipal boundaries his controlling principle, rather than the equalization of population, which the Dominion Tories had once favoured. Second, he adopted Laurier's mechanism of a bipartisan special committee on redistribution. There Whitney's similarity to Laurier ended. Laurier's special committee had worked out the details of the redistribution. Whitney's special committee, in contrast, was a mere rubber-stamp "ratifying body" for details issuing from a committee of cabinet.

Whitney's 1908 Representation Act was a gerrymander. Based on Liberal-majority statistics for the 1905 election, the Act increased the prospective Tory majority from forty to fifty-two. Of this twelve-seat gain, four came from the creation of new ridings in Northern Ontario, four came from the doubling of representation for Toronto, and four came from the rearrangement of the county ridings. Whitney's redistribution held gerrymanders. These worked in the 1908 general election, gaining the government party five seats (two in Toronto and one each in Brockville, Essex, and Peel).

W.J. HANNA'S 1914 REDISTRIBUTION

Ontario's 1914 redistribution boosted the number of provincial ridings from 106 to 111. To arrive at an increase of five ridings, Premier Whitney's provincial secretary, William J. Hanna, abolished the electoral county of Monck and added six ridings. His redistribution touched thirty-one of the 106 ridings (29 percent) and boosted the percentage in the optimum zone from a dismal 12 to 23. It shrunk the electoral district of Ottawa to exclude the unincorporated village of Mechanicsville, but otherwise the electoral and municipal territories of Ottawa matched. No matches obtained for Hamilton, London, or Toronto. The Representation Act also left intact Toronto's four double-member, double-election ridings.

Overall, the 1914 redistribution was a mild gerrymander. The opposition-party voice was a dead letter on Hanna's special committee. Hanna orchestrated local gerrymanders to boost Tory prospects in the Niagara region, Toronto, and Bruce County. The gerrymanders worked in the 1914 general election. Votes in the townships, towns, and villages of the gerrymandered ridings went as predicted, and the government party did better than predicted in those elections. The Conservative Party was less successful overall, with eighty-four members elected, five short of prediction.

The 1914 redistributions, Dominion and provincial, were the last hurrah for the two-party system of Conservatives and Liberals, which had dominated Ontario since Confederation. Chapter 9 discusses the redistributions of the 1920s, which featured new parties, the United Farmers of Ontario (or the Progressives) and a new Independent Labour Party.

9

Mackenzie King and Howard Ferguson: Redistributions of the 1920s

The 1920s produced four redistribution Bills and three Representation Acts for Ontario. The special committee for a 1923 Dominion Bill failed to produce a schedule of ridings for Ontario, but an identical committee delivered one for enactment in 1924. The Provincial Legislative Assembly passed a Representation Act in 1925, and amended it with an Act in 1926. The Dominion Act was mandatory, following issuance of the 1921 national census. The Ontario Acts were optional.

During the decade 1911–21, the Ontario population grew by 16 percent. The regional statistics were the GTA, 42 percent; the northland districts, 18; Western Ontario, 12; and Eastern Ontario, 3. Ontario cities increased in number from nineteen to twenty-five, and their population rose by 43 percent. In 1921 cities held 40 percent of the provincial population, up from 33 in 1911. In 1921 the population of Toronto was 521,893. That of the northland districts was 313,341.

The post-war rise of the Progressives, a political movement of farmers and labourers, transformed Ontario's traditional two-party rivalry into a three-party competition in both parliaments. In the 1921 Dominion general election, the Progressives contested sixty-nine of the eighty-two Ontario ridings and won twenty.[1] After the 1919 Ontario general election, the forty-five members-elect of the United Farmers of Ontario (UFO) – the provincial branch of the Progressives – joined with eleven members-elect of the Independent Labour Party (ILP) to form a UFO–ILP coalition ministry. Although Howard Ferguson's Conservatives toppled the Farmers' government in the general election of 1923, the UFO contested seventy-six of the one hundred eleven ridings and won seventeen, and the ILP contested twenty-nine ridings and won four.[2]

The three-party system mattered in the 1924 Dominion parliament, where Mackenzie King, the Liberal prime minister, headed Canada's first-ever minority government (one hundred sixteen Liberals, sixty-four Progressives, fifty Conservatives, and five others) and held a minority of the Ontario seats (Conservative, thirty-seven; Progressive, twenty-two; Liberal, twenty-one; Independent, two). King's style of politics also shaped the fate of his redistribution Bills. As John English argues, Robert Borden, prime minister for the 1914 redistribution, had favoured "creative" politics and avoided expedient-based compromise. In contrast, Mackenzie King embraced brokerage politics, "which minimizes differences, avoids conflict, and makes politics an end in itself."[3] This may account for King's stunning lack of direction to Parliament for his doomed 1923 Bill.

The three-party system mattered less in the provincial parliament, where Howard Ferguson, the Conservative premier, led a strong majority government (Conservatives, seventy-five; UFO–ILP, twenty-one; Liberal, fourteen; Independent, one). In both parliaments, the Progressives held the second greatest number of seats but declined to become the official opposition. Thus, the third-place party filled this role – the Conservatives under the Hon. Arthur Meighen in the Dominion parliament, and the Liberals under William E.N. Sinclair in the provincial parliament.

THE 1923–24 DOMINION REDISTRIBUTION BILLS

The Abortive 1923 Redistribution Bill

Prime Minister King named a special committee of nineteen to draw up a revised schedule of ridings. The special committee, in turn, struck a six-member subcommittee to deal with Ontario.[4] The large size of the national committee resulted from the circumstances of the hung parliament. The Hon. Arthur Meighen, leader of the third-place Conservative Party, pressed successfully for a minimum of four Tory members to give coverage to Canada's five regions. On the basis of party strengths in the House, this entitled the Progressives, the second-place party, to five members, and the governing Liberals to ten (a bare majority). Edward Macdonald (Liberal, Pictou, Nova Scotia), the acting Defence minister, chaired the national committee. The Hon. Thomas Low (Liberal, Renfrew South), King's minister of Trade and Commerce, chaired the six-man subcommittee for Ontario, which comprised two Liberals, two Conservatives, and two Progressives.

The Ontario subcommittee failed to complete a schedule of ridings during the parliamentary session, and so the national committee recommended successfully that the mandatory redistribution be put over for one year. Progress had been painfully slow on the subcommittee. A Conservative on the subcommittee, Donald Sutherland (Oxford South), faulted the general committee for want of direction "as to how redistribution should be brought about."[5] Indeed, Prime Minister King stated no principles for redistribution on moving the second reading of the Bill, which passed without debate. The following day, W.F. Maclean (Independent Conservative, York South), a champion of full representation by population for cities as defined by their municipal boundaries, asked the prime minister "whether an opportunity will be given to members of the House to discuss the principle of the Bill before it goes to committee?" King evaded the question, so Maclean repeated it. King's blunt reply: "Yesterday my hon. friend had that opportunity, as every member of the House had [on second reading of the Bill], and if he missed that opportunity, he will no doubt on the third reading have a chance to say something."[6]

The 1924 Representation Act

The 1921 census entitled Ontario to eighty-two seats in the Dominion parliament, the same as its previous quota. Although the province held just 80.9 Quebec-standard populations, section 51.4 of the 1867 BNA Act provided that a province's quota could not decline if the ratio of its population to the Canadian population had diminished by less than one-twentieth. The 1924 Representation Act added seven seats and eliminated seven seats. It touched thirty-seven of the eighty-two ridings (45 percent) and raised the percentage of ridings with population in the optimum zone (0.90–1.10) from 17 to 22.

King reappointed the special committee of 1923, with its six-man subcommittee for Ontario. Thomas Low (Liberal, Renfrew South), King's minister of Trade and Commerce, chaired the subcommittee of six, which comprised two members from each of the three parties.[7] The other five were: James Rankin (Liberal, Perth North), a future senator (1925); John Kennedy (Progressive, Glengarry-Stormont); John King (Progressive, Huron North); Hugh Stewart (Conservative, Leeds), future minister of Public Works in the R.B. Bennett administration; and Donald Sutherland (Conservative, Oxford South), a future minister-without-portfolio in the short-lived Arthur Meighen ministry (1926) and a senator (1935). On 3 July 1924, Low left the special committee due to ill health, and Harold McGiverin (Liberal, Ottawa), replaced him as chair.[8]

Following the procedures of the 1903 redistribution, the 1924 subcommittee set the number of seats for Toronto and then calculated the unit of population for all other Ontario ridings.[9] That done, the subcommittee drafted the schedule of ridings, which the special committee and the House accepted without major alteration.

Principles for the Dominion Redistribution

This time King stated four principles to guide the special committee.[10] First, the committee was to observe county lines: "the municipal organization is the basis of our entire judicial system, of our municipal system, and by holding to the county unit, municipal organization, we are following a basis that is familiar to the citizens of the country generally." Second, the committee was to set a larger unit of population for urban constituencies than for rural ridings. Rural ridings had more scattered populations, were less easily organized, and in several cases had city men representing them. Third, the ridings should be compact "so that public opinion within one given area will be as nearly true to the feeling of the whole community as it is possible to get it." Fourth, the committee was to equalize population separately for city ridings and rural ridings. King opined that the work of equalization could not be done with "mathematical precision," but was to be guided by "fair play."

Progressives, predominantly a farmers' movement, emphasized the prime minister's first principle, county lines. John Kennedy, a Progressive on the subcommittee, agreed "with the principle that as far as possible county boundaries should be maintained, for the reasons already given by the Prime Minister. I might refer also to [Prime Minister King's] fourth principle, that of maintaining as far as possible, as between rural constituencies, a uniformity of population. Where there is a conflict between these two principles, the principle of maintaining county boundaries and that of maintaining uniformity in population … the people are more concerned in maintaining their county boundaries than they are in having population nearly equal as between county constituencies. So in my opinion the fourth principle should be sacrificed to the first when there is a conflict between the two."[11]

Conservatives, whose party polled strongly in cities, gave primacy to population as the basis of representation, and rejected King's second and fourth principles, which dealt with rural-urban differences in the unit of population. Donald Sutherland, a Tory on the subcommittee, opined that the adoption of universal suffrage (in 1918) had based the franchise on human rights, not property rights, as of old.[12] Inasmuch as human rights were equal across the ridings, so too should be the weight of a vote, and hence the population of the ridings. Equality was not the case in 1924, decried Horatio Hocken (Conservative, Toronto West), and he asked: "Why should a mechanic have less influence than a farm labourer? ... Why does it take two men living in a city to have the same influence as one farmer?"[13] As his fellow Tory, Sutherland, noted, "There are fourteen constituencies where the unit of population averages 55,109, [and] the other sixty-eight have an average unit of 31,796 ... Placing them upon an equality with the other sixty-eight, there are 26,192 in every one of these fourteen constituencies who are not entitled to exercise the franchise to the same degree ... They are absolutely disenfranchised to that extent."[14]

A key argument for giving rural constituencies a smaller unit of population than cities had been that their populations were more scattered and less easily organized than city ridings. "That argument might have been good enough twenty-five or thirty years ago," countered Hocken, "but it is not of any weight to-day. The rural districts of every province enjoy good roads and the people there own motor cars; the press is scattered daily by the rural mailmen to every home in the farming districts; and I presume that by the time we have another general election radio will be added to these means of communication."[15] Arthur Meighen, past prime minister and now leader of the opposition, agreed that "improved methods of transportation, the additional railway advantages, the better roads, and particularly the newer and more rapid methods of getting about, have now all combined to bring the country constituency almost to a level with the city constituency in so far as the ease with which a member can reach his constituents is concerned." In the circumstances, the current low representation for cities amounted to "a virtual disenfranchisement of half the cities of Canada."[16]

Effectively, Conservatives differed from the other parties in their principles for redistribution. It remained to be seen how two Liberals, two Progressives, and two Conservatives would function on the subcommittee for Ontario. Also of interest was how the mid-session change in the subcommittee's chair would affect its decisions.

The Work of the Subcommittee

The 1924 Representation Act increased Toronto City from six to nine seats; added two seats to the northland districts; increased Essex-County ridings from two to three; and divided Glengarry-Stormont into the separate ridings of Glengarry and Stormont. To balance those seven additions, it reduced York County from four ridings to three and eliminated six county ridings through mergers.

"The first thing settled in committee," noted Donald Sutherland, a Conservative on the subcommittee, "was the representation to which the city of Toronto would be entitled."[17] As a preliminary step, the subcommittee expanded Toronto's electoral territory to capture the city's municipal fragments in the York ridings. This boosted the city's electoral population from 375,437 to 521,486. Then it set the number of city ridings at nine (up from six), which yielded 57,943 as the unit of population for the Toronto ridings (the city's population divided by nine). This left the unit of population for all other ridings at 32,982 (the balance of the provincial population divided by the seventy-three ridings remaining in the Ontario quota). In this fashion, the Toronto ridings were to have a mean of 1.62 standard populations, and all other ridings, 0.92.

Sutherland lambasted the special committee for having "refused" to lay down some general principles to guide the subcommittee, "ignored almost in their entirety" the principles set forth by the prime minister, and denied the Tory minority on the subcommittee "the right of presenting a minority report either to the main committee or to the House." He detected a conspiracy between the Liberals and Progressives "to put down Toryism in this country."[18] "Some of our most acute difficulties," recalled his Tory colleague Hugh Stewart, "arose from the fact that in the Province of Ontario we had three [political parties], each contending for a point of view which was difficult to harmonize when they were all brought together." Given the "trying" circumstances, Stewart intended "to stand by the report of the committee."[19]

PRINCIPLES AND PRACTICE ON THE SUBCOMMITTEE

The Liberal prime minister's first principle was the observance of county lines, which Progressives argued should be a controlling principle. That is, where the principles of county lines and population equalization clashed, county lines should prevail.

That did not happen when the subcommittee dealt with small-population ridings within counties, such as Peterborough East (0.38), Ontario North (0.43), Elgin East (0.48), and Hastings East (0.64). The solution in these cases, if county lines were to be observed, was to merge the two Peterborough-County ridings, the two Ontario-County ridings, and the two Elgin-County ridings. These hypothetical mergers would have formed the county ridings of Peterborough (1.20), Ontario (1.30), and Elgin (1.25). Hastings County had sufficient population (1.60) for its two ridings, so in this case, the solution was to equalize the populations of Hastings East (0.64) and Hastings West (0.96). A downside of these hypothetical within-county mergers, however, was that their populations were notably higher than 0.92, the unit of population for ridings outside Toronto. Effectively, the equalization of population, coupled with the observance of county lines, meant a reduction of rural representation. Thus, in several cases, discussed below, the subcommittee departed from county lines to equalize populations.

RIDINGS IN THE COUNTIES OF PETERBOROUGH AND HASTINGS

Before redistribution, the riding of Peterborough East (0.38) had insufficient population to warrant separate representation. Second, the two ridings within each county were unequal in population (Peterborough East, 0.38, and Peterborough West, 0.82; Hastings East, 0.64, and Hastings West, 0.96). Third, Peterborough County (1.20) had insufficient population for two ridings (1.50), yet too large a population for one rural riding.

In a compromise, the subcommittee folded the four ridings into three: a mixed-county riding, Hastings-Peterborough (0.81); Peterborough West (0.95); and Hastings South (1.05). The two Conservatives – perhaps mischievously – moved to preserve county lines, first by merging the Peterborough ridings, and second, by leaving alone the Hastings ridings; but they were outvoted by the two Liberals and two Progressives.[20] Effectively, the Liberals and Progressives on the subcommittee sacrificed county lines – the prime minister's first principle and the Progressives' pick for a controlling principle – to equalize populations and maintain a low unit of population for country ridings – the prime minister's second and fourth principles. As the Tory Hugh Stewart summarized, "We have not, unfortunately, been able to follow altogether the county municipal boundaries. I want to say frankly it would be impossible to do so in all cases and at the same time preserve the unit of population."

The clash of principles was difficult for all concerned. In the House, George Brethen (Progressive, Peterborough East) moved an amendment to preserve county lines by merging the Peterborough ridings and leaving the Hastings ridings as they were.[21] John Kennedy, one of the Progressives on the subcommittee, had gone along with the subcommittee's compromise, but spoke against it in the House and voted for the Brethen amendment.[22] The Hon. Edward Macdonald, King's Defence minister[23] and chair of the national committee, defended the subcommittee's compromise, as did George Gordon, the Liberal MP for Peterborough West, and the Brethen amendment was lost, forty to eighty-six.

The transformation of four ridings into three prospectively eliminated one Progressive-held seat; the Tories stood to retain two and the Liberals one. The 1925 general election returned the Conservative candidate in all three seats.

RIDINGS IN THE UNITED-MUNICIPAL COUNTIES OF GRENVILLE-LEEDS AND GLENGARRY-STORMONT-DUNDAS

The province's Territorial Division of Ontario Act compressed five counties into the two united-municipal counties of Glengarry-Stormont-Dundas and Grenville-Leeds. The united county was the municipal county, not its constituent counties, which had no municipal function. From this perspective, neither united-county lines nor population equalization was well served in the redistribution for Grenville (0.47), Dundas (0.68), Glengarry-Stormont (1.08), and Leeds (0.98). First, the subcommittee merged Grenville and Dundas to form the riding of Grenville-Dundas (0.95) – which trespassed on united-county lines. Second, it divided Glengarry-Stormont (1.08) into two ridings, Glengarry (0.57) and Stormont (0.70), and left alone Leeds (0.98). This increased population inequality. Third, it over-represented the two united counties, allowing them four ridings for just 3.21 standard populations.

The redistribution had no effect on prospective party strengths. Like the original ridings, the redistributed ridings were likely to return two Tories and two Progressives. A likely motivation for dividing Glengarry-Stormont was to recognize Glengarry's historical, Highland-Scotch community, which Borden's 1914 redistribution had overturned. John Kennedy, the Progressive incumbent for Glengarry-Stormont and a native of Glengarry, was on the subcommittee.

RURAL-URBAN DIFFERENCES IN POPULATION

The prime minister's second principle was to give city ridings larger populations than country ridings. The subcommittee applied this principle to London (1.50, compared to 0.78 and 0.70 for the Middlesex-County ridings), the two Hamilton ridings (1.52 and 1.49, versus 1.29 for Wentworth), and the two Ottawa ridings (each 1.31, versus 0.91 for

Carleton and 1.21 for Russell). It ignored the principle for Kingston (0.67, compared with 0.85 for Frontenac-Addington) and the nine Toronto ridings (a mean of 1.62, compared with 1.72 for York West).

THE EQUALIZATION OF POPULATION IN THE COUNTIES

The subcommittee increased the percentage of Ontario ridings in the optimum zone from 17 to 22, and, in five cases, it sacrificed county lines to equalize population. It could have done more. In five cases, it declined to equalize riding populations within a county. It left alone four county ridings with less than 0.60 standard populations and seven county ridings with more than 1.20.

Case Studies

ESSEX COUNTY

The redistribution for Essex County evidenced the subcommittee's half-hearted application of the population principle. It divided the two Essex-County ridings (1.99 and 0.88) into three ridings with unequal populations (Essex East, 0.71; Essex South, 0.82; and Essex West, 1.38). The Essex West riding included Windsor City, Sandwich Town, and the townships of Sandwich East and Sandwich West. The subcommittee declined to give separate representation to Windsor City (1.08 standard populations) by giving the Sandwich townships and Sandwich Town to the other Essex ridings. Such redistribution would have rendered the populations more equal among the Essex-County ridings (Essex East, 0.84; Essex South, 0.99; and Windsor, 1.08), while observing city-county lines and leaving the city riding with more population than the county ridings. The Essex-County ridings were Liberal strongholds, prospectively remained so with the redistribution, and would have remained so with the hypothetical alternative redistribution.

WELLINGTON COUNTY: THE LIBERAL MAJORITY PROTECTS PARTY INTERESTS

By 1924 the two Wellington-County ridings had unequal populations: Wellington South, 0.96, and Wellington North, 0.55. The incumbents, John Pritchard (Progressive, Wellington North) and Hugh Guthrie (Conservative, Wellington South), believed that they had an understanding with the subcommittee's chair (Thomas Low, Liberal) to transfer the townships of Nichol and Pilkington from the South riding to the North riding, which would have "made the population of the divisions more nearly even" (0.89 and 0.63). However, Harold McGiverin (Liberal, Ottawa), Low's replacement as subcommittee chair, and Edward Macdonald (Liberal, Pictou, Nova Scotia), chair of the general committee, found that the proposed transfer was "not satisfactory," for reasons unstated. Thus, the general committee, with the unanimous support of the subcommittee, left "the Wellingtons ... as they were in the last redistribution." The matter ended in the Commons when a Pritchard-Guthrie motion to restore the transfer failed, twenty-two to sixty-eight.[24]

Political considerations probably moved the two Liberals to find the proposed transfer "not satisfactory." Despite Pritchard's claim that the proposed transfers would not "affect the political complexion of the county in any way," they in fact would have benefited the incumbents, both of whom were in opposition parties.[25] The proposed transfers mattered little for the North riding, a massive Progressive hive (+1,264), but they would have boosted Conservative prospects in the South riding from reasonably safe (-131) to very safe (-412).

The Politics of Electoral Boundaries for Cities

Each incorporated city was "a county of itself" for municipal purposes. Thus, the city limits were a county line for purposes of redistribution. Over time, Ontario cities extended their municipal territories through annexations. Principle required that a redistribution enlarge the city's electoral district to match its civic territory. Laurier's 1903 redistribution made the match-ups, but Borden's 1914 redistribution did not.

During the years 1903–24, Toronto had annexed twenty-five territories; Hamilton, thirteen; Ottawa, six; and London, five. In addition, Ottawa's Rideau Ward, annexed in 1887, was still in the riding of Russell. The 1921 census reported 28 percent of Toronto's population (521,893) in three York ridings; 22 percent of Hamilton's population (114,151) in Wentworth; 13 percent of Ottawa's population (107,843) in Russell and Carleton; and 11 percent of London's population (65,959) in Middlesex East.

RIDINGS IN TORONTO AND YORK COUNTY

The subcommittee transferred 146,049 Toronto-City residents from the York ridings to city ridings. Then it increased the number of Toronto-City ridings from six to nine, for 14.59 standard populations, and reduced the number of York-County ridings from four to three, for 3.52 standard populations. The redistribution was positive for population equality: the mean standard population for the city ridings dropped from 1.74 to 1.62, and the mean for the York ridings dropped from 1.90 to 1.17. However, populations remained unequal within York County (1.01, 0.78, and 1.73) and within Toronto (ranging from 1.38 for Toronto South to 1.78 for Toronto East).

Donald Sutherland and Hugh Stewart, the Tory minority on the subcommittee, had tried and failed to secure eleven ridings for Toronto, instead of the nine given, and four ridings for York County, instead of the three given. The subcommittee's parsimonious increase of representation for Toronto prospectively gave the Conservatives two additional seats, but only two. Before redistribution, the six city ridings and the three York-County ridings with Toronto-resident populations were Tory hives. York North, the fourth York riding, which held no city fragments, was a Liberal hive. After redistribution, the nine city ridings, prospectively, were Tory hives, a gain of three for the Tories, but the consolidation of the York ridings reduced the Tory gain to two. As predicted, the Tories swept the nine city ridings and the two city-border ridings in York County in the 1925 general election. Against prediction, they won the Liberal stronghold of York North.

RIDINGS IN HAMILTON CITY AND WENTWORTH COUNTY

The Wentworth-County riding included 25,033 city residents in eleven territories that Hamilton had annexed since 1903 (Map 9.1). This gave the county riding a larger population (1.80) than either of the two city ridings (Hamilton East, 1.39, and Hamilton West, 1.10). A transfer of the city fragments to the city ridings would have corrected the problem (giving Wentworth 1.10 standard populations, compared with a mean of 1.60 for the two city ridings).

Politics muddied the waters of the issue. The city ridings were Tory strongholds (-1,496 and -1,952). Wentworth was reasonably safe (-129), but entirely due to city-fragments within the county riding (-2,214). Wentworth without the fragments would have returned the Progressive candidate with a majority of +2,085. Clearly, a transfer of the fragments to city ridings would have "hived" the Tories into Hamilton. Unsurprisingly, Thomas Stewart (Conservative, Hamilton West), "the member for Hamilton for fifteen or sixteen years," wanted the city's electoral boundaries left as they were.[26] Stewart did not get his way. The subcommittee, with its two members from each of the three parties, transferred 18,328 of the 25,033 city residents from Wentworth to city ridings. The change was positive for equalizing populations for the Hamilton ridings

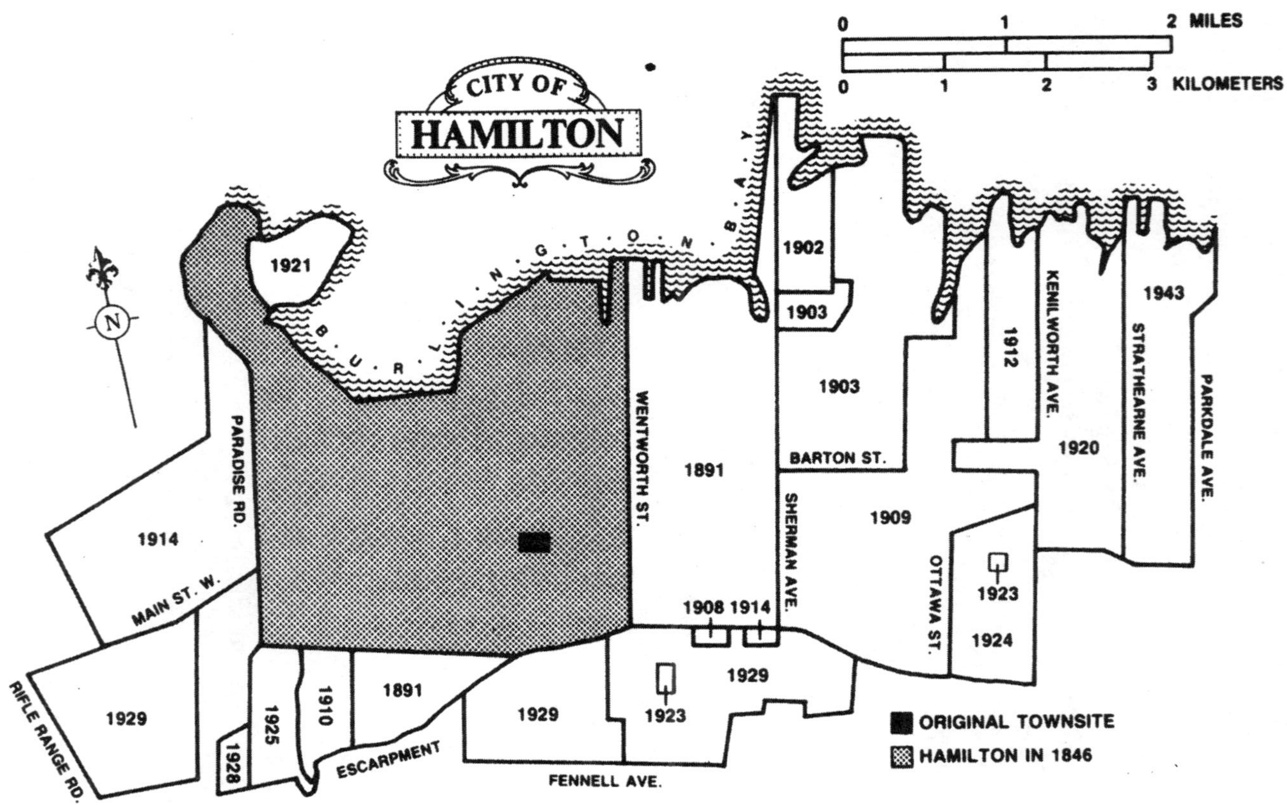

Map 9.1 Annexations by the City of Hamilton to 1945

(1.52 and 1.49) and giving the county riding a smaller population than the city ridings (1.29). It turned Wentworth from reasonably safe, Conservative (-129) into a Progressive hive (+1,492). Prospectively, the opposition Conservatives lost a seat to the other opposition party. Against prediction, the Tories swept the Hamilton and Wentworth ridings in the 1925 general election.

RIDINGS IN OTTAWA AND THE COUNTIES OF CARLETON AND RUSSELL

The 1924 redistribution left alone the ridings of Ottawa, Carleton, and Russell. This flouted county lines, first by leaving the city's Rideau Ward (annexed in 1887) in Russell and parts of its Dalhousie and Victoria Wards (six annexations from the years 1907–11) in Carleton; and second by leaving the Carleton-County townships of Gloucester and Osgoode in Russell. The no-change redistribution was negative for equalizing population.[27] It mattered not at all for prospective party fortunes.[28]

RIDINGS IN LONDON CITY AND MIDDLESEX COUNTY

Politics and complications of principle worked against the extension of London's electoral district to match its municipal territory. The status quo was the ridings of London City (1.50), Middlesex East (0.78), and Middlesex West (0.70). Middlesex East included 7,121 city residents (0.20) in five territories that London had annexed during the years 1912–13. The transfer of the city-fragments from Middlesex East to the London riding would have boosted the city riding's population to 1.70. However, it also would have given the two county ridings a population of 1.28 – well below the threshold for two ridings, yet high for a merged county riding (the rural unit was 0.92). Inasmuch as the incumbents of the county ridings were Progressives, a merger of their ridings would cost their party a seat. The in-transfer of the city fragment (-435) would have strengthened the Tory hold on the London riding, boosting its Liberal-majority statistic from -1,746 to -2,121.

John White (Conservative, London) proposed, unsuccessfully, a division that would have placed more of the municipal city in the rural ridings (London, 1.18, and the county ridings, 0.97 and 0.86).[29] This would have equalized the riding populations, given the city riding a larger population than the county ridings, and given the two county ridings sufficient population to avoid merger. It also would have de-hived Tories out of London, thereby boosting Tory prospects in the county ridings.

Not unreasonably, the subcommittee left the status quo alone. The Conservatives retained London in the 1925 general election. Against prediction, the Progressives lost both county ridings, one to the Liberals and one to the Conservatives.

BRANTFORD

William Good (Progressive) and William Raymond (Liberal) represented the ridings of Brant and Brantford. Good urged that "to separate the rural from the urban populations, other things being equal," was "a wise principle."[30] Thus, he proposed the transfer of Oakland Township and the eastern half of Brant Township into his rural riding, leaving the Brantford riding "as the city alone." He was "quite sure this would meet the wishes of the few farmers who are now thrown into a very large city." His proposal would equalize the riding populations (from 0.56 and 0.93, to 0.66 and 0.83).

Raymond, the Brantford Liberal, defended the status quo: the two townships "had always been associated with the city of Brantford, and [he saw] no reason why they should be removed." The proposed transfer, prospectively, would have boosted the Progressive majority in rural Brant (from +159 to +327), while diminishing the Liberal majority in urban Brantford (+1,987 to +1,819).[31] In the event, the subcommittee left the ridings alone. Both incumbents lost to a Conservative in the 1925 general election.

Overview of the 1924 Dominion Redistribution

The 1924 Representation Act added seven seats and eliminated seven seats to match the Ontario quota of eighty-two. It touched thirty-seven of the eighty-two ridings (45 percent) and raised the percentage of ridings with population in the optimum zone (0.90–1.10) from 17 to 22. It continued the practice, enshrined in principle since the 1890s, of leaving Toronto under-represented in relation to its population. It enlarged Toronto's electoral district to capture territories in York-County ridings that the city had annexed, and Hamilton's electoral district to capture most but not all territories in the Wentworth riding that the city had annexed. It did not match electoral and civic boundaries for Ottawa or London.

On balance, the redistribution was not a gerrymander. Rather, it evidenced the Ontario subcommittee's difficulties in reconciling the prime minister's four cardinal principles; partisan differences over choice of

Table 9.1 Distribution of Dominion seats by party and level of safety, before and after the 1924 redistribution

	Before 1924 redistribution				*After redistribution: Predictions for 1925 election*			
	Cons.	*Lib.*	*Prog.*	*Ont.*	*Cons.*	*Lib.*	*Prog.*	*Ont.*
hive (500+)	78%	76%	50%	70%	79%	77%	63%	75%
very safe (200+)	8%	5%	23%	11%	8%	14%	19%	12%
reasonably safe (100+)	8%	19%	18%	14%	11%	9%	13%	11%
possibly safe (50+)	5%	0%	0%	4%	3%	0%	0%	1%
precarious (< 50)	0%	0%	0%	1%	0%	0%	6%	1%
acclamation	0%	0%	0%	0%	0%	0%	0%	0%
# of ridings	37	21	22	80	38	22	16	76
not counted	2 (independents)				6 (2 independents, 4 unknown)			

controlling principle; and the weakness of the government party, with its minority in Parliament, two opposition parties, and a tripartisan special committee and Ontario subcommittee.

As shown in Table 9.1, the redistribution forecast a gain of one seat each for the governing Liberals and the Conservatives, an advance of four seats to the category of "unknown," and a loss of six seats for the Progressives. The 1925 general election was a Tory rout (Tories, sixty-eight; Liberals, twelve; Progressives, two) that owed nothing to King's 1924 redistribution.

THE PROVINCIAL REDISTRIBUTION OF 1925–26

Ontario's population underwent robust growth and urbanization during the decade 1911–21. It rose by 42 percent in the GTA, more than double the 16 percent increase for the province. The number of cities and towns with 10,000+ people increased from nineteen to twenty-five, and their net population rose by 43 percent. The percentage gains were average for the northlands (18 percent), and below average for the western counties (12 percent) and the eastern counties (3 percent).

The electoral territories of Toronto, Hamilton, and London dated from 1885, and that of Ottawa from 1914. In the interim, Toronto had annexed thirty-seven suburban territories; Hamilton, sixteen; and

London, seven (see Appendix A). The Ottawa-City ridings excluded the village of Mechanicsville, annexed in 1911. In the 1923 general election, 17 percent of the Toronto-City electors were in the ridings of York East and York West, where they comprised 58 and 39 percent respectively of the electors in those ridings. Fifteen percent of the Hamilton-City electors were in the ridings of Wentworth North and Wentworth South, where they comprised 46 percent of the electors. Nine percent of the London-City electors were in Middlesex East, where they comprised 14 percent of the electors. One percent of Ottawa-City electors (Mechanicsville) were in the riding of Carleton, where they comprised 4 percent of the electors.

In this context, Howard Ferguson, Ontario's Conservative premier, and William Sinclair, leader of the official-opposition Liberals, agreed to a redistribution before the next general election.[32] Their agreement produced the Representation Act, 1925, and amendments to the Representation Act, 1926.

Principles

The Conservative government's general principle was to increase representation for cities and suburbs. As the premier opined, "large increases in population in Hamilton and Wentworth had to be taken care of." Toronto and York County held "a quarter of the population of the Province, [but] had only one-sixth of the representation." The government's second, unstated principle was to cap the size of Parliament at 112 seats, an increase of one. From this self-imposed quota followed a third principle: the elimination of county ridings to make room for the increase of representation for cities, while holding the line on representation for Northern Ontario. Absent was the notion that city ridings should have larger populations than country ridings. However, Premier Ferguson did say that he kept the rural unit of population as low as possible, by which he meant a minimum population of 15,000 (0.57) for representation.[33] A fourth principle was the observance of county lines. The government, declared the Hon. William Price, the provincial treasurer and a member of the special committee, "had been careful not to cut up counties [and] in the case of Toronto had done its best to preserve the ward boundaries." Price likened "wards in the city to counties in the country. There was a definite organization for municipal purposes in each ward, and it was only right and proper that the wards be preserved as far as possible." He did not mention matching the electoral districts of cities to their civic territories. Minimal interference was a fifth principle. As the Toronto *Globe* reported, "it had been the government's earnest desire to effect redistribution with a minimum of change, and the Premier expressed the opinion that this had been done."

The Special Committee

Premier Ferguson named a tripartisan special committee of fifteen to draft a schedule of ridings for the 1925 redistribution. This departed from Tory practice for the 1908 and 1914 redistributions, whereby a committee of cabinet had drafted the schedule, and the special committee had been a mere ratifying body. The special committee represented parties according to their strength in the House: thus, ten Conservatives, two United Farmers, two Liberals, and one Labour. The committee included three ministers: Premier Ferguson (Grenville); the Hon. George Henry (York East), minister of Highways and the committee chair; and the Hon. William Price (Toronto Parkdale), provincial treasurer.

The Redistribution

The redistribution increased the number of ridings from 111 to 112, thirty more than the number of Dominion ridings. It added nine ridings for cities: five for Toronto; third ridings for Ottawa and Hamilton; and second ridings for London and Windsor. It increased York County from three ridings to four. It divided Cochrane into two ridings, an increase of one seat for Northern Ontario. To make room for its eleven additions to Parliament, the redistribution eliminated ten county seats. Simcoe County went from four ridings to three. The counties of Bruce, Grey, Huron, Middlesex, Lennox & Addington, Frontenac, and Wellington went from three ridings to two. The counties of Durham, Norfolk, and Northumberland went from two ridings to one.

The 1925–26 redistribution touched fifty-six of the one hundred eleven ridings (51 percent) and raised the percentage of ridings in the optimum-population zone (0.90–1.10) from 15 to 24. The select committee pegged the minimum population for representation at 15,000. The number of county ridings below this threshold dropped from nineteen to two. Even so, Victoria North (14,841) and Lanark North (14,286), two Tory-held seats, survived the chop, while Bruce West, a Liberal-held seat with a population of 15,247, did not.

The Conservative government had little reason to gerrymander, given its large majority in the House (seventy-five of the one hundred eleven seats, with the thirty-six opposition seats divided between two opposition parties). Without gerrymanders, moreover, the redistribution was likely to benefit the government party. The Tories polled well in cities, which were gaining seats, but less well in the counties, whose ridings were undergoing consolidation. Indeed, declared William Price, the provincial treasurer, the government "had refrained entirely from anything approaching a gerrymander." It had made "no effort to hive Opposition ridings," stated George Henry, the committee's chair.[34]

But the 1925–26 redistribution was a gerrymander against the Progressive–United Farmers Party, which prized strong representation for rural populations. The 1925 Act, opined the Hon. William E. Raney, leader of the Progressives, was crafted to guarantee the Conservatives a majority "for 15 to 20 years." Raney, who had been attorney-general in the UFO–ILP coalition ministry (1919–23), was a staunch supporter of the Ontario Temperance Act, 1916 (OTA), which banned the sale of alcoholic beverages in the province. Thus, he lamented that "nine ridings have been taken from rural Ontario and ten urban constituencies added. The rural ridings gave [a] 72,000 majority in favour of the Ontario Temperance Act, while every one of the new urban divisions is assumed to be wet." Raney subsequently "named Addington, Northumberland, Middlesex, Wellington, Bruce, Huron, Norfolk, and Grey, all returning large dry majorities in the [1924 OTA] plebiscite, as losing in total nine ridings, and ten new wet ridings are created – five in Toronto, one in London, one in Hamilton, one in Ottawa, one in the rural Yorks, and one in Windsor."[35] Raney received more bad news from the 1926 Act, which reduced Simcoe County from four dry ridings to three.[36]

Matthew Lang (Liberal, Cochrane), a member of the special committee and a champion for Northern Ontario, was outraged that the committee had "laid aside" a claim for additional representation for the northlands from "a committee of four New Ontario members." He "went on to declare, pounding his desk, that this [Act] would go down in the history of the Province as the worst gerrymander that was ever perpetrated." Lang was especially piqued that the 1925 Act had not divided his own riding into two. First, he was certain that the 1921 census statistic for Cochrane, 29,500, was low; a new census would find more than 60,000. Second, the huge territories and scattered populations of the northlands warranted a below-average threshold of population for representation. Thus, he "condemned the proposal to put fifteen members in Toronto, in ridings … 'the members could step across.' Why there were parts of his northern riding that he had never seen!" An editorial in the Toronto *Globe*, a Liberal organ, supported Lang's grievance: "New Ontario is left without augmented representation, though one riding there is said to have a population of about 50,000, compared with a Toronto seat at 29,000."[37]

Tories dominated the northland ridings. Eight of the thirteen incumbents were Conservative, two were Liberal, two were Labour, and one was UFO. However, Lang's riding of Cochrane had the largest population and was the only serious candidate for division. Thus, an additional seat for the northlands would predict a gain of one seat for the opposition Liberal Party.

Lang's plea fell on deaf ears: "Northern Ontario, Mr. Ferguson said, was largely represented, so far as population was concerned, along railway lines, giving ready access to population. There was no necessity for Northern Ontario to have large representation with the organization that had been built up for Northern Ontario development. He referred to the large increases in population in Hamilton and Wentworth [that] had to be taken care of."[38] But a year later, the premier yielded. The 1926 Representation Act divided Lang's Cochrane riding into Cochrane North and Cochrane South, and reduced Simcoe County from four ridings to three.

Case Studies

TORONTO CITY AND YORK COUNTY: A GERRYMANDER

Ferguson's redistribution for the Toronto and York-County ridings unfolded in two stages. First, it enlarged the Toronto electoral district to match the city's municipal territory, which included nineteen territories annexed since 1908.[39] The population of the city's electoral district was 431,666 before redistribution and 521,893 after, a rise of 21 percent; and the population of the York ridings was 215,997 before redistribution and 125,770 after, a drop of 72 percent. Toronto's electoral district moved from 16.48 to 19.9 standard populations; that of the Yorks plunged from 10.19 to 4.80.

Second, the redistribution raised the representation for Toronto from ten ridings to fifteen, and that for York County from three ridings to four.[40] The provincial redistribution paid little heed to the principle that Toronto ridings should have larger populations than county ridings. The fifteen Toronto ridings had a mean of 1.33 standard populations. As estimated from statistics for electors, their populations were unequal (ranging from 0.89 to 1.99); three had below-average populations (less than 1.00); and two of the four York ridings had larger populations than the mean for Toronto (1.38, 0.84, 1.35, and 1.23). In terms of principle, Ferguson's redistribution over-represented municipal Toronto ("a county of itself") by two ridings and under-represented the municipal county of York by one riding.[41]

The redistribution for the GTA was positive for the government party. In the 1923 general election, every Toronto and York riding was a Tory hive. Thus, the rise in their number of ridings, from thirteen to nineteen, portended six additional Tory seats (one more than was warranted on principle). Ferguson's Conservatives won eighteen of the nineteen ridings in the 1926 general election.

HAMILTON CITY AND WENTWORTH COUNTY: A GERRYMANDER

Hamilton City presented two issues for redistribution. First, the city's electoral territory excluded five parcels of land that the city had annexed during the years 1914–25. Second, the municipal city was under-represented, with just two ridings for its 4.32 standard populations. Ferguson's response to the first issue was unprecedented and contrary to principle: he increased the population of city residents in the county ridings, from 3,229 to 17,100.[42] Then he gave the city's shrunken population (3.71) a third riding.

Harry Nixon (UFO, Brant North) "objected to the practice of placing [parts of] large cities in rural ridings. That, in my mind, is certainly a most objectionable form of gerrymandering ... [I do] not object in the case of small cities, but, instancing Hamilton and the Wentworths, [such placing could] throw enough of the city vote into the rural ridings to carry those ridings." Premier Ferguson's response – with a straight face? – was that this "has always been done."

The redistribution for Hamilton and Wentworth County was a gerrymander: one that trampled on several principles, while improving the prospects of the government party in the next general election. First, as noted above, it increased the population of city residents in the county ridings, a trespass on county lines. Second, it gave a county riding a larger population than two city ridings. The populations were Hamilton Centre, 1.26; Hamilton East, 1.38; Hamilton West, 1.06; Wentworth North, 0.74; and Wentworth South, 1.42.[43] Third, the populations were unequal for city ridings, and for the two county ridings. Fourth, it split townships, giving each of the Wentworth ridings portions of Ancaster and Barton.

The redistribution clearly benefited Ferguson's governing Tories. Before redistribution, the Hamilton ridings had been Tory hives (Hamilton East, -5,992; Hamilton West, -2,791); Wentworth South, a Tory hive (-889), with the party helped by its city fragment (-455); and Wentworth North, a UFO hive (+939). By creating a third city riding, the redistribution forecast a gain of a seat for the government party. Similarly, its transfer of city populations to the county ridings prospectively increased the Tory margin of safety in Wentworth South (4,307 city electors) and cut deeply into the UFO majority in Wentworth North riding (12,792 city electors). The gerrymander worked in the 1926 general election: the three city ridings and Wentworth South returned Tories – a gain of one for the government party. The UFO held on to Wentworth North.

OTTAWA AND CARLETON: NO GERRYMANDER

The redistribution left alone Ottawa East (1.37), a predominantly Francophone riding, but touched Ottawa West, a predominantly Anglophone riding. First, it transferred part of the city's Victoria Ward (including Mechanicsville Village, annexed in 1911) from the riding of Carleton to Ottawa West. This transfer matched the city's electoral territory to its civic boundaries. Then it divided Ottawa West (2.32) into the ridings of Ottawa North (1.50) and Ottawa South (1.23). The population of the Carleton riding was high for a county riding before the transfer (1.25), but not after (0.86). The division of the Ottawa West riding, a Liberal hive (+892), boded well for the opposition Liberals. However, both redistributed ridings returned Tories in the 1926 general election.

LONDON AND MIDDLESEX: THE TORIES BENEFIT, BUT NO GERRYMANDER

The redistribution transferred the bulk of the annexed territories in Middlesex East to the city's electoral district (all but a small parcel annexed in 1913).[44] Then it divided London City (1.97) into the ridings of London North (1.14) and London South (1.09), and folded three Middlesex ridings (0.94, 0.52, and 0.48) into two (0.84 and 0.85). The redistribution equalized populations and gave the city ridings larger populations than the county ridings. The division of London City, a massive Tory hive (-7,611), into two ridings, and the transfer of the Tory-leaning annexed territories (-583) to the London North riding, forecast the gain of a seat for the Conservatives. The three Middlesex ridings had two UFO and one Tory incumbents; with two ridings, the UFO, prospectively, lost a seat.[45] Although the government party prospectively benefited, the redistribution squared with principles and was no gerrymander. The Conservatives took both London seats in the 1926 general election, but the two county ridings returned Progressives.

WINDSOR AND ESSEX COUNTY: A GERRYMANDER

Essex County received a fourth riding for its 3.86 standard populations. Windsor, one of three ridings before redistribution, included two towns, Walkerville and Sandwich. The redistribution divided the riding of Windsor (1.89) into two: Windsor East, including Walkerville (1.01), and Windsor West, including Sandwich (0.91). It left alone the ridings of Essex North (1.17), a Liberal hive (+1,674), and Essex South (0.81), a possibly safe Tory riding (-60). The redistribution flouted principles. It left the county ridings with unequal populations (1.17 and 0.81) and Essex North with a larger population than either of the all-urban Windsor ridings. It declined to make Windsor (1.47 without its two towns) an all-city riding, thereby failing to observe the municipal city as "a county of itself" for representation.

The redistribution benefited the government party. The Liberal-majority statistics for the ridings before redistribution were: Windsor, a Tory hive (-1,871); Essex North, a Liberal hive (+1,674); and Essex South, possibly safe, Tory (-60). The division of the Windsor riding forecast a gain of one seat for the government party. Conversely, by not transferring municipalities from the Liberal-hive riding of Essex North to Essex South, to equalize their populations, it avoided the prospective loss of a seat in the fighting riding of Essex South. The gerrymander produced mixed results in the 1926 general election: the government party won both Windsor seats; won Essex North, where they had not had a candidate in the 1923 general election; but lost Essex South, against prediction.

Alternative redistributions would have been more in line with principle, but less favourable to the government party. A hypothetical transfer of Anderdon and Malden Townships from Essex North to Essex South, for example, would have equalized the county-riding populations (1.03 and 0.93), but also would have turned the South riding from possibly safe, Tory (-60) into a Liberal hive (+1,092). A second alternative, noted above, was to transfer the towns of Sandwich and Walkerville from the Windsor riding to county ridings and give a third riding to the county. This would have created Windsor as an all-city riding (1.47) and three county ridings with about 0.81 standard populations each. Without a division of the Windsor riding, however, the government party would not have gained a seat.

Consolidation in the Counties

The consolidation of twenty-eight small-population ridings in eleven counties eliminated nine ridings. Simcoe County dropped from four ridings to three. The counties of Lennox & Addington, Frontenac, Bruce, Grey, Huron, Middlesex, and Wellington each dropped from three ridings to two. The counties of Durham, Norfolk, and Northumberland each dropped from two ridings to one. These consolidations were positive for equalizing populations.

The government party fared remarkably well from the consolidations. The incumbents of the twenty-eight consolidated ridings included sixteen Tories, eight UFO, and four Liberals. Yet the incumbents who stood to lose their ridings included just three Tories, three UFO, and all four Liberals! Ferguson might have picked the counties of Hastings, Lanark, and Victoria for consolidation. The government party held all seven ridings in these counties, so consolidation in any one of them would have eliminated a Tory seat. That said, riding populations in these counties were higher than in the counties selected, which works against a judgment of a gerrymandered selection. In the event, the results of the 1926 general election belied the predicted outcomes in the consolidated ridings. The government party lost nine seats and the Liberals won seven seats, including all four for which redistribution had predicted their loss.

Overview of the 1925–26 Redistribution

Whereas the bipartisan special committee had been a mere ratifying body for cabinet decisions in the 1908 and 1914 redistributions, Ferguson's 1925 tripartisan committee actually redrew the ridings. The redistribution boosted the percentage of ridings in the optimum zone from 17 to 22. The redistribution enlarged the electoral districts of Toronto and Ottawa to match their respective municipal territories, and came close to doing so for London. For Hamilton, in contrast, the redistribution transferred city populations to Wentworth County ridings, a reversal of principle that was unique in Ontario's history of provincial redistribution.

The redistribution added city seats and subtracted county seats to increase the size of the House from 111 to 112. As Table 9.2 shows, this added six to the Tory count of seats, and removed two from the Liberal count and three from the Progressive count. The redistribution predicted a gain of nine seats for the Conservatives from the increase of

Table 9.2 Distribution of provincial seats by party and level of safety, before and after the 1925–26 redistribution

	Before 1925–26 redistribution				*After redistribution: Predictions for 1929 election*			
	Cons.	*Lib.*	*Prog.*	*All parties*	*Cons.*	*Lib.*	*Prog.*	*All parties*
hive (500+)	77%	50%	35%	67%	85%	42%	71%	79%
very safe (200–499)	16%	0%	29%	16%	10%	33%	14%	13%
reasonably safe (100–199)	1%	29%	0%	5%	0%	8%	0%	0%
possibly safe (50–99)	1%	0%	24%	5%	1%	0%	7%	2%
precarious (< 50)	3%	14%	12%	6%	2%	8%	7%	4%
acclamation	1%	7%	0%	2%	1%	8%	0%	2%
# of ridings	75	14	17	106	81	12	14	107
not counted	5 (4 Labour, 1 independent)				5 (4 Labour, 1 independent)			

representation for cities, where the Tories polled strongly, against a loss of three seats from the elimination of nine county ridings. The redistributions for London and Middlesex, Hamilton and Wentworth, and Windsor and Essex were gerrymanders. The elimination of ten county ridings was suspiciously favourable to the government party, which prospectively lost just three seats, despite holding sixteen of the twenty-eight consolidated ridings.

In the 1926 general election the Tories did well in Toronto and York, winning eighteen of the nineteen seats (a gain of five seats versus the predicted six), and also small cities (gaining five ridings versus the predicted three). The government part did worse than expected in consolidated county ridings, dropping ten seats versus the predicted two.

SUMMARY AND INTERPRETATION

Ontario experienced major shifts in population between the 1911 and 1921 censuses. There was above-average population increase in the GTA, average increases in small cities and the northlands districts, and lagging rates in the counties. The municipal boundaries of Toronto, Ottawa, Hamilton, and London extended beyond their electoral districts into adjacent county ridings. Government responded with the 1924 Dominion redistribution, which was mandatory, and the 1925–26 Ontario-provincial redistribution, which was not.

Whereas previous redistributions took place in a two-party system, composed of Liberals and Conservatives, those of the 1920s took place in a three-party system, which included the Progressive-ILP, a coalition of farm and labour parties. The three parties mattered for the Dominion redistribution, given that the prime minister, Mackenzie King, presided over a hung parliament. They mattered little for the Ontario redistribution, given that the Tory premier, Howard Ferguson, enjoyed a massive majority in the provincial parliament.

Both governments struck large tripartisan special committees on redistribution. The nineteen-man Dominion committee included ten Liberals, five Progressives, and four Conservatives, and its six-man Ontario subcommittee comprised two members from each of the three parties. In Ontario's provincial parliament, the fifteen-man special committee included ten Conservatives and five from opposition parties. Unlike previous provincial committees, which had been mere ratifying bodies, the 1925 committee drafted the schedule of ridings.

The Dominion and Ontario parliaments, and the parties represented therein, diverged somewhat in their principles for redistribution. The Dominion parliament remained committed to a higher unit of population for city ridings than for county ridings, but the provincial parliament abandoned the practice. Compared with the Liberals and Progressives, Conservatives in both parliaments favoured more representation for cities and less representation for counties. This mattered little in the Dominion parliament, where the Tories were a minority party, but a great deal in the provincial parliament, where the Tories enjoyed a massive majority.

Mackenzie King went out of his way to avoid discussion of principles in his abortive 1923 redistribution Bill. He did articulate conventional Liberal principles for his 1924 Bill, but his Ontario subcommittee had difficulty reconciling them in particular cases, and did not follow any of them consistently. Overall, the 1924 Dominion redistribution was not a gerrymander. Rather, it evidenced the weakness of King's minority government, party differences of principle on a three-party Ontario subcommittee, and the subcommittee's difficulties in reconciling the prime minister's four cardinal principles in particular cases.

The provincial redistribution raised the percentage of ridings in the optimum zone from 15 to 24. Ferguson's redistributions for Toronto and

York, Hamilton and Wentworth, and Windsor and Essex were gerrymanders. The elimination of nine county ridings was suspiciously favourable to the government party, which prospectively lost just three ridings, despite holding sixteen of the twenty-eight consolidated ridings.

The provincial gerrymanders produced mixed results in the 1926 general election. The Tories did well in Toronto and York, winning eighteen of the nineteen seats (a gain of five seats versus the predicted six), and small cities (gaining five ridings versus the predicted three). The government party did worse than expected in the twenty-eight consolidated county ridings, dropping ten seats versus the predicted two.

The matching-up of a city's electoral territory with its larger municipal territory was an issue in both redistributions, but their responses differed. Both matched up the electoral and municipal territories for Toronto. The Dominion redistribution left alone the electoral districts of Ottawa and London, but the provincial redistribution matched the electoral and municipal territories for both. The Dominion redistribution enlarged Hamilton's electoral district to include 72 percent of the population of city fragments, but the provincial redistribution transferred city populations into the county ridings, turning the principle of city-county lines upside-down.

The sharply contrasting 1924-Dominion and 1925-provincial redistributions for the Hamilton and Wentworth-County ridings evidenced how a government party's political calculations could influence outcomes. In both cases, Wentworth-County ridings included suburban populations that the city had annexed; the Hamilton-City ridings were Tory hives; city-fragments in the county ridings were Tory-leaning; and the transfer of the city fragments into the all-city ridings would hive the Tories into Hamilton, to the benefit of the Progressive Party in the county ridings.

A crucial difference was that the government party was Liberal for the Dominion redistribution and Conservative for the provincial redistribution. Thus, the Liberal-administered Dominion redistribution transferred some 18,000 city residents from the Wentworth riding into city ridings: effectively, hiving Tory-opposition supporters into the city ridings to strengthen Liberal prospects in Wentworth-County ridings. In contrast, the Tory-administered provincial redistribution transferred some 14,000 city residents out of city ridings into two Wentworth ridings: effectively, de-hiving government-party supporters from the city ridings to strengthen the party's prospects in the county ridings.

The redistributions of the 1920s were no template for the redistributions of the Great Depression. As chapter 10 reveals, the three-party system had largely collapsed in Dominion politics by the 1930s, and the Conservatives were in office with a large majority. Meanwhile, the provincial redistribution eliminated twenty-two seats as an economy measure, a reversal of its long-standing practice of creating new ridings for cities and the northlands, while leaving the county ridings alone.

10

R.B. Bennett and George Henry: Redistributions during the Great 1930s Depression

Ontario underwent Dominion and provincial redistributions in 1933. Conservatives held office in both Ottawa and Queen's Park, in each case with a large majority. Prime Minister R.B. Bennett's majority was one hundred ten nationally and twenty-three among the Ontario members (fifty-nine Conservatives, twenty-two Liberals, and one Progressive). The Tory majority was seventy in the provincial parliament (ninety-two Tories, fourteen Liberals, and six Progressives). George S. Henry (York East), Howard Ferguson's successor as premier of Ontario (1930–34), administered the provincial redistribution.

Ontario electors had effectively reverted to a two-party system in the 1930 Dominion general election, but less so in the 1929 provincial general election. The Conservatives had run candidates in all eighty-two Dominion ridings, the Liberals in eighty, and the Progressives in just five. In the provincial general election, the Conservatives had contested all one hundred twelve seats, the Liberals eighty-six, and the Progressives twenty-one.[1]

The Movement of Population

The Ontario population increased by 17 percent during the 1920s, a boom headed by cities. In 1931 Ontario had thirty-two cities,[2] up from twenty-five in 1921. The population of cities had increased by 28 percent and held 45 percent of the provincial population. Toronto held the lion's share of the city populations (42 percent), followed by Hamilton (10 percent), Ottawa (9 percent), London (5 percent), and Windsor (4 percent).[3]

By 1931, sixty years of population growth and urbanization had transformed Ontario's northland districts. Algoma and Nipissing had originated in 1858 as judicial districts in "unsettled territories."[4] Ontario's eleven districts now held 406,993 people, up 30 percent from 1921. The twin cities of Port Arthur and Fort William held 71 percent of the population in Thunder Bay District; Sault Ste. Marie City, 50 percent in Algoma District; Sudbury City, 32 percent in Sudbury District; and the town of Timmins, 25 percent in Cochrane District.

The issue of county lines for cities was unimportant in the Dominion and provincial redistributions of 1933.[5] No action was needed for Toronto, whose Dominion and provincial ridings extended to the city limits. Little action was taken where the electoral and municipal territories differed. The Dominion redistribution left 21 percent of Hamilton-City electors in the riding of Wentworth and 13 percent of London-City electors in the riding of Middlesex East; it transferred Ottawa's Rideau Ward from the riding of Russell to the riding of Ottawa East, but left 3 percent of Ottawa-City electors in the riding of Carleton. The provincial redistribution left 15 percent of Hamilton-City electors in the riding of Wentworth and another 22 percent in the hybrid riding of Hamilton-Wentworth; 13 percent of London-City electors in the riding of Middlesex North; and 3 percent of Ottawa-City electors in the riding of Carleton.

Otherwise the movement of population played upon the province's principles for redistribution. Could redistribution maintain county lines when consolidating ridings with small, shrinking rural populations? Should city populations be represented in all-city ridings, or hybrid (semi-urban) ones? Should hybrid ridings have larger populations than all-rural ones? Was it possible politically to give cities additional representation if this entailed an equivalent decrease in representation for the counties? The latter consideration obtained for the 1933 Dominion redistribution, with its fixed quota of seats (eighty-two), but also for the 1933 provincial redistribution, which cut the number of ridings from one hundred twelve to ninety, as an economy measure.

THE 1933 DOMINION REDISTRIBUTION

Ontario's allocation was eighty-two seats, the same as its 1921 quota. The province held 79.9 Quebec standard populations, enough for just eighty seats. Under Section 51.4 of the 1867 BNA Act, however, a province's quota could not decline if the ratio of its population to the Canadian population had diminished by less than one-twentieth.[6]

Prime Minister Bennett named a twenty-member special committee, which represented the parties according to their strength in the House:

thus, eleven Tories, seven Liberals, and two Progressive-Labour members. The subcommittee for Ontario comprised three Tories and one Liberal. Its chair was John MacNicol (Toronto Northwest), past president of the Ontario Liberal-Conservative Association (1923–30); president and founder of the Dominion Liberal-Conservative Association (1924–43); a prominent, albeit ineffectual, party organizer; and a newly elected MP.[7] MacNicol's fellow Tories on the subcommittee were the Hon. Hugh Stewart (Leeds), minister of Public Works, a veteran of the 1924 subcommittee and chair of the 1933 national committee; and Dr Ira Cotnam (Renfrew North), an MP since 1926. The lone Liberal was the Hon. John Elliott (Middlesex West), past minister of Public Works (1926–30).

Elliott decried being the sole Liberal on the subcommittee. His recommendations for the next redistribution were, first, that the national committee represent provinces, not just parties, according to their strength in the House; and second, that the Ontario subcommittee represent parties according to their strength in the Ontario ridings. Had Elliott's recommendation applied in 1933, the Ontario subcommittee would have comprised five Tories and two Liberals.

Principles

Mackenzie King, leader of the opposition, restated the principles that he had advocated as prime minister in 1924. These were to "follow as largely as possible municipal organizations in defining and delimiting the constituencies"; give "urban centres" a larger "unit of representation ... than that in rural constituencies"; ensure "an effort at compactness in the shaping of constituencies"; and plan "an equalization of the representation as between the different urban constituencies and as between the different rural constituencies." King regarded "the trend of population from rural to urban ... [as] a trend headed in the wrong direction. The fact that the urban population in Canada is to-day larger than the rural, notwithstanding the vast size of this country, is the strongest evidence that our industrial policies have been wrong; that the policy of protection has had the effect of bringing people into the cities, over-industrializing the manufacturing side of our country and as a consequence helping to deplete the rural sections." By extension, protection for rural representation could help to reverse the trend.[8]

Prime Minister Bennett, a veteran of Robert Borden's 1914 special committee, declined to "anticipate the principles upon which the committee will act." In a rambling, error-filled, incoherent speech on the final version of the Representation Bill, he spoke against the application of the Quebec standard population (44,186), or any one principle, to ridings in rural Ontario. In Bennett's words,

> If you applied the rule of dividing the population of the province of Ontario, outside the great cities, by 44,000 and saying, "There are your seats," you would create complete chaos and dissatisfaction throughout that province ... in the rural part of Ontario there has been no application of the rule I have referred to, namely the division of the population by 44,000 ... because it has not been done ... you have in Welland to-day 83,000 people represented by one member, just as they were at confederation in that constituency. That cannot be said to be fair; and yet if you endeavoured to apply the 44,000 rule and set about doing so, you would so disorganize the whole rural population of Ontario as to create a condition not only of dissatisfaction but of chaos.

Bennett opposed the application of principles that Wilfrid Laurier had espoused in 1903:

> I would point out that the very principles which in 1903 were moved for on the third reading of the redistribution bill – the first redistribution bill of the Liberal party – were principles such as are now asserted by the opposition here [county lines, rural-city differences in the unit of population, compact shape of ridings]. But when the government of Sir Robert Borden were charged with the responsibility of redistribution [in 1914], they realized that you could not apply these principles, and the committee unanimously arrived at this conclusion: you had here a small constituency and there a large one; you had county boundaries and municipal lines, the convenience of a large population, and in some instances the historic and traditional circumstances connected with the riding itself. The committee have not departed from *that* [it is unclear what he refers to here]; if they did, it would be such a radical and complete change ... that I do not believe that the house would adopt any such redistribution.[9]

Simply put, the special committee was on its own, without guidance from the prime minister. "The Ontario section" of the national committee, recalled John MacNicol, "established our own rules and regulations."[10]

Like his party leader, Prime Minister Bennett, MacNicol had a muddled grasp of past practice for redistribution. "A great number of seats have very small populations," ventured MacNicol, "and as there was no rule before the committee stating a rural seat should have a minimum population of so many thousands, a rural-urban seat so many thousands minimum, and a city seat so many thousands minimum, we had no rule to go by, with the exception of what was done in past redistributions, namely to respect as much as possible the county boundaries ... that has been the plan followed since confederation."[11] Apparently MacNicol was unaware of his party's "gerrymander Acts" of 1882 and 1892, which had trashed county lines. Conversely, he might have considered his own party's Borden-Haggart rules of 1903 as a possible template for rules in 1933. An alternative template, used in the Liberal redistributions of 1903 and 1924, was to set the number of ridings for Toronto, and then calculate a lower unit of population for all other ridings.

In the event, MacNicol summarized the subcommittee's principles as follows. First, it adhered to county lines "as much as possible ... we made eighteen seats out of full counties ... four seats consisted of two counties each ... Thirty-two seats were wholly within their counties. Seven seats were within the county and included part of another county."[12] Even so, "under the present redistribution there will be only a few counties left in all Ontario that will have their own boundaries as the boundaries of their new ridings ... The counties of Brant, Durham, Elgin, Glengarry, Haldimand, Essex, Wentworth, Welland, Lincoln, Lanark, Middlesex, Norfolk, Northumberland, Leeds, Prescott, Peel, Halton, Renfrew, York, and Waterloo are the only counties in this province to-day that it is not proposed to associate under this redistribution with other counties, and I doubt if in the next redistribution there will be more than two or three counties in that category."[13]

Second, MacNicol – unusually for a Toronto Tory – refined the principle that rural ridings should have smaller populations than ridings in large cities. Several county ridings were "semi-urban" in that they included a city and towns. By extension, such ridings presented degrees of urbanity (as measured by city and towns). Thus, a riding with a low "urban" proportion of its population should have a smaller population than a riding with a high proportion. The subcommittee's proposed riding of Perth, elaborated MacNicol, included Stratford City and the towns of Listowel, St. Mary's, and Mitchell, whose populations totalled 25,808, "or an urban population of over one-half of the new riding with a population of 47,816." In North Huron, "with a population of 26,095, there [was] an urban population of 6,239, and in Huron-Perth, with a population of 22,656, there [was] an urban population of 3,352." Thus, Huron-Perth was "almost entirely rural. The riding of North Huron [was] not as rural as Huron-Perth, having twice the latter's urban population, and therefore it should have a larger unit than Huron-Perth. The riding of Perth itself, being over fifty percent urban, should have a larger population than either of the other two."[14]

Third, allowing for rural-urban differences in the unit of population, the subcommittee sought to equalize populations of the ridings. MacNicol calculated that forty-six seats (56 percent) were within "thirty-three and a third per cent" above or below the quota. He conceded that this distribution was "not very close to the quota," but that getting closer was difficult "in many cases."[15]

Fourth, the subcommittee tried to ensure that each incumbent could return to his riding for re-election "without being in opposition to anyone now in the house." This principle's sole exception was the two Perth ridings, whose merger left their incumbents, one a Liberal and the other a Conservative, to face each other in the next election.

Fifth, fair play between the parties mattered. MacNicol himself "would not hesitate to go into any seat which has been called a gerrymander, but for which I was not responsible, and do my best against whoever opposed me."[16] As discussed below, the Perth ridings escaped his ethical gaze.

Sixth, the subcommittee considered "community of interest or the diversity of the community of interest," "the tradition and history of the ridings," "communications, such as railways and highways," and "topographical characteristics of the ridings."

Finally, as any redistribution committee would find out, "the principles cannot be followed exactly; so many factors have to be considered before and against. We did the best we could and ... our final recommendations went through the house unanimously."[17]

"The leaders of all parties," added Hugh Stewart, Tory chair of the national committee and member of the subcommittee, "recognized and confirmed ... that the unit of representation in cities should be larger than the unit in the rural municipalities, and that there should be no greater disturbance of conditions than was absolutely necessary" (minimalism). "The urban population," noted Stewart,

> has created a problem which is difficult to deal with. On the one hand we have the contention that you must not decrease rural representation, and on the other hand we have the contention that you

> must increase urban representation. We have endeavoured to keep both these in mind and to give to cities an increase, though not as much as they desire, while not disturbing too greatly county boundaries or conditions as we find them. Particularly have we endeavoured to avoid tearing up the map, as it were, where it had all been torn up only ten years ago and the electors in those areas which had then been disturbed had just got quietly settled down and had adapted themselves to the changed conditions.

Stewart had "no confidence in gerrymanders. I do not believe either of the parties think that you can count on any definite advantage being gained in an election from a redistribution ... If my hon. friends think that as far as I am concerned in this redistribution we have been primarily and principally concerned in endeavouring to secure some small, petty party advantage, which I think we will all agree is extremely doubtful, then they are absolutely mistaken."[18]

In echo of Mackenzie King, the Hon. John Elliott, the lone Liberal on the subcommittee, warned against increasing the representation for cities, which would require the "elimination of certain ridings that have existed practically ever since confederation." Government was "spending money to bring people back to the land." Thus, any adjustments to city ridings should be made "if possible at the expense of urban representation rather than at the expense of rural representation ... There are 82 seats in the province of Ontario, and it is not an easy matter to delimit boundaries by which certain constituencies which have existed ever since confederation shall be wiped out. I think that ... 31 of those constituencies were not touched. Some of them are small in population, but if you affect one riding by taking townships from adjoining ridings, then all these other ridings are more or less affected so that the number of ridings actually affected becomes very considerable."[19] The Conservative majority's desire for unanimity on the subcommittee gave clout to Elliott's views.

Deliberations of the Subcommittee

MacNicol's subcommittee initially "set out to take five seats from the rural communities. It was our intention to give three of those five seats to the urban communities and two to rural seats which had largely increased in population ... In that connection we decided to give two more seats to Toronto, one more to York, one to Welland, and one to

Nipissing." However, for the sake of "unanimity in all seats," the subcommittee took only three seats from the counties, which caused it to jettison planned second seats for Welland (1.87), a Tory hive, and Nipissing (1.63), a Liberal hive.[20] Simply put, the subcommittee was highly protective of representation for the counties. In this regard, all subcommittee members except MacNicol represented left-alone county ridings: John Elliott, the lone Liberal (Middlesex West, 0.53 standard populations); Dr Ira Cotnam (Renfrew North, 0.62); and Hugh Stewart (Leeds, 0.80).

The redistribution touched forty-five of the eighty-two ridings (55 percent). It added three ridings, two for Toronto and one for York County. And it eliminated three county ridings by folding four Bruce and Grey County ridings into three; four Perth and Huron ridings into three; and two Oxford ridings into one.

It gave low priority to representation by population. The percentage of ridings in the optimum zone (0.90–1.10) rose from 7 to 9, an all-time low in Ontario's history of redistribution. Thirty-nine percent of the ridings had less than 0.80 standard populations, and 29 percent had more than 1.20. Glengarry (0.42), Brant (0.48), and Haldimand (0.48) were at the low end, with Elliott's constituency, Middlesex West (0.53), close behind. At the high end was Welland (1.97), a Conservative hive left alone, much to the dismay of local Tories.[21] The redistribution prospectively gave the government party a gain of two seats (from fifty-nine to sixty-one), and took one seat from the Liberals (from twenty-two to twenty-one) and one from the Progressives (their only seat).

Case Studies

PERTH AND HURON: "POLITICAL ASSASSINATION" WITH A SMILE

MacNicol's subcommittee folded four ridings in Huron and Perth Counties (Map 10.1) into three (Huron North, Perth, and Huron-Perth). Its transfer of two Perth townships to the newly created Huron-Perth riding interfered with county lines and made the riding populations *less* equal.[22] The redistribution helped the government party.[23] Before redistribution, each party held two seats: the Liberals, Huron South (+349) and Perth South (+717), and the Tories, Huron North (-233) and Perth North (-876). Redistribution, prospectively, gave the government party two seats (Perth, -449, and Huron North, -654) and the Liberals one (Huron-Perth (+1,028). Effectively, MacNicol's redistribution "hived the Grits" into Huron-Perth to boost Tory prospects in Perth and Huron North.

The odd man out in the shift from four ridings to three was Frederick Sanderson (Perth South), chief whip of the Liberal Party, who was to be situated in the redistributed Tory-leaning riding of Perth (-449). MacNicol, a "gentleman, manufacturer, and teacher," delivered his message with a smile. As Sanderson acknowledged, MacNicol had been "very courteous and fair in conversations with me."[24]

In vain, Sanderson pled for "justice, fair play, an even break and a chance for the Liberal party in the next general election in the county of Perth." He saw "no justification for disturbing townships in South Perth. I have always been under the impression that county boundaries should be adhered to as far as possible." He linked Perth's county lines to its "community spirit" and tradition that dated from Confederation. Although a merged Perth riding, with its county lines intact, would have 1.23 standard populations, which was high for a county riding, "the unit of population is not always the only factor in redistribution. There are many constituencies far below the unit and many far above."[25] The Liberal Toronto *Globe* was sympathetic to Sanderson's

> valiant effort to convince the Redistribution Committee that it should not "deliberately reach over the fence and take two historic townships which have been in Perth since Confederation, for purely political purposes to take them out of Perth County and put them in another county." The two townships are Hibbert and Fullarton, which together gave him a majority of 290 in the last election, and removal of which in his opinion, will give the Conservative candidate an advantage of 436 in Perth County in the next contest … The mysteries of redistribution are deep when in the hands of a committee governed by one party. But one point seems clear: that, party politics being what it is, the "ins" take advantage of the "outs."[26]

MacNicol defended his redistribution on a novel principle: his subcommittee had adjusted the constituencies according to the urban percentage of their populations. Yet his subcommittee did not apply this principle elsewhere. According to MacNicol, the subcommittee tried to ensure that each incumbent could return to his riding for re-election "without being in opposition to anyone now in the house." As he acknowledged, however, the incumbents for the two Perth ridings could

Map 10.1 The Huron and Perth ridings before redistribution

expect to face each other in the merged riding of Perth in the next general election. John Elliott, the lone Liberal on the subcommittee, did not rise to Sanderson's defence during MacNicol's presentation to the House. Perhaps he felt bound by log-rolling agreements of the subcommittee.

The redistribution was a gerrymander. First, its ranking of riding populations by their percentages of "urban" population was novel. Second, the subcommittee applied that ranking method solely to Perth and Huron. Third, the novel principle clashed with established principles: county lines, of course, but also representation by population and the equalization of riding populations. Together, the counties of Huron and Perth had 2.19 standard populations, enough for two ridings, not the three given. Equal populations for the three given ridings required standard populations of approximately 0.73 each; the statistics for MacNicol's ridings were 0.62, 0.54, and 1.14.

MacNicol eschewed alternative redistributions for Huron and Perth that were more defensible in principle, though less beneficial to his party. One was to merge the Huron ridings into one, while equalizing population in the Perth ridings by transferring the townships of North Easthope and Ellice to the South riding. This alternative redistribution observed county lines and was marginally the better for equalizing population (1.08, 0.66, and 0.62 versus MacNicol's 0.62, 0.54, and 1.14). In its predictions for the next election, however, the government party, not the Liberals, would lose a seat.[27] In the event, the Huron-Perth gerrymander failed disastrously in the 1935 general election. The Liberals swept the three ridings by large majorities. Frederick Sanderson won Perth with a majority of 5,215. David Wright, the Tory incumbent for the former riding of Perth North, and the prospective instrument of Sanderson's "political assassination," was not a candidate, having quit politics for business reasons.[28]

KENT AND LAMBTON

The redistribution for these counties slightly benefited the government party, as measured by Liberal-majority statistics. But it also calls into question the appropriateness of the Liberal-majority statistic in a three-party setting.

The combined population of the Kent and Lambton counties (2.62) sufficed for their current three ridings: one for each county and the other a mixed-county riding. With redistribution, the ridings of Kent, Lambton East, and Lambton West became the ridings of Kent, Lambton-Kent, and Lambton West. The mixed-county constituency was Lambton East before redistribution and Lambton-Kent after.

The redistribution was consistent with principles. First, it advanced the equalization of the riding populations.[29] Second, it observed county lines. Although it gave the Kent riding two municipalities from Essex-County ridings – Tilbury Town from Essex East, and Wheatley Village from Essex South – those municipalities straddled the border between the two counties. Interestingly, the subcommittee disregarded MacNicol's novel principle for Perth and Huron, of ranking population by percentage "urban." In the counties of Kent and Lambton, Lambton West, 55 percent "urban," had 0.75 standard populations; Kent, 43 percent "urban," had 1.08; and Lambton-Kent, 26 percent "urban," 0.85.

The redistribution benefited the government party. Before redistribution, two ridings were Liberal hives: Kent (+1,474) and Lambton West (+554); the third riding, Lambton East, was precarious, Tory (-13). Redistribution prospectively reversed the party tallies by hiving the Grits into the Kent riding (+2,630).[30] Lambton West was now a Tory hive (-3,138), and Lambton-Kent (formerly Lambton East) was reasonably safe, Conservative (-176), up from precarious (-13).

Nevertheless, Liberal-majority statistics are problematic for transfers in Ontario's three-party system. As shown in Table 10.1, the Conservative Party had contested all three Kent and Lambton ridings in the 1930 general election; the Liberals, two; and the Progressives, one. Wallaceburg Town was then in the riding of Kent, which Liberal and Conservative candidates had contested. Its transfer to Lambton-Kent gave that new riding 1,328 Tory votes and 718 Liberal votes, but no Progressive votes. Similarly, transfers from the pre-redistribution Lambton East riding added Tory votes and Progressive votes, but no Liberal votes, to the receiving ridings.

Table 10.1 compares the Liberal-majority statistics for the three-party system (the actual case) with a hypothetical two-party system in which the Conservatives faced a single Liberal-Progressive opposition party in all three ridings – imagine that Progressives, as Mackenzie King believed, were "Liberals in a hurry." The results for the hypothetical two-party system are distinctly less favourable to the government party, with Lambton West now a prospective Liberal hive instead of a reasonably safe Tory seat. Lambton-Kent remains a Tory hive, but with a greatly reduced majority. In the event, Liberals won all three ridings in the 1935 general election.

ESSEX COUNTY: REDISTRIBUTION WITHOUT PURPOSE

Essex County had 3.87 standard populations – sufficient for four ridings – but the redistribution maintained three ridings, Essex East (1.03), Essex South (0.87), and Essex West (1.97). Before redistribution and after, Essex West included most of the city of Windsor, but Essex East included "part of the City of Windsor south of Tecumseh Road." The redistribution transferred Sandwich South Township from Essex South (0.79) to Essex East (0.97), and Tilbury Town (Essex South) and

Table 10.1 Party prospects after redistribution: With three parties (the actual case) and one Liberal-Progressive opposition party (hypothetical)

		Liberal-majority statistic after redistribution	
Ridings before redistribution	*Candidates in the 1930 general election*	*Two opposition parties*	*One opposition party*
Kent	Liberal, Conservative	-2,630	-2,630
Lambton East	Progressive, Conservative	-2,462	-712
Lambton West	Liberal, Conservative	-176	+579

Wheatley Village (Essex East) to the riding of Kent. The transfers were negative for population equality.[31] They had no prospective consequences for party strengths; the three ridings were massive Tory hives (-2,120, -1,980, and -6,460) before redistribution and remained so. Before and after redistribution, the size of population in the Essex ridings increased with the percentage "urban" (MacNicol's measure for the Huron and Perth ridings). However, this feature predated MacNicol's novel principle.[32]

The changes to the Essex ridings were trivial, which raises the question of why the subcommittee bothered with them. The subcommittee could have done more. For example, it could have made Windsor City a stand-alone riding with 1.51 standard populations, along with two county ridings, each 1.15 – or three county ridings, each 0.77 – a prospective gain of a seat for the government party. A fourth riding for Essex, of course, would have required the elimination of a county riding elsewhere.

BRUCE AND GREY: NOT A GERRYMANDER

The counties of Bruce (1.01) and Grey (1.37) each held two ridings. The subcommittee reduced the four ridings (2.38) to three: Bruce, Grey North, and Grey-Bruce, a mixed-county riding. The redistribution was positive for equalization of the riding populations.[33] The subcommittee disregarded MacNicol's supposed principle that population sizes in the ridings should correspond with their percentage of "urban" population.[34]

The redistribution, prospectively, cost the Progressives a seat. The incumbents for the four pre-redistribution ridings were two Liberals, one Conservative, and one Progressive (the first female MPP, Agnes MacPhail). Party prospects for the three post-redistribution ridings wiped out the Progressive candidate. The three-party system doomed the

Progressives with this book's Liberal-majority-statistic method of calculation. Whereas in the 1930 general election, the Liberals ran candidates in all four ridings and the Conservatives in three, the Progressives contested just one. Thus, transfers in redistribution tended to favour the Liberals, less so the Conservatives, and the Progressives not at all. Against prediction, the Progressive, Agnes MacPhail, won her riding in the 1935 general election, and Liberals won the two other seats. Thus, the government party, not the Progressives, lost a seat.

THE NORTHLAND DISTRICTS

The subcommittee redistributed the northland ridings, primarily Temiskaming and Nipissing, without adding to their number. The names changed in two cases: Temiskaming and Cochrane replaced Temiskaming North and Temiskaming South. The redistribution was slightly positive for equalizing populations.[35]

OTTAWA, CARLETON, AND RUSSELL

The subcommittee divided the two-member Ottawa riding into two ridings with contrasting "communities of interest." Ottawa East (1.17) was predominantly Francophone, and Ottawa West (1.78) was predominantly Anglophone. The subcommittee transferred the city's Rideau Ward (annexed in 1887) to Ottawa East; transferred two Carleton municipalities (Eastview Village and Rockcliffe Park) from Russell to Ottawa East; and placed parts of two west-side city wards in the riding of Carleton, not Ottawa West. It transferred the Carleton-County township of Osgoode from Russell to Carleton, but left the Carleton-County township of Gloucester in Russell. Thus, the redistribution advanced the principles of municipal lines and city limits as county lines, but applied them incompletely.

Summary of the 1933 Dominion Redistribution

The 1933 redistribution was muddled in principle, chaotic in design and execution, and highly protective of county ridings, which furnished three of the four members of the subcommittee. It touched many ridings but achieved little. The muddle started with Prime Minister Bennett and continued with John MacNicol and his subcommittee.

The Dominion redistribution increased the percentage of ridings in the optimum zone (0.90–1.10) from 7 to 9, an all-time low in Ontario's history of redistribution. Of the eighty-two ridings after redistribution,

45 percent had less than 0.80 standard populations. Three seats with less than 0.50 standard populations were undisturbed. Eight undisturbed county ridings had more than 1.20 standard populations. Welland (1.87) was left alone, even though the division of this Tory hive (-2,466), ardently desired by local Tories,[36] would have forecast a gain of a seat for MacNicol's government party. Traditionally the northland ridings had below-average populations to allow for their vast territories and scattered populations. This was not the case in 1933. Exclusive of Muskoka and Parry Sound, the districts had eight ridings for 8.45 standard populations, for an above-average mean (1.06). Arguably, the northlands merited an additional riding; the redistribution did not give them one.

Like the Tory redistribution of 1914, the 1933 Tory redistribution declined to observe the city limits of Toronto, Hamilton, Ottawa, and London as municipal-county lines. It left annexed parts of Toronto, Hamilton, and London in their contiguous county ridings. It transferred Ottawa's Rideau Ward from the riding of Russell to the city riding of Ottawa East, but left parts of two city wards in the riding of Carleton; conversely it transferred two Carleton-County villages to the city riding of Ottawa East.

The subcommittee arranged population size for the Huron and Perth ridings according to percentage "urban" in their populations, but ignored this novel principle elsewhere. The task of reconciling the principles of population and county lines was difficult. MacNicol's novel principle made it more so, with the saving grace that he applied it to only one local redistribution.

The redistribution forecast a gain of two seats for the government party (from fifty-nine to sixty-one) and a loss of one seat each for the Liberals (from twenty-two to twenty-one) and Progressives (from one to zero). Two sets of transfers (Kent and Lambton, Huron, and Perth) were local gerrymanders. However, the 1935 general election returned fifty-six Liberals, twenty-six Tories, and one Progressive. The Liberal tide swept through all six gerrymandered ridings for Huron-Perth and Kent-Lambton, for which redistribution had predicted four wins for the governing Tories. Frederick Sanderson, targeted for "political assassination," won Perth.

THE 1933 ONTARIO REDISTRIBUTION

Premier Howard Ferguson led his Conservatives to a crushing victory in the 1929 Ontario general election. His government party's fortunes improved from seventy-five seats to ninety-two, and the opposition parties fell from thirty-seven to twenty seats (fourteen Liberals and six Progressives). The Tory candidate was acclaimed in eight ridings, and his opponent was an Independent Conservative in another eight. The three-party system barely survived. Whereas the Conservatives ran candidates in all one hundred twelve ridings and the Liberals in eighty-six, the Progressives contested just twenty-one – down from thirty-seven in the 1926 general election, and seventy-six in 1923.

In 1930 Ferguson stepped down as premier and leader of the Ontario Conservative Party. His replacement, the Hon. George S. Henry (York East), minister of Highways, was a graduate of Upper Canada College, the University of Toronto, and Ontario Agricultural College, and a lawyer who farmed near Todmorden Mills in the Don River Valley, East York Township.[37]

In January 1933, Premier Henry announced his government's plan, developed by a committee of cabinet, to cut the number of provincial ridings from one hundred and twelve to ninety.[38] To Henry, the government party's majority had "become so burdensome as to become noticeably unwieldy or unworkable." Second, a smaller House would be more efficient than the current one, with its hundred twelve ridings. Apart from reducing the salary bill for members, it would lower the "general cost of administration" and reduce "over-government." "Larger numbers," for example, "meant longer debates and, therefore, a waste of the Legislature's time. Moreover, 'other items of expenditure are reduced when the membership is cut down.'" Third, a reduction in the size of the Legislature appealed to Henry as an economy measure in the Great 1930s Depression.

Nevertheless, added the premier, "We have not been able to see our way clear to adopt the suggestion which has been made, to make the Federal and Provincial ridings co-terminate. Our interests are somewhat different from what they are at Ottawa, and we feel that a definite variation was essential, and that possibly a greater number of seats would be justified [ninety versus eighty-two] – in light of the fact that members of the Legislature deal with more intimate problems; with problems, one can say, that more nearly touch the home of the average citizen."[39]

To guide the elimination of twenty-two ridings, Henry set the minimum population for city ridings at 50,000, and the minimum for other ridings at 25,000. Staff at Queen's Park worked out the populations of the current ridings. Based on the 50,000 minimum, Toronto was to lose three seats, from fifteen to twelve, and Hamilton and Ottawa one each.

When the Liberal-Conservative Association of Toronto protested, Henry left Toronto with thirteen ridings.[40] That meant one more rural seat for elimination.

In March the premier faced a rebellious Tory caucus. "It is no secret," reported the *Globe*,

> that rural members, both Conservatives and those in the Opposition, feel they are being sacrificed so that cities can continue to have more members in the House than they really require, thereby making the Province safe for Tory democracy ... what they will not say for publication now will be said quite vehemently behind the closed doors of [the] secret enclave, they declare.
>
> TOO MUCH FOR TORONTO?
>
> 'Why should Toronto have twelve or thirteen seats to handle the affairs of one municipality when we rural members look after the interests of several municipalities and travel great distances to do it?' is a summary of the objections raised. Or: 'Why should our ridings be enveloped into others when we are already doing more than any city member thought of doing?' And again this pointed objection has been raised: 'We rural members travel to Toronto at much expense to ourselves during the year in the interests of many sections of our ridings and stay in the House throughout the session, while three or four Toronto members do all the work for the municipality, and then are absent from the Legislature many days of the session.'[41]

Premier Henry did not budge, telling his caucus to "take it or leave it."[42]

In mid-April Henry assigned the details of redistribution to a special committee of seventeen (ten Tories, four Liberals, two Progressives, and one Labour).[43] The composition by parties was generous to the opposition. If assembled by party strengths in the house, the seventeen would have included fourteen Tories, two Liberals, and one Progressive-Labour. The special committee extended this generosity to the opposition parties on striking a four-person subcommittee to design a schedule of ridings that could obtain unanimity in the House. The subcommittee comprised two Conservatives and two opposition members. The Hon. William Finlayson (Conservative, Simcoe East), minister of Lands and Forests, chaired the subcommittee; its other members were the Hon. Leopold Macaulay (Conservative, York South), minister of Highways; Dr George

A. McQuibban (Liberal, Wellington Northeast), Liberal whip; and David Taylor (Progressive, Grey North).[44] In mid-April the special committee reached unanimous agreement on the cuts.[45] The Bill passed without serious opposition in the House.

Equalizing Population

The elimination of twenty-two ridings raised the standard population (the provincial mean) from 30,797 to 38,325. The percentage of ridings in the optimum zone for standard populations (0.90–1.10) rose from 13 to 16, primarily through the consolidation of small-population county ridings. Redistribution cut much, but not all, of the fat, as defined by the government's population thresholds (50,000 for all-city ridings and 25,000 for others). It gave Toronto thirteen ridings, though its entitlement was twelve. The revised representation included thirty ridings with less than the 25,000 minimum population for country ridings, down from forty-four.

County Lines Take a Beating

The redistribution split four townships: the Prescott-County townships of Hawkesbury East and Hawkesbury West between the ridings of Prescott and Glengarry; North York Township between the ridings of York East and York North; and the township of York between the ridings of York South and York West. In eight transfers, it detached twenty-eight municipalities from their municipal counties. It folded six county ridings into three two-county ridings, each of which trespassed on either county or united-county lines: Grenville-Dundas included part of the united county of Stormont-Dundas-Glengarry; Haldimand-Norfolk included part of the county of Norfolk, the balance of the county going to the riding of Brant; and Muskoka-Ontario included part of Ontario County. Of the sixteen municipalities in Lennox & Addington County, the redistribution placed seven in the riding of Prince Edward–Lennox and one in the riding of Kingston.

Predicted Party Strengths

The elimination of twenty-two ridings favoured the old parties at the expense of the Progressives. A partisan-neutral redistribution would have replicated the current strength of the parties in the House:

seventy-four Tories, eleven Liberals, and five Progressives. The actual redistribution predicted seventy-six Tories, twelve Liberals, and two Progressives.

Nevertheless, the predicted party strengths were partly an artefact of the Liberal-majority statistic in a three-party setting. The statistics, calculated from transfers of municipalities from one riding to another, diminished the prospects of a party that lacked candidates in one or more of the redistributed ridings. In the 1929 general election, the Conservatives ran candidates in all hundred twelve ridings, the Liberals in eighty-six, and the Progressives in twenty-one.[46] Thus, all transfers of municipalities added Conservative votes to the receiving ridings; most transfers included Liberal votes; and very few included Progressive votes.

Given the method of prediction, the five Progressive incumbents had above-average prospects of losing their seats through redistribution. The Progressive incumbents for Grey North and Grey South survived because the 1933 redistribution left their their ridings alone. The three other Progressive incumbents prospectively perished because their ridings were disturbed. The redistribution "wiped out" Dufferin, the riding of one Progressive. The Progressive incumbents for the ridings of Brant and Huron South perished statistically for want of Progressive candidates in ridings from which their ridings received transfers.[47]

Testing for Gerrymanders

Gerrymandering seemed unlikely in the 1933 provincial redistribution. Premier Henry's legislative majority was huge; he regarded his party caucus as so large as to be unwieldy; and his special committee and its subcommittee over-represented the opposition parties. Yet he gave one too many seats to Toronto, and his redistribution for the ridings of Glengarry, Prescott, and Russell was a gerrymander.

Glengarry, Prescott, and Russell were county ridings within two united-municipal counties: Prescott-Russell and Stormont-Dundas-Glengarry. As such, they had no municipal functions and therefore no county lines to be observed in redistribution. But the united-county lines were another matter.

The redistribution for those ridings was problematic for the observance of principles. First, it did not reduce the number of ridings, which was the principal objective of the 1933 redistribution. Second, it transferred Caledonia Township and parts of two townships (East

Hawkesbury and West Hawkesbury) from the Prescott riding to Glengarry. These transfers split townships and trespassed on united-county lines.[48]

To complete the gerrymander, the redistribution benefited the government party. The Prescott riding was a massive Tory hive (-4,788); Prescott not only returned a Conservative in the 1929 general election, but another Tory was the runner-up, while the Liberal candidate was a distant third. Prescott was situated between two fighting ridings, Glengarry (+45) and Russell (-291). To reduce wasted government-party votes in Prescott, the redistribution moved two of its rock-solid Tory municipalities (-1,036) to Glengarry, which prospectively turned Glengarry from precarious, Liberal (+45) into a Tory hive (-1,081). In return, Prescott absorbed four Liberal-leaning municipalities (+313) from Russell, which moved the prospective Tory advantage in Russell from very safe, Tory (-291) to hive (-620). The end product was three Tory hives and the prospective gain of a seat for the government party.

Interestingly, James Sangster, the Liberal incumbent for Glengarry, pronounced himself "satisfied with the redistribution, and said that his own Glengarry riding had been fairly treated." Joseph St. Denis, the Conservative incumbent for Prescott, also opined that the "redistribution committee had done its job fairly."[49] Perhaps both men were relieved that their ridings had survived the government chop. In the event, the gerrymander failed. Liberals swept the three ridings in the 1934 general election. Glengarry returned Sangster with a large majority (+2,398). St. Denis was not a candidate in Prescott.

SUMMARY AND INTERPRETATION

Urbanization produced major shifts in population after 1901, a trend that continued during the 1920s. By 1931, cities held 45 percent of the provincial population, and Toronto held 41 percent of the population in cities. The shift in population put pressure on traditional principles for redistribution, such as the observance of county lines, rural-city differences in the unit of population, and the matching-up of the electoral and municipal territories for cities.

For the 1933 Dominion redistribution, Prime Minister Bennett named a twenty-member special committee, whose composition by parties matched their relative strengths in the House. The subcommittee for Ontario comprised three Conservatives and one Liberal. In the absence of direction from the prime minister or the national committee, the subcommittee, chaired by John MacNicol, set its own guidelines for redistribution. Ignorant of practice in previous redistributions, it acted without a comprehensive plan for the work. In the event, the 1933 redistribution was muddled in principle, chaotic in design, and inconsistent in execution.

The subcommittee's signature was its resistance to eliminating county ridings: it removed just three from the county tally, thereby giving it just three new seats for high-population constituencies. In this regard, three of the four subcommittee members, all except MacNicol, represented county ridings.

The subcommittee touched many ridings, but accomplished little. The percentage of ridings in the optimum zone for population (0.90–1.10) rose from 7 to 9, an all-time low in Ontario's history of redistribution. It did not match the electoral and municipal territories for any of the cities, thereby leaving their annexed city fragments in county ridings. In introduced the novel principle of arranging population size for county ridings by their percentage "urban," but applied the principle to one local redistribution only, possibly with the "political assassination" of a Liberal incumbent in mind.

The 1933 Dominion redistribution forecast a gain of two seats for the government party (from fifty-nine to sixty-one) and a loss of one seat each for the Liberals (from twenty-two to twenty-one) and Progressives (from one to zero). However, the 1935 general election returned fifty-six Liberals, twenty-six Tories, and one Progressive. The Liberal tide swept all five gerrymandered ridings for which redistribution had predicted wins for the governing Tories. The mild gerrymander of 1933 had little to do with the defeat of the Bennett government in Canada's 1935 general election. Far more important an influence was the Bennett government's record in the Great 1930s Depression.

George Henry's 1933 provincial redistribution reduced the size of the House, from one hundred twelve to ninety, as an economy measure and to increase efficiency. His chief opposition came from his own Tory caucus, whose members represented many of the eliminated seats. As a concession to the Liberal-Conservative Association of Toronto, the premier stripped the city of two seats rather than the planned three, but he held firm against Tory rebels from county ridings, to the point of over-representing the opposition parties on the special committee and its tripartite subcommittee. The redistribution slightly equalized riding populations – the percentage of ridings in the optimum zone for population rose from 13 to 17. It also trespassed on county lines, splitting townships in Prescott County and detaching twenty-eight municipalities from their home counties.

With one exception (Glengarry, Prescott, and Russell), Henry's redistribution was a fair one. The elimination of twenty-two ridings favoured the old parties at the expense of the Progressives. The predicted losses borne by the Progressives were partly an artefact of the Liberal-majority statistics, which were skewed by the lack of a Progressive candidate in many of the redistributed ridings.

In the event, the 1934 general election was a Tory rout. Led by Mitchell Hepburn, the Grits took sixty-five seats, versus the twelve statistically projected, and the Tories fell to seventeen seats, versus the seventy-six predicted. The Tories lost every seat in the five case-study groups of ridings for which redistribution predicted a Tory win. Clearly the 1933 provincial redistribution had no discernible impact on the outcome of the 1934 Ontario general election.

The ridings of 1933 served for six consecutive provincial general elections. The next provincial redistribution, and Ontario's last parliamentary redistribution ever, was to take place in 1954, twenty-one years later, and, remarkably, was to leave most of the ridings of 1933 undisturbed.

11

The Last of Ontario's Parliamentary Redistributions, 1947–54

Liberal ministries managed Dominion redistributions in 1947 and 1952, the first under Prime Minister Mackenzie King, and the second under Prime Minister Louis-Stephen St-Laurent. In 1947 Mackenzie King had a bare working majority nationally, and held a minority of the Ontario ridings (thirty-four Liberals and forty-eight Conservatives).[1] King's circumstances were similar to those of his 1924 redistribution, when he had headed a minority government. In 1952, by contrast, the St-Laurent Liberals had a majority nationally and within the Ontario ridings: fifty-seven Liberals, twenty-five Conservatives, and one CCF (Co-operative Commonwealth Federation).

A Tory ministry under Premier Leslie Frost administered a provincial redistribution in 1954, the province's first in twenty-one years. Frost headed a massive majority in the Legislative Assembly, with seventy-nine Tories, eight Liberals, two CCF, and one LPP (Labour-Progressive Party). Thus, unlike King in 1947, but like St-Laurent in 1952, Frost in 1954 faced negligible pressure to conciliate opposition parties.

THE 1947 DOMINION REDISTRIBUTION

The 1941 census – the basis for the 1947 Dominion redistribution – expressed Ontario's 10 percent growth of population during the Great 1930s Depression. The percentages by region were the northland districts, 25; the GTA, 11; Eastern Ontario, 9; and Western Ontario, 7. In 1941 the province had thirty-two cities, the same as in 1931. Three newcomers to the list were Brockville, Pembroke, and Forest Hill; dropped from the list were East Windsor (Ford City), Sandwich, and Walkerville, all of which Windsor had annexed in 1935.

Although a Dominion redistribution was mandatory following the issuance of the 1941 census, the Second World War intervened. In 1943, Parliament obtained an amendment to the imperial BNA Act to postpone redistribution "until the cessation of hostilities." The upshot was the Representation Act, 1947, which was "out of season," with the 1941 census now dated and a new census due in 1951.

In a break with tradition, the 1947 redistribution did not use a Quebec-standard population to allocate seats to the provinces. A 1946 amendment to Section 51 of the BNA Act fixed the number of seats in Parliament at 255, an increase of ten, and provided for a redistribution of seats according each province's share of the national population. Under the revised formula, Ontario's allocation increased from eighty-two to eighty-three.[2]

Prime Minister King struck a special committee of twenty-five, with the parties represented according to their strength in the House: fourteen Liberals, seven Tories, three CCF, and one Social Credit. However, the tail wagged the dog on the subcommittee for Ontario. Although the opposition Tories held 59 percent of the Ontario ridings, the subcommittee numbered four Liberals and two Conservatives. The chair was Walter Harris (Grey-Bruce), a trusted advisor and parliamentary assistant to the minister of External Affairs, Louis-Stephen St-Laurent.[3] The other Liberals were Leoda Gauthier (Nipissing), Robert McCubbin (Middlesex West), and George McIlraith (Ottawa West). The Tories were John MacNicol (Toronto Davenport), who had chaired R.B. Bennett's 1933 subcommittee, and Park Manross (London). None of the members had ministerial experience. Gauthier and Manross were newly elected to Parliament.

The Work of the Ontario Subcommittee

Minimalism was the subcommittee's dominant principle. Indeed, the subcommittee considered making no changes, with the next census due only four years hence, but decided against "postponing those changes which were equitable and unlikely to be affected materially by the census of 1951."[4]

To arrive at eighty-three ridings from the 1933 allocation of eighty-two, the subcommittee added two ridings and eliminated one. Its redistribution touched twenty-seven ridings and left alone fifty-five. "Of the 82 constituencies established by the 1933 Representation Act," reported Walter Harris, "sixteen are either increased or decreased slightly, 6 are the subject of three changes involving from 10,000–12,000 people in each case, and four are the subject of major changes." In the end, the subcommittee report was "unanimous except for one constituency."[5]

To determine the changes, the subcommittee sorted ridings into "six main divisions of the province recognized by everyone – eastern, central, western, northern, southern, and Toronto and York" – and calculated the "unit of population" (the mean) for each of them. It ignored the "Toronto and York division," which had the highest unit of population, presumably on the principle that city ridings should have above-average populations. This left the "northern division," the second-highest unit, with the greatest need for increased representation.[6] Indeed, the subcommittee gave the "northern division" two additional seats, by rearranging Nipissing, Cochrane, and Temiskaming into the five ridings of Nipissing, Cochrane, Temiskaming, Sudbury, and Timmins. With the redistribution now over the Ontario quota of eighty-three seats, the subcommittee had to eliminate one riding, ostensibly in the "central division," which had the lowest unit of population.

The subcommittee's approach to redistribution boded ill for the opposition party. Conservatives held ten of the eleven ridings in the ill-fated "central division," and all ten had smaller populations (0.51 to 0.88) than the sole Liberal-held riding (1.06). If constituencies rather than "divisions" had mattered, then the subcommittee might have merged Glengarry, the riding with the smallest population in Ontario (0.38), with Prescott, the fourth smallest (0.51). Glengarry was Prime Minister King's constituency, however, and a merger of these two Liberal-held ridings would have eliminated a Liberal seat. Hence "divisions," not ridings, mattered in 1947. Conveniently for the government party, Glengarry and Prescott were safely lodged in the left-alone "eastern division."

The subcommittee's redistribution for the "central division" held surprises, however. To eliminate a riding, the subcommittee chose Muskoka-Ontario (0.71) rather than any of the six Tory ridings in the "central division" with smaller populations. Muskoka-Ontario comprised the Muskoka District and part of Ontario County, with the balance of Ontario County located in the riding of Ontario. The subcommittee made four changes, two of which involved units from outside the "central division." First, it divided Muskoka-Ontario into its Muskoka and Ontario-County portions. Second, it divided the Ontario-County portion between the redistributed "central-division" ridings of Ontario and Victoria. Third, it removed Baxter Township,[7] Muskoka District, to Simcoe East – in the subcommittee's "western division." Fourth, it joined the balance of the Muskoka District to Parry Sound – in the subcommittee's "northern division" – to form the riding of Parry Sound–Muskoka. These transfers prospectively reduced by one the opposition Tory count of seats. Whereas the Parry Sound riding had been very safe, Liberal (+392) and Muskoka-Ontario very safe, Conservative (-769), the proposed Parry Sound–Muskoka riding was possibly safe, Liberal (+60).[8]

In a memorandum to James Macdonnell, the Tory incumbent for Muskoka-Ontario, Walter Harris, the subcommittee's Liberal chair, struggled to justify the subcommittee's selection and dismemberment of Macdonnell's riding. "Some of us," explained Harris, "decided on Muskoka-Ontario simply because it was the nearest geographically to what is generally referred to as the north and on the ground that the unit of representation for Parry Sound would be almost the same as the average of the northern constituencies."[9] He elaborated the position in a statement to the House:

> the people in Muskoka and Parry Sound have a great deal in common. They engage almost exclusively in lumbering, hunting, and fishing and catering to the tourist trade. There are two common railway and highway systems which touch practically all the larger centres in both districts; there is no town over 6,000 so that it could not be said that undue influence was given to any municipality … [Conversely,] the townships in Ontario county are purely agricultural and have nothing in common with districts to the north. Their communications and markets are to the east and south and the transfer of these townships to Victoria and Ontario [riding] has restored them to more convenient and logical electoral districts. Further, the new constituency of Parry Sound-Muskoka is nearer than any other in central Ontario to that part of northern Ontario requiring extra representation – in fact it adjoins the constituency of Nipissing.[10]

Macdonnell was having none of this. The Ontario municipalities in his Muskoka-Ontario riding were "dealt around like a pack of cards" across county lines. Whereas his riding had "a population of 35,000," there were "nineteen Ontario ridings with a population of under 30,000, and the smallest of course … is Glengarry … which heads or tails the list, whichever you like, with a population of 18,732." Muskoka-Ontario had twice the territory of the prime minister's Glengarry riding, and the proposed Parry Sound–Muskoka constituency would have three times its territory. Moreover, Prime Minister Mackenzie King was on record as opposing any special treatment for himself as prime minister or for his constituency. King had made the statement in 1933, when he had been leader of the opposition, but with reference to the 1924 redistribution, when he had been prime minister.[11]

Two speculations are in order. One is that the Liberal majority on the subcommittee aimed to "politically assassinate" James M. Macdonnell, the Conservative incumbent for Muskoka-Ontario. Macdonnell, writes J.L. Granatstein, was "an extraordinary man ... a Rhodes scholar [who] had served with great distinction in the Great War." He had been a prominent and successful party organizer before his election to Parliament in 1945.[12] In one of several achievements, he had been a key organizer of the party's Port Hope Conference of 1942, which had crafted a left-leaning platform to blunt the rising popularity of the CCF and displace the Liberal hold on the middle ground.

The second speculation is that John MacNicol, the senior Tory on the subcommittee, was complicit in Macdonnell's "political assassination." MacNicol, the founding president of the Dominion Liberal-Conservative Association (1924–43), had motive. In 1943, Richard A. Bell, the Conservative Party's national director and Macdonnell's close ally, had orchestrated MacNicol's ouster as president of the Association. "Gordon Graydon was elected president," writes J.L. Granatstein, "and MacNicol was ushered out with praises, honours, and finality."[13]

In the event, MacNicol accepted the Liberal majority's lethal focus on "divisions" rather than constituencies, which would have made the Glengarry riding a prime target for extinction. Indeed, MacNicol wanted Liberal-held Glengarry left alone, ostensibly "owing to the fact that it is represented by the Prime Minister."[14] As he elaborated, "we could easily have changed Glengarry by adding to it [three townships] from the adjacent county of Stormont ... [but] we did not do that because it did not gain a seat, and what the [sub]committee wanted to do was to gain an extra seat for Ottawa." He "could not understand this attack on Glengarry [by Macdonnell and others]. I cannot see it at all, because nothing could have been gained by changing it." He also opposed a merger of King's Glengarry (0.32) and Liberal-held Prescott (0.46), which would have gained a seat, and eliminated a seat from the government party's prospective tally in the next general election.[15]

MacNicol endorsed the subcommittee's work overall. His advice, "to let the ridings remain very largely as they are because within five years we shall have another census and another redistribution, was largely followed ... the Ontario committee, following that advice, made very few changes ... I do not know what I could have done in Ontario different[ly] from what I did." He "could defend everything that was done to the province of Ontario, even as to [Muskoka-Ontario]. I did my best, as the subcommittee will admit, to prevent that seat from being changed; but another seat in northern Ontario was required ... It finally came down to the point where my hon. friend's seat and another one were put together. I did not support it then and I am not supporting it now; but outside of that one seat I believe our whole schedule in Ontario was a good record, eighty-two out of eighty-three."[16]

Summary of the 1947 Redistribution

The minimalist redistribution of 1947 did little to equalize population. It boosted the percentage of ridings in the optimum zone (0.90–1.10) from 20 to 24. Its dismemberment of the Muskoka-Ontario riding, with its contrived "division" method of selection and tortured application of the method, was a gerrymandered attempt at "political assassination." Of equal moment, it avoided the extinction of Glengarry, the prime minister's riding.

The 1947 redistribution benefited the government party. The redistribution prospectively added three to the Liberal count of seats and subtracted two from the Tory total. The two additional seats for northern Ontario were likely to favour the Liberals, inasmuch as the feeder ridings of Nipissing, Cochrane, and Temiskaming were Liberal hives.[17] Conversely, the Conservatives prospectively lost one seat from the liquidation of Muskoka-Ontario. No other changes in the 1947 redistribution significantly altered party prospects.

However, the 1949 general election delivered twenty-three additional Liberal seats in Ontario. In Parry Sound–Muskoka, the Liberal candidate, "Bucko" McDonald, a retired NHL hockey player, crushed James Macdonnell by 1,820 votes, a great deal more than the predicted Liberal majority (+60). Redistribution had little to do with the Tory rout, nor did Macdonell's "political assassination."[18]

THE DOMINION REDISTRIBUTION OF 1952

The 1951 census captured Ontario's robust 21 percent increase of population during the 1940s. The boom was in suburbs of the major cities. The increase was minuscule for Toronto City (1 percent), but much higher for suburban townships: Scarborough (132 percent), Etobicoke

(109 percent), and Vaughan (66 percent). The statistic was average for Hamilton City (25 percent), but above average in the townships of Barton (88 percent), East and West Flamborough (49 percent), and Ancaster (45 percent). Ottawa's suburban sprawl boosted population in the townships of Nepean and Gloucester until the years 1949–50, when the city annexed suburban parts of those townships. The suburban population boom continued into the 1950s, as evidenced by statistics from the 1956 census. In the circumstances, observes MacGregor Dawson, "an equitable allocation of population among urban and suburban areas could quickly become obsolete."[19]

Ontario's 1951 census population entitled the province to eighty-five seats, up from eighty-three. The 1952 redistribution reached the new quota in two steps. First, it added five seats through division of current ridings: three for suburban York County (York Centre, York-Humber, and York-Scarborough), one for Sudbury (Nickel Belt), and one for Welland (Niagara Falls). Then it eliminated three county ridings through mergers: Glengarry with Prescott, Brant with Haldimand,[20] and Hastings-Peterborough with Frontenac-Addington. The redistribution touched thirty-three of the eighty-three ridings.

Prime Minister St-Laurent named a special committee of thirty-seven, the largest ever, to draft the schedule. Twenty-two Liberals were the majority; the others were ten Conservative, three CCF, and two Social Credit members. Five Liberals and three Conservatives constituted the subcommittee for Ontario. The Liberals were George McIlraith (Ottawa West), the subcommittee's chair; the Hon. Walter Harris (Grey-Bruce), minister of Citizenship and Immigration, past parliamentary assistant and trusted advisor to Prime Minister St-Laurent, and chair of the 1947 and 1952 special committees; Leoda Gauthier (Sudbury); Robert McCubbin (Middlesex West); and William Robinson (Simcoe East). The Conservatives were Donald Fleming (Toronto-Eglinton), Joseph Murphy (Lambton West), and William Blair (Lanark). Experience favoured the Liberal side. All Grit members except Robinson were veterans of the 1947 subcommittee, and Harris had been its chair.

Work of the Subcommittee

The 1952 subcommittee focussed on ridings, not the six "divisions" of its 1947 predecessor. Its primary goal was to equalize populations. For the purpose, it selected the seven Ontario ridings with less than 0.50 standard populations and the seven ridings with 1.67 or more standard populations. It eliminated three ridings in the first group through mergers and added five ridings to the second group through division. McIlraith conceded "that maybe we did not go far enough, or that we should have continued and tried to adjust all constituencies. [But] there are endless problems if you get into that field."[21]

The compressed time frame for the redistribution truncated what the subcommittee could accomplish and exacerbated partisan tensions. The Tory opposition had stalled the appointment of the special committee in a failed effort to give redistribution to an independent commission. Consequently, the government appointed the committee two months into the parliamentary session, not at its beginning; this gave the committee just two and a half months to complete the schedule of ridings, rather than the normal duration of three to seven months.

On the 1947 subcommittee, when the Liberals had a bare working majority nationally and a minority of seats in Ontario, the majority party's desire for unanimity led it to make concessions to the minority. This did not happen in 1952, when the Liberals had a large majority nationally and a majority of the Ontario ridings. The redistribution, charged Joseph Murphy (Conservative, Lambton West), "was brought about on a political basis, and no argument we in the opposition could make had any effect. I do hope that no future member of this house will have to go through the mess we had on this committee. As an opposition member you could accomplish nothing. Those on the government side rode roughshod over everyone else. They had their plans prepared in advance and they were announced in the newspapers. Those plans were carried out in spite of the opposition of members on this side."[22]

Donald Fleming alleged that the government side made "ruthless use" of its majority on the subcommittee, which paid lip service to principles but showed no regard for their consistent application: "We see one principle invoked to justify what is done in connection with one riding, but when we move to another riding where the political situation happens to be a little different, that particular principle seems to be completely forgotten; it is abandoned and something else arises to dictate the decision in that particular case." Fleming noted "a great deal of pulling and hauling at all times, and gerrymandering … created by the fact that government representatives on such a committee are the objects of a great deal of pressure from within the ranks of their own party." Glaring inequalities in population remained, ranging from 30,000 to 90,000. The subcommittee extinguished tiny Haldimand (0.44), but neighbouring Lincoln (1.32) was undisturbed. It treated with kid gloves ridings whose sitting members were ministers. Fleming had in mind Renfrew South, represented by the minister of National Revenue, the Hon. James McCann, and Algoma East, represented by the Hon. Lester Pearson, secretary of state for External Affairs.[23]

Norman Ward and the "Save the Leaders" Principle

In a 1953 article, Norman Ward detected a save-the-leaders "dogma" as a general feature of parliamentary redistribution.[24] By this, he meant a bipartisan understanding to leave untouched the seats of party leaders, cabinet ministers, and opposition front-benchers. This "*preposterous notion*," wrote Ward, "had been lost sight of in 1947, when the three seats most adversely affected in the entire country had by a coincidence been held by three leading members of the Progressive Conservative Party: Mr. Bracken, Mr. Macdonnell, and Mr. Diefenbaker." However, the dogma was resurrected in 1952 for George Drew, the Tory leader, who pressed successfully to have his riding of Carleton left alone. Drew's gain came at the expense of Ottawa City, whose population warranted a third seat, which, if given, would have destroyed Carleton, "a large part of which was within city limits."

Ward overlooks a contrary practice to "saving the leaders": that of "politically assassinating" opposition leaders through gerrymander. Targets of this practice include the Hon. Sir Richard Cartwright, Huron Centre, 1882; the Hon. David Mills, Bothwell, 1882; James Clancy, Bothwell, 1903; Frederick Sanderson, Perth South, 1933; Sam Hughes, Victoria North, 1903; and James Macdonnell, Muskoka-Ontario, 1947. Thus, "political assassination" may explain the adverse redistributions for the "three leading members of the Progressive Conservative Party in 1947" – one of them being Macdonnell. Conversely, the 1947 redistribution had not "lost sight of" the dogma. Rather, the leader of the Tory minority on the Ontario subcommittee, John MacNicol, wanted tiny Glengarry left alone, "owing to the fact that it is represented by the Prime Minister."

Second, due to the brief time period available for the work of redistribution in 1952, the subcommittee focussed on the top seven and bottom seven ridings by population. The subcommittee left Drew's riding of Carleton undisturbed, not because Drew was a party leader, but because his riding ranked seventeenth in standard populations. Third, Ward's assumption of three all-city Ottawa ridings, in which the city's electoral district matched its municipal boundaries, ignores local history. Previous redistributions had left, or placed, some city residents in the ridings of Russell and Carleton. In 1951 Carleton was already a third Ottawa riding in all but name: city residents comprised 75 percent of its population.[25]

Annexations and the Electoral Territories of Cities

Before redistribution, the electoral and municipal territories matched for Toronto, but not for Hamilton, Ottawa, or London. In 1941, 38 percent of Hamilton City's municipal population was in Wentworth; 17 percent of London's municipal population was in East Middlesex; 21 percent of Ottawa's municipal population was in the riding of Carleton and 3 percent was situated in Russell. Ottawa's annexation of two parcels during the years 1949–50 added to the city's electoral diaspora. The 1952 redistribution matched the electoral and municipal territories for Hamilton, but not for Ottawa or London. This left 24 percent of London City's population in the riding of East Middlesex, and 35 percent of Ottawa City's population in the ridings of Carleton and Russell.

Some Consequences of the 1952 Redistribution

The 1952 redistribution boosted the percentage of ridings in the optimum zone (0.90–1.10) from 24 to 31. Stanley Knowles (NDP, Winnipeg North Centre) congratulated the Ontario subcommittee for moving riding populations in the right direction, although in his view, it had not gone far enough.

The 1952 redistribution boosted the government party's prospects. With the two-seat increase in the Ontario quota, the Liberals prospectively gained three seats (from fifty-seven to sixty) and the Conservatives prospectively lost one (from twenty-five to twenty-four). The CCF count held at one. The creation of five new ridings prospectively added three to the Liberal count of seats and two to the Conservative count. The elimination of three ridings, and a transfer in the Middlesex ridings, prospectively removed three from the Tory count of seats and left the Liberal count unchanged.

The 1953 general election denied the government party its predicted gains. It returned fifty-one Liberals, nine fewer than the sixty predicted. The Conservatives won thirty-three seats, seven more than predicted, and the CCF held at one. The impact of redistribution on this outcome was minimal.

THE PROVINCIAL REDISTRIBUTION OF 1954

In 1954 Ontario was ripe for a major overhaul of its provincial ridings, which had been undisturbed for twenty-one years. During the years 1931–51, the Ontario population had increased by 25 percent. The increases by region were, northlands, 45 percent; GTA, 39 percent; Eastern Ontario, 25 percent; and Western Ontario, 31 percent. In the redistribution of 1933, just 16 percent of the ridings had been in the optimum zone for population; before redistribution in 1954, the statistic was 19 percent. Clearly, there was much to do. What the Frost government delivered in 1954 was a mockery of redistribution.

The weakness of the opposition parties was striking. Frost headed a massive majority in the Legislative Assembly (seventy-nine Tories, eight Liberals, two CCF, and one Communist). Neither leader of the opposition parties – Walter Thomson for the Liberals and Donald C. Macdonald for the CCF – had a seat in the House. In 1936 the Toronto *Globe*, a dependable Liberal organ, had given way to the Toronto *Globe and Mail*, the product of a merger of the *Globe* with the Toronto *Mail and Empire*. By the 1950s, this newspaper was a Conservative organ. One of its editorials urged voters in the 1955 provincial general election to "Make it a Landslide" for Frost's government party.[26]

Premier Frost struck an eleven-person special committee to work out the details, with parties represented according to their strength in the House: eight Conservatives, two Liberals, and one CCF.[27] William Collings (Toronto Beaches) chaired the committee, which included one minister, the attorney-general, Dana H. Porter (Toronto St. George's). The Liberals were the party's House leader, Farquhar Oliver, and Harry Nixon (Brant), a former party leader. The CCF member was the party's House leader, Bill Grummett (Cochrane South).

Principles

Frost's sole declared motivation was to increase representation for the province's rapidly growing suburban populations. Otherwise, *do nothing* was his guiding principle. A "redistribution which cuts people away from their moorings," opined the premier, "is a great mistake … the cutting up of historic ridings and disturbing historic associations is a mistake."[28] Effectively, he styled the ridings of 1933 as historical, a designation once restricted to the ridings of Confederation. With this subterfuge, he aimed to feather the nests of seventy-nine Tory incumbents. The chair of Frost's special committee, William Collings (Toronto Beaches), saw "no advantage in a wholesale changing of boundaries ... [he had] canvassed all the members and that was the consensus."

Details of the Redistribution

Collings's special committee increased the size of the Legislature from ninety to ninety-eight seats, but touched only sixteen of the ninety ridings (18 percent). It divided the four York-County constituencies into seven; added one seat each for Hamilton, Ottawa, and London; divided Sudbury into two ridings; and added one seat to Muskoka District and Ontario County.[29] The redistribution was barely positive for equalizing population. The percentage of ridings in the optimum zone (0.90–1.10) increased from 19 to 20. The redistribution showed scant regard for county lines, splitting three York-County townships and three townships in Ontario County. Before redistribution, the government party held seventy-nine of the ninety seats. The redistribution furnished eight additional seats, all of which, prospectively, went to the Tory count of ridings.

ANNEXATIONS AND THE ELECTORAL TERRITORIES OF CITIES

Before redistribution, the electoral and municipal territories of cities matched for Toronto, but not for Hamilton, Ottawa, or London. As noted above, Ottawa's annexation of two parcels in 1949 and 1950 added to the city's electoral diaspora. The 1954 redistribution left Ottawa alone, which stranded 3 percent of the city's electors in the riding of Carleton and 11 percent in the riding of Russell. It gave Hamilton a set of hybrid ridings: the distribution of the city's electors by ridings was Wentworth, 14 percent; Wentworth East, 16 percent; Hamilton Centre, 32 percent; Hamilton East, 29 percent; and Hamilton-Wentworth, 9 percent. It gave each of the London-City ridings a part of London Township; one surmises that these transfers were city fragments left from the 1933 redistribution. If so, then London City's electoral and municipal territories were one.

MUSKOKA DISTRICT AND ONTARIO COUNTY: A GERRYMANDER

The redistribution turned Muskoka-Ontario (0.77) and Ontario (1.42) into three ridings: Muskoka (0.53), Ontario (0.69), and Oshawa (1.16). It was a gerrymander. With only 1.93 standard populations, the two current ridings manifestly fell short of the threshold for three ridings (2.50). The Tories held Muskoka-Ontario (-2,807) and the CCF held Ontario (+2,608). The redistribution hived the CCF into the Oshawa riding (+3,867), and set up two Tory hives: Muskoka (-1,221) and Ontario (-22,024): thus, prospectively, a gain of one seat for the government party.

The partition of the Ontario riding split three municipalities – the townships of Pickering and Whitby and the town of Whitby. The Oshawa riding received the southern sections of the split municipalities, and the Ontario riding the northern sections. Change in the provincial road network underlay the trespasses on county lines. The new electoral boundary ran eastwards along a concession road in Pickering, continued east along the north town line of Ajax, turned south at Whitby Township to the newly christened Highway 401, and then moved eastwards along Highway 401 to Oshawa.[30] The new ridings had unequal populations (0.69 and 1.16). Had township lines prevailed, then the statistics would have improved to 0.72 and 1.14.[31]

"Many members," reported the Toronto *Globe and Mail*, expected that the redistribution "would turn out to be a cut and dried proposition." Indeed, the committee planned to complete its work with a single meeting, and nearly did so, creating seven new ridings "in less than an hour, [with] little discussion of the location of the new ridings or their boundaries." However, the proposed partition of Muskoka-Ontario was "the rock upon which the Committee on Redistribution foundered."[32] The Hon. Col. George Welsh, the provincial secretary, "was on hand to support his request that [his riding of] Muskoka-Ontario be made into two ridings, Muskoka and Ontario, the latter to take in what is left over of the old Ontario riding when Oshawa and other urban areas are taken out." The populations for Welsh's proposed ridings would be Muskoka, 0.53, and Ontario, 0.69. The Hon. Dana Porter (Toronto St. George's) objected "when he discovered that the division would leave each riding with about 12,000 voters." "If we tamper with it," he said, "we are departing from our general principle of not disturbing the riding boundaries and that we should only deal with places that should be cut in half." Interestingly, Porter's evidence was voters, not *population*, which was the statutory basis for representation. Nor did he refer to trespasses on county lines, although the proposed partition split three municipalities in the proposed riding of Ontario.[33] In the event, Col. Welsh's request prevailed. At its second meeting, the committee divided Muskoka-Ontario (0.77). It refused the request of Bill Grummett, the CCF House leader and a member of the special committee, to divide his Cochrane South riding (1.33) due to its vast extent of territory.[34]

Criticism of Frost's handiwork was minimal. Neither the *Globe and Mail* nor the opposition parties remarked upon an outstanding feature of the redistribution: its passive gerrymander to protect the ridings of the incumbents (drawn from the redistribution of 1933). The Liberals offered no criticism of any kind. The Liberal and CCF members on the special committee signed its report, which, as Premier Frost noted, had been "unanimously endorsed by the committee."[35] Donald C. Macdonald, leader of the CCF who lacked a seat in the House, roasted the redistribution in a public broadcast, but only for what the redistribution did, not what it did not do (the passive gerrymander).[36] He lambasted the process: the special committee was "a rubber stamp … It merely went through the motions of approving cut-and-dried decisions worked out behind the scenes by the Conservatives"; and although seven new seats went to areas that were heavily populated, "the new riding boundaries had been drawn up beforehand by the Conservative members affected." Above all, there was the Muskoka gerrymander. "Although Premier Frost had declared the Government's intention not to disturb historical boundaries, this principle had gone out the window when it came to Col. Welsh's riding … the provincial secretary carved out for himself a little pocket borough, with about 15,000 voters. The [rubber-stamp] committee okayed it." The Frost redistribution benefited the government party. Its eight new ridings were Tory-leaning. The redistribution for Muskoka-Ontario and Ontario was an outright intentional gerrymander. The do-nothing feature for seventy-four ridings feathered the nests of the party's army of incumbents. In the 1955 general election, Frost's multi-dimensional gerrymander helped his party to win eighty-four seats, including seven of the eight additional seats, and Col. Welsh's scandalously under-populated riding of Muskoka.

SUMMARY AND INTERPRETATION

Two Dominion redistributions and one provincial redistribution responded to a post-war population boom in city suburbs and the northlands. The Liberal-Party administrations of Mackenzie King and Louis-Stephen St-Laurent administered the Dominion redistributions of 1947 and 1952. The Tory premier, Leslie Frost, directed the provincial redistribution of 1954. In 1947, the King government, with a bare working majority nationally and a minority of the Ontario constituencies, was conciliatory to the Tory minority on the subcommittee for Ontario. The St-Laurent and Frost administrations, each with a large parliamentary majority, did little to placate the opposition parties. With the remarkably feeble opposition in Ontario provincial politics following the 1951 general election, Frost had no need to.

The 1947 Dominion redistribution had been delayed by the Second World War, was "out of season" with the 1941 and 1951 censuses, and made few changes. To arrive at the province's quota of eighty-three seats, the Ontario subcommittee added two ridings and eliminated one. An unusual feature of its work, supported by its senior Tory member, John MacNicol, was to proceed by "divisions" to determine where to add two ridings and eliminate one. This enabled the subcommittee to leave alone Prime Minister King's Glengarry constituency, which had the smallest population of the eighty-two Ontario ridings. The subcommittee's misapplication of its so-called "divisions" stratagem was a gerrymander. Its objective was to "politically assassinate" the talented Tory politician James Macdonnell, with MacNicol complicit. Prospectively, the redistribution added one to the Liberal count of seats. It did little to equalize populations.

The 1952 redistribution, the second in five years, added five ridings and eliminated three to arrive at the province's quota of eighty-five seats. Whereas the 1947 subcommittee had proceeded by "divisions," the 1952 subcommittee touched the ridings with the seven lowest and seven highest populations, and made few changes between the extremes. Faced with a compressed time frame for the work, the Liberal majority imposed decisions over the bitter opposition of the Tory minority. This contrasted with the bipartisan harmony of the 1947 subcommittee. The 1952 redistribution, prospectively, added three to the Liberal count of seats and subtracted one from the Tory tally. With its focus on the high and low extremes of population, it increased the percentage of ridings in the optimum zone from 24 to 31. It did little to equalize population for the sixty-nine ridings in the neglected middle.

The Tory-administered provincial redistribution of 1954 showed a near-total disregard for traditional principles such as county lines and the equalization of population. Despite being the province's first redistribution since 1933, it touched only sixteen of the ninety ridings. Although not recognized as such by contemporaries, it was a passive gerrymander that protected the ridings of Tory incumbents. It added eight seats, all of which were Tory-leaning and favoured to add to the Frost government's already massive majority. It was a patchwork affair, to increase representation for suburban and northern populations and boost prospects for the government party. The breakup of the Muskoka-Ontario riding was an intentional gerrymander and the product of bullying by the government's provincial secretary, Col. Welsh.

In 1951, the electoral and municipal territories of cities matched for Toronto, but not for Hamilton, Ottawa, or London. The 1952 Dominion redistribution matched the territories for Hamilton, but not Ottawa or London. The 1954 provincial redistribution united the electoral and municipal territories for London, but not for Ottawa or Hamilton.

Each of the three post-war redistributions boosted the prospects of the government party. None of the three redistributions mattered much to the outcome of the next election. The 1952 redistribution was notably free of gerrymanders. The 1947 Dominion and 1954 provincial redistributions held gerrymanders, and they worked, respectively, in the 1949 Dominion and 1955 provincial general elections. Such was the last hurrah for parliamentary redistribution. The 1960s ushered in commissioned ridings.

Conclusion

Redistribution matters in parliamentary systems. It adjusts representation to the movement of population, sets limits on democracy, and influences the fortunes of incumbents and political parties. The fairness of a given redistribution affects the legitimacy of the next general election and the confidence of the people in the institutions that govern them. A key issue in parliamentary redistribution is its vulnerability to gerrymandering – attempts by the majority party to redraw, or leave alone, electoral districts for partisan advantage. A related issue is whether or not gerrymanders work.

Since 1840, Ontario has had two contrasting systems for administering redistribution. Before the 1960s, Parliament managed the work. Since the 1960s, arm's-length provincial boundary commissions, headed by a judge, have been the authority. This chapter summarizes the book's findings for 120 years of parliamentary redistribution. It closes with a discussion of the transition to commissioned ridings.

Ontario underwent twenty-three parliamentary redistributions before the 1960s: five for Canada West (1840–67); nine for Dominion ridings (1872–1952); and nine for Ontario-provincial ridings (1874–1954). Two redistributions came from imperial statutes: the Act to Re-Unite the Provinces of Upper and Lower Canada, 1840 (Union Act), and the British North America Act, 1867 (BNA Act). Lord Sydenham, the governor of Canada, and Britain's colonial office arranged the ridings of 1840. John A. Macdonald, leader of the Great Coalition Party in the colonial Legislative Assembly, set up the ridings of Confederation, with the compliance of colonial officials and without discussion in the Canadian parliament. All other redistributions issued from the colonial parliaments.

With the development of political parties by the 1860s, parliamentary authority meant the majority party in Parliament.

Representation and the Movement of Population

The Ontario population grew by 15 percent or more in all but three decades: the 1880s (10 percent), the 1890s (3 percent), and the 1930s (10 percent). The rate of growth was above average for the Greater Toronto Area (GTA) and the northland districts during the years 1871–1941. It was below average in the largely rural counties of Eastern Ontario, and also in Western Ontario counties after 1881. Population urbanized. The number of cities increased from five in 1852 to forty-four in 1956. The percentage of the population living in cities rose steadily, from 9 in 1852 to 46 in 1941, then slipped to 43 in 1956.

Population growth in Ontario outstripped the supply of ridings. Between Confederation and 1951, the number of seats per 100,000 population fell from 5.9 to 1.9 for the Dominion parliament, and from 5.9 to 2.1 for the provincial parliament. In both jurisdictions, representation was below average for the GTA; above average for Eastern Ontario; below average for Western Ontario until 1900, and then above average; and below average for small cities after the 1890s. Representation for the northland districts was above average into the 1870s for both jurisdictions, then average for Dominion ridings and slightly above average for provincial ridings. The statistics reflect conventional wisdom, beginning in the 1890s, that rural populations in the counties and settler populations in the northland districts merited fuller representation than population in cities, notably Toronto. The bias was pronounced in the Dominion parliament, with its constitutional quota for the number of Ontario ridings. Whenever the quota was unchanged or declined, the addition of seats for Toronto required the elimination of ridings in the counties. The provincial parliament, without a quota, could increase the size of the House.

The Redistribution in Canada West, 1840–67

Ontario's history of redistribution began when it was Canada West, Province of Canada, 1840–67. The 1840 imperial Union Act made Parliament the authority for redistribution. The Act gave the province a start-up set of ridings, but empowered its Legislative Assembly to "alter the Divisions and Extent of the several Counties, Ridings, Cities, and Towns which shall be represented." The Union Act added a constitutional limitation: Canada West and Canada East were to have equal representation in the province's Legislative Assembly. The two sections of the province had forty-two seats each until 1853, and then sixty-five each.

The years of Canada West served up five redistributions, two by imperial statute (1840 and 1867) and three by Acts of the Legislative Assembly (1845, 1851, and 1853). In the meantime, Parliament developed the framework for redistribution in Canada West. It reorganized counties (1845, 1849, 1851, and 1860), made counties municipal as well as electoral entities (1849), and undertook two modern census enumerations (1852 and 1861).

The pre-Confederation years lacked widely accepted unwritten principles for redistribution. In redrawing the ridings, neither representation by population nor the observance of municipal-county lines carried much weight. The percentage of the ridings in the optimum range for standard populations (0.90–1.10) was 28 in 1852 and 21 in 1867. The 1853 and 1867 redistributions retained the tiny town ridings of Niagara, Cornwall, and Brockville. The 1853 redistribution split townships in three cases and removed townships from their counties in three. The 1867 redistribution created three purely-electoral counties (Bothwell, Monck, and Cardwell) from parts of seven municipal counties.

Intentional gerrymandering was unimportant in Canada West, for want of stable political parties. Nevertheless, based on returns for the 1863 general election, Macdonald's 1867 redistribution left Liberal-held ridings with larger populations than obtained for Tory-held ridings.

The imperial BNA Act, 1867, turned Canada West, the western section of the united Province of Canada, into the province of Ontario in the new Dominion of Canada. It gave the House of Commons the authority for Dominion redistribution and, by default, made Ontario's Legislative Assembly the authority for provincial redistribution. It imposed timing and quota requirements for Dominion redistribution, but not provincial redistribution. The timing requirement required a Dominion redistribution on the completion of each decennial census. The quota requirement issued a precise number of Dominion seats for Ontario, based on its population in the most recent census. The imperial Act was silent about redistribution within the province – such as altering the territories of ridings. The imperial Act placed "municipal institutions" in the jurisdiction of provinces. Thus, only the provincial parliament could change the number and territories of county, township, and urban municipalities. Yet observance of provincially mandated municipal lines developed as a major principle in the redrawing of Dominion ridings, as well as provincial ridings.

Principles for Redistribution, 1867–1954

Parliament decided redistribution during the years 1840 to 1954. Thus, the majority party in the House administered redistribution, without statutory guidelines, principles, or fixed rules. Perforce, Parliament had a free hand in formulating principles for redistribution.

Its handiwork developed historically. The principle of observing municipal lines, for example, awaited the 1849 "Baldwin Act," which made counties municipal units in addition to their previous function as electoral units. The principle of representation by population required official counts of population, which awaited the issuance of Canada's first modern census enumerations in 1852 and 1861. Politicians in the western sections of Canada West sought to apply representation by population on a sectional basis (although blocked by the Union Act's constitutional requirement for equal representation between Canada West and Canada East). They rarely valued the principle for redistribution within the province. The BNA Act, 1867, made population the basis for allocating Dominion parliamentary seats to Ontario (the Ontario quota), but representation by population was but one of several principles for redrawing the Dominion and provincial ridings within Ontario.

A collage of principles influenced redistribution after Confederation. Although certain of the principles sometimes clashed, they were not invariably mutually exclusive, but, rather, were open to combination. For example, a redistribution Bill could determine each county's number of ridings on the basis of representation by population, after which it could equalize riding populations within counties, thereby observing county lines. Similarly, the principle that city ridings should have larger populations than country ridings was not mutually exclusive with representation by population; rather, a Bill could apply the principle in two streams, one for city ridings, and the other for county ridings.

The collage of principles included the following:

1 Minimalism. Ridings were best left undisturbed where no principle warranted intervention. Minimalism differed from doing nothing

for ridings that warranted adjustment on principle; and from passive gerrymandering (doing nothing to gain partisan advantage).

2 No gerrymander. The majority party should not use redistribution to rig the results of the next election.

3 Municipal lines. County and township boundaries, and ward boundaries within a city, should be observed in the drawing of electoral districts. Conversely, riding boundaries should not divide counties or split townships and wards. Certain counties were united for municipal purposes; in such cases, the united county was the municipal county; the counties within it had no municipal functions and no county lines to be observed in redistribution. Similarly, northland districts had no municipal function; hence redistribution could disregard district lines.

4 Population. Redistribution should equalize population across the ridings, provided that the principle was not applied mathematically or "carried too far."

5 City ridings, especially those of Toronto, should have larger populations – less representation – than county ridings. This principle took root in the 1890s, but was less popular with Toronto MPs than with MPs from the counties. The principle held more weight in Dominion redistribution, with its quota of seats for Ontario, than in the provincial parliament, which could increase representation for cities without eliminating county ridings.

6 Ridings should be compact and symmetrical in shape, with contiguity among the municipalities composing them. Conversely, an odd shape was symptomatic of gerrymander.

7 Historical ridings, such as the town ridings of Cornwall and Niagara, or the ridings of Confederation, should be undisturbed.

8 Representation should recognize distinctive communities, such as cities in opposition to country regions, counties with their shared experience of local government, the Highland Scots of Glengarry County, the French-English ethnic divide between East Ottawa and West Ottawa, and the German-Scottish ethnic divide between the north and south ridings of Waterloo County.

9 Redistribution should enlarge the electoral territory of a large city (its city ridings) to match its municipal territory, which periodically expanded through annexations of suburban territories. Under provincial statutes dating from 1849, an incorporated city was "a county of itself" for municipal purposes; effectively, the city limits of Toronto (incorporated 1834), Hamilton and Kingston (1846),

and Ottawa and London (1856) were county lines, to be observed in redistribution.

10 A low unit of population was appropriate for northland district ridings, owing to the vastness of their territories, scattered populations, and attendant difficulties of organization.

11 Opposing principles also were in play – for example, that Toronto should be fully represented by population, or that municipal lines mattered for the provincial parliament, but not the House of Commons, which dealt with great national issues.

The order of importance among the various principles evolved. Both Conservatives and Liberals had accepted representation by population *and* municipal boundaries as key principles for Dominion redistributions in 1872. A decade later the Tories championed representation by population *without* regard to municipal lines. In reaction, the Liberals made municipal boundaries their top priority on coming into office in 1896.

Annexations and the Electoral Territories of Cities

From time to time, Ontario cities enlarged their civic territories by annexing suburban populations (see Appendix A). Toronto annexed forty-nine parcels of land during the years 1883–1967; Ottawa, ten during the years 1887–1946; Hamilton, twenty-three during the years 1891–1945; and London, eight during the years 1885–1950. Annexations made a city's civic population larger than its electoral population. An issue in redistribution was therefore whether or not to expand a city's electoral territory to its civic boundaries.

Redistribution responded unevenly, and not always in timely fashion, to dissonance between the electoral and civic populations of cities. It enlarged Toronto's provincial electoral territory in 1885 and 1933, and its Dominion electoral territory in 1903, 1924, and 1925; London's Dominion electoral territory in 1903, and its provincial electoral territory in 1914 and 1954; and Ottawa's Dominion electoral territory in 1933, and its provincial electoral territory in 1894, 1914, 1925, and 1954. It enlarged Hamilton's Dominion electoral territory in 1903, 1924, and 1952, and its provincial electoral territory in 1914. The 1925 provincial redistribution, however, turned principle on its head, transferring parts of Hamilton-City territory out of city ridings into Wentworth-County ridings. The 1954 provincial redistribution built on this legacy to draw two all-city Hamilton ridings and three hybrid city-county ridings.

The sharply contrasting 1924-Dominion and 1925-provincial redistributions for the Hamilton and Wentworth-County ridings evidenced how a government party's political calculations could influence outcomes. In both cases, Wentworth-County ridings included suburban populations that the city had annexed; the Hamilton-City ridings were Tory hives; city-fragments in the county ridings were Tory-leaning; and the transfer of the city fragments into the all-city ridings would hive the Tories into Hamilton, to the benefit of the Progressive Party in the county ridings.

A crucial difference was that the government party was Liberal for the Dominion redistribution and Conservative for the provincial redistribution. Thus, the Liberal-administered Dominion redistribution transferred some 18,000 city residents from the Wentworth riding into city ridings: effectively, hiving Tory-opposition supporters into the city ridings to strengthen Liberal prospects in Wentworth-County ridings. In contrast, the Tory-administered provincial redistribution transferred some 14,000 city residents out of city ridings into two Wentworth ridings: effectively, de-hiving government-party supporters from the city ridings to strengthen the party's prospects in the county ridings.

Mechanisms: The Bipartisan Special Committee

Before the 1960s, the creation of an arm's-length mechanism for redistribution seemed impossible politically. Although in 1900 Sir Charles Tupper, the leader of the Conservative opposition party, moved to adopt "a commission consisting of the chief justices in each of the provinces of Canada" for the entire redistribution process, his amendment, due to its precise wording, failed.[1] "Up to the present time," observed Sir Wilfrid Laurier in 1914, "neither one party nor the other has been willing to part with the authority that is vested in this Parliament. Neither one party nor the other has been willing to transfer to any other hands than its own the duty and responsibility ... to determine what shall be the representation in this House."[2] Thus, throughout the nineteenth century, the government party (Conservative) imposed redistribution on Parliament. On introducing a Representation Bill, the government party gave the Liberal opposition no time for mastering its details and used its majority to crush objections and amendments.

However, Britain's Redistribution of Seats Act, 1885, provided a model for dampening partisan warfare in the redistribution process. The prelude to this British Act was a series of conferences between the two parties to arrive at neutral ground for discussion. Then a deal was struck. The government appointed commissioners from the British civil service, with an eye to balancing the party preferences of the men appointed. It directed the commissioners to create single-member constituencies with approximately equal populations, while working within municipal lines, giving the ridings a compact shape, and balancing representation for rural and urban "communities of interest." In the course of their work the commissioners held court and consulted with the public.[3]

Canada's Dominion politicians drew selectively from the British model. Laurier's doomed redistribution Bills of 1899 and 1900 provided for a commission of judges to administer the second stage of his proposed redistribution process. The government party would determine the number of ridings to which a county or city was entitled. Where the allocation for a county or city was two or more ridings, the judges would draw the boundary lines within the county or city. The Conservative opposition party accepted the judicial commission in principle, provided that the judges administer the entire process. In the event, the Tory majority in the Senate killed Laurier's Bills.

In his 1903 Bill, which the Senate accepted, Laurier struck a bipartisan special committee to work out the details of redistribution. To this end, his Bill received its first reading with the schedule of ridings left blank, it being the task of the special committee to work out the details. The two parties were represented on the committee in proportion to their strengths in the House, which ensured that government members were a majority. Thus, Laurier's 1903 committee included four Liberals and three Conservatives.

Laurier's purpose for the special committee was to give the minority party a voice and thereby remove or dampen partisan rancour from the redistribution process. To this end, he intended the special committee to act as a conference, a partisanship-free neutral ground for discussion. He reasoned also that a small number of men – in this case, seven – could negotiate a fair redistribution more readily than could the full membership of the House.

The bipartisan special committee became standard in Canadian practice. Every Dominion and provincial redistribution after 1903 had one. Typically, in Dominion redistribution, the prime minister appointed the committee near the beginning of the parliamentary session and directed the committee to complete its work within the life of the session, which ranged from three to seven months. In 1952, however,

Parliament debated whether to continue with the special-committee mechanism or adopt redistribution by an independent commission. This delayed the appointment of a special committee until two months into the session, and left the committee just two and a half months to submit its final report.

Over time the Dominion committee grew in size, from seven under Laurier in 1903 to nine under Robert Borden in 1914, nineteen under Mackenzie King in 1924, twenty under R.B. Bennett in 1933, twenty-five under Mackenzie King in 1947, and thirty-seven under Louis St-Laurent in 1952. The Dominion special committee functioned passably as a conference in 1903 and successfully in 1914. It functioned ineptly in 1923–24, harmoniously in 1933 and 1947, and badly in the fractious parliament of 1952.

Beginning in 1914 the national committee delegated the details of redistribution to regional subcommittees. The 1924 subcommittee for Ontario, for example, comprised two government members (Liberals), two Progressives, and two Conservatives, with one of the Liberals as chair. As of 1924, the subcommittee was the key decider for Ontario.

The special committee for the provincial parliament numbered eight in 1908 and 1914, fifteen in 1925, seventeen in 1933, and ten in 1954. The committees of 1908 and 1914 were a farce that gave the opposition parties a negligible voice. A committee of cabinet drafted the schedule of ridings, with the special committee deprived of advance information and reduced to a ratifying role. The 1925 redistribution was the first in which the provincial special committee revised the schedule of ridings. In the 1933 redistribution, the Tory premier gave the opposition parties exceptional voice, in order to contain a rebellion in his own caucus. The special committee was irrelevant in the 1954 redistribution, in that it committed itself in advance, on direction from the premier, to adding seven ridings for rapidly growing city and suburban populations, and one northland riding, and leaving all other ridings as they were.

Redistribution after Confederation, 1867–1954

The 1867 BNA Act imposed timing and quota requirements for Dominion redistribution, but not for provincial redistribution. This contrast in constraints produced important differences between the two jurisdictions.

THE QUOTA OF RIDINGS FOR ONTARIO

The imperial BNA Act set up a Quebec-standard population to determine the allocation of seats among the provinces. With Quebec's representation fixed at sixty-five seats, the standard population was Quebec's census population divided by sixty-five. Ontario's quota of seats was the number of standard populations in its census population. Quebec's population grew over time, while its sixty-five seats were constant. Thus, the standard population rose, from 18,331 at Confederation (1861 census) to 36,283 in the 1921 census. A 1915 amendment to Section 51.4 of the BNA Act secured a higher quota for Ontario in the 1924 and 1933 redistributions than would have obtained from a strict application of the Quebec-standard population.[4] A 1946 amendment to the BNA Act jettisoned the Quebec-standard population, first by fixing the number of seats in the House of Commons at 255, and then by setting each province's quota according to its share of the national population.

The Dominion quota was an important constraint on redistribution. During the years 1867–1952, urbanization in southern Ontario and robust population growth in Northern Ontario pressed government to create new ridings. Due to the quota, government had to eliminate county ridings to make room for new ones. The difficulty mounted in 1891 when, for the first time, Ontario's quota did not increase; in 1901, when it dropped by six; and in 1911, when it decreased by four.

The provincial parliament, having no quota, could create new ridings without having to eliminate existing ones. Beginning in 1894, the provincial parliament provided for additional ridings by increasing the size of the House. The province's number of ridings surpassed Ontario's Dominion quota by two in 1894, six in 1902, twenty in 1908, twenty-nine in 1914, eight in 1933, and thirteen in 1954.

THE TIMING REQUIREMENT

The BNA Act, 1867, required a Dominion redistribution "on the completion of each decennial census," but did not bar a redistribution Bill at other times. Laurier's Liberal administration passed nearly identical Representation Bills in 1899 and 1900, well after the completion of the 1891 census, and on the eve of a new census in 1901, which would necessitate another redistribution. The Conservatives opposed these "out-of-season" Bills and used their majority in the Senate to defeat them. Robert Borden's 1914 redistribution was late due to political deadlock over his naval policy. Mackenzie King's 1947 redistribution was late, the Second World War having postponed the mandatory redistribution until the cessation of hostilities. The constitution did not prescribe a timing requirement for Ontario's provincial parliament. In the circumstance, the province enacted provincial redistributions midway between censuses (1874, 1885, 1894, 1908, 1914, 1925, 1933, and 1954). The exception, George Ross's 1902 redistribution, was a small, special-purpose affair, limited to northern Ontario. The province evidenced two notable hiatuses between major redistributions (1885–1908, twenty-three years; 1933–54, twenty-one years).

Statistical Overview of Ontario's Parliamentary Redistributions

Table C.1 gives a statistical overview for twenty redistributions.[5] In the Table data, the between-county transfers violated the rule of municipal lines, and each transfer involved one or more municipalities. The twenty-two transfers of the 1882 Dominion redistribution, for example, moved fifty-five townships, towns, and villages out of their home counties.[6]

The 1867 (Confederation), 1882-Dominion, and 1885-Ontario interventions were notably aggressive. In six cases – 1903, 1914, 1921, 1933, and 1947 Dominion, and 1908 provincial – a change in the government party preceded the redistribution. The 1924 Dominion redistribution involved a hung parliament and three political parties: the Liberals, Conservatives, and Progressives, the latter a farmers' political movement. Most redistributions followed municipal lines during the years of study, but the Conservative-Party redistributions of 1867, 1882, and 1892 did not.

Tables C.2 and C.3 report inequalities of riding populations. The percentage of ridings in the optimum zone for population (±10 percent of the standard population, 1.00) ranged from 12 to 43 for Dominion redistributions and from 16 to 39 for provincial redistributions.[7] In both cases, the percentage peaked during the 1880s and then declined.

Gerrymanders

A gerrymander refers to the government party's use of redistribution to boost its prospects in the next election. The gerrymander takes the forms of outright intentional (no support from understood principles), thinly disguised (principles used to mask partisan manipulation), and passive (leaving alone, to preserve partisan advantage, ridings that warrant change). Gerrymanders involve two ridings or larger clusters of ridings. Target ridings are opposition-held ridings within a gerrymandered cluster that the government party expects to win in the next general election, or precarious government-party-held ridings that have been strengthened to forestall their loss to the opposition. A gerrymander works if the next-election outcomes for the target ridings and their municipal subdivisions

Table C.1 Statistical summary of Ontario redistributions, 1853–1954

	Government party	*Seats before revision*	*Seats added or subtracted*	*# of ridings revised*	*Revisions as % of ridings*	*Between-county transfers*	*# of municipalities in transfers*
				Canada West			
1853	Reform	42	23	–	–	2	3
1867	Conservative	65	17	39	48%	8	31
				Dominion			
1872	Conservative	82	6	14	17%	1	1
1882	Conservative	88	4	50	57%	22	53
1892	Conservative	92	0	12	15%	2	3
1903	Liberal	92	-6	76	83%	0	0
1914	Conservative	86	-4	32	39%	2	4
1924	Liberal	82	0	47	57%	3	8
1933	Conservative	82	0	42	51%	–	–
1947	Liberal	82	1	27	32%	–	–
1952	Liberal	83	2	33	40%	–	–
				Ontario			
1874	Liberal	82	6	22	27%	2	5
1885	Liberal	88	2	45	51%	2	4
1894	Liberal	90	4	4	4%	0	0
1902	Liberal	94	4	3	3%	0	0
1908	Conservative	98	8	22	23%	–	–
1914	Conservative	106	5	31	29%	–	–
1925	Conservative	111	1	52	48%	–	–
1933	Conservative	112	-22	84	75%	–	–
1954	Conservative	90	8	16	18%	–	–

match up with the electoral outcomes predicted from the redistribution. Otherwise it fails.

STRATAGEMS

One stratagem was "hiving." With this stratagem, the government party transferred an opposition-party-leaning township from a fighting riding into an adjacent hive riding, which the opposition seemed certain to win. The out-transfer helped the government party in the fighting riding,

Table C.2 Dominion ridings after redistribution, percentage of ridings within 10% of the standard population, 1872–1966 (* = commissioned ridings)

Redistribution	*1872*	*1882*	*1892*	*1903*	*1914*	*1924*	*1933*	*1947*	*1952*	*1966**
<0.80	22%	15%	17%	21%	28%	39%	45%	34%	24%	14%
0.80–0.89	15%	14%	21%	19%	20%	10%	13%	14%	15%	14%
0.90–1.10	**23%**	**43%**	**36%**	**31%**	20%	**22%**	9%	24%	31%	38%
1.11–1.19	22%	11%	14%	14%	9%	2%	5%	05%	06%	35%
1.20+	19%	16%	12%	15%	24%	27%	28%	23%	25%	0%
# of ridings	88	92	92	86	82	82	82	83	85	88

Table C.3 Provincial ridings after redistribution, percentage of ridings within 10% of the standard population, 1874–1954

Redistribution	*1874*	*1885*	*1894*	*1902*	*1908*	*1914*	*1925*	*1933*	*1954*
<0.80	20%	17%	20%	23%	20%	32%	28%	32%	33%
0.80–0.89	21%	11%	22%	21%	15%	17%	13%	17%	10%
0.90–1.10	**30%**	**39%**	**39%**	**27%**	35%	23%	22%	16%	20%
1.11–1.19	18%	12%	7%	12%	5%	5%	8%	13%	11%
1.20+	18%	21%	11%	16%	25%	23%	29%	22%	26%
# of ridings	88	90	94	98	106	111	112	90	98

from which the township was taken, while the in-transfer merely added to the opposition party's certain majority. Another stratagem was to over-represent populations that favoured the government party. This took the form of leaving alone small-population ridings that merited consolidation (passive gerrymandering), or inflating representation by adding more new ridings than were warranted on principle, an issue for Toronto from the 1890s on. On certain special committees, majority-party bullying, blackmail, and outright cheating played a role. Two examples were an outrageous misuse of population statistics for Eastern Ontario in Wilfrid Laurier's 1903 Dominion redistribution, and the use and misapplication of contrived "divisions" in Mackenzie King's 1947 Dominion redistribution.

"Political assassination" was the government party's gerrymandering of a prominent opposition politician's riding in an attempt to secure the politician's defeat in the next general election. Liberal targets of Tory

Table C.4 Dominion and provincial redistributions with one or more intentional gerrymanders, and whether or not the gerrymander(s) worked, 1872–1954

Dominion redistributions		*Included a gerrymander*	*Success*	*Provincial redistributions*		*Included a gerrymander*	*Success*
1872	Tory	Yes	Yes	1874	Liberal	No	NA
1882	Tory	Yes	No	1885	Liberal	No	NA
1892	Tory	Yes	No	1894	Liberal	No	NA
1903	Liberal	Yes	Yes	1902	Liberal	Yes	No
1914	Tory	Yes	Yes	1908	Tory	Yes	Yes
1924	Liberal	No	NA	1914	Tory	Yes	Yes
1933	Tory	Yes	No	1925	Tory	Yes	Yes
1947	Liberal	Yes	Yes	1933	Tory	No	NA
1952	Liberal	No	NA	1954	Tory	Yes	Yes

assassination attempts were Sir Richard Cartwright (Huron Centre, 1882), the Hon. David Mills (Bothwell, 1882), and Frederick Sanderson (Perth South, 1933). Tory targets of Liberal assassination attempts were James Clancy (Bothwell, 1903), Sam Hughes (Victoria North, 1903), and James Macdonnell (Muskoka-Ontario, 1947).

FREQUENCY, SCOPE, AND SUCCESS RATE

As Table C.4 summarizes, twelve of eighteen redistributions included one or more intentional gerrymanders (outright and thinly disguised). Passive gerrymandering was a feature of every redistribution, the most extreme example of which was Premier Leslie Frost's 1954 provincial redistribution.

Intentional gerrymandering was extensive in some redistributions, such as those of John A. Macdonald in 1882, Laurier in 1903, and Whitney in 1908, but slight in others, such as Robert Borden's 1914 redistribution. Most redistributions included a gerrymander, but rarely did the term apply sweepingly to whole redistributions.

Five redistributions followed a change in the government party, which raises the question of whether or not the new ministry used gerrymanders to settle scores. Such indeed was the case with Wilfrid Laurier's Dominion redistribution of 1903 and James Whitney's provincial redistribution of 1908, but not with Robert Borden's Dominion redistribution of 1914 or Mackenzie King's Dominion redistributions of 1924 and 1947.

As indicated in Table C.4, gerrymanders worked in eight redistributions and failed in four. Small wonder that government politicians were tempted to use them, given the favourable odds for their success. In the 1882 Dominion general election, John A. Macdonald's failed gerrymanders contributed to his loss of seats across the province. In the 1904 Dominion general election, Wilfrid Laurier's Liberals lost ground in Ontario, but his gerrymanders worked; effectively, his gerrymanders successfully staunched losses. In the 1908 provincial general election, James Whitney's gerrymanders worked, but he would have won without them in his sweeping victory across the province. In the 1935 Dominion general election, R.B. Bennett's gerrymanders failed, but nothing could have prevented his defeat across the province: he was too closely identified with the Great Depression.

FROM PARLIAMENTARY REDISTRIBUTION TO COMMISSIONED RIDINGS

The 1954 provincial redistribution was Ontario's last under the parliamentary system. In 1962, Premier John Robarts created an independent commission on redistribution, with instructions to consider "the population of the province as revealed by the 1961 census, rural as opposed to urban representation, the existing and traditional boundaries of constituencies, the diversity and community interests of the population, and the means of communication between the districts. With particular relevance to rural districts the commission will be asked to try to include whole municipalities within the electoral districts."[8] E.A. Richardson, an Ontario Supreme Court judge, headed the commission; J.R. Simonett (Conservative, Frontenac-Addington) was its chair; and the other members were Grant Crawford, professor of Political Science at Queen's University, and Roderick Lewis, clerk of the Legislature and chief electoral officer. Robarts designed the commission "to remove the whole question from politics." The commission made recommendations for the provincial redistributions of 1962 and 1966. In each case, the Legislature made the final decision.

In 1973, Premier William Davis named a three-man commission on redistribution, headed by Justice Campbell Grant of the Ontario Supreme Court and including Roderick Lewis and Robert Sansom, an assistant professor of Political Science at the University of Western Ontario. This commission was the final authority for the provincial redistributions of 1974 and 1986.[9]

Meanwhile, the Dominion government's Electoral Boundaries Adjustment Act, 1964, removed Dominion redistribution from Parliament to arm's-length provincial boundary commissions, each headed by a judge. The Act made representation by population the controlling principle and gave mathematical precision for its application: "in no case shall the population of any electoral district ... depart from the electoral quota for that province to a greater extent than twenty-five percent more or twenty-five percent less" (0.75–1.25 standard populations). The Bill initially provided for a 20 percent tolerance (0.80–1.20); the increase to 25 was the government's compromise with the Conservative opposition, which had pushed for a one-third tolerance (0.67–1.33). A few members had advocated for 10 percent (0.90–1.10), this book's optimum zone.

Apart from compliance with the rule of 25 percent tolerance, the Act (s. 13, i–ii) allowed for "special geographic considerations, including in particular the sparsity, density or relative rate of growth of population, the accessibility of such regions or the size or shape thereof" and consideration of "special community or diversity of interests of the inhabitants."

Otherwise, Section 13 was silent about traditional Ontario principles for redistribution. On introducing the Bill, Jack Pickersgill, minister of Transport, stated that "you need a tolerance to follow municipal boundaries as far as possible."[10] Yet the Act made no mention of county lines. On another issue, Pauline Jewett (Liberal, Northumberland) and W.H.A. Thomas (Conservative, Middlesex West) urged that rural ridings should have smaller populations than urban ridings. By contrast, Reid Scott (NDP, Toronto Danforth) called for a strict application of the population principle to "finally abolish the rural tyranny that has dominated this parliament for decades."[11] In the event, the Act made no mention of rural-urban differences in riding populations. G.H.A. Aitken (Conservative, Parry Sound–Muskoka), for one, lamented the Act's lack of "sufficiently detailed instructions."

Nevertheless, the 1964 Act was a turning point in the history of redistribution for Ontario. Foremost was that it gave final authority for redistribution to an arm's-length provincial commission. Second, it made representation by population the controlling principle and gave it mandatory mathematical precision. Lastly, the 25 percent "tolerance," large though it might be, advanced the equalization of riding populations. Beginning with the first commissioned redistribution in

Table C.5 The 1952 and 1966 Dominion redistributions: Riding populations by number of standard populations (SPs)

	25% tolerance (1964)		*SP =>*	*54,777*	*70,865*
N. of SPs	*After 1952*	*After 1966*	*N. of SPs*	*After 1952*	*After 1966*
<0.75	21%	0%	<0.80	24%	14%
0.75–1.25	60%	100%	0.80–0.89	15%	14%
>1.25	19%	0%	0.90–1.10	31%	38%
			1.11–1.19	6%	35%
			1.20+	25%	0%
	85	88		85	88

1966, 100 percent of Dominion ridings were within 25 percent of the provincial mean. By contrast, the percentage was 60 for the 1952 Dominion-parliamentary redistribution and 54 for the 1954 provincial-parliamentary redistribution. Under the 1966 commissioned redistribution, as shown in Table C.5, 38 percent of the ridings were in the optimum zone (10 percent tolerance), up from the 1952 Dominion redistribution (31 percent), though less than John A. Macdonald's gerrymandered redistribution of 1882 (43 percent) and Mowat's 1885 provincial redistribution (39 percent).

In 1996, the Ontario government adopted Dominion ridings for provincial purposes. Effectively, the federal government's boundary commission for Ontario decided the provincial ridings. For the first time since 1867–72, Dominion and provincial ridings for Ontario were identical.[12] For the first time ever, albeit indirectly, provincial redistribution took on the Dominion redistribution's timing and quota requirements under the BNA Act.

Although the commission system seems to be entrenched in Canada's parliamentary democracy, it remains fragile. First, it is derived from statutes, which a partisan government could amend or overturn. Second, the speaker of the House, a member of the government party, appoints two of the three members of each provincial boundary commission (the third is a judge). This opens the possibility of partisan appointments. Last, although the commission has the last word, the redistribution process provides for submissions from interested parties, which exposes the commissioners to partisan pressures.

Nevertheless, judges John C. Courtney, "independent electoral boundary commissions stand as one of the success stories of the last half-century of Canadian political institutions ... With the replacement of government-dominated redistributions by independent commissions, partisan gerrymandering as it was once practised in Canada was relegated to history."[13] A recent dust-up in Saskatchewan, which involved Courtney as a boundary commissioner, allows optimism about the future of commissioned ridings (see Appendix B).

APPENDIX A

Municipal Annexations of Toronto, Hamilton, Ottawa, and London[1]

TORONTO 1883–1967

1883 Village of Yorkville (St. Paul's Ward)
1884 Town of Brockton (including High Park)
1884 Village of Riverside (Riverdale when annexed)
1887 Rosedale
1887 Strip north of Queen Street
1887 Annex
1888 Walker and Woodlawn Avenues
1888 Poplar Plains Road
1888 North of Bloor and west of Bathurst Streets
1888 Sunnyside
1889 Village of Parkdale
1890 Greenwood sideline
1893 Lakeshore Road
1893 Summerhill Avenue
1903 Part of Humber Bay and Lake west of Island
1905 Avenue Road (district) (*Globe*, 12 October 1905: 1,839 pop.)
1906 North Rosedale (*Globe*, 12 July 1905: the "scotch settlement," 20 acres at the north end of Rosedale district)
1907 Annex west of Avenue Road
1908 Deer Park (*Globe*, 15 December 1908: 4,000 pop.)
1908 Baldwin Estate (*Globe*, 15 December 1908: part of Baldwin farm; rural annex)
1908 East Toronto (*Globe*, 15 December 1908: 7,000 pop.)
1909 Wychwood and Bracondale (*Globe*, 15 Dec. 1908: 7,000 pop.)

1909 West Toronto – The Junction (*Globe*, 1 May 1909: 12,967 pop., police census)
1909 Midway
1909 Balmy Beach
1910 Dovercourt and Earlscourt
1912 Helliwell property (*Globe*, 2 March 1912: 36.4 acres, probably rural)
1912 Montclair (Park) District (*Globe*, 6 June 1912: 19 acres)
1912 North Toronto (pop. 5,362, census)
1912 Moore Park (*Globe*, 20 November 1912: 1,500 pop.)
1914 Glebe estate (*Globe*, 7 February 1914: 80 acres)
1914 Mount Pleasant Cemetery
1920 South side of Bloor Street West (Swansea) (thin slice on north boundary of Swansea)
1920 North of Danforth, east of Woodbine Ave.
1921 Davies estate
1922 Annette Street, north side
1922 Runnymede Road, west side
1922 Rowntree Avenue, north side
1924 Forest Hill (block on east boundary of Forest Hill)
1924 Gunn's Road and Northland Avenue
1925 Newmarket and Meagher Avenues
1930 Bayview Avenue, street only
1934 Lakeshore bridge approach
1947 Belt Line Railway
1947 Eglinton and Bayview Avenues
1950 Nursewood Road
1954 Victoria Park Avenue
1967 Forest Hill
1967 Swansea

OTTAWA 1887–1946

1887 New Edinburgh Village (Rideau Ward)
1889 Parts of Nepean and Gloucester Townships
1907 Bayswater, Hintonburg, Ottawa East, Ottawa South, Rideauville
1909 Part of Nepean Township
1911 Village of Mechanicsville

1939 Hampton Park
1946 Part of Nepean Township
1947 Part of Nepean Township
1949 Part Nepean, Westboro (location of Nepean Town Hall)
1950 Part of Gloucester (14,605 acres). Includes Overbrook, Hurdman's Bridge, Billings Bridge, Ellwood, Manor Park, Rideau Park, Hawthorne, Riverview, Alta Vista, Hogsback

HAMILTON 1891–1945

1891 (2 parcels) 924 acres
1902 17.3 acres
1903 (2 parcels) 694.7 acres
1908 30 acres
1909 Barton, 1,272 acres
1910 89 acres
1912 170 acres
1913 14.5 acres
1914 869.0 acres
1920 767.9 acres
1921 99.4 acres
1922 7.6 acres
1924 253.8 acres
1925 86.2 acres
1928 470.5 acres
1929 (3 parcels) 878.5 acres
1943 638.3 acres
1948 293.1 acres
1949 3,451 acres

LONDON 1885–1950

1885 East London
1890 London South
1898 London West (Petersville)
1912 Ealing, Potterburg, Knollwood Park, Chelsea Green (2,200 acres)
1913 Small part of London Township (London Annex)
1950 Part of London Township

KINGSTON

1952 Portsmouth Village and part of Kingston Township. Annexations by Kingston, if any before 1952, were irrelevant for redistribution. The municipal city always had less than one standard population. At a minimum, in both the Dominion and provincial parliaments, the riding comprised the whole of the municipal city. The Dominion riding included the village of Portsmouth (annexed in 1952) during the years 1903–47, and in 1952 five Frontenac-County townships (Pittsburgh, Storrington, Kingston, Howe Island, Wolfe Island). The provincial riding included Kingston Township and Portsmouth Village in 1885–1914; Portsmouth Village only in 1925; and Portsmouth Village, Howe Island, Wolfe Island, and Amherst Island (taken from Lennox & Addington County) in 1933–54.

WINDSOR

1935 Walkerville, Sandwich, East Windsor (Ford City)

APPENDIX B

The Harper Government and the Saskatchewan Boundary Commission, 2013

An uproar in Saskatchewan in 2013 elaborated the nature of the 1960s revolution. In its preliminary report, the Saskatchewan Boundary Commission proposed five all-urban ridings for Regina and Saskatoon, in place of the current pie-shaped hybrid ridings, which combined city parts with suburban and rural populations. The premise of the proposed redistribution was that city populations were distinctive communities of interest, and, as such, warranted separate representation. The premise of the status quo, the hybrid ridings, was that no meaningful differences were obtained between rural and urban populations.

Apart from that premise, the redistribution had political implications. Under the status quo, in the 2011 general election, the Conservatives had polled 56 percent of the vote and won all but one of the province's fourteen ridings. The NDP had won no ridings, but had polled 32 percent of the vote and had been competitive with the Conservatives in city polls of Regina and Saskatoon. In the hybrid ridings, the Tory-leaning rural tail had wagged the urban dog. In the circumstances, the creation of all-urban ridings boosted the prospects of the NDP.[1]

The commissioners were themselves divided. The majority report issued from the judicial chair, the Hon. Ronald C. Mills, and John C. Courtney, a political scientist at the University of Saskatchewan and author of *Commissioned Ridings*. A minority report was issued by David Marit, president of the Saskatchewan Association of Rural Municipalities. Interestingly, one of the MPs affected was none other than the Speaker of the House of Commons, Andrew Scheer (Conservative, Regina-Qu'Appelle), who had appointed the two non-judicial commissioners.

Shortly after the issuance of the Commission's report, recounted the Saskatoon *StarPhoenix*,

> Saskatchewan citizens were bombarded with a robocall push poll[2] meant to convince them the commission was trying to tear apart the province's fabric. Although the Conservatives initially denied involvement, they were caught out after *Postmedia News* used voice-recognition software to identify the voice on the calls as belonging to Matt Meier of telemarketer *RackNine* – a company used extensively by the party. Prime Minister Stephen Harper then told Parliament that while the party may have been behind the calls, it [had done] nothing wrong.
>
> This opinion was overturned by the CRTC, which fined the Conservatives $78,000 for violating its rules.[3] [As stated by the CRTC's chief compliance and enforcement officer, "Canadians have a right to know who is calling them."[4]]
>
> In submissions to a parliamentary committee, Tory MPs accused commissioners of "denigrating" the process by being biased and, in a bizarre switching of blame, of gerrymandering the ridings – a process by which boundaries are determined for partisan, rather than practical purposes.

Certainly the Harper government (2006–present) had been partisan to an extreme. In particular, it had pioneered an American-style "permanent campaign," with a sustained "carpet-bombing" of opposition leaders with negative "attack ads" before, not just after, an election writ was dropped. Tom Flanagan, once Harper's chief organizer, notes Harper's "dark, almost Nixonian side ... He believes in playing politics right up to the edge of the rules, which inevitably means some team members will cross ethical and legal guidelines in their desire to win for the boss."[5]

Two aspects of the Saskatchewan episode apply across the nation. First, the commission system keeps government-party partisanship at bay. As Courtney judges, "partisan gerrymandering as it was once practised in Canada was relegated to history." Second, one must view with caution the notion that the commission system is politically neutral. In the case at hand, redistribution does boost the prospects of the NDP, at the expense of the government party. Clearly, in a parliamentary redistribution, all-urban ridings in Saskatchewan would be a non-starter under the hyper-partisan Harper government.

Notes

INTRODUCTION

1 Ward, *Canadian House of Commons*, 19.
2 *Debates*, 1939, Power, 1808.
3 *Debates*, 1882, Mackenzie, 1209.
4 *Debates*, 1892, Charlton, 3136–7, 3824.
5 The comparable American terms are *redistricting* or *reapportionment*. See Argersinger, "Introduction," in *Representation and Inequality*. According to George Drew, leader of the Conservative opposition in 1952, "the term 'riding' was commonly accepted for electoral districts in Ontario; 'constituency' was employed in most of the rest of Canada, and 'district' in the province of Quebec." *Debates*, 1952, Drew, 4080.
6 Courtney, *Commissioned Ridings*, 4.
7 Ibid., 237–8, 315n5.
8 Ward, *Canadian House of Commons*. In 1964 Stanley Knowles (NDP, Winnipeg North Centre) quoted from Ward's book in debates that culminated in Canada's landmark Electoral Boundaries Adjustment Act, 1964. For Newfoundland, see Rothney, "The Denominational Basis of Representation in the Newfoundland House of Assembly, 1919–1962."
9 Ward, *Canadian House of Commons*; Courtney, *Commissioned Ridings*.
10 Kerr, "The 1867 Elections in Ontario."
11 *Debates*, 1952, Power, 421; 1964, Jewett, 800.
12 Dawson, "The Gerrymander of 1882." For example, Dawson writes (205): "If Lambton, for example, which was being made into 2 districts for the first time, had been divided as for the provincial legislature, the districts would have had populations of 21,115 and 21,501, almost mathematically perfect, as the quota was 20,905. But both these districts would have been

Liberal. A somewhat different division was therefore made so as to give each party 1 seat (on the basis of the election of 1878) with populations of 21,725 and 20,891."

Here Dawson mistakenly equates the Dominion riding of Lambton with the county of Lambton. In fact, the Dominion riding excluded three Lambton townships (Sombra, Dawn, and Euphemia), which were in the riding of Bothwell; hence the Dominion riding included only 42,616 of the municipal county's 53,648 people. The combined territories of the two provincial Lambton ridings, in contrast, were that of the municipal county. The populations of the provincial ridings – 23,906 and 29,742 – were unequal, not Dawson's "21,115 and 21,501, almost mathematically perfect."

13 Beck, *Pendulum of Power*, 40–3, 52, 425. Beck's book surveys party formations, policies, and outcomes for 28 Dominion general elections during the century after Confederation.
14 Creighton, *John A. Macdonald, the Old Chieftain*, 129, 335–6.
15 Waite, *The Man from Halifax*, 333.
16 Schull, *Laurier, the First Canadian.*
17 Brown, *Robert Laird Borden*, 255.
18 Neatby, *William Lyon Mackenzie King, 1924–1932*, 23.
19 Graham, *Arthur Meighen.*
20 Boyko, *Bennett, the Rebel*; Waite, *In Search of R.B. Bennett*; Glassford, *Reaction and Reform.*
21 Thomson, *Louis St. Laurent, Canadian*, 325–7.
22 Pickersgill, *My Life with Louis St. Laurent*, 167–70.
23 Evans, *Sir Oliver Mowat*, 92–3, 102–3, 131, 240–1, 243–6, 308.
24 Humphries, *'Honest Enough to be Bold,'* 171; Prang, *N.W. Rowell: Ontario Nationalist*, ch. 8.
25 Oliver, *G. Howard Ferguson: Ontario Tory*, 167.
26 Johnston, *E.C. Drury*; Drury, *Farmer Premier*, 152.
27 Spanner, "'The Straight Furrow,'" 337–47.
28 Graham, *Old Man Ontario.*
29 McDougall, *John P. Robarts: His Life and Government*; Steve Paikin, *Public Triumph, Private Tragedy.*
30 Dawson, *Gerrymander*, 197–8.
31 Ward, *Canadian House of Commons*, 26–7.
32 Courtney, *Commissioned Ridings*, 20.
33 Ward, *Canadian House of Commons*, 42–3.
34 Ibid., 32.

35 Dawson, *Gerrymander*, 206–7. For Liberal-Party sources, see Anonymous, "The Alleged 'Gerrymander' by Mr. Mowat, in 1874"; Ontario Liberal Association, *The Record of the Mowat Government*.

36 "It is fair to say," writes Paul Romney, "that Mowat's government established standards of public conduct that were in salutary contrast to the excesses of Macdonald's government and those of several Quebec administrations." Romney, "Mowat, Sir Oliver."

37 Stewart, "John A. Macdonald's Greatest Triumph," 3–33, esp. 3. For the Franchise Act, see Forster et al., "The Franchise, Personators, and Dead Men."

38 Skelton, *Life and Letters of Sir Wilfrid Laurier*, 270.

39 English, *The Decline of Politics*, 18. See also Ward, ed., *A Party Politician*, 18.

40 Siegfried, *The Race Question in Canada*, ch. 19–21; English, *Decline of Politics*, 8.

41 English, *Decline of Politics*.

42 Forster et al., "The Franchise, Personators, and Dead Men." See also Stewart, "Macdonald's Greatest Triumph."

43 Noel, *Patrons, Clients, Brokers*.

44 Siegfried, *Race Question in Canada*, ch. 19–21.

45 Emery, *Elections in Oxford County*.

46 Ward, *Canadian House of Commons*, 29, 35.

47 Courtney, *Commissioned Ridings*, 20–1.

48 Dawson, *The Government of Canada*, revised by Norman Ward, 340–2. Dawson's book was published in 1947 and Ward's revision of the book in 1963. See also Courtney, *Commissioned Ridings*, v–ix.

49 Courtney, *Commissioned Ridings*, 21–2.

50 This list excludes the province's creation of the Nipissing riding by statute in 1889.

CHAPTER ONE

1 Emery, *Elections in Oxford County*, 20–4.

2 Province of Canada, *Statutes*, 1845, An Act for Better Defining the Limits of Counties and Districts.

3 The united-county ridings were: *Kent* (Kent and Lambton); *Huron* (Huron, Perth, and Bruce); *Middlesex* (Middlesex and Elgin); *Wentworth* (Wentworth and Brant); *Waterloo* (Waterloo, Wellington, and Grey); *Peterborough* (Peterborough and Victoria); *Lennox & Addington* (Lennox and Addington); and *Lanark* (Lanark and Renfrew).

4 Province of Canada, *Statutes*, 1860, Cap. XXXIX.
5 Anonymous, "Alleged 'Gerrymander' by Mr. Mowat," 5–6.
6 Nicholson, *The Boundaries of the Canadian Confederation*, 95–9.
7 *Ontario Archives* website, "The Changing Shape of Ontario, the Districts of Northern Ontario."
8 Province of Canada, *Statutes*, 1849, Cap. 78, An Act Abolishing the Territorial Division of Upper Canada into Districts, and for Providing Temporary Unions of Counties for Judicial and [Municipal] Purposes, s. II.V and Schedule A. The united-municipal counties were Essex-Kent, Frontenac-Lennox-Addington, Lanark-Renfrew, Leeds-Grenville, Lincoln-Haldimand-Welland, Northumberland-Durham, Prescott-Russell, Stormont-Dundas-Glengarry, and Wentworth-Halton.
9 Province of Canada, *Statutes*, 1851, An Act to Make Certain Alterations in the Territorial Divisions of Upper Canada, Schedules B and C.
10 *Consolidated Statutes of Upper Canada, 1859*, Cap. III, An Act Respecting the Territorial Division of Upper Canada.
11 Province of Canada, *Statutes*, 1861, Act to Provide for the Separation of the County of Victoria from the County of Peterborough; 1861, Act to Provide for the Separation of the County of Renfrew from the County of Lanark; 1866, Act to Complete the Separation of the County of Peel from the County of York.
12 BNA Act, 1867, s. 92.8.
13 Ontario, *Statutes*, An Act Respecting the Territorial Division of Ontario for Municipal and Judicial Purposes, in *Revised Statutes of Ontario* (*RSO*), 1877, 1887, 1897, 1914, 1927, 1937, 1950, and 1960.
14 Province of Canada, *Statutes*, 1849, Municipal Act, Cap. 81, s. VI, ss. LXXXV. See also Cap. 78, s. XXX, ss. XVIII–XVIX.
15 *Consolidated Statutes of Upper Canada*, 1859, Cap. III, An Act Respecting the Territorial Division of Upper Canada; *rso*, 1877, An Act Respecting the Territorial Division of Ontario for Municipal and Judicial Purposes. If the city lacked population for separate representation, then its civic limits did not matter for redistribution.
16 Noel, *Patrons, Clients, Brokers*, 13–15, 89–90, 218, 275–7; Emery, *Elections in Oxford County*, 89; Ward, ed., *A Party Politician*, 11, 18.
17 Noel, *Patrons, Clients, Brokers*, 275.
18 Crawford, *Pioneer Public Service*; Emery, *Elections in Oxford County*, 22–4.
19 Crawford, *Pioneer Public Service*, 36.
20 Ibid.; Province of Canada, *Report of the Postmaster-General*, Sessional Paper 3, 1865.

21 Ingersoll *Chronicle*, 22 August 1862.
22 Canada, *Report of the Postmaster-General*, Sessional Paper 3, 1865.
23 Noel, *Patrons, Clients, Brokers*, 275–7.
24 English, *Decline of Politics*, 222–30.
25 Ibid., ch. 2–3.
26 Courtney, *Commissioned Ridings*, 11.
27 Rush, *Does Redistricting Make a Difference?* 2.
28 *Debates*, 1892, Charlton, 3136.
29 *Debates*, 1903, Thomson, 11529.
30 The comparable American term is "packing" or "bunching." The opposite of these terms is "cracking," which means dispersal of the votes of the opposition party. See Argersinger, "All Politics Are Local," 10.
31 *Debates*, 1882, Blake, 1205.
32 Ibid., 1207.
33 Ibid., 1372, 1374.
34 *Debates*, Mills, 1393.
35 *Debates*, 1892, Charlton, 3144.
36 Dawson, *Gerrymander*, 199–200.
37 http://www.collectionscanada.gc.ca/primeministers/h4-4035-e.html. The Toronto *Globe*, 1 June 1882, confirms the date and content of the address. The internet source incorrectly dates the mass meeting to 1881.
38 Dawson, *Gerrymander*, 208.
39 Cartwright, *Reminiscences*, 226–7. See also Lower, "Determinism in Canadian Politics," 234–5.
40 Campbell, "Voters and Non-voters."
41 Dawson, *Gerrymander*, 211. The Liberal-majority statistics for Macdonald's gerrymander forecast a Tory gain of 7 seats in the 1882 general election (from 61 to 68). That election, however, lost them 8 seats (from 61 to 53).
42 The ridings and their Liberal-majority statistics are Bothwell (-189); Brant South (-43); Bruce East (-520); Bruce North (-331); Huron East (-122); Huron West (-170); Lincoln & Niagara (-152); Monck (-62); Norfolk South (-111); Ontario North (-198); Ontario South (+8); Perth North (-288); Perth South (-118); Wentworth South (-103); and York North (-202).
43 Cartwright, *Reminiscences*, 228–30, 232. Cartwright believed that Macdonald "owed at least fourteen or fifteen" seats to the gerrymander in the 1887 general election.
44 Beck, *Pendulum of Power*, 40–3, 52, 425.
45 Province of Canada, *Consolidated Statutes of Upper Canada*, 1859, Cap. III, An Act Respecting the Territorial Divisions of Upper Canada, s. 21.

CHAPTER TWO

1 Great Britain, *Statutes*, Act to Re-Unite the Provinces of Upper and Lower Canada, 1840, Sections XIII–XVII, XXVI.

2 Great Britain, *Statutes*, 1791 Constitutional Act, s. XIV, authorized "the Governor to issue a Proclamation to divide the Province into Districts, Counties, Towns, and Townships and declare the number of representatives to be chosen by each of such Districts, Counties, Towns, and Townships." For Sydenham, see Buckner, "Thomson, Charles Edward Poulett, 1st Baron Sydenham."

3 Canada, *Statutes*, 1841, District Councils Act; 1849, Act for Abolishing the Territorial Division of Upper Canada into Districts, and for Providing for Temporary Unions of Counties for Judicial and other purposes, and for the future dissolutions of such Unions, as the increase of wealth and population may require; 1849, Municipal Act ("Baldwin Act"). The Baldwin Act provided one general law for municipal corporations (counties, townships, cities, towns, and villages).

4 Canada, *Statutes*, 1845, Act for Better Defining the Limits of Counties and Districts in Upper Canada, Cap. 7.

5 Brant, Elgin, Grey, Ontario, Peel, Victoria, and Wellington.

6 The 1841 census of Canada reported heads of household only, not each individual in the population.

7 Ingersoll *Chronicle*, 24 May 1861.

8 The statute gave Toronto one riding only, a clerical error, soon corrected.

9 Lennox & Addington and Huron & Bruce were the united-electoral county ridings.

10 The 1853 Act placed Georgina Township, Ontario County, in the riding of York North. The province transferred the township to York County for municipal purposes at some point, possibly in 1853 and certainly by 1859. See text for the counties of Ontario and York in the 1853 statute (ridings for Upper Canada, s. 4 and 10); Province of Canada, *Consolidated Statutes of Upper Canada, 1859*, Cap. III, An Act Respecting the Territorial Divisions of Upper Canada, s. 21.

11 For critique of the 1852 and 1861 census data, see Curtis, *The Politics of Population*. For my critique of Curtis's book, see *Canadian Historical Review* 82, no. 4 (Dec. 2001): 751–4.

12 Emery, *Elections in Oxford County*, ch. 4, 5, 6–8. Pro-coalition Reformers were known as *Hincksites*, named after Francis Hincks, who had approved of the formation of the province's first coalition administration in 1854.

13 Careless, "Brown, George," and *Brown of the Globe*, vol. 1, ch. 7.

14 Section XXVI of the 1840 imperial Union Act enabled the Legislative Assembly to "make a new and different Apportionment of the number of Representatives to be chosen in and for those Parts of the Province of Canada which now constitute the said provinces of Upper and Lower Canada respectively," conditional on a two-thirds majority vote in both Houses (an enabling provision). The 1854 imperial Act to Empower the Legislature of Canada to alter the Constitution of the Legislative Council for that Province and for Other Purposes (Section 5) abolished Section XXVI of the 1840 Act, which left Section XII (the equal representation provision) without possible remedy.

15 Pope, *Confederation Documents Hitherto Unpublished*, 20, 29, 38, 41, 98, 111, 133, 141, 158, 212, 298–9; Whitelaw, "Reconstructing the Quebec Conference." Ward's discussion of Macdonald's role may mislead (see Ward, *Canadian House of Commons*, 21–2). As Ward writes, "Although for a time it appeared that the provinces were to be charged with the duty, Sir John [he had yet to be knighted] subsequently altered the relevant portion of the Quebec resolutions on this point [Resolution 24], and in debates of the Legislative Assembly in 1865 blandly explained the amendment away on the ground that the resolutions were in error." But Macdonald himself had moved the original resolution; the Canadian delegates, not just Macdonald, altered the original motion; and "blandly" is a gratuitous value judgment. Whitelaw notes that the delegates at Westminster in 1866 used "copies of the resolutions … in their unaltered form" (the original Resolution 24): so much for Macdonald's amendment. In the event, neither the original resolution nor the altered version made it into the British North America bill.

16 Désilets, "Taché, Sir Étienne-Paschal."

17 Regarding the note on the draft bill, that readjustments to representation were "to be made by an independent authority, as some of the judges," Ward writes, "As if to support this point, the BNA Act itself did not specifically empower the House of Commons to execute changes, but stated that representation 'shall be adjusted by such authority … as the Parliament of Canada decides.'" Ward's interpretation is dubious. Arguably the text does specifically empower Parliament. As Ward concedes, "it has never been seriously suggested that Parliament does not have the power to adjust constituencies."

18 Toronto *Globe and Mail*, 25 January 1954.

19 *Debates*, 1882, 1366.

20 By "Reform colleagues," he appeared to mean Great-Coalition Reformers, not those who had followed George Brown into opposition. In this regard,

the Parliament of Canada website classes one-third of the 49 Ontario Conservative-Party MPs elected in 1867 as "Liberal-Conservative." The divide between coalition Reformers (Hincksites) and anti-coalition Reformers (Brownites) dated from 1854; see Emery, *Elections in Oxford County*.

21 Macdonald to Monck, 22 June 1866, in Pope, *Memoirs of the Right Honourable Sir John Alexander Macdonald*, 301. On Macdonald and Confederation, see Johnston and Waite, "Macdonald, Sir John Alexander."

22 Charles Stanley Monck, 4th Viscount Monck, was the last governor-general of the Province of Canada. Edward Cardwell, 1st Viscount Cardwell, was colonial secretary, 1864–66.

23 Riding of Russell, marginalia, in *Returns* for the 1867 Dominion general election. Schedule I of the BNA Act refers to Carleton and Russell, incorrectly, as county ridings, under the heading "Existing Electoral Divisions." An 1853 statute had "provided always, that the Townships of Gloucester and Osgoode shall, for purposes of representation only, be detached from the County of Carleton and attached to the County of Russell." See Province of Canada, *Statutes*, 1853, "An Act to Enlarge the Representation of the People of the Province in Parliament," Upper Canada, s. 20.

24 The 27 Conservatives included seven men who had been elected as anti-coalition Reformers in 1863 but remained with the Great-Coalition ministry in 1867. These were John Sandfield Macdonald, Cornwall; Lewis Wallbridge, Hastings South; Francis Jones, Leeds & Grenville North; Crowell Willson, Middlesex East; William McDougall, Ontario North; James Cowan, Waterloo South; and William Howland, York West. Wallbridge, McDougall, and Howland were ministers in the Macdonald-Sicotte cabinet, 1863–65. Howland and McDougall were ministers in the last Province of Canada cabinet. McDougall, Willson, Jones, and Cowan ran as Conservatives in the 1867 Dominion election.

25 Liberal-majority statistics are unavailable for ridings with acclamation outcomes (e.g. Simcoe South, Huron & Bruce, Lambton, Wellington South, Hastings South, Peterborough); ridings with same-party contests (e.g. Victoria, Lennox & Addington); and ridings whose detailed returns were not printed in the Toronto *Globe* (e.g. Victoria).

26 Morgan and Brown, "Cartwright, Sir Richard John."

27 *Debates*, 1892, Wilson, 4330–1.

28 Without Camden, however, the Addington riding would have been less compact, with Sheffield Township an awkward eastern appendage of the riding's Frontenac-County townships. Moreover, the retention of Camden

in Lennox would have been negative for equalizing the populations of the two ridings; Lennox would have changed from 0.94 to 1.38, and Addington from 1.26 to 0.82.

29 Details for the three electoral counties were as follows. Bothwell, a prospective Liberal seat, drew townships from Lambton and Kent Counties. The out-transfers moved the riding of Kent from very safe, Liberal (+296) to precarious (+62). Their effect on the Lambton riding is unknowable (Liberal, acclamation). Cardwell, a prospective Conservative seat, drew townships from the municipal counties of Simcoe (Simcoe South riding) and Peel. The out-transfers moved the riding of Peel from very safe, Conservative (-212) to very safe (-324). Their effect on the riding of Simcoe South is unknowable (Conservative, acclamation). Monck, reasonably safe, Liberal (+133), drew townships from Haldimand, Lincoln, and Welland municipal counties. The out-transfers moved the Haldimand riding moved from precarious, Liberal (+11) to possibly safe (+114); the Lincoln riding from very safe, Liberal (+499) to very safe (+393); and the Welland riding from reasonably safe, Conservative (-152) to very safe (-334).

30 Toronto *Globe*, 18 March 1867.

31 Swainson, "Street, Thomas Clark (Clarke)."

CHAPTER THREE

1 Ontario, *Statutes*, 1889, An Act to Give Representation in the Assembly to the District of Nipissing; Canada, *Statutes*, 1892, Representation Act; 1893, Act to Readjust Representation.

2 *Debates*, 1872, Macdonald, 926–31, 934–5.

3 *Debates*, 1872, Blake, 931–2.

4 *Debates*, 1872, Cameron, 934; Russell, "Cameron, Malcolm Colin."

5 *Debates*, 1872, McKenzie, 1049, 1058–9, 1066.

6 *Debates*, 1872, Mills, 1065.

7 Toronto received a third riding for its 3.06 standard populations.

8 *Debates*, 934–5.

9 The Liberal-majority statistics for the hypothetical redistribution were -478, +53, +469, and +671.

10 On the basis of geography, either Proton Township or St. Vincent Township was suitable for redeployment to an adjacent Grey-County riding. Only Proton, however, had a population that was sufficiently small to balance the riding populations.

11 *Debates*, 1872, Cameron, 934.

12 Rea, "Greenway, Thomas."

13 Bothwell and Niagara were abolished. Dufferin and Muskoka & Parry Sound were new ridings. Additional ridings went to the counties of Grey, Kent, Essex, Huron, and Lambton.

14 *Debates*, 1892, Blake, 1366.

15 Settlers in the Haliburton townships cited the remoteness of the county towns of Grey, Simcoe, and Wellington, and the difficulties that caused for persons participating in municipal government or legal processes. Also, the settlers wished to tax themselves to bonus a proposed Victoria Railway, which the Peterborough County Council opposed. Accordingly, Mowat separated twenty townships from Peterborough County and three townships from Victoria County to create Haliburton. Mulvaney, *History of the County of Peterborough*, 463–4; history of Dufferin County at http://www.dufferinmuseum.com/About/DufferinCounty.aspx.

16 Dawson, *Gerrymander*, 206–7. For Liberal-Party sources, see Anonymous, "The Alleged 'Gerrymander' by Mr. Mowat," and Ontario Liberal Association, *The Record of the Mowat Government*.

17 As noted, his redistribution divided Goderich Township to the north and south of "the line known as the 'cut line,'" and the townships of Hullett and Turnberry to the east and west of "the road commonly called the Gravel Road." However, the printed 1875 election returns reported the whole population of Goderich Township twice, once for each of its parts; the returns gave the whole population of Hullett and Turnberry Townships to one of their parts, with nothing given for their companion parts. For purposes of calculation, each part of a split township was awarded population and Liberal-majority statistics in proportion to its percentage of voters at the township polls. The split was 50-50 for Goderich Township and one-third/two-thirds for Turnberry and Hullett Townships.

18 The population and Liberal-majority statistics in the actual redistribution were 1.12, 1.24, and 1.25 and +332, +133, and +213. The statistics for the alternative three-riding redistribution are 1.15, 1.14, and 1.22 and +315, +186, and +171.

19 The Liberal-majority statistics for the four-riding model are +183, +174, +1, and +314. The population statistics are 0.87, 0.86, 0.98, and 0.90.

20 The four new ridings had approximately equal populations in or close to the optimum range: Kent East, 1.08; Kent West, 1.14; Lambton East, 1.05; and Lambton West, 1.07.

21 Toronto *Globe*, 18 December 1874.

22 Toronto *Globe*, 15 December 1874, editorial.

23 Hodgins, "Macdonald, John Sandfield."

24 The contributing ridings were Cardwell, Grey South, Wellington North, Wellington South, and Simcoe South.
25 Toronto *Globe*, 15 December 1874, editorial.
26 The census population for the Algoma riding, Dominion and provincial, was 7,018. The 1875 Ontario election returns incorrectly reported 5,007 people, which omits the population of Manitoulin Island.
27 The standard populations for the Peterborough and Victoria ridings were 1.02, 0.64, 0.60, and 1.05 before redistribution, and 0.84, 0.71, 0.74, and 1.05 after. Victoria North had been possibly safe for the Tories (-90), and now it was very safe (-203). Peterborough West moved from possibly safe, Liberal (+53) to reasonably safe, Tory (-105).

CHAPTER FOUR

1 These populations are taken from the 1881 census. Table 7 of the 1931 census, based on "areas as of 1931," reports higher populations for four cities: Toronto, 96,196; Hamilton, 36,661; Ottawa, 31,307; and London, 27,867.
2 *Debates*, Macdonald, 1203, 1209.
3 Ibid., 1205.
4 Ibid., 1207; Vipond, "Blake, Edward."
5 *Debates*, Mackenzie, 1209.
6 A rise from 39 percent of 41 counties in 1872.
7 *Debates*, Macdonald, 1208.
8 *Debates*, Blake, 1365–7.
9 *Debates*, Bowell, 1378.
10 *Debates*, 1882, Boultbee, 1211; Anonymous, "The Alleged 'Gerrymander' by Mr. Mowat"; Ontario Liberal Association, *The Record of the Mowat Government*.
11 For list of counties and their municipalities, see RSO, 1877, Territorial Division, Section II.
12 Ontario, *Statutes*, 1874, Act Respecting the Provisional County of Haliburton. Haliburton was united with the County of Victoria for judicial purposes.
13 *Debates*, Charlton, 1212. The Liberal-majority statistic was -102 for the two municipalities.
14 *Debates*, 1882, Paterson, 1478.
15 *Debates*, 1882, Blake, 1369.
16 *Debates*, 1899, Robertson, 6539.
17 *Debates*, 1892, McCarthy, 3411. Mowat was knighted in 1892.

18 Debates, 1892, O'Brien, 3447–8.
19 *Debates*, 1892, Weldon, 3468.
20 *Debates*, 1882, Mackenzie, 1209–10.
21 *Debates*, 1882, Blake, 1207.
22 de Bonville, *La Presse Québécoise de 1884 à 1914*, 63.
23 Ibid., 131, 152n264.
24 The full text of the letter is available in *Debates*, 1900, Charles Heyd (Liberal, Brant South), 1626–7; *Debates*, 1903, Heyd, 10930; Toronto *Globe*, 10 July 1899.
25 Toronto *Globe*, 10 July 1899.
26 Ward, *Canadian House of Commons*, 29.
27 Cochrane, ed., *Men of Canada*, vol. I, 49; Morgan, ed., *Canadian Men and Women of the Time* (1898), 420–1; Morgan, ed., *Canadian Men and Women of the Time* (1912), 488.
28 *Debates*, 1903, Sproule, 10944–6.
29 1.23, 1.33, and 1.12 standard populations before redistribution, and 1.00, 1.05, and 1.12 after.
30 Toronto *Globe*, 18 May 1882.
31 Toronto *Globe*, 9 and 14 March, 18 and 24 May, and 18 June 1882. For an excellent biography of Cartwright, see Morgan and Brown, "Cartwright, Sir Richard John."
32 Toronto *Globe*, 30 November 1883. This was on the understanding that Cartwright would yield the riding back to McMillan in the next general election. See Toronto *Globe*, 7 July 1886. Thus, Cartwright found a safe seat in Oxford South for the next four general elections – 1887, 1891, 1896, and 1900. For the Liberal-leaning politics of this riding, see Emery, *Elections in Oxford County*.
33 Wentworth South took Grimsby Township and Grimsby Village (+60) from Lincoln and Caister Township (+34) from Monck, and gave up Ancaster (+271) to Brant North.
34 In other changes, Perth North gave up Wallace Township and Palmerston Town (-84) to Wellington North, and Perth South acquired Usborne Township (-2) from Huron South.
35 The other transfers: West Gwilliambury Township and Bradford Village (pop. 4,170; -71) from Simcoe South to York North; the townships of Morrison, Draper & Oakley, Ryde, McLean, Macaulay, and Bracebridge Village from Muskoka to Ontario North (pop. 4,685; +1); and Reach Township and Port Perry Village from Ontario North to Ontario South. Simcoe South was very safe, Conservative (-443) and remained so (-372).

36 The three ridings moved from 1.44, 1.12, and 1.01 before redistribution to 1.20, 1.12, and 1.23 after.

37 As predicted (-156), Artemesia Township gave a Tory majority (-123).

38 First, it removed three Liberal-leaning municipalities – Orford Township, Howard Township, and Ridgetown Village (+321) – from Bothwell to West Elgin. Second, it relocated two Tory-leaning municipalities, Chatham Township and Wallaceburg Village (-183), from Kent to Bothwell. Third, it removed Tory-leaning Euphemia Township (-30) from Bothwell to Middlesex West. Fourth, it transferred South Dorchester Township and Springfield Village (+6) from East Elgin to Middlesex East. The changes boosted West Elgin from reasonably safe, Liberal (+112) to very safe (+468), and reduced Kent from Tory hive (-533) to very safe (-321). There were no significant changes for East Elgin, Kent, or the two Middlesex ridings.

39 1882 General Election Returns for Bothwell, marginalia; Toronto *Globe*, 26 February 1884; Morgan, ed., *Dominion Annual Register and Review, 1883*, 20, 22.

40 From 0.62, 0.96, and 0.60 for Leeds & Grenville, Lanark South, and Brockville, to 0.59, 0.86, and 0.72.

41 Before redistribution, the Liberals held Niagara (+2), Wentworth South (+74), and Brant North (+198), and the Tories held Monck (-28) and Lincoln (-94). The 1882 redistribution predicted a Liberal win in Brant North (+704), and Tory wins in Lincoln & Niagara (-152), Monck (-62), and Wentworth South (-103).

42 The Tory gerrymanders failed in Huron East, Brant South, Wentworth South, Perth South, Ontario North, Ontario South, York North, Bruce East, Grey South, and, after a two-year delay, Bothwell. They succeeded in Huron West and Bruce North.

43 Toronto *Globe*, 5 March 1885; for Hardy, see David, "Hardy, Arthur Sturgis."

44 These were: three townships from Addington to Frontenac; Caledon from Cardwell to Peel; and East Luther from Wellington Centre to Dufferin.

45 The statistics for Toronto were 1.71 and 2.43 (two ridings) before redistribution, and a mean of 1.47 for the redistributed three-member riding. The statistics for the York ridings (East, North, and South) moved from 1.11, 1.17, and 0.86 to 0.93, 1.17, and 0.76.

46 Before redistribution, Conservatives held the two Toronto ridings (-124 and -207) and York West (-31), and the government party held York North (+854) and York East (+243). Redistribution favoured the Tories in the three-member Toronto riding (-368), but the government party in the three York ridings (East, +289; North, +854; and West, +16).

47 *Debates*, 1892, McMullen, 3499.
48 Mowat created Dufferin as a provisional municipal county in 1874. The new county took Aramanth Township, East Garafraxa Township, and the town of Orangeville from Wellington County. In 1880 the province divided Luther Township into East Luther and West Luther Townships. On its proclamation as a municipal county in 1881, Dufferin included East Luther Township. The awkwardly shaped Wellington County was the leftover rump.
49 With redistribution, the statistics were Wellington East (the former Centre riding) now very safe (+391); Wellington West, very safe (+498); and Wellington South, reasonably safe (+151).
50 From 0.94, 0.97, and 1.19 before redistribution to 1.06, 1.06, and 0.90 after.
51 From 1.23, 1.01, and 1.14 before redistribution to 1.03, 1.17, and 1.17 after.
52 From 0.86 (Cardwell), 1.15 (Simcoe East), 0.82 (Simcoe South), 1.25 (Simcoe West), and 0.78 (Peel) to 1.07, 0.83, 0.97, 0.96, and 1.04.

CHAPTER FIVE

1 The new riding of Nipissing included 521 persons from Head, Clara, and Maria Townships, which were taken from Renfrew North. The riding also included part of Algoma District.
2 Waite, *The Man from Halifax*, 333.
3 Stevens, "Edgar, Sir James David."
4 *Debates*, 1892, Edgar, 3858.
5 *Debates*, 1892, Thompson, 1856.
6 Ibid., 1862ff.
7 *Debates*, 1892, Haggart, 3439–40.
8 Kulisek, "McCarthy, D'Alton"; P.B. Waite, *The Man from Halifax*, 238–40.
9 *Debates*, 1892, McCarthy, 3414; O'Brien, 3447.
10 *Debates*, 1892, Weldon, 3468. Of 92 Ontario seats in the three elections (1882, 1887, and 1891), the Conservatives won 55, 55, and 48 seats respectively, with popular votes of 50.4, 50.7, and 49.4. All three outcomes were below those statistically projected from Macdonald's 1882 gerrymander.
11 *Debates*, Mills, 3898; Bowell, 3926; Weldon, 3873–5.
12 *Debates*, 1892, Mills, 1874.
13 *Debates*, 1892, Cartwright, 3930–1.
14 *Debates*, 1892, Hughes, 3495–99.

15 Haycock, *Sam Hughes*, 15; Brown, "Hughes, Sir Samuel."
16 As Hughes recounted, "wherever two Conservatives contested a riding, as in Carleton, and wherever two Reformers contested a riding, as in West[ern?] Ontario, I have referred back to the previous election when a Conservative was opposed by a Reformer." Perhaps he handled four ridings with acclamation outcomes in the same fashion. Hughes's description of his adjustments for Toronto was confusing. In the provincial parliament, Toronto was a three-member riding in which an elector could vote for up to two candidates. Thus, the city's 31,116 votes could have been polled from as few as 15,558 voters.
17 This total excludes four ridings with acclamation outcomes. It misleads for any riding whose rival candidates were from the same party. It assumes that each Toronto voter voted for two candidates (his entitlement), although an unknown number of electors voted for one.
18 Province of Canada, *Statutes*, Representation Act, 1853, s. II, 16.
19 *Debates*, 1892, McMullen, 3499.
20 Calculated from the 1881 and 1891 censuses. Table 7 of the 1931 census, for "areas as of 1931," reports higher populations (96,196 and 181,215).
21 *Debates*, 1892, Weldon, 3874–6.
22 *Debates*, 1892, Laurier, 3119; Weldon, 3873–5; Edgar, 3862–3; Cockburn, 4071. Laurier spoke of Montreal, but his logic applied equally to Toronto.
23 Debates, 1892, Charlton, 3136–7, 3824.
24 *Debates*, 1892, Laurier, 3115, 3127, 3130.
25 Ibid., 3118, 3127ff, 3130; Weldon, 3873–5.
26 The statistics were: Lincoln & Niagara, 1.18; Wentworth South, 1.17; Welland, 1.10; Wentworth North & Brant, 0.94; Haldimand & Monck, 0.94; and Norfolk South, 0.99.
27 Waite, *The Man from Halifax*, 333.

CHAPTER SIX

1 Ward, ed., *A Party Politician*, 69–70, 77. Chubby Power, a Liberal-Party organizer, remembered Borden for his "tact and the consideration of others."
2 *Debates*, 1899, Mulock, 3442–7.
3 *Debates*, 1899, Tupper, 3449–56; Borden, 6659, 6748ff; McNeill, 6597–9.
4 Ward, *Canadian House of Commons*, 38.
5 *Debates*, 1900, Wallace, 1607–8.
6 Rossiter et al., *The Boundary Commissions*, 34–44.
7 *Debates*, 1892, Laurier, 3118, 3127ff.

8 *Debates*, 1899, Mulock, 3442–7.
9 *Debates*, 1899, Robertson, 6539.
10 *Debates*, 1900, Tupper, 1585–7.
11 *Debates*, 1899, Laurier, 3497, 6758.
12 *Debates*, 1899, Macdonald, 6625–6.
13 *Debates*, 1899, Laurier, 3445; 1899, Landerkin, 6639–46; 1900, Postmaster General (William Mulock), 1214.
14 *Debates*, 1899, Wallace, 3459.
15 *Debates*, 1899, Laurier, 6799.
16 *Debates*, 1899, Mulock, 6771.
17 *Debates*, 1899, McGregor, 6625–6.
18 *Debates*, 1899, Robertson, 6539.
19 *Debates*, 1899, Haggart, 6904.
20 *Debates*, 1899, Henderson, 6995.
21 *Debates*, 1899, Wallace, 3459–60.
22 *Debates*, 1899, Tisdale, 3463–5.
23 *Debates*, 1899, Bennett, 3481.
24 *Debates*, 1903, Sutherland, 11486.
25 *Debates*, 1903, Tisdale, 12372–99.
26 Ontario abolished the property qualification for provincial elections in 1888. Dominion elections had used the provincial franchise until 1885, when Sir John A. Macdonald's corrupt Dominion Franchise Act introduced a Dominion franchise with a property qualification. The Laurier government's Franchise Act, 1898, restored the franchise of the various provinces for Dominion elections and with it, for Ontario, the abolition of the property qualification. No longer could a man vote in all Dominion ridings in which he held property (plural voting). Under universal manhood suffrage he could vote in one riding, the constituency in which he resided.
27 *Debates*, 1900, Tupper, 1585–7.
28 *Debates*, 1903, Borden, 1294.
29 The provincial Act respecting the Territorial Division of Ontario, 1897, lists the municipalities within each county, including incorporated cities, which were "counties unto themselves" for municipal purposes. It says nothing about the city's territory, which was subject to enlargement through annexations.
30 *Debates*, 1903, Borden, 10840–1, 11441–2. For clarity, the numbering of the rules differs from the original.
31 *Debates*, 1903, Sutherland, 10842.
32 *Debates*, 1903, Monk, 10833.
33 Ibid., 10837, 10845–6.

34 *Debates*, 1903, Borden, 11439, 11441–2, 11477.
35 *Debates*, 1903, Haggart, 10886.
36 *Debates*, 1903, Laurier, 10850; Borden, 11441–2.
37 *Debates*, 1903, Haggart, 12414, 12430–1.
38 *Debates*, 1903, Clancy, 11043, 11572.
39 Clancy was defeated in Lambton West in the 1904 general election. Mills was named to the Senate in 1896 and became Laurier's minister of Justice in 1897.
40 Under the proposed, but rejected, Borden-Haggart rules 4 and 5, the committee would have fixed the representation for all five cities (Toronto, Hamilton, Ottawa, Kingston, and London), not just Toronto, before treating the counties.
41 The three ridings (East, West, and North) moved from 1.59, 2.12, and 0.74 standard populations to 0.85, 0.82, and 0.88 (Centre, South, and North). Statistics for the Toronto ridings moved from 1.13, 1.80, and 1.61 (the two-member West riding) to 1.73, 1.58, 1.61, 1.50, and 1.77.
42 As Laurier noted, England was able to equalize population between borough and county ridings because, unlike Canada, it had no restriction on the total number of seats in its House of Commons. *Debates*, 1903, Laurier, 11431, 11681.
43 *Debates*, 1903, Hyman, 11686.
44 The transfer of the city fragments (-194) to the city riding helped the Liberal cause in the county ridings without wrecking it in the city. London, a Liberal hive (+547), was still very safe (+353) after redistribution.
45 The evidence that the redistribution left the annexed territories of 1902–03 in the county riding is as follows. The 1911 census reported that the city fragments in the Wentworth riding totalled 2,100 acres. This corresponds with the sum of the acreages (2,103) reported in tax rolls for all annexations during the years 1902–10 (Appendix A). It follows that the 1903 redistribution left the three parcels of 1902–03 in the county riding. The 1901-census populations of the city fragments are unknown.
46 *Debates*, 1903, Ingram, 11596–601.
47 *Debates*, 1903, Hyman, 10864–5.
48 *Debates*, 1903, Haggart, 11048. The details for Haggart's understanding of Leeds are unclear. With the riding's population reconstructed along municipal-county lines (exclusive of Brockville, three townships, and one village), it held 0.79 units of population, which was well above the minimum for one riding.
49 *Revised Statutes of Ontario*, 1897, Section II, Territorial Division, Cap. 3, s. 1. Section 1 introduces the "Territorial division of Counties and Districts

... for municipal and judicial purposes." Chapter 3 is the statutory reference for the identification of county lines.

50 *Debates*, 1903, Borden, 11441–2.

51 *Debates*, 1903, 11625–34.

52 Personal communication from Ronald Graham Haycock.

53 Haycock, *Sam Hughes*, 103.

54 Using Liberal-majority statistics for the 1896 election (two elections previously), the revision indicated a Tory hive (-1,093) for the North riding and a Liberal hive (+893) for the South riding. The North riding had an acclamation outcome (Tory) in the 1900 election, hence no Liberal-majority statistic. The partial prediction for 1900 was similar to the full prediction for 1896: a Tory win in the North riding (-523 plus three Tory-acclamation townships) and a Liberal win in the South riding (+305 plus three Tory-acclamation townships).

55 Toronto *Globe*, 9 November 1900, quotation from comments in the Clinton *News-Record* (Conservative) on the Huron South election but not on the Morris-Township polls. 5 of the 11 Morris-Township polls were in Huron South, and 36 percent of its votes were polled there.

56 For list of Ontario counties and the municipalities in each of them, see *Revised Statutes of Ontario*, 1877, 1887, 1897 and 1914, Cap. 3, s. 1, "The Territorial Division of Ontario for Municipal and Judicial Purposes."

57 In all but one of the ten affected counties (Renfrew) the trespass dated from 1867. In Renfrew it dated from 1892 for Dominion ridings and 1902 for Ontario-provincial ridings.

CHAPTER SEVEN

1 Interestingly, Prime Minister Laurier was returned for two ridings in the 1911 general election (Québec East and Soulanges) and sat for both – which, I speculate, was unique in Canada's parliamentary history. He had been elected for two constituencies in the 1904 and 1908 general elections, but in each case had resigned one of them.

2 Brown, "Borden, Sir Robert Laird"; Hall and Smith, "Lougheed, Sir James Alexander"; Toronto *Globe*, 13 June 1914; *Debates*, debate on Borden's Redistribution Bill, February to June 1914.

3 Toronto *Globe*, 11 September and 24 December 1912 and 14 and 19 February 1913. For the Liberal perspective on the upcoming redistribution, see Mackenzie and Dutil, *Canada 1911*, ch. 5 and 6.

4 The Senate accepted Borden's Constitution Bill in 1915. Its enactment recognized Canada's four western provinces as a distinct "section" under the

BNA Act, and as such, entitled to 24 senators, an increase of 11. See Parliament of Canada, "A Legislative and Historical Overview of the Senate of Canada."

5 Toronto *Globe*, 12 June 1914.

6 Toronto *Globe*, 6 March 1914.

7 The merged ridings were Glengarry & Stormont, Leeds & Brockville, and the two ridings in each of the counties of Kent, Lanark, and Northumberland. The counties of Grey, Huron, and Middlesex were each reduced from three ridings to two.

8 *Debates*, 1914, Borden, 617–19.

9 Debates, 1923, E.M. Macdonald (Pictou, N.S.), a Liberal member of the 1914 special committee and of Mackenzie King's special committees of 1923 and 1924, 4736.

10 *Debates*, 1914, Borden, 927.

11 English, *Decline of Politics*, 15–16, 47, 63, 74, 76, 81.

12 Toronto *Globe*, 9 January and 21 February 1914.

13 *Debates*, 1903, Borden, 11439, 11441–2, 11477.

14 *Debates*, 1914, Laurier, 830–42.

15 *Debates*, 1923, E.M. Macdonald (Pictou), 4736.

16 Toronto *Globe*, 11–12 June 1914.

17 Canada, *Statutes*, Representation Act, 1914; amendment to the Act, 1915, section pertaining to the city of London. In a preamble to the schedule of ridings for Ontario, taken verbatim from Laurier's Representation Act, 1903, Borden's Representation Act, 1914 referred to counties and territorial districts as "those constituted by or under chapter 3 of the Revised Statutes of Ontario (RSO), 1897, entitled 'An Act Respecting the Territorial Division of Ontario for Municipal and Judicial Purposes.'" An amended version of the provincial statute (RSO 1914) was available to the special committee, but not chosen. In either version, the statute merely lists the municipalities by counties. It does not delineate city municipalities by their civic boundaries for the year of the statute (1897 or 1914). The Dominion special committee ignored the preamble in its reference to districts. In the 1914 schedule, the new riding of Temiskaming was to include the district of Temiskaming and part of the district of Algoma. The district of Temiskaming, created in 1912, had not existed in 1897.

18 The standard populations were Carleton, 0.79; Ottawa, 1.25 per member; and Russell, 1.28. With full application of municipal lines they would have been Carleton, 1.22; Ottawa, 1.29 per member; and Russell, 0.77.

19 *Debates*, 1872, Macdonald, 926–31, 934–5.

20 Toronto *Globe*, 11 June 1914, special despatch to the *Globe*.
21 Ibid.
22 The merger and out-transfers did not advance the equalization of riding populations. Glengarry, Stormont, and Dundas had held 0.69, 0.80, and 0.59 standard populations; with redistribution the statistics were Glengarry-Stormont, 1.24, and Dundas, 0.79.
23 *Debates*, 1892, Haggart, 3439–40.
24 Ward, ed., *A Party Politician*, 69–70, 77. Chubby Power, a Liberal-Party organizer, remembered Borden for his "tact and the consideration of others." Laurier "in the House ... was suave and courteous, speaking always with smooth fluency, and without the slightest sign of recrimination."

CHAPTER EIGHT

1 The 1885 Act created 90 seats; the ministry added the riding of Nipissing in 1889. The Toronto *Globe* reported a parliamentary debate over the transfer of Kingston Township from Kingston City to Frontenac, but otherwise gave no details about the debate on the 1894 Bill. Toronto *Globe*, 23 February, 30 March, and 11 April to 6 May 1894.
2 Toronto *Globe*, 11 April 1894. The provincial secretary, John Morison Gibson, reported the "voting populations" (electors) of the Toronto ridings as follows: East, 7,686; North, 7,611; West, 8,722; and South, 10,666.
3 Toronto *Globe*, 11 April 1894.
4 Ross, *Getting into Parliament and After*, 210ff; Burley, "Ross, Sir George William."
5 As the 1892 Dominion Representation Act had done, the province's 1902 Representation Act transferred the townships of Head, Clara, and Maria from Renfrew North to the new riding of Nipissing East.
6 Toronto *Globe*, 4 March 1898.
7 Toronto *Globe*, 2 and 3 March and 4 and 15 April 1908.
8 Toronto *Globe*, 10, 11, and 21 March 1908.
9 Toronto *Globe*, 8 and 10 March and 2 April 1908.
10 Toronto *Globe*, 7 April 1908, "A Straight Gerrymander Charges Hon. A.G. McKay."
11 Toronto *Globe*, 8 April and 20 May 1908.
12 Toronto *Globe*, 3 April 1908, regarding the report of the Liberal minority on the special committee.
13 Interestingly, the arrangement harkened back to Confederation, when each riding held simultaneous Dominion and provincial general elections.
14 The distribution across the ridings is estimated from statistics for electors.

15 The standard populations before redistribution were Cardwell, 0.84, and Peel, 0.82; then Peel, 1.04, and Simcoe South, 0.68, after. Within Simcoe County, the statistics before redistribution for three ridings were 0.88, 1.18, and 0.90; after redistribution the statistics for four ridings were 0.94, 1.43. 0.68, and 0.94.
16 Toronto *Globe*, 2 April 1908.
17 Their standard populations moved from 0.65 and 0.71 to 0.72 and 0.64.
18 The standard populations for the ridings were as follows: status quo, 0.82, 0.97, and 1.01; Tory proposal, 1.02, 0.99, and 1,00; and Liberal proposal, 0.98, 1.04, and 1.00.
19 Of eight redistributed ridings that were precarious, possibly safe, or reasonably safe for the incumbent (±199, either party) the changes benefited the Tories in six cases and the Grits in two.
20 Comeau, "Hanna, William John."
21 English, *Decline of Politics*, 46, 61–2.
22 Toronto *Globe*, 6 March 1914.
23 Toronto *Globe*, 6 March, 9, 10, 17, 23, 24, and 30 April, and 1 May 1914.
24 Humphries, *'Honest Enough to be Bold,'* 208.
25 Toronto *Globe*, 9 April 1914.
26 Toronto *Globe*, 23 April 1914.
27 From 0.60, 0.82, and 0.68 to 0.74, 0.73, and 0.70.
28 The predicted outcomes were Bruce North, Tory (-234); Bruce South, Tory (-6); and Bruce West, Liberal (+1,041). The initial results of the election were Bruce North, Tory (-23); Bruce South, Tory (-317); and Bruce West, Liberal (+647).
29 Cécillon, *Prayers, Petitions, and Protests*, ch. 3.
30 From Monck, 0.64; Haldimand, 0.65; Lincoln, 1.33; and Welland, 1.53, before redistribution, to St. Catharines, 0.93; Niagara Falls, 0.89; Welland, 0.84; Haldimand, 0.95; and Lincoln, 0.75, after.
31 The redistribution for Lincoln combined municipalities with a Liberal-majority surplus (+361) in 1911 with municipalities having a Tory acclamation.
32 Toronto *Globe*, 5 May 1894.
33 "Mechanicsville, or Number 9 Ottawa City," was one poll in the Carleton riding in the 1914 general election, and two Victoria-Ward polls in the 1923 general election.

CHAPTER NINE

1 The Conservatives contested 79 of the 82 seats and won 37, and the Liberals contested 66 seats and won 17.

2 The Conservatives contested 102 of the 111 seats, won 75, and formed the government; the Liberals contested 77 ridings and won 14. For party affiliations of the candidates, see Toronto *Globe*, 15 June 1929, "Nominations to the Sixteenth Legislature of Ontario."
3 English, *Decline of Politics*, 6.
4 *Debates*, 1923, Macdonald (Liberal, Pictou), 4736. The special committee appointed three-member subcommittees to deal with the regions of the Maritimes, Quebec, the prairies, and British Columbia.
5 *Debates*, 1923, Sutherland, 4740–1.
6 *Debates*, 1924, King, 250–4; King and W.F. Maclean (Conservative, York South), 488.
7 *Debates*, 1924, King, 1068.
8 *Debates*, 1924, Macdonald, 4550; Toronto *Globe*, 3 July 1924. The *Globe* described McGiverin as "an extremely able parliamentarian," whose "chairmanship of the Private Bills Committee during the Church Union controversy [had] won him the esteem and admiration of all parties."
9 *Debates*, 1924, Sutherland, 4513.
10 *Debates*, 1924, King, 660ff.
11 *Debates*, 1924, Kennedy, 669.
12 *Debates*, 1924, Sutherland, 4512–13. Universal male suffrage in Ontario dated from 1888 for provincial elections and 1903 for Dominion elections; equal suffrage for women dated from 1918.
13 *Debates*, 1924, Hocken, 663.
14 *Debates*, 1924, Sutherland, 1413–14.
15 *Debates*, 1924, Hocken, 663; see also Joseph Harris (Conservative, York East), 673.
16 *Debates*, 1924, Meighen, 4531–3.
17 *Debates*, 1924, Sutherland, 4512–13.
18 Ibid., 4512.
19 *Debates*, 1924, Stewart, 4527.
20 Ibid., 4544.
21 *Debates*, 1924, Brethen, 4542–4. Brethen's amendment, identical to what Conservatives on the subcommittee claimed to have supported, was neutral for party prospects and would have done less than the "compromise" to equalize populations.
22 *Debates*, 1924, Kennedy, 4544–5.
23 No longer acting minister.
24 *Debates*, 1924, Pritchard, Macdonald, 4550.
25 James Singer, a farmer, ran as a Labour candidate in the heavily urbanized South riding, but was a Progressive.

26 *Debates*, 1924, Stewart, 4551.

27 The statistics for the status quo were Ottawa, 1.31, for each of its two members; Russell, 1.22; and Carleton, 0.91. If the redistribution had observed county lines, then the statistics would have been 1.50, 0.75, and 0.63.

28 The Liberal-majority statistics for the two-member Ottawa riding, Russell, and Carleton were +6,258, +2,223, and -1,395. If the redistribution had restored county lines, by transferring the Ottawa-City fragments to the Ottawa riding and the townships of Gloucester and Osgoode to the riding of Carleton, then the statistics would have been +7,755, +2,153, and -1,315.

29 *Debates*, 1924, White, 4547–8.

30 *Debates*, 1924, Good, 4551–2.

31 Meanwhile, fate placed the Parkdale district, a part of Brantford's Ward 5 with some 800 population, in the rural Brant riding. This happened by accident in 1921, explained William Good. The city had incorporated Parkdale after the release of the electors' list, but before the 1921 general election. Perforce, its residents voted in Brant. Parkdale then remained in the Brant riding by statute. Whereas the 1914 redistribution referred simply to "the city of Brantford," the 1924 redistribution referred to the city "as it existed in 1914," which did not include Parkdale.

32 Toronto *Globe*, 10 April 1925.

33 Toronto *Globe*, 10 April 1925, Howard Ferguson; 10 February 1933, Premier George Henry.

34 Toronto *Globe*, 10 April 1925.

35 Toronto *Globe*, 10 April and 9 June, 1925. The 1916 OTA banned the sale of alcoholic beverages, but provided for the Act's repeal, subject to obtaining a wet majority in a plebiscite. In a 1924 plebiscite, 51.5 percent voted to continue the OTA, and 48.5 percent voted to allow government-regulated sale of alcoholic beverages. The cities, where the Conservatives were strong, gave majorities to the wet side. County ridings, where the Progressives did well, gave majorities to the drys. In 1925 the Ferguson government amended the OTA to allow government-regulated sale of beer with 4.4 percent alcoholic content ("Fergies foam"). The government repealed the OTA in 1927.

36 For the results of the 1924 plebiscite on the OTA, see Toronto *Globe*, 25 Oct 1924.

37 Toronto *Globe*, 11 April 1925, editorial.

38 Toronto *Globe*, 10 April 1925. The 13 northern districts held 10 percent of the province's population and 10 percent of the province's ridings. The northern districts had 3.0 constituencies per 100,000 population, which

was more than the statistics for small cities and the GTA (2.3 and 2.1), though less than the statistics for the eastern and western counties (3.3 and 3.1).

39 The Toronto *Globe*, 10 March 1925, noted that Wards 7 and 8, then part of the West York and East York ridings respectively, "may be detached from the rural ridings." The 1925 Representation Act confirmed that the Toronto riding of High Park included Ward 7. The 1923 general election returns for the York ridings included city fragments, but the 1926 general election returns did not.

40 York North was a left-alone rural riding. It was the southern ridings on the city's fringe that increased from two to three.

41 Holding constant York North (0.84), a rural riding not contiguous with the city, York's three city-border ridings had 3.96 standard populations, sufficient for four ridings, as opposed to the three given. The mean for 15 Toronto ridings was 1.33, but for 13 would have been 1.53.

42 Population is estimated from statistics for electors; 3% of the city's electors were in county ridings before redistribution, and 15% after.

43 The pre-redistribution populations were: Hamilton East, 2.89; Hamilton West, 1.40; Wentworth North, 0.62; and Wentworth South, 1.02.

44 The London North riding excluded "that portion of the City of London annexed since the year 1912."

45 The three county ridings were very safe, UFO (+377), very safe, UFO (+206), and very safe, Conservative (-381). The two replacement ridings were very safe, Conservative (-363) and a Progressive hive (+2,180).

CHAPTER TEN

1 Toronto *Globe*, 22 July 1930; 29 October 1929.

2 For 1931 only, the total for cities includes four towns with 10,000+ population. "Greater Windsor" includes the cities of East Windsor, Sandwich, and Walkerville, which Windsor was to annex in 1935.

4 Province of Canada, *Statutes*, 1857, Act to Allow the Proclamation of Judicial Districts in Unsettled Territories.

5 Canada, *Statutes*, 1933, Representation Act and Ontario, *Statutes*, 1933 Representation Act; *Returns* for the 1935 Dominion general election and the 1934 provincial general election. See entries for the ridings of Carleton, Middlesex, Wentworth, and York.

6 *Debates*, 1932, Bennett, 1590. BNA Act, 1867, s. 51.4. With 82 seats rather than 80, the mean population for the Ontario ridings – the de facto standard population for calculating the units of population for Toronto and all other

ridings – was 41,850. This compares with the Quebec-standard population of 44,186, which was referenced in parliamentary debates.

7 Glassford, *Reaction and Reform*, 19–20, 54–5.

8 *Debates*, 1932, King, 1590–1; 1933, King, 5422–3.

9 *Debates*, 1932, Bennett, 1598; 1933, Bennett, 1540–4.

10 John MacNicol discussed the Ontario subcommittee's principles for the 1933 redistribution on two occasions, first in 1933, and fourteen years later, during debates on the 1947 redistribution Bill. *Debates*, 1933, MacNicol, 5492–3; 1947, MacNicol, 692, 725–31.

11 *Debates*, 1933, MacNicol, 5246.

12 *Debates*, 1947, MacNicol, 726–7.

13 The list should have included Oxford and Stormont. It should not have included Northumberland.

14 *Debates*, 1933, MacNicol, 5492. MacNicol's statistical calculations of urban population (cities and towns) were incorrect. His count for Huron North missed the town of Clinton. His count for Huron-Perth incorrectly included Exeter, a village. In 1947 MacNicol drew on an Australian rule of "five, seven, and nine" to argue that "in a widely extended riding like West Algoma or Algoma, they [Australians] would count five votes equivalent to nine votes in a city riding; or in a riding which was semi-city or semi-rural, like Oxford or Norfolk, for instance, they would count seven votes equivalent to nine votes in a large city riding."

15 *Debates*, 1947, MacNicol, 726.

16 Ibid., 727.

17 Ibid., 726.

18 *Debates*, 1933, Stewart, 1539, 5296.

19 *Debates*, 1933, Elliott, 5245.

20 *Debates*, 1933, MacNicol, 5245.

21 Toronto *Globe*, 19 May 1933.

22 Their standard populations changed from 0.54, Huron North; 0.54, Huron South; 0.81, Perth North; and 0.42, Perth South; to 0.62, Huron North; 0.54, Huron-Perth; and 1.14, Perth.

23 Goderich Township and Clinton Town (-410) moved from Huron South to Huron North, and the Perth-County townships of Hibbert and Fullarton (-290) moved from Perth South to Huron-Perth.

24 *Debates*, 1933, Sanderson, 5487.

25 Ibid., 5486–91.

26 Toronto *Globe*, 30 May 1933. The *Globe*'s solution was to give redistribution to a non-political tribunal, which would be a committee of High Court judges.

27 The united Huron riding would have been Liberal, +126, in comparison with -233 and +349 for the pre-merger ridings. The statistics for the Perths would have been -876 and +717 before redistribution and -1,355 and +1,176 after. The statistic for the transferred townships, North Easthope and Ellice, was +479.
28 Toronto *Globe*, 12 April 1935.
29 The standard populations before redistribution were Kent, 1.24; Lambton East, 0.60; and Lambton West, 0.78. After redistribution they were Kent, 1.08; Lambton-Kent, 0.85; and Lambton West, 0.75.
30 The transfer of Tilbury Town and Wheatley Village (+560) added to the Liberal hive in the Kent riding.
31 Their populations before redistribution were Essex East, 1.07; Essex South, 0.87; and Essex West, 1.97; and after redistribution, 1.24, 0.76, and 1.80.
32 The pre-redistribution statistics are Essex West, 88% "urban," 1.97 standard populations; Essex East, 77%, 1.07; and Essex South, 27%, 0.87. The post-redistribution statistics are Essex West, 94%, 1.80; Essex East, 65%, 1.24; and Essex South, 30%, 0.76.
33 From 0.45, 0.50, 0.69, and 0.62 for four ridings to 0.68, 0.81, and 0.78 for three.
34 Grey North, 45% "urban," had 0.82 standard populations, while Grey-Bruce, 25% "urban," had 0.85.
35 Populations for the pre-redistribution ridings are estimated from statistics for electors.
36 Toronto *Globe*, 19 May 1933.
37 Spanner, "'The Straight Furrow,'" 1, 59–60, 75.
38 Toronto *Globe*, 25 and 28 January 1933; Spanner, "'The Straight Furrow,'" 340.
39 Toronto *Globe*, 10 February 1933.
40 Spanner, "'The Straight Furrow,'" 345.
41 Toronto *Globe*, 28 March 1933.
42 Toronto *Globe*, 29 March 1933.
43 Toronto *Globe*, 31 March 1933.
44 Toronto *Globe*, 11 April 1933.
45 Toronto *Globe*, 25 January, 10 and 15 February, 11 and 28 March, and 11 April 1933.
46 For party affiliations of the candidates, see Toronto *Globe*, 29 (nominations) and 31 (returns) October 1929.
47 The Brant riding, for example, acquired Oakland Township from the Brantford riding; Townsend, Windham, and Waterford Villages from Norfolk; and Blenheim from Oxford North. In the 1929 general election,

the Conservatives had run candidates in all four ridings (Brant, Brantford, Norfolk, and Oxford North) and the Liberals in three (all but Brant), but the Progressives had contested Brant only. Thus, the in-transfers from Brantford, Norfolk, and Oxford North added 5,712 Tory votes and 3,717 Liberal votes, but no Progressive votes. In Huron South, the in-transfer of Goderich Town added Liberal and Conservative votes to the post-redistribution tallies, but no Progressive votes.

48 The redistribution had some positives for principles. It slightly equalized the riding populations: Glengarry, 0.61, Prescott, 0.80, and Russell, 1.27 before redistribution (112 ridings) and 0.59, 0.88, and 0.75 after (90 ridings). The redistribution also returned the Carleton-County village of Casselman to the Carleton riding.

49 Toronto *Globe*, 14 April 1933.

CHAPTER ELEVEN

1 The Conservative Party changed its name to "Progressive Conservative" in 1942.

2 *Debates*, 1947, Gibson, 690–1.

3 Pickersgill, *My Life with Louis St. Laurent*, 65. In the 1940 Grey-Bruce general election, Harris had defeated Agnes MacPhail, the first woman Member of Parliament.

4 *Debates*, 1947, Walter Harris, chair of the subcommittee, 5676.

5 Ibid. Harris reported that 26 constituencies were touched.

6 I reconstituted Harris's "districts" from information on riding populations and geographical locations. This revealed that Harris miscalculated the census populations for two "divisions." With correct totals, Harris's "southern division" had a larger unit of population (54,372) than his "northern division" (53,785) and hence the greater need for increased representation; its Welland riding (1.98), a Liberal hive (+4,895), was overdue for division, which would have gained a seat for his Liberal Party.

7 Baxter was an unorganized township, situated on the Georgian Bay shore, immediately to the north of Tay Township, Simcoe County. Road and water transportation routes linked the township more closely to the riding of Simcoe East than to the rest of Muskoka District. Indeed, one of its two polls was situated in Port Severn, Tay Township. With its 1941 census population of 866, its transfer made little difference to population in the Simcoe East and Parry Sound–Muskoka ridings. In the 1945 general election, however, 255 men had polled their votes in Baxter, giving a majority of 83 to the Liberal candidate.

8 The Ontario riding had been and remained a Liberal hive, and Victoria had been and remained a Tory hive.
9 *Debates*, 1947, Macdonnell, quote from Harris's memorandum, 5583.
10 *Debates*, 1947, Harris, 5676.
11 *Debates*, 1947, Macdonnell, 5583–7; 1933, King, 5379.
12 Granatstein, *The Politics of Survival*, 69–72.
13 Ibid., 157–8.
14 *Debates*, 1947, MacNicol, 701. King had been defeated in the Prince Albert riding in the 1945 general election, but won Glengarry in a 1945 by-election.
15 *Debates*, 1947, MacNicol, 730, 5677.
16 Ibid., 5679. Interestingly, the merger of Muskoka District and Parry Sound set up a contest between two sitting members in the next election. This broke a "principle" that John MacNicol had espoused as chair of the 1933 subcommittee, but which his subcommittee had violated in its redistribution for the Perth-County ridings. In retribution for MacNicol's sin of 1933, the Parry Sound Liberal, "Bucko" McDonald, a retired professional hockey player with three Stanley Cups to his credit, was to defeat James Macdonnell, the Muskoka-Ontario Conservative, in the 1949 Parry Sound–Muskoka general election.
17 Nipissing, +6,067; Cochrane, +5,930; and Temiskaming, +1,548.
18 The 1945 general election returned 34 Liberals and 48 Tories. The 1947 redistribution predicted 37 Liberal and 46 Tory seats. The outcome of the 1949 general election was 57 Liberals, 25 Tories, and 1 CCF.
19 Dawson, *Government of Canada*, 242.
20 Brant had been combined with part of Wentworth County; the Wentworth portion of Brant-Wentworth was merged with the Wentworth riding.
21 *Debates*, 1952, McIlraith, 3984–7. The subcommittee started with six ridings in each group, but ended with the first seven in each case.
22 *Debates*, 1952, Murphy, 3991.
23 *Debates*, 1952, Fleming, 3914, 3978ff. Following their defeat in the subcommittee, the minority moved losing amendments at meetings of the national committee and then in the House.
24 Ward, "The Redistribution of 1952."
25 City residents were 33 percent of population in Russell. With 3.8 standard populations, the city qualified for four all-urban ridings on the basis of population.
26 Toronto *Globe and Mail*, 2 June 1955, editorial, "Make it a Landslide." For the 1936 merger, see Young, "C. George McCullagh and the Leadership League." The newspaper had supported the Liberal Party through to 1942.

27 Toronto *Globe and Mail*, 10 March 1954.
28 Ontario, *Legislature of Ontario Debates*, 1954, 421.
29 It left alone the ridings of Addington and Wellington North, but renamed them Frontenac-Addington and Wellington-Dufferin.
30 A "dual highway" running from Scarborough to Oshawa was completed in 1939. In 1952 the road became a founding section of the proposed Highway 401.
31 The alternative division, along municipal lines, would have given the Oshawa riding the townships of Whitby and East Whitby, and the town of Whitby; and would have given Pickering, including the town of Ajax, to the riding of Ontario.
32 Toronto *Globe and Mail*, 2 March 1954.
33 The proposed Muskoka riding had 14,030 electors, 10,250 voters, and 23,880 population; the proposed Ontario riding had 14,191 electors, 7,041 voters, and 32,593 population. The statistics for the riding of Ontario include estimates for three split municipalities (Pickering, Whitby Township, and Whitby Town).
34 Toronto *Globe and Mail*, 30 March 1954.
35 Toronto *Globe and Mail*, 13 April 1954.
36 Toronto *Globe and Mail*, 15 April 1954.

CONCLUSION

1 *Debates*, 1900, Tupper, 1585–7. Tupper's amendment closed by providing "that such commission shall be appointed as soon as possible *after the completion of the next census*." If passed, the amendment would have killed Laurier's "out of season" Bill.
2 *Debates*, Laurier, 1914, 830–42.
3 Rossiter et al., *The Boundary Commissions*.
4 A province's quota could not decline if the ratio of its population to the Canadian population had diminished by less than one-twentieth.
5 All but the 1840, 1845, 1849, and 1851 redistributions for Canada West.
6 The statistics for between-county transfers exclude transfers to set up new ridings and repatriations of municipalities to their municipal-home counties.
7 Courtney used the ±10 percent range in "The Unfinished Agenda of Electoral Redistributions," 684.
8 Toronto *Globe and Mail*, 19 and 25 April 1962.
9 Toronto *Globe and Mail*, 1 and 25 December 1973; 8 June, 28 August, and 12 September 1974; 31 July 1986.

10 *Debates*, 1964, Pickersgill, 744. See also Jewett, 803, and Aitken, 771–3.
11 *Debates*, 1964, Scott, 829. See also M.J. Moreau (Liberal, York-Scarborough), 852ff.
12 *Elections Ontario* website. Previously, under the Representation Act, 1996, Ontario was divided into electoral districts whose names and boundaries were identical to those of its federal electoral districts, and required redistribution whenever a readjustment took place at the federal level under the Electoral Boundaries Readjustment Act (Canada). With the passing of the Representation Act, 2005, Ontario's electoral boundaries for 11 northern ridings differ slightly from the federal electoral boundaries.
13 Ibid., 237–8, 315n5.

APPENDIX A

1 References: Curtis, "The Boundary Adjustment Process"; Taylor, *Ottawa: An Illustrated History*, 115; Doucet and Weaver, *Housing the North American City*, 88; Weaver, *Hamilton: An Illustrated History*, 92–3, 199 table IX; Toronto Archives, *Annexation Map, 1967*, map displaying the amalgamation dates of various Toronto neighbourhoods and geographical areas; Careless, *Toronto to 1918*.

APPENDIX B

1 Colby Cosh, "The Scheer Madness of Saskatchewan's Boundary Battle," *Maclean's*, 30 January 2013; Harris, *Party of One*, ch. four.
2 *Robocall* is a term for automated phone calls. A *push poll* is "an interactive marketing technique, most commonly employed during political campaigning, in which an individual or organization attempts to influence or alter the view of voters under the guise of conducting a poll. In a push poll, large numbers of voters are contacted, and little or no effort is made to collect and analyze response data. Instead, the push poll is a form of telemarketing-based propaganda and rumour mongering, masquerading as a poll. Push polls may rely on innuendo or knowledge gleaned from opposition research on an opponent. They are generally viewed as a form of negative campaigning." *Wikipedia*, derived from Mark Blumenthal, "So What is a Push Poll?" Pollster.com, 22 August 2006.
3 *Saskatoon StarPhoenix*, "Commissioners Showed Courage," 23 August 2013. John Courtney, author of *Commissioned Ridings*, was one of the commissioners.

4 Ibid.; *Toronto Globe & Mail*, 29 May 2013. "These attacks on an independent commission," averred the *StarPhoenix*,

> have become pro forma for the Harper government. In the seven years it has been in power, it has gone after such arm's-length offices as federal judges, the budget officer, the nuclear regulator, the RCMP ombudsman, the veterans' ombudsman, Elections Canada, native and other non-government advocacy groups, aid organizations, and most recently the Senate, which was brought to its lowest ebb in public support because of malfeasance conducted primarily by Mr. Harper's appointees. As have been its attacks on its political opponents, those directed at these organizations have been brutal, personal and underhanded. Unlike attacks on political opponents that serve primarily to denigrate trust in elected officials, including government members, attacking those organizations established to protect Canadian rights undermines confidence in how this country works.

5 Flanagan, *Persona Non Grata*, ch. 1. See also Flanagan, *Winning Power*; Martin, *Harperland*; Wells, *The Longer I'm Prime Minister*; Harris, *Party of One*.

BIBLIOGRAPHY

1 Since 1956, national censuses have been issued at five-year intervals (1951, 1956, 1961, 1966, etc.).

2 Curtis, *The Politics of Population*.

3 For example, Toronto's 1881 population is 96,196 in *Table 6*, but 86,415 in *the 1881 census*.

4 Ward, "The Formative Years of the House of Commons," 444–6.

5 Legislature of Ontario *Debates*, daily edition, 1954, 420, 693–5, 1245.

Bibliography

OFFICIAL RECORDS

Election Returns

The Toronto *Globe* reports the outcomes of pre-Confederation general elections. The Dominion *Sessional Papers* hold the returns for Dominion general elections through to 1931, after which government published the returns in separate volumes. The Ontario *Sessional Papers* hold the returns for Ontario general elections, with the exception of the first one, in 1867. The returns report the candidates, their tallies of votes, the number of electors (persons eligible to vote), and population for the riding and its subdivisions. The returns for provincial general elections do not report population after 1900. The *Globe* and the *Elections Canada* website report party affiliations of nominated candidates. *Wikipedia* lists the MPPs and their party affiliation in Ontario parliaments from 1867 to the present (to be used with caution).

Census Statistics

Population statistics for the ridings and their municipalities are taken from the decennial censuses. The 1852 and 1861 statistics are organized by counties. With Confederation, the statistics through to 1921 are organized by Dominion ridings, which came to differ from provincial ridings. As reported in the 1891 census, for example, the territories of two provincial ridings, Oxford North and Oxford South, coincided with the territory of Oxford County. In contrast, the Dominion ridings, Oxford North and Oxford South, included two Perth-County townships and two Brant-County townships and excluded three Oxford-County municipalities.

Reporting practices in published census statistics change for the years 1931–56. The 1931 census reports population by counties, not Dominion ridings. The 1941 census does not report population for either municipal or electoral districts. However, the 1951 and 1956[1] censuses report both for 1941 and 1951. Table 5 of the 1951 census reports population for Dominion ridings of the 1947 redistribution, for 1941 and 1951. Table 5 of the 1956 census (the start of censuses at five-year intervals) reports population for Dominion ridings of the 1952 redistribution, for 1951 and 1956. In both censuses, Table 6 reports population for counties and sub-divisions for every census since Confederation.

Nineteenth-century census data are biased and incomplete and must be used with caution.[2] Retrospective data in later censuses present another pitfall. In the 1931 census, for example, Table 8. "Population of cities, towns, and villages ... 1871–1931 (areas as of 1931)" gives Toronto and Ottawa larger populations in 1871, 1881, and 1891 than do the original censuses for those years.[3] The areas as of 1931 include territories that the cities had annexed over the years, hence the difference in the tallies. For analysis, the book uses the original census data, which is what nineteenth-century parliamentarians used for redistribution.

Parliamentary Debates (Hansard)

An edited, official record of debates in the House of Commons (*Hansard*) reports debates on Dominion Representation Bills.[4] A *Hansard* for Ontario's Legislative Assembly dates from 1944. For debates on provincial redistribution Bills, one must rely upon newspaper reportage, which is selective, non-verbatim, and partisan. This book uses the Toronto *Globe* (available online from 1844) for its proxy *Hansard*. Coverage of the debates in the provincial *Hansard* for Ontario's 1954 redistribution Bill is much inferior to that in the Toronto *Globe and Mail*.[5]

Statutes of Canada, Ontario, and the United Kingdom

These include the Representation Acts, which are the official record of redistributions. The *Revised Statutes of Upper Canada*, 1859 and the *Revised Statutes of Ontario*, 1877, 1887, 1897, 1914, 1927, 1937, 1950, and 1960 include Territorial Division Acts, which list the province's municipalities by counties (or northland districts) for the years concerned.

Websites

The Canadian County Atlas Digital Project (McGill University, 2001) hosts a comprehensive collection of digitalized county maps (ca. 1870s and 1880s).

REFERENCES

Anonymous. "The Alleged 'Gerrymander' by Mr. Mowat, in 1874." Microform, ca. 1882.

Argersinger, Peter H. "All Politics Are Local: Another Look at the 1890s." *Journal of the Gilded Age and Progressive Era* 8, no. 1 (January 2009): 7–24.

– *Representation and Inequality in Late Nineteenth-Century America: The Politics of Apportionment*. Cambridge: Cambridge University Press, 2012.

Beaulieu, Eugene, and J.C. Herbert Emery. "Pork Packers, Reciprocity, and Laurier's Defeat in the 1911 Canadian General Election." *Journal of Economic History* 61, no. 4 (2001): 1083–1101.

Beaven, Brian P.M. "Bunting, Christopher William." *Dictionary of Canadian Biography* [hereafter DCB] vol. XII (1891–1900).

Beck, J. Murray. *Pendulum of Power, Canada's Federal Elections*. Scarborough, ON: Prentice-Hall, 1968.

Bélanger, Réal. "Laurier, Sir Wilfrid." *DCB* vol. XIV (1911–1920).

Bengough, J.W. *A Caricature History of Canadian Politics*, vols. 1–2. Toronto: *The Grip*, 1886.

Bonville, Jean de. *La Presse Québécoise de 1884 à 1914, Genèse d'un media de masse*. Quebec: Les Presses de l'université Laval, 1988.

Bothwell, Robert. "St-Laurent, Louis-Stephen." *DCB* vol. XX (1971–1980).

Boyko, John. *Bennett, the Rebel who Challenged and Changed a Nation*. Toronto: Key Porter, 2010.

Brown, Robert Craig. "Borden, Sir Robert Laird." *DCB* vol. XVI (1931–1940).

– *Robert Laird Borden: A Biography*, vol. 1. Toronto: Macmillan of Canada, 1975.

– "Hughes, Sir Samuel." *DCB* vol. XV (1921–1930).

Brown, Robert Craig, and Ramsay Cook. *Canada: A Nation Transformed*. Toronto: McClelland & Stewart, 1974.

Browne, G.P., ed. *Documents on the Confederation of British North America. A Compilation Based on Sir Joseph Pope's Confederation Documents Supplemented by Other Official Material*. Introduction by Janet Ajzenstat. Montreal and Kingston: McGill-Queen's University Press, 2009.

Buckner, Phillip. "Thomson, Charles Edward Poulett, 1st Baron Sydenham." *DCB* vol. VII (1836–1850).

– "Tupper, Sir Charles." *DCB* vol. XIV (1911–1920).

Burley, David G. "Hardy, Arthur Sturgis." *DCB* vol. XIII (1901–1910).

– "Ross, Sir George William." *DCB* vol. XIV (1911–1920).

Campbell, Gail G. "Voters and Non-voters: Voter Turnout in the Nineteenth Century – Southwestern Ontario as a Case Study." *Social Science History* 11, no. 2 (1987): 187–210.

Campbell, S. Lynn. "McMillan, John." *DCB* vol. XIII (1901–1910).

Careless, J.M.S. "Brown, George." *DCB* vol. X (1871–1880).

– *Brown of the Globe, vol. 1: The Voice of Upper Canada, 1818–1859*. Toronto: Macmillan, 1959.

– *Brown of the Globe, vol. 2: Statesman of Confederation, 1860–1880*. Toronto: Macmillan, 1963.

– *The Union of the Canadas: The Growth of Canadian Institutions, 1841–1857*. Toronto: McClelland & Stewart, 1967.

– *Toronto to 1918*. Toronto: James Lorimer & Co., 1984.

Cartwright, Sir Richard. *Reminiscences*. Toronto: William Briggs, 1912.

Cécillon, Jack D. *Prayers, Petitions, and Protests: The Catholic Church and the Ontario Schools Crisis in the Windsor Border Region, 1910–1928*. Montreal and Kingston: McGill-Queen's University Press, 2013.

Clarke, Brian P. "Sproule, Thomas Simpson." *DCB* vol. XIV (1911–1920).

Clippingdale, Richard. *Laurier, His Life and World*. Toronto: McGraw-Hill-Ryerson, 1979.

Cochrane, William, ed. *Men of Canada*, vol. I. Brantford, ON: Bradley, Garretson & Co., 1891.

Comeau, Gayle M. "Hanna, William John." *DCB* vol XIV (1911–1920).

Cook, Ramsay. "Bengough, John Wilson." *DCB* vol XV (1921–1930).

Courtney, John C. "The Unfinished Agenda of Electoral Redistributions." *Canadian Journal of Economics and Political Science* 21, no. 4 (Dec. 1988): 675–90.

– *Commissioned Ridings: Designing Canada's Electoral Districts*. Montreal and Kingston: McGill-Queen's University Press, 2001.

– *Elections*. Vancouver: UBC Press, 2004.

Crawford, J.E. *Pioneer Public Service, An Administrative History of the United Canadas, 1841–1867*. Toronto: University of Toronto Press, 1955.

Creighton, Donald. *John A. Macdonald, the Young Politician*. Toronto: Macmillan, 1952.

– *John A. Macdonald, the Old Chieftain*. Toronto: Macmillan, 1965.

Curtis, Bruce. *The Politics of Population: State Formation, Statistics, and the Census of Canada 1840–1875*. Toronto: University of Toronto Press, 2001.

– "The Boundary Adjustment Process: The Case of Arbitration in the Greater London Area." London, ON: MPA thesis, University of Western Ontario, 1992.

Dawson, R. MacGregor. "The Gerrymander of 1882." *Canadian Journal of Economics and Political Science* 1, no. 2 (May 1935): 197–221.

– *The Government of Canada*. Revised by Norman Ward. Toronto: University of Toronto Press, (1947) 1963.

– *William Lyon Mackenzie King, a Political Biography*. Toronto: University of Toronto Press, 1958.

Désilets, Andrée. "Taché, Sir Étienne-Paschal." *DCB* vol. IX (1861–1870).

Doucet, Michael, and John Weaver. *Housing the North American City*. Montreal and Kingston: McGill-Queen's University Press, 1991.

Drury, E.C. *Farmer Premier. Memoirs of the Hon. E.C. Drury*. Toronto: McClelland & Stewart, 1966.

Emery, George. *Facts of Life: The Social Construction of Vital Statistics, Ontario, 1869–1952*. Montreal and Kingston: McGill-Queen's University Press, 1993.

– *Noxons of Ingersoll: The Family and the Firm in Canada's Agricultural Implements Industry, 1856–1918*. Ingersoll, ON: Ingersoll Historical Society, 2001.

– "Review of Bruce Curtis, *The Politics of Population: State Formation, Statistics, and the Census of Canada 1840–1875* (Toronto: University of Toronto Press, 2001)." *Canadian Historical Review* 82, no. 4 (Dec. 2001): 751–4.

– *Elections in Oxford County, 1837–1875: A Case Study of Democracy in Canada West and Early Ontario*. Toronto: University of Toronto Press, 2012.

Emery, George, with Glenna Jamieson. *Adam Oliver of Ingersoll, 1823–1882: Lumberman, Millowner, Contractor, and Politician*. Ingersoll, ON: Ingersoll Historical Society, 2002.

English, John. *The Decline of Politics: The Conservatives and the Party System 1901–20*. Toronto: University of Toronto Press, 1977.

Evans, Anna Margaret. *Sir Oliver Mowat*. Toronto: University of Toronto Press, 1992.

Ferns, Thomas H., and Robert Craig Brown. "Charlton, John." *DCB* vol. XIII (1901–1910).

Flanagan, Tom. *Persona Non Grata: The Death of Free Speech in the Internet Age*. Toronto: McClelland & Stewart / Signal, 2014.

– *Winning Power: Canadian Campaigning in the Twenty-First Century*. Montreal and Kingston: McGill-Queen's University Press, 2014.

Forster, Ben, Malcolm Davidson, and R. Craig Brown. "The Franchise, Personators, and Dead Men: An Inquiry into the Voters' Lists and the Election of 1891." *Canadian Historical Review* LXVII, no. I (1986): 17–41.

– "Mackenzie, Alexander." *DCB* vol. XII (1891–1900).

Forster, Ben, and Jonathan Swainger. "Blake, Edward." *DCB* vol. XIV (1911–1920).

Girard, Philip. "Weldon, Richard Chapman." *DCB* vol. XV (1921–1930).

Glassford, Larry A. *Reaction and Reform: The Politics of the Conservative Party under R.B. Bennett, 1927–1938*. Toronto: University of Toronto Press, 1992.

– "Hepburn, Mitchell Frederick." *DCB* vol. XVIII (1951–1960).

Godbout, Jean-François, and Bjørn Høyland. "The Emergence of Parties in the Canadian House of Commons (1867–1908)." *Canadian Journal of Political Science* 46, no. 4 (Dec. 2013): 773–97.

Graham, Roger. *Arthur Meighen, a Biography*, vols. 1–3. Toronto: Clark-Irwin & Co. Ltd., 1960–65.

– *Old Man Ontario: Leslie M. Frost*. Toronto: University of Toronto Press, 1990.

Granatstein, J.L. *The Politics of Survival: The Conservative Party of Canada, 1939–1945*. Toronto: University of Toronto Press, 1967.

Granger, Jennifer. *Vanished Villages of Middlesex*. Toronto: Natural Heritage/Natural History, 2002.

Gray, Carolyn E. "Gibson, Sir John Morison." *DCB* vol. XV (1921–1930).

Grittner, Colin. "Review of George Emery, *Elections in Oxford County, 1837–1875: A Case Study of Democracy in Canada West and Early Ontario* (Toronto: University of Toronto Press, 2012)." *Canadian Historical Review* 94, no. 2 (June 2013): 322–4.

– "Macdonald and Women's Enfranchisement." In *Macdonald at 200: New Reflections and Legacies*, edited by Patrice Dutil and Roger Hall, ch. 1. Toronto: Dundurn, 2014.

Hall, David J., and Donald B. Smith. "Lougheed, Sir James Alexander." *DCB* vol. XV (1921–1930).

Harris, Michael. *Party of One: Stephen Harper and Canada's Radical Makeover*. Toronto: Penguin Random House Canada, 2014.

Haycock, R.G. *Sam Hughes, the Public Career of a Controversial Canadian, 1885–1916*. Waterloo, ON: Wilfrid Laurier University Press, 1986.

Hodgins, Bruce W. "Macdonald, John Sandfield." *DCB* vol. X (1871–1880).

Hodgins, Bruce W., and Paul W. White. "Macdonald, Donald Alexander." *DCB* vol. XII (1891–1900).

Humphries, Charles W. "Whitney, Sir James Pliny." *DCB* vol. XIV (1911–1920).

– *'Honest Enough to be Bold': The Life and Times of Sir James Pliny Whitney*. Toronto: University of Toronto Press, 1985.

Johnston, Charles M. *E.C. Drury: Agrarian Idealist.* Toronto: University of Toronto Press, 1986.

Johnston, J.K., and P.B. Waite. "Macdonald, Sir John Alexander." *DCB* vol. XII (1891–1900).

Jones, Elwood H. "Rymal, Joseph." *DCB* vol. XII (1891–1900).

Kerr, D.G.G. "The 1867 Elections in Ontario: The Rules of the Game." *Canadian Historical Review* 60, no. 4 (1970): 369–85.

Kulisek, Larry L. "McCarthy, D'Alton." *DCB* vol. XII (1891–1900).

Lower, A.R.M. "Determinism in Canadian Politics." *Canadian Historical Review* XXVII, no. 3 (1946): 233–48.

Mackay, Ian. "The Liberal Order Framework: A Prospectus for a Reconnaissance of Canadian History." *Canadian Historical Review* 81, no. 4 (Dec. 2000): 617–45.

Martin, Ged. *Britain and the Origins of Canadian Confederation, 1840–67.* Houndmills, UK: Macmillan, 1995.

Martin, Lawrence. *Harperland, the Politics of Control.* Toronto: Viking Canada, 2010.

May, J. "'John A. & John May,' or, the struggle between Carleton and the Clique; also, the battle of Ephesus, an Epic after Campbell." Microform, 1882.

Mackenzie, David, and Patrice Dutil. *Canada 1911: The Decisive Election that Shaped the Country.* Toronto: Dundurn, 2011.

McDougall, Allan Kerr. *John P. Robarts: His Life and Government.* Toronto: University of Toronto, 1986.

McMurray, Thomas. *Free Grant Lands of Muskoka and Parry Sound.* Bracebridge, Muskoka, ON: Northern Advocate, 1871.

Metcalf, George. "Draper, William Henry." *DCB* vol. X (1871–1880).

Monet, Jacques. "Monck, Charles Stanley, 4th Viscount Monck." *DCB* vol. XII (1891–1900).

Morgan, Cecelia, and Robert Craig Brown. "Cartwright, Sir Richard John." *DCB* vol. XIV (1911–1920).

Morgan, Henry James, ed. *Dominion Annual Register and Review, 1883.* Toronto: Hunter, Rose & Company, 1884.

– ed. *Canadian Men and Women of the Time.* Toronto: William Briggs, 1898.

– ed. *Canadian Men and Women of the Time.* Toronto: William Briggs, 1912.

Morton, W.L. *The Critical Years: The Union of British North America, 1857–1873.* Toronto: McClelland & Stewart, 1964.

Mulvaney, Charles Pelham. *History of the County of Peterborough, Ontario.* Toronto: C. Blackett Robinson, 1884.

Neatby, H. Blair. *William Lyon Mackenzie King, 1924–1932: The Lonely Heights.* Toronto: University of Toronto Press, 1958.

– *William Lyon Mackenzie King, 1932–1939: The Prism of Unity.* Toronto: University of Toronto Press, 1976.

– "King, William Lyon Mackenzie." DCB vol. XVII (1941–1950).

Nelles, H.V. "Beck, Sir Adam." DCB vol. XV (1921–1930).

Nicholson, Norman L. *The Boundaries of the Canadian Federation.* Toronto: Macmillan Canada, 1979.

Noel, S.J.R. *Patrons, Clients, Brokers: Ontario Society and Politics, 1791–1896.* Toronto: University of Toronto Press, 1990.

Oliver, Peter. *G. Howard Ferguson: Ontario Tory.* Toronto: University of Toronto Press, 1977.

Ontario Liberal Association. *The Record of the Mowat Government, 22 Years of Progressive Legislation and Honest Administration, 1872–1894.* Toronto: Hunter Rose, 1894.

Osborne, Brian S., and Donald Swainson. *Kingston: Building on the Past.* Westport, CT: Butternut Press, 1988.

Paikin, Steve. *Public Triumph, Private Tragedy: The Double Life of John P. Robarts.* Toronto: Viking Press, 2005.

Parliament of Canada. "A Legislative and Historical Overview of the Senate of Canada." Ottawa: Author, 2001. http://www.parl.gc.ca/About/Senate/LegisFocus/legislative-e.htm.

Pickersgill, J.W. *My Life with Louis St. Laurent: A Political Memoir.* Toronto: University of Toronto Press, 1975.

Pollin, Stanley. "Hay, Robert." DCB vol. XI (1881–1890).

Pope, Joseph. *Confederation Documents Hitherto Unpublished.* Toronto: Carswell Company, 1895.

– *Memoirs of the Right Honourable Sir John Alexander Macdonald G.C.B., First Prime Minister of the Dominion of Canada*, vol. I. Ottawa: J. Durie & Son, 1894.

Prang, Margaret E. "Rowell, Newton Wesley." DCB vol. XVII (1941–1950).

– *N.W. Rowell: Ontario Nationalist.* Toronto: University of Toronto Press, 1975.

Rea, J.E. "Greenway, Thomas." DCB vol. XIII (1901–1910).

Robertson, Norman. *The History of the County of Bruce.* Toronto: William Briggs, 1906.

Roland, Charles G. "Bergin, Darby." DCB vol. XII (1891–1900).

Romney, Paul. "Mowat, Sir Oliver." DCB vol. XIII (1901–1910).

Ross, George W. *Getting into Parliament and After.* Toronto: William Briggs, 1913.

Ross, Margaret. *Sir George W. Ross, A Biographical Study.* Toronto: Ryerson Press, 1923.

Rossiter, D.J., R.J. Johnston, and C.J. Pattie. *The Boundary Commissions, Redrawing the UK's Map of Parliamentary Constituencies*. Manchester, UK: University of Manchester Press, 1999.

Rothney, Gordon O. "The Denominational Basis of Representation in the Newfoundland House of Assembly, 1919–1962." *Canadian Journal of Economics and Political Science* 28 (1962): 557–70.

Russell, Peter A. "Cameron, Malcolm Colin." *DCB* vol. XII (1891–1900).

Rush, Mark E. *Does Redistricting Make a Difference? Partisan Representation and Electoral Behavior*. Baltimore, MD: Johns Hopkins University Press, 1993.

Saywell, John T. *Just Call Me Mitch: The Life of Mitchell F. Hepburn*. Toronto: University of Toronto Press, 1991.

Schull, Joseph. *Laurier, the First Canadian*. Toronto: Macmillan of Canada, 1965.

– *Ontario Since 1867*. Toronto: McClelland and Stewart, 1978.

Siegfried, André. *The Race Question in Canada*. London: Eveleigh Nash, 1907; reprinted Toronto: McClelland and Stewart, 1968.

Skelton, Oscar Douglas. *Life and Letters of Sir Wilfrid Laurier*. Toronto: Oxford University Press, 1921.

Smith, David E. *Across the Aisle: Opposition in Canadian Politics*. Toronto: University of Toronto Press, 2013.

Sotiron, Minko. "Maclean, William Findlay." *DCB* vol. XV (1921–1930).

Spanner, Donald Ross. "'The Straight Furrow': The Life of George S. Henry, Ontario's Unknown Premier." London, ON: PhD thesis, University of Western Ontario, 1994.

Stevens, Paul. "Edgar, Sir James David." *DCB* vol. XII (1891–1900).

Stewart, Gordon. "John A. Macdonald's Greatest Triumph." *Canadian Historical Review* 63, no. 1 (1982): 3–33.

Stott, Greg R. "The Maintenance of Suburban Autonomy: The Story of Petersville-London West, Ontario, 1874–1897." London, ON: MA thesis, University of Western Ontario, 1999.

Swainson, Donald. "Street, Thomas Clark (Clarke)." *DCB* vol. X (1871–1880).

Taylor, John H. *Ottawa: An Illustrated History*. Toronto: Lorimer, 1986.

Thomas, Paul E.J., Peter John Loewen, and Michael K. MacKenzie. "Fair Isn't Always Equal: Constituency Population and the Quality of Representation in Canada." *Canadian Journal of Political Science* 46, no. 2 (2013): 273–93.

Thompson, John Herd. *Canada 1922–1939: Decades of Discord*. Toronto: McClelland & Stewart, 1985.

Thomson, Dale C. *Louis St. Laurent, Canadian*. Toronto: Macmillan of Canada, 1967.

Turley-Ewart, John A. "Kemp, Sir Albert Edward." *DCB* vol. XV (1921–1930).
Turner, Larry. "Haggart, John Graham." *DCB* vol. XIV (1911–1920).
Vipond, Robert C. "Blake, Edward." *DCB* vol. XIII (1901–1910).
– "Mills, David." *DCB* vol. XIII (1901–1910).
Waite, P.B. "Bowell, Sir Mackenzie." *DCB* vol. XIV (1911–1920).
– "Thompson, Sir John Sparrow David." *DCB* vol. XII (1891–1900).
– "Bennett, Richard Bedford, 1st Viscount Bennett." *DCB* vol. XVII (1941–1950).
– *The Man from Halifax, Sir John Thompson, Prime Minister.* Toronto: University of Toronto Press, 1985.
– *Canada 1874–1896: Arduous Destiny.* Toronto: McClelland & Stewart, 1988.
– *In Search of R.B. Bennett.* Montreal & Kingston: McGill-Queen's University Press, 2012.
Ward, Norman. *The Canadian House of Commons: Representation.* Toronto: University of Toronto Press, 1950.
– "The Formative Years of the House of Commons, 1867–91." *The Canadian Journal of Economics and Political Science / Revue canadienne d'économique et de science politique* 18, no. 4 (Nov. 1952): 431–51.
– "The Redistribution of 1952." *The Canadian Journal of Economics and Political Science / Revue canadienne d'économique et de science politique* 19, no. 3 (Aug. 1953): 341–60.
– ed. *A Party Politician, the Memoirs of Chubby Power.* Toronto: Macmillan of Canada, 1966.
Weaver, John C. *Hamilton: An Illustrated History.* Toronto: James Lorimer, 1982.
Wells, Paul. *The Longer I'm Prime Minister: Stephen Harper and Canada, 2006–.* Toronto: Random House Canada, 2013.
Whitelaw, W. Menzies. "Reconstructing the Quebec Conference." *Canadian Historical Review* XIX, no. 2 (June 1938): 122–37.
Young, Brian J. "C. George McCullagh and the Leadership League." *Canadian Historical Review* XLVII, no. 3 (Sep. 1966): 202–26.

Index